THE BELLARMINE SERIES

Published by the Jesuit Fathers of Heythrop College

General Editor
EDMUND F. SUTCLIFFE, S.J.
*Sometime Professor of Old Testament Exegesis
and Hebrew at Heythrop College*

BY THE SAME AUTHOR

*

THE BELLARMINE SERIES XVI

A HISTORY OF PHILOSOPHY

VOLUME V

HOBBES TO HUME

BY

FREDERICK COPLESTON, S.J.

*Professor at the Pontifical Gregorian University, Rome,
and at Heythrop College*

THE NEWMAN PRESS
WESTMINSTER · MARYLAND

De Licentia Superiorum Ordinis:
J. D. BOYLE, S.J.
Praep. Prov. Angliae

Nihil obstat:
J. L. RUSSELL, S.J.
Censor Deputatus

Imprimatur:
✠ FRANCISCUS
Archiepiscopus Birmingamiensis

Birmingamiae
die 25 Julii 1957

First published 1959
Second impression 1961
Third impression 1964
Fourth impression 1968

PRINTED IN GREAT BRITAIN

CONTENTS

PREFACE

As I remarked in the preface to the fourth volume of this work, my original intention was to cover the philosophy of the seventeenth and eighteenth centuries, including the system of Kant, in one book. But it did not prove possible to do this. And I have divided the matter between three books, treating each as a separate volume. My original plan has, however, been preserved to this extent, that there is a common introductory chapter and a common Concluding Review for Volumes IV, V and VI. The former has been placed, of course, at the beginning of Volume IV, *Descartes to Leibniz*. The Concluding Review, in which I propose to discuss, not only from an historical but also from a more philosophical point of view, the nature, importance and value of the various styles of philosophizing in the seventeenth and eighteenth centuries, will form the last chapter of Volume VI, *Wolff to Kant*, which will comprise the French Enlightenment, the German Enlightenment, the rise of the philosophy of history, and the system of Kant. The present volume, therefore, *Hobbes to Hume*, which is devoted to British philosophical thought from Hobbes up to and including the Scottish philosophy of common sense and which represents the second part of the originally projected fourth volume, *Descartes to Kant*, does not contain either an introductory chapter or a Concluding Review. As its arrangement differs to this extent from that of the first three volumes, I thought it desirable to repeat here the explanation which has already been offered in the preface to Volume IV.

CHAPTER I

HOBBES (1)

*Life and writings—The end and nature of philosophy and its
exclusion of all theology—The divisions of philosophy—
Philosophical method—Hobbes's nominalism—Causality and
mechanism—Space and time—Body and accidents—Motion
and change—Vital motions and animal motions—Good and
evil—The passions—Will—Intellectual virtues—Atomic individualism.*

1. THOMAS HOBBES, author of one of the most celebrated political
treatises in European literature, was born at Westport near
Malmesbury in 1588. His father was a clergyman. In 1608, when
Hobbes went down from Oxford, he entered the service of the
Cavendish family and spent the years 1608–10 travelling in France
and Italy as tutor to the son of Lord Cavendish, future earl of
Devonshire. On his return to England he occupied himself with
literary pursuits and translated Thucydides into English, the
translation being published in 1628. He had relations with Francis
Bacon (d. 1626) and with Lord Herbert of Cherbury; but he had
not yet given himself to philosophy.

From 1629 until 1631 Hobbes was again in France, this time as
tutor to the son of Sir Gervase Clifton; and it was during a visit to
Paris that he made acquaintance with the *Elements* of Euclid.
Historians have pointed out that for all his labours Hobbes was
never able to acquire that degree of mathematical knowledge and
insight which Descartes had attained at a far earlier age. But
though he was never a great mathematician, it was this encounter
with geometry which supplied him with his lasting ideal of
scientific method. During his visit to Paris his attention was also
drawn to problems of sense-perception, the relation of sensation
to the motions of bodies and the status of secondary qualities.

On returning to England Hobbes again entered the service of
the Cavendish family, and from 1634 until 1637 he was once more
on the Continent. He met Galileo at Florence, and at Paris he was
introduced by Mersenne into philosophical and scientific circles.
He thus came to know the Cartesian philosophy, and at Mersenne's invitation he submitted to Descartes his objections against

the latter's *Meditations*. This period was of great importance in the development of Hobbes's mind and in determining his philosophical interests. He was already a middle-aged man when he turned his attention to philosophy; but he formulated for himself the idea of a system and projected a presentation of it in three parts. In actual fact his mind was first seriously occupied with social and political problems, and in 1640 he wrote *The Elements of Law, Natural and Politic*, of which two portions appeared in 1650 under the titles *Human Nature or the Fundamental Elements of Policy* and *De corpore politico*. The text of the whole work did not appear until 1889, when it was edited and published by F. Tönnies.

In 1640 Hobbes, thinking that his safety was menaced in England because of his royalist convictions, took refuge in France. In 1642 he published at Paris his work *De cive*, the third part of his projected philosophical system; and it was at Paris that he wrote his famous *Leviathan or the Matter, Form and Power of a Commonwealth, Ecclesiastical and Civil*, which appeared in London in 1651. In 1649 Charles I was beheaded, and one might perhaps expect that Hobbes would have remained in France, especially as he had been for a time mathematical tutor to Charles, Prince of Wales, who was living in exile at Paris. However, he made his peace with the Commonwealth in 1652 and settled down in the household of the earl of Devonshire. Some of the ideas which he was known to have expounded in the *Leviathan* were not acceptable in royalist circles at Paris, and in any case the civil war, which had constituted Hobbes's chief reason for remaining abroad, was over. As will be seen later, his political convictions enabled him to accept any *de facto* government which was in effective control of the State. After the Restoration in 1660 Hobbes enjoyed the favour of Charles II and received a pension.

In 1655 and 1658 Hobbes published the first and second sections of his philosophical system, the *De corpore* and the *De homine*. And until the end of his life he occupied himself with literary labours, translating the whole of Homer into English and writing a book on the Long Parliament. He was also much engaged in controversy. Thus he conducted a literary debate with Bramhall, bishop of Derry, on the subject of freedom and necessity, in which he maintained a determinist point of view. He was also engaged in controversy with the mathematician Wallis, who published an *Elenchus geometriae hobbinae* in which Hobbes's mathematical errors were subjected to sharp criticism. He was also attacked, particularly by ecclesiastics, on the score of heresy and atheism. However, having successfully weathered both Commonwealth and Restoration, he was not to be killed by verbal polemics, and he survived until the winter of 1679 when he died at the age of ninety-one.[1]

2. Hobbes, like Bacon, stresses the practical purpose of philosophy. 'The *end* or *scope* of philosophy is that we may make use to our benefit of effects formerly seen; or that, by application of bodies to one another, we may produce the like effects of those we conceive in our mind, as far forth as matter, strength and industry will permit, for the commodity of human life. . . . The end of knowledge is power . . . and the scope of all speculation is the performance of some action or thing to be done.'[2] Natural philosophy confers obvious benefits on mankind. But moral and political philosophy also possesses great utility. For human life is afflicted by calamities, of which civil war is the chief, that arise because men do not understand sufficiently the rules of conduct and of political life. 'Now, the knowledge of these rules is moral philosophy.'[3] Both in the sciences and in politics knowledge is power.

But though philosophical knowledge is power, in the sense that its function is to contribute to man's material prosperity and to social peace and security, it does not follow that all knowledge is philosophical. As far as the remote basis of philosophical knowledge is concerned, Hobbes is an empiricist. The philosopher starts with the given, with sense-impressions made on us by external bodies, and with our memories of such impressions. He starts with the empirical data, from what Hobbes calls 'effects' or 'appearances'. But though our immediate awareness of appearances or phenomena and our memory of them constitute knowledge, and though they form the remote basis of philosophy, they are not philosophical knowledge. 'Although sense and memory of things, which are common to man and all living creatures, be knowledge, yet because they are given us immediately by nature, and not gotten by ratiocination, they are not philosophy.'[4] Everyone knows that the sun exists, in the sense that they have the

---

[1] W. Molesworth edited two collections of Hobbes's writings: *Opera philosophica quae latine scripsit* in five volumes (1839–45) and *The English Works of Thomas Hobbes* in eleven volumes (1839–45). In the references given in this and in the next chapter the letters *O.L.* and *E.W.* refer respectively to these editions.
[2] *Concerning Body*, 1, 1, 6; *E.W.*, 1, p. 7.
[3] *Concerning Body*, 1, 1, 7; *E.W.*, 1, p. 8.
[4] *Concerning Body*, 1, 1, 2; *E.W.*, 1, p. 3.

experience which we call 'seeing the sun'; but nobody would say that such knowledge is scientific astronomical knowledge. Similarly, that human actions take place is known by all; but all do not possess a scientific or philosophical knowledge of human actions. Philosophy is concerned with causal relations. 'Philosophy is such knowledge of effects or appearances as we acquire by true ratiocination from the knowledge we have first of their causes or generation. And again, of such causes or generations as may be (had) from knowing first their effects.'[1] The philosopher discovers effects from known causes and causes from known effects. And he does so by 'ratiocination'. He is not concerned with simply stating empirical facts, that this or that is or was a fact, but with the consequences of propositions, which are discovered by reasoning and not by observation.

We can understand, therefore, what Hobbes means when he divides knowledge into knowledge of fact and knowledge of consequence. 'There are of Knowledge two kinds; whereof one is *knowledge of fact:* the other *knowledge of the consequence of one affirmation to another.'*[2] When I see something done or remember seeing it done, I have knowledge of fact. This, says Hobbes, is the kind of knowledge required of a witness in a court of law. It is 'absolute' knowledge, in the sense that it is expressed absolutely or in assertoric form. And the 'register' of knowledge of fact is called history, which may take the form either of natural or of civil history. Knowledge of consequence, on the contrary, is conditional or hypothetical, in the sense that it is knowledge that, for example, if A is true, B is also true. To use Hobbes's example, 'If the figure shown be a circle, then any straight line through the centre shall divide it into two equal parts'.[3] This is scientific knowledge, the kind of knowledge which is required of a philosopher, 'that is to say, of him that pretends to reasoning'.[4] And the 'registers of science' are books containing the demonstrations of the consequences of propositions and 'are commonly called *books of philosophy*'.[5] Scientific or philosophical knowledge can therefore be described as knowledge of consequences. And such knowledge is always conditional: 'if this be, that is; if this has been, that has been; if this shall be, that shall be'.[6]

We have seen that for Hobbes philosophy is concerned with causal explanation. And by causal explanation he means a

[1] *Concerning Body*, I, I, 2; *E.W.*, I, p. 3.   [2] *Leviathan*, I, 9; *E.W.*, III, p. 71.
[3] *Ibid.*   [4] *Ibid.*   [5] *Ibid.*   [6] *Leviathan*, I, 7; *E.W.*, III, p. 52.

scientific account of the generative process by which some effect comes into being. From this it follows that if there is anything which does not come into existence through a generative process, it cannot be part of the subject-matter of philosophy. God, therefore, and indeed all spiritual reality, is excluded from philosophy. 'The *subject* of Philosophy, or the matter it treats of, is every body of which we can conceive any generation, and which we may, by any consideration thereof, compare with other bodies, or which is capable of composition and resolution; that is to say, every body of whose generation or properties we can have any knowledge. . . . Therefore it (philosophy) excludes theology, I mean the doctrine of God, eternal, ingenerable, incomprehensible, and in whom there is nothing neither to divide nor compound, nor any generation to be conceived.'[1] History is also excluded, because 'such knowledge is but experience (memory) or authority, and not ratiocination'.[2] And pseudo-sciences, such as astrology, cannot be admitted.

Philosophy, therefore, is concerned with the causes and properties of bodies. And this means that it is concerned with bodies in motion. For motion is the 'one universal cause', which 'cannot be understood to have any other cause besides motion'; and 'the variety of all figures arises out of the variety of those motions by which they are made'.[3] This account of the nature and subject-matter of philosophy may not, Hobbes observes, be acceptable to everyone. Some will say that it is a matter of definition and that anyone is free to define philosophy as he wishes. This is true, 'though I think it no hard matter to demonstrate that this definition of mine agrees with the sense of all men'.[4] Hobbes adds, however, that those who seek another kind of philosophy must adopt other principles. If his own principles are adopted, philosophy will be what he conceives it to be.

Hobbes's philosophy, therefore, is materialistic in the sense that it takes no account of anything but bodies. And in so far as the exclusion of God and of all spiritual reality is simply the result of a freely chosen definition, his materialism can be called methodological. He does not say that there is no God; he says that God is not the subject-matter of philosophy. At the same time it seems to me to be a great mistake to represent Hobbes as saying no more than that according to his use of the word 'philosophy' the

[1] *Concerning Body*, 1, 1, 8; *E.W.*, 1, p. 10.   [2] *Ibid.*, p. 11.
[3] *Concerning Body*, 1, 6, 5; *E.W.*, 1, pp. 69–70.
[4] *Concerning Body*, 1, 1, 10; *E.W.*, 1, p. 12.

existence and nature of God are not philosophical topics. Philosophy and reasoning are for him coextensive; and from this it follows that theology is irrational. To all intents and purposes he identified the imaginable and the conceivable. And from this he drew the conclusion that we can have no idea of the infinite or of the immaterial. 'Whatsoever we imagine is *finite*. Therefore there is no idea or conception of any thing we call infinite.'[1] A term such as *incorporeal substance* is just as contradictory as *incorporeal body* or *round quadrangle*. Terms of this sort are 'insignificant'[2], that is, meaningless. Some people do indeed think that they understand them; but all that they really do is to repeat the words to themselves without any real understanding of their content. For they have no content. Hobbes explicitly asserts that words such as *hypostatical, transubstantiate, eternal-now* and so on 'signify nothing'.[3] 'Words whereby we conceive nothing but the sound are those we call *absurd, insignificant* and *nonsense*. And therefore if a man should talk to me of a *round quadrangle* . . . or *immaterial substances* . . . or of a *free subject* . . . I should not say he were in an error, but that his words were without meaning, that is to say, absurd.'[4] He makes it abundantly clear that theology, if offered as a science or coherent body of true propositions, is absurd and irrational. And to say this is to say very much more than that one proposes to confine one's attention in philosophy to the realm of the corporeal.

At the same time one cannot legitimately conclude without more ado that Hobbes is an atheist. It would indeed appear to follow from his empiricist analysis of the meaning of names that all talk about God is so much gibberish and that belief is simply a matter of emotion, that is, of an emotive attitude. But this is not precisely what Hobbes says. As regards natural religion he says that curiosity or love of the knowledge of causes naturally draws a man to conceive a cause which itself has no cause, 'so that it is impossible to make any profound inquiry into natural causes without being inclined thereby to believe that there is one God eternal; though they (men) cannot have any idea of him in their mind, answerable to his nature'.[5] For 'by the visible things in this world, and their admirable order, a man may conceive there is a cause of them, which men call God; and yet not have an idea or image of him in his mind'.[6] In other words, Hobbes emphasizes

---

[1] *Leviathan*, I, 3; *E.W.*, III, p. 17.   [2] *Leviathan*, I, 4; *E.W.*, III, p. 27.
[3] *Leviathan*, I, 5; *E.W.*, III, pp. 34-5.   [4] *Ibid.*, pp. 32-3.
[5] *Leviathan*, I, 11; *E.W.*, III, p. 92.   [6] *Ibid.*, p. 93.

the incomprehensibility of God. If a word such as 'infinite' is
predicated of God, it does not stand for any positive idea of God
but expresses our inability to conceive Him. 'And therefore the
name of God is used, not to make us conceive him, for he is incomprehensible; and his greatness and power' are inconceivable, but
that we may honour him.'[1] Similarly, terms such as *spirit* and
incorporeal are not in themselves intelligible. 'And therefore, men
that by their own meditation arrive to the acknowledgement of
one infinite, omnipotent, and eternal God, choose rather to confess
he is incomprehensible and above their understanding than to
define his nature by *spirit incorporeal*, and then confess their
definition to be unintelligible: or if they give him such a title, it is
not *dogmatically*, with intention to make the divine nature *understood*; but *piously*, to honour him with attributes, or significations,
as remote as they can from the grossness of bodies visible.'[2] As
for Christian revelation, expressed in the Scriptures, Hobbes does
not deny that there is a revelation, but he applies the same
principles in his interpretation of the terms used. The word *spirit*
either signifies a subtle and fluid body or is used metaphorically
or is purely unintelligible. 'For the nature of God is incomprehensible; that is to say, we understand nothing of *what he is*, but
only *that he is*; and therefore the attributes we give him are not to
tell one another *what he is*, nor to signify our opinion of his nature,
but our desire to honour him with such names as we conceive most
honourable amongst ourselves.'[3]

Some commentators have seen in all this a continuation and
intensification of the tendency, already visible in fourteenth-
century thinkers such as Ockham and those who belonged to the
movement of which he was the most eminent representative, to
draw a sharp distinction between theology and philosophy and to
relegate all theology, including natural theology, to the sphere of
faith, so that philosophy would have little or nothing to say about
God. And there is certainly a good deal to be said in favour of this
interpretation. As we have seen, Hobbes makes explicit use of the
famous distinction, common enough in the Middle Ages, between
knowing of God *that* He is and knowing *what* He is. But the
mediaeval theologians and philosophers who emphasized this
distinction believed that God is incorporeal substance and infinite
spirit. And this is true both of a writer such as St. Thomas Aquinas

---

[1] *Leviathan*, 1, 3; *E.W.*, III, p. 17.   [2] *Leviathan*, 1, 12; *E.W.*, III, p. 97.
[3] *Leviathan*, 3, 34; *E.W.*, III, p. 383.

who combined the use of the distinction with belief in a philosophical though analogical knowledge of God, and of a fourteenth-century philosopher such as Ockham, who evidently considered that philosophy is incapable of telling us much about God. Hobbes, however, seems to have affirmed the corporeality of God, at least if one can judge by what he says in the course of his controversy with Bishop Bramhall. For there he says explicitly that God is 'a most pure and most simple corporeal spirit' and that 'the Trinity, and the persons thereof, are that one pure, simple and eternal corporeal spirit'.[1] The phrase 'simple, corporeal spirit' seems at first sight to be a contradiction in terms. But a pure and simple body is said to be 'body of one and the same kind in every part throughout'.[2] And spirit is said to be 'thin, fluid, transparent, invisible body'.[3] If, then, the terms are given these meanings, the contradiction disappears. But in this case God's corporeality is affirmed. True, this does not mean that God possesses secondary qualities; but it means that He possesses magnitude. 'By corporeal I mean a substance that has magnitude.'[4] And magnitude, as will be seen later, is the same as extension. God, therefore, is infinite, invisible extension. And to make this statement is to say very much more than that God is incomprehensible and that because of His incomprehensibility philosophy has nothing to say about Him. However, if Hobbes, who appeals not only to Tertullian but also to Scripture in support of his theory, is serious in all this, as presumably he is, he cannot be called an atheist, unless under the term 'atheist' one includes the man who affirms God's existence but denies that He is infinite, incorporeal substance. And in Hobbes's opinion to affirm the latter would be itself atheism; for to say that God is incorporeal substance is to say that there is no God, since substance is necessarily corporeal.

3. To say, however, that philosophy is concerned exclusively with bodies and their properties and causes is not to say that it is concerned exclusively with bodies in the ordinary sense and that it is coextensive with what we call the natural sciences. 'For two chief kinds of bodies, and very different from one another, offer themselves to such as search after their generation and properties.'[5] The one is called a *natural body*, because it is made by nature; the other is called a *commonwealth*, and 'it is made by the wills and agreement of men'.[6] Philosophy can thus be subdivided into two

---

[1] *E.W.*, IV, p. 306. [2] *Ibid.*, p. 309. [3] *Ibid.* [4] *Ibid.*, p. 313.
[5] *Concerning Body*, I, I, 9; *E.W.*, I, p. 11. [6] *Ibid.*

parts, natural and civil. Further, civil philosophy can be sub-divided. For in order to understand the nature, function and properties of a commonwealth we have first to understand the dispositions, affections and manners of man; and the part of philosophy which treats of this subject is called *ethics*, whereas the part which treats of man's civil duties is called *politics* or takes to itself alone the general term *civil philosophy*. And from this analysis of the subject-matter of philosophy there follows the division of headings which Hobbes adopted for his systematic exposition: *De corpore*, treating of natural bodies, *De homine*, treating of man's dispositions, affections and 'manners', and *De cive*, treating of the commonwealth and of man's civic duties.

This division is not, however, complete. In the dedicatory epistle to the *De cive* Hobbes remarks that just as the British, Atlantic and Indian seas make up the ocean, so do geometry, physics and morals make up philosophy. If we consider the effects produced by a body in motion and confine our attention exclusively to the motion of the body, we see that the motion of a point generates a line, the motion of a line a plane surface, and so on. And from this study there sprang 'that part of philosophy which is called geometry'.[1] We can then consider the effects produced by one moving body on another when the bodies are considered as wholes. And we can thus develop a science of motion. We can also consider the effects produced by the motion of the parts of a body. We can arrive, for example, at knowledge of the nature of secondary qualities and of phenomena such as light. And these 'considerations comprehend that part of philosophy which is called physics'.[2] Finally, we can consider the motions of the mind, such as appetite and aversion, hope, anger and so on, and their causes and effects. And then we have moral philosophy.

The completest division which Hobbes gives of the subject-matter of philosophy is derived from applying the definition of science or philosophical knowledge as the 'knowledge of consequences'.[3] The two main divisions are knowledge of consequences from the accidents of natural bodies and knowledge of consequences from the accidents of political bodies. The former is called natural philosophy, the latter politics or civil philosophy. In politics we study what follows from the institution of commonwealths, first as regards the rights and duties of the sovereign, secondly as

---

[1] *Concerning Body*, I, 6, 6; *E.W.*, I, p. 71.　　　　[2] *Ibid.*, p. 72.
[3] Cf. *Leviathan*, I, 9; *E.W.*, III, pp. 72–3.

regards the duty and rights of subjects. Natural philosophy, however, comprises a considerable number of further divisions and subdivisions. If we study the consequences which follow from the accidents common to all bodies, namely, quantity and motion, we have either 'first philosophy', if it is indeterminate quantity and motion which are being considered, or mathematics, if we are considering the consequences from quantity and motion determined by figure and number, or astronomy or mechanics according to the special kinds of bodies we are considering. If we study the consequences from the qualities of bodies, we have physics. And physics in turn can be subdivided according to the different kinds of bodies considered. For instance, study of the consequences from the passions of men yields ethics, which is classified, therefore, under the general heading of natural philosophy, since a human being is a natural and not an artificial body in the sense in which a commonwealth is an artificial body.[1]

4. The description of philosophical knowledge or science as 'knowledge of the consequences of one affirmation to another', coupled with the assertion that such knowledge is hypothetical or conditional, naturally suggests that Hobbes attached great importance to deduction; that is, to the mathematical method. And some commentators have given the impression that in his opinion philosophy is, or rather should be, a purely deductive system. 'Rationalism' or reasoning, which is the essential characteristic of philosophy, is described in mathematical terms. 'By *ratiocination* I mean *computation*.'[2] And Hobbes proceeds to say that to compute is to add or subtract, terms which obviously suggest arithmetical operations. The whole system of Hobbes, it has been said, was designed to be a deduction from an analysis of motion and quantity, even though he did not in fact succeed in fulfilling his purpose. In his insistence on the practical function and end of philosophy or science he was akin to Bacon; but his concept of the proper method to be employed in philosophy was very different from Bacon's. The latter stressed experiment, whereas Hobbes took a dim view of the experimenters and upheld an idea of method which clearly resembles that of continental rationalists such as Descartes.

---

[1] The study of the consequences from the qualities of men in particular includes, besides ethics, study of the functions of speech. Study of, for example, the technique of persuading gives us rhetoric, while study of the art of reasoning gives us logic.
[2] *Concerning Body*, I, I, 2; *E.W.*, I, p. 3.

This interpretation of Hobbes's conception of philosophical method contains a great deal of truth. But I think that it is an over-simplified view and stands in need of qualification. For one thing, Hobbes certainly never imagined that he could start with an abstract analysis of motion and then proceed in a purely deductive manner without the introduction of any empirical material drawn from experience. He was, indeed, a systematizer. He was convinced that there is a continuity between physics, psychology and politics, and that a coherent and systematic view of the different branches of philosophy is possible in the light of general principles. But he was well aware that one cannot deduce man and society from abstract laws of motion. If anything can be deduced, it is the laws governing man's 'motions', not man himself. As we have already seen, there are empirically given data which form the remote subject-matter of philosophy, even though knowledge of these data, considered as mere given facts, is not philosophy.

When Hobbes says that ratiocination means computation, and that computation means addition and subtraction, he goes on to explain that he is using these last-mentioned terms in the sense of 'composition' and 'division or resolution'. 'And the resolutive (method) is commonly called *analytical* method, as the compositive is called *synthetical*.'[1] Philosophical method or ratiocination comprises, therefore, analysis and synthesis. In analysis the mind proceeds from the particular to the universal or to first principles. For example, if a man starts with the idea of gold, he can come by 'resolution' to the ideas of solid, visible, heavy 'and many others more universal than gold itself; and these he may resolve again, till he comes to such things as are most universal. . . . I conclude, therefore, that the method of attaining to the universal knowledge of things is purely *analytical*.'[2] In synthesis, on the contrary, the mind starts with principles or general causes and proceeds to construct their possible effects. The whole process of determining or discovering causal relations and establishing causal explanations, the method of invention as Hobbes calls it, is partly analytical and partly synthetical. To use terms which he borrowed from Galileo, it is partly resolutive and partly compositive. Or, to use terms more familiar to us, it is partly inductive and partly deductive. We can say, I think, that Hobbes envisaged the method

[1] *Concerning Body*, 1, 6, 1; *E.W.*, 1, p. 66.
[2] *Ibid.*

of framing explanatory hypotheses and deducing their consequences. The fact that he asserts that the deduced effects are
'possible' effects, at least in what we would call physical science,
shows that he had some awareness of the hypothetical character
of the explanatory theories concerned.

A distinction is made by Hobbes between the method of
invention and the method of teaching or demonstrating. In using
the latter method we start with first principles, which stand in
need of explanation but not of demonstration, since first principles
cannot be demonstrated, and proceed deductively to conclusions.
'The whole method, therefore, of demonstration is *synthetical*,
consisting of that order of speech which begins from primary or
most universal propositions, which are manifest of themselves,
and proceeds by a perpetual composition of propositions into
syllogisms, till at last the learner understands the truth of the
conclusion sought after.'[1]

It is perhaps this ideal of continuous demonstration which has
given the impression that Hobbes aimed at the construction of a
purely deductive system. And if we press this point of view, we
shall have to say that he failed, at least in part, in his attempt. But
in estimating what Hobbes was trying to do it seems reasonable
to take into account what he actually says about the method or
methods which he in fact employs.

Hobbes certainly emphasizes the debt which science and man
owe to mathematics. 'For whatsoever assistance doth accrue to
the life of man, whether from the observation of the heavens or
from the description of the earth, from the notation of times or
from the remotest experiments of navigation; finally, whatsoever
things they are in which this present age doth differ from the rude
simpleness of antiquity, we must acknowledge to be a debt which
we owe to geometry.'[2] The advances in astronomy, for example,
were rendered possible by mathematics, and without mathematics
there would have been no advance. And the benefits conferred by
applied science are also due to mathematics. If moral philosophers
took the trouble to ascertain the nature of human passions and
actions as clearly as mathematicians understand 'the nature of
quantity in geometrical figures'[3] it would be possible to banish
war and secure a stable peace.

This suggests that there is a close link between mathematics and

---

[1] *Concerning Body*, 1, 6, 12; *E.W.*, 1, p. 81.
[2] *Concerning Government and Society*, dedicatory epistle; *E.W.*, 11, p. iv.
[3] *Ibid.*

physics. And in point of fact Hobbes insists on this link. 'They that study natural philosophy study in vain, except they begin at geometry; and such writers or disputers thereof, as are ignorant of geometry, do but make their readers and hearers lose their time.'[1] But this does not mean that Hobbes endeavoured to deduce from the abstract analysis of motion and quantity and from mathematics the whole of natural philosophy. When he comes to the fourth part of his treatise *Concerning Body*, which he entitles 'Physics or the Phenomena of Nature', he remarks that the definition of philosophy which he gave in the first chapter shows that there are two methods: 'one from the generation of things to their possible effects, and the other from their effects or appearances to some possible generation of the same'.[2] In the foregoing chapters he has followed the first method, affirming nothing but definitions and their implications.[3] He is now about to use the second method, 'the finding out by the appearances or effects of nature, which we know by sense, some ways and means by which they may be, I do not say they are, generated'.[4] He is not now starting with definitions but with sensible phenomena or appearances, and he is seeking their possible causes.

If, therefore, Hobbes asserts a connection between the use of these two methods and his own definition of philosophy, it can reasonably be claimed that his introduction of fresh empirical material is not properly described as a 'failure' to fulfil his aim. And in this case we are not justified in accusing him of inconsistency because he makes, as it were, a fresh start when he comes to psychology and politics. He does, indeed, say that to obtain a knowledge of morals and politics by the synthetical method it is necessary to have first studied mathematics and physics. For the synthetical method involves seeing all effects as conclusions, proximate or remote, from first principles. But I do not think that he means much more by this than following out the exemplification of general principles in progressively particularized subject-matter according to an architectonic scheme. One cannot deduce men from the laws of motion, but one can study first the laws of motion in themselves and their application to body in

---

[1] *Concerning Body*, 1, 6, 6; *E.W.*, 1, p. 73.
[2] *Concerning Body*, 4, 1, 1; *E.W.*, 1, pp. 387–8.
[3] For example, given a certain definition of motion or a certain definition of body, motion or body will necessarily possess certain properties. But it does not follow immediately that there is motion or body. What follows is that if there is motion or if there is body, it will have these properties.
[4] *Ibid.*, p. 388.

general, secondly their application to different kinds of natural bodies, inanimate and animate, and thirdly their application to the artificial body which we call the commonwealth. In any case Hobbes observes that it is possible to study moral and political philosophy without previous knowledge of mathematics and physics if one employs the analytical method. Let us suppose that the question is asked whether an action is just or unjust. We can 'resolve' the notion *unjust* into the notion *fact against law*, and the notion of *law* into the notion *command* of him who has *coercive* power. And this notion of coercive power can be derived from the notion of men voluntarily establishing this power that they may live a peaceful life. Finally we can arrive at the principle that men's appetites and passions are of such a kind that they will be constantly making war on one another unless they are restrained by some power. And this 'may be known to be so by any man's experience, that will but examine his own mind'.[1] One can then decide, by employing the synthetical method, whether the action in question is just or unjust. And in the total process of 'resolution' and 'composition' one remains within the sphere of morals and politics without introducing remoter principles. Experience provides the factual data, and the philosopher can show systematically how they are connected in a rational scheme of cause and effect without necessarily having to relate the cause or causes to remoter and more general causes. Hobbes doubtless considered that a philosopher should show the connections between natural philosophy and civil philosophy. But the fact that he asserted the relative independence of morals and politics shows clearly enough that he was well aware of the need for fresh empirical data when treating of human psychology and of man's social and political life. I have no intention of denying the affinity between Hobbes and the continental rationalists. Among English philosophers he is one of the few who have tried to create systems. But it is also important to emphasize the fact that he was not a fanatical worshipper of pure deduction.

5. Now, it is obvious that philosophical knowledge, as envisaged by Hobbes, is concerned with the universal and not simply with the particular. Philosophy aims at a coherent and systematic knowledge of causal relations in the light of first principles or of universal causes. At the same time Hobbes clearly asserts a nominalist position when he is treating of names. The

---

[1] *Concerning Body*, 1, 6, 7; *E.W.*, 1, p. 74.

individual philosopher, he says, requires marks to help him to remember or recall his thoughts; and these marks are names. Further, if he is to communicate his thoughts to others, these marks must be able to serve as signs, which they can do when they are connected together in what we call 'speech'. Hence he gives the following definition. 'A *name* is a word taken at pleasure[1] to serve for a mark, which may raise in our mind a thought like to some thought we had before, and which being pronounced to others, may be to them a sign of what thought the speaker had or had not before in his mind.'[2] This does not mean that every name should be the name of something. The word *nothing* does not connote a special kind of something. But of the names which do designate things some are proper to one thing (such as *Homer* or *this man*), while others are common to many things (such as *man* or *tree*). And these common names are called 'universal'. That is to say, the term 'universal' is predicated of the name, not of the object designated by the name. For the name is the name of many individual things taken collectively. No one of them is a universal; nor is there any universal thing alongside of these individual things. Further, the universal name does not stand for any universal concept. 'This word *universal* is never the name of any thing existent in nature, nor of any idea or phantasm formed in the mind, but always the name of some word or name; so that when *a living creature, a stone, a spirit*, or any other thing, is said to be *universal*, it is not to be understood that any man, stone, etc., ever was or can be universal, but only that the words, living creature, stone, etc., are *universal names*, that is, names common to many things; and the conceptions answering them in our mind are the images and phantasms of several living creatures or other things.'[3] As Hobbes tended to identify the conceivable with the imaginable, he naturally found no place for a universal concept or idea, and he therefore attributed universality to common names only. He gives no very thorough explanation of the justification of our use of common names for sets of individual things, beyond referring to the likeness between things. 'One universal name is imposed on many things, for their similitude in some quality, or other accident.'[4] But his statement of a nominalistic position is unambiguous.

[1] Hobbes is here referring to the conventional character of language. Names are conventional marks and signs.
[2] *Concerning Body*, 1, 2, 4; *E.W.*, 1, p. 16.
[3] *Concerning Body*, 1, 2, 9; *E.W.*, 1, p. 20.   [4] *Leviathan*, 1, 4; *E.W.*, III, p. 21.

Like Ockham[1] and other mediaeval predecessors, Hobbes distinguishes between names or terms of 'first intention' and names of 'second intention'. Logical terms such as *universal, genus, species* and *syllogism* are, he tells us, 'the names of names and speeches'; they are terms of second intention. Words such as *man* or *stone* are names of first intention. One might expect perhaps that Hobbes would follow Ockham in saying that while terms of second intention stand for other terms, terms of first intention stand for things, universal terms of first intention standing for a plurality of individual things, not, of course, for any universal thing. But this is not what he actually says. He does, indeed, remark that names such as 'a man', 'a tree', 'a stone', 'are the names of things themselves';[2] but he insists that because 'names ordered in speech are signs of our conceptions, it is manifest that they are not signs of the things themselves'.[3] A name such as *stone* is the sign of a 'conception', that is, of a phantasm or image. If John uses this word when speaking to Peter, it is a sign to the latter of John's thought. 'The general use of speech is to transfer our mental discourse into verbal; or the train of our thoughts into a train of words.'[4] And if the 'thought' or 'conception' is an image, it is obvious that universality can be attributed only to words. But even if a universal word or term signifies directly a mental representation or 'fiction', as Hobbes sometimes puts it, this does not necessarily mean that it has no relation to reality. For it can have an indirect relation, inasmuch as the mental representation is itself caused by things. A 'thought' is 'a representation or appearance of some quality or other accident of a body without us, which is commonly called object. Which object worketh on the eyes, ears, and other parts of a man's body; and by diversity of working produceth diversity of appearances. The original of them all is that which we call *sense*, for there is no conception in a man's mind, which hath not at first, totally or by parts, been begotten upon the organs of sense. The rest are derived from that original.'[5] Thus although universality belongs only to words, which signify 'thoughts', there is an indirect relation between universal statements and reality, even if 'reality' must be here taken to mean the sphere of appearances or phenomena. There is, indeed, a great difference between experience,

[1] For an account of Ockham's doctrine on this point, see vol. III of this *History*, pp. 55 f.   [2] *Concerning Body*, 1, 2, 6; *E.W.*, I, p. 17.
[3] *Concerning Body*, 1, 2, 5; *E.W.*, I, p. 17.   [4] *Leviathan*, I, 4; *E.W.*, III, p. 19.
[5] *Leviathan*, I, I; *E.W.*, III, p. 1.

which Hobbes identifies with memory, and science. 'Experience,' to quote his famous statement, 'concludeth nothing universally.'[1] But science, which does 'conclude universally', is based on sense-experience.

If, therefore, we press the empiricist aspect of Hobbes's philosophy, it is possible to argue that his nominalism is not necessarily infected with scepticism; that is to say, with doubt about the real reference of scientific propositions. It may, indeed, follow that science is concerned with the realm of phenomena. For appearances produce images, and images are translated into words, the connection of which in speech renders science possible. But the conclusions of science, it might be said, are applicable within the realm of phenomena. And of any other realm the philosopher or scientist can say nothing. On a nominalistic basis constructed theories and causal explanations would be, as Hobbes says they are, hypothetical and conditional. But it would be possible to verify, or at least to test, scientific conclusions in experience, though Hobbes, who had no great esteem for the experimental method in science, does not in fact talk about verification.

Hobbes is, of course, very far from being only an empiricist, though there is certainly an important empiricist element in his thought. What he emphasizes when speaking of philosophy and science is deduction of consequences from first principles. As we have seen, he explicitly recognizes the use of the analytical or inductive method in arriving at the knowledge of principles; but what he emphasizes as the mark of scientific procedure is the deduction of the consequences of affirmations. And it is important to notice his clear statement that the principles from which deduction starts are definitions, and that definitions are nothing but the explication of the meanings of words. Definitions are the 'settling of significations' or 'settled significations of words'.[2] More exactly, a definition is 'a proposition, whose predicate resolves the subject, when it may; and when it may not, it exemplifies the same'.[3] Definitions are the sole principles of demonstration, and they are 'truths constituted arbitrarily by the inventors of speech, and therefore not to be demonstrated'.[4] If this is taken to mean that definitions are no more than arbitrary determinations of the meanings of words, the conclusions

---

[1] *Human Nature*, 1, 4, 10; *E.W.*, IV, p. 18.
[2] *Leviathan*, 1, 4 and 5; *E.W.*, III, pp. 24 and 33.
[3] *Concerning Body*, 1, 6, 14; *E.W.*, I, pp. 83–4.
[4] *Concerning Body*, 1, 3, 9; *E.W.*, I, p. 37.

derived from such definitions must partake of their arbitrariness. And then we are confronted with a divorce between scientific propositions and reality. There is no guarantee that scientific propositions are applicable to reality. In Hobbes's objections against the *Meditations* of Descartes we find the following remarkable passage. 'But what shall we now say if reasoning is perhaps nothing else but the joining and stringing together of names or appellations by the word *is*? In this case reason gives no conclusions about the nature of things, but only about their names; whether, indeed, or not we join the names of things according to conventions which we have arbitrarily established about their meanings. If this is the case, as it may be, reasoning will depend on names, names on the imagination, and the imagination perhaps, as I think, on the motion of the bodily organs.'[1] Even though Hobbes does not state dogmatically in this passage that reasoning establishes the connections between words only, he certainly suggests it. And it is no matter for surprise that a number of commentators have drawn the conclusion that philosophy or science is, for Hobbes, inevitably affected by subjectivism, and that they have spoken of his nominalistic scepticism.

Sometimes, indeed, it is possible to interpret Hobbes's assertions in a different light. He says, for example, that 'the first truths were arbitrarily made by those that first of all imposed names upon things, or received them from the imposition of others'.[2] But this statement could at any rate be taken to mean that if people had used the terms involved to mean something else than what they have in fact been made to mean, the propositions would not be true.[3] 'For it is true, for example, that *man is a living creature*, but it is for this reason, that it pleased men to impose both those names on the same thing.'[4] If the term *living creature* had been made to mean *stone*, it could not have been true to say that man is a living creature. And this is obviously the case. Again, when Hobbes asserts that it is false to say that 'the definition is the essence of any thing',[5] he is rejecting a form of expression used by Aristotle. And the remark which immediately follows, that 'definition is not the essence of any thing, but a speech signifying what we conceive of the essence thereof', is not by itself a

---

[1] *Objection*, IV; *O.L.*, pp. 257–8.   [2] *Concerning Body*, I, 3, 8; *E.W.*, I, p. 36.
[3] Hobbes insists that truth and falsity are predictable of propositions, never of things. Truth 'is not any affection of the thing, but of the proposition concerning it' (*Concerning Body*, I, 3, 7; *E.W.*, I, p. 35).
[4] *Ibid.*   [5] *Concerning Body*, I, 5, 7; *E.W.*, I, p. 60.

'sceptical' assertion. For it can be taken to imply that we have some idea or conception of the essence,[1] an idea which is signified by the name that is explained in the definition. Further, it can be pointed out that when Hobbes says that a word is a 'mere name', he does not necessarily mean that the idea signified by the word is without any relation to reality. For example, when he adopts for his own purposes the Aristotelian term 'first matter', he asks what this first matter or *materia prima* is, and he answers that it is a 'mere name'.[2] But he immediately adds, 'yet a name which is not of vain use; for it signifies a conception of body without the consideration of any form or other accident except only magnitude or extension, and aptness to receive form and other accident'.[3] 'First matter' and 'body in general' are for Hobbes equivalent terms. And there is no body in general. 'Wherefore *materia prima* is nothing.'[4] That is to say, there is no thing which corresponds to the name. In this sense the term is a 'mere name'. But it signifies a way of conceiving bodies; and bodies exist. Therefore, even though the name is not the name of any *thing*, it has some relation to reality.

However, even if the statement that Hobbes is a sceptic constitutes an exaggeration, it remains true that whether we proceed from cause to effect or from effect to cause, we attain knowledge only of possible effects or of possible causes. The only certain knowledge we can acquire is knowledge of the implications of propositions. If A implies B, then if A is true, B is true.

It seems to me that in Hobbes's interpretation of philosophy or science there are different strands of thought which he failed to distinguish clearly. The idea that in what we would call 'natural science' explanatory theories are hypothetical in character and that we can at best attain only a very high degree of probability may perhaps be said to represent one strand of thought. The idea that in mathematics we start with definitions and develop their implications, so that in pure mathematics we are concerned only with formal implications and not with the 'real world', represents another strand. And both these ideas reappear in modern empiricism. But Hobbes was also influenced by the rationalist ideal of a deductive philosophical system. For him the first principles of mathematics are 'postulates' and not true first

---

[1] The 'essence' of a thing is 'that accident for which we give a certain name to a body, or the accident which denominates its subject . . . as extension is the essence of a body' (*Concerning Body*, 2, 8, 23; *E.W.*, 1, p. 117).

[2] *Concerning Body*, 2, 8, 24; *E.W.*, 1, p. 118.   [3] *Ibid.*   [4] *Ibid.*

principles, because he considered them to be demonstrable. There are ultimate first principles, antecedent to mathematics and to physics. Now, for a rationalism of the continental type the truth of first principles must be known intuitively, and all the propositions which can be deduced from them will be certainly true. And sometimes Hobbes appears to indicate that this is what he thinks. But at other times he speaks as though the first principles or definitions were 'arbitrary', in the sense in which a modern empiricist might say that mathematical definitions are arbitrary. And then he draws the conclusion that the whole of science or philosophy is nothing but a reasoning about 'names', about the consequences of definitions or meanings which have been arbitrarily established. We are then confronted with a divorce between philosophy and the world which was alien to the spirit of continental rationalism. Further, we can find in Hobbes a monolithic idea of science, according to which there is a progressive development from first principles in a deductive manner, and which, if consistently maintained, would neglect the important differences between, for example, pure mathematics and empirical science. And at the same time we find a recognition of the relative independence of ethics and politics, on the ground that their principles can be known experimentally without reference to the parts of philosophy which logically precede.

If, therefore, these diverse ideas and lines of thought are present together in Hobbes's mind, it is not surprising that different historians have interpreted him in different ways according to the varying degrees of emphasis which they have placed on this or that aspect of his philosophy. As regards the view that he was a 'sceptical nominalist', his nominalism, as we have seen, is clearly stated, and the charge of 'scepticism' is not without support in his writings. But I do not think that anyone who reads his philosophical writings as a whole would naturally form the impression that 'sceptic' is the most appropriate label to give to Hobbes. It is doubtless arguable that nominalism leads, or should lead, to scepticism. But Hobbes happily combined his nominalism with points of view that are scarcely compatible with it. A great deal of the confusion arose, no doubt, from the failure to distinguish adequately between philosophy, mathematics and empirical science. But we can hardly blame Hobbes for this. In the seventeenth century, philosophy and science were not clearly distinguished, and it is no matter for surprise that Hobbes failed to distinguish them adequately. But, of course, by confining philosophy to the study of bodies he made it even more difficult for him to do so than it would have been in any case.

6. Philosophy, as we have seen, is concerned with the discovery of causes. What does Hobbes understand by 'cause'? 'A cause is the sum or aggregate of all such accidents, both in the agents and the patient, as concur to the producing of the effect propounded; all which existing together, it cannot be understood but that the effect existeth with them; or that it can possibly exist if any one of them be absent.'[1] But to understand this definition we must first understand what Hobbes means by 'accident'. He defines the latter as 'the manner of our conception of body'.[2] And this is, he asserts, the same as saying that 'an accident is that faculty of any body by which it works in us a conception of itself'.[3] If, therefore, we choose to call accidents 'phenomena' or 'appearances', we can say that for Hobbes the cause of any given effect is the sum of phenomena, both in the agent and in the patient, which concur in the following way in producing the effect. If the whole set of phenomena is present, we cannot conceive the absence of the effect. And if any one of the set of phenomena is absent, we cannot conceive the production of the effect. The cause of any thing is thus the sum of all the conditions required for the existence of that thing; the conditions required, that is to say, both in the agent and in the patient. If body A generates motion in body B, A is the agent and B is the patient. Thus if fire warms my hand, fire is the agent and the hand is the patient. The accident generated in the patient is the effect of the action of the fire. And the cause (that is, entire cause) of this effect is to vary the definition slightly, 'the aggregate of all the accidents both of the agents, how many soever they be, and of the patient, put together; which when they are all supposed to be present, it cannot be understood but that the effect is produced at the same instant: and if any one of them be wanting, it cannot be understood but that the effect is not produced'.[4]

Within the 'entire cause', as defined above, Hobbes distinguishes between 'efficient cause' and 'material cause'. The former is the aggregate of accidents in the agent or agents which are required for the production of an effect which is actually produced, while

---

[1] *Concerning Body*, 1, 6, 10; *E.W.*, 1, p. 77.
[2] *Concerning Body*, 2, 8, 2; *E.W.*, 1, p. 104.
[3] *Ibid.*, p. 103.
[4] *Concerning Body*, 2, 9, 3; *E.W.*, 1, pp. 121-2.

the latter is the aggregate of requisite accidents in the patient. Both together make up the entire cause. We can, indeed, talk about the power of the agent and the power of the patient, or, rather, about the active power of the agent and the passive power of the patient. But these are objectively the same as the efficient cause and the material cause respectively, though different terms are used because we can consider the same things from different points of view. The aggregate of accidents in the agent, when considered in relation to an effect already produced, is called the efficient cause, and when considered in relation to future time, to the effect to be produced later, it is called the active power of the agent. Similarly, the aggregate of actions in the patient is called the material cause when it is considered in relation to the past, to the effect already produced, and the passive power of the patient when it is considered in relation to the future. As for the so-called 'formal' and 'final' causes, these are both reducible to efficient causes. 'For when it is said that the essence of a thing is the cause thereof, *as to be rational is the cause of man*, it is not intelligible; for it is all one, as if it were said, *to be a man is the cause of man;* which is not well said. And yet the knowledge of the *essence* of anything is the cause of the knowledge of the thing itself; for, if I first know that a thing is *rational*, I know from thence that the same is *man*; but this is no other than an efficient cause. A *final cause* has no place but in such things as have sense and will; and this also I shall prove hereafter to be an efficient cause.'[1] For Hobbes final causality is simply the way in which efficient causes operate in man, with deliberation.

In the foregoing account of Hobbes's analysis of causality we can note how he uses Scholastic terms, interpreting them or assigning them meanings in accordance with his own philosophy. To all intents and purposes we are left with efficient causality alone. Now, if the entire efficient cause is present, the effect is produced. Indeed, this statement is necessarily true, once given Hobbes's definition of a cause. For if the effect were not produced, the cause would not be an entire cause. Furthermore, 'in what-soever instant the cause is entire, in the same instant the effect is produced. For if it be not produced, something is still wanting, which is requisite for the production of it; and therefore the cause was not entire, as was supposed.'[2]

[1] *Concerning Body*, 2, 10, 7; *E.W.*, 1, pp. 131–2.
[2] *Concerning Body*, 2, 9, 5; *E.W.*, 1, p. 123.

From these considerations Hobbes draws an important conclusion. We have seen that when the cause is present, the effect always and instantaneously follows. Therefore it cannot but be produced, once given the cause. Therefore the effect follows necessarily from the cause. Hence the cause is a necessary cause. The conclusion is, then, that 'all the effects that have been, or shall be produced, have their necessity in things antecedent'.[1] This at once rules out all freedom in man, at least if freedom is taken to imply absence of necessity. If, indeed, to call an agent free is simply to say that he is not hindered in his activity, this way of speaking has a meaning; but if anyone means by the epithet something more than 'free from being hindered by opposition, I should not say he were in error, but that his words were without meaning, that is to say, absurd'.[2] Once given the cause, the effect necessarily follows. If the effect does not follow, the cause (that is, the entire cause) was not present. And that is all there is to it.

Philosophy, therefore, is concerned with necessary causality; for there can be no other. And causal activity consists in the production of motion by an agent in a patient, both agent and patient being bodies. Creation out of nothing, immaterial causal activity, free causes; such ideas have no place in philosophy. We are concerned simply with the action of bodies in motion on contiguous bodies in motion, with the laws of dynamics operating necessarily and mechanically. And this applies to human activity as much as to the activity of unconscious bodies. True, the deliberate activity of rational beings differs from the activity of inanimate bodies; and in this sense the laws operate in different ways. But for Hobbes mechanistic determinism has the last word, in the human as in the non-human sphere. In this respect it can be said that his philosophy is an attempt to see how far the Galilean dynamics can be pushed as an explanatory principle.

7. The fact that Hobbes believed that every effect has a necessary antecedent cause does not mean that he believed that we can determine with certainty what is the cause of a given event. As we have already seen, the philosopher argues from effects to possible causes and from causes to possible effects. And all our knowledge of the 'consequences' of facts is hypothetical or conditional. That this must be só is, indeed, indicated by the use of the word 'accident' in the definition of a cause. For accident is

---

[1] *Concerning Body*, 2, 9, 5; *E.W.*, I, p. 123.
[2] *Leviathan*, I, 5; *E.W.*, III, p. 33.

itself defined as 'the manner of our conception of body'. Thus accidents, the aggregate of which form the entire cause, are defined as having a relation to the mind, to our way of looking at things. We cannot attain absolute certainty that causal relations are in fact what we think them to be.

A similar tendency towards subjectivism (I should not care to put it more strongly) can be seen in Hobbes's definitions of space and time. For space is defined as 'the phantasm of a thing existing without the mind simply'[1] and time as 'the phantasm of before and after in motion'.[2] Hobbes does not mean, of course, that the thing existing outside the mind is a phantasm or image: he did not doubt the existence of bodies. But we can have a phantasm or image of a thing 'in which we consider no other accident, but only that it appears without us' (that is, the fact of its externality); and space is defined as being this image. The image has, indeed, an objective foundation, and Hobbes has no intention of denying this. But this does not alter the fact that he defines space in terms of a subjective modification. Time too has an objective foundation, namely, the movement of bodies; but it is none the less defined as a phantasm and so is said to be 'not in the things without us, but only in the thoughts of the mind'.[3]

Given these definitions of space and time, Hobbes naturally answers the question whether space and time are infinite or finite by remarking that the reply depends simply on our imagination; that is, on whether we imagine space and time as terminated or not. We can imagine time as having a beginning and an end, or we can imagine it without any assigned limits, that is, as extending indefinitely. (Similarly, when we say that number is infinite, we mean only that no number is expressed, or that number is an indefinite name.) As for the infinite divisibility of space and time, this is to be taken in the sense that 'whatsoever is divided, is divided into such parts as may again be divided' or as 'the least divisible thing is not to be given, or, as geometricians have it, no quantity is so small, but a less may be taken'.[4]

8. The objective foundation of space is, as we have seen, existent body, which can be considered in abstraction from all accidents. It is called 'body' because of its extension, and 'existing' because it does not depend on our thought. 'Because it depends not upon our thoughts, we say (it) is *a thing subsisting* of itself; as

---

[1] *Concerning Body*, 2, 7, 2; *E.W.*, 1, p. 94.   [2] *Ibid.*, p. 95.
[3] *Concerning Body*, 2, 7, 3; p. 94.   [4] *Concerning Body*, 2, 7, 13; *E.W.*, 1, p. 100.

also *existing*, because without us.'[1] It is also called the 'subject', 'because it is so placed in and *subjected* to imaginary space, that it may be understood by reason, as well as perceived by sense. The definition, therefore, of *body* may be this, *a body is that, which having no dependence upon our thought, is coincident or coextended with some part of space*.'[2] Objectivity or independence of human thinking thus enters into the definition of body. But at the same time the latter is defined in relation to our thought, as not dependent upon it and as knowable because subjected to imaginary space. If one takes this idea by itself, it has a remarkably Kantian flavour.

A body possesses accidents. The definition of an accident as 'the manner of our conception of body' has already been given. But some further explanation may be appropriate here. If we ask 'what is hard?', we are asking for the definition of a concrete name. 'The answer will be, hard is that, whereof no part gives place, but when the whole gives place.'[3] But if we ask 'what is hardness?', we are asking a question about an abstract name, namely, why a thing appears hard. And therefore 'a cause must be shown why a part does not give place, except the whole give place'.[4] And to ask this is to ask what it is in a body which gives rise in us to a certain conception of body. According to Hobbes, as has been mentioned before, to say that an accident is the manner in which we conceive a body is the same as to say that an accident is the faculty in a body of producing in us a certain conception of itself. The force of this assertion comes out most clearly in Hobbes's theory of secondary qualities.

A distinction must be made between accidents which are common to all bodies and which cannot perish unless the body also perishes and accidents which are not common to all bodies and which can perish and be succeeded by others without the body itself perishing. Extension and figure are accidents of the first kind, 'for no body can be conceived to be without extension or without figure'.[5] Figure varies, of course; but there is not, and cannot be, any body without figure. But an accident such as hardness can be succeeded by softness without the body itself perishing. Hardness, therefore, is an accident of the second type.

Extension and figure are the only accidents of the first type. Magnitude is not another accident: it is the same as extension. It

[1] *Concerning Body*, 2, 8, 1; *E.W.*, I, p. 102.   [2] *Ibid.*
[3] *Concerning Body*, 2, 8, 2; *E.W.*, I, p. 103.   [4] *Ibid.*
[5] *Concerning Body*, 2, 8, 3; *E.W.*, I, p. 104.

is also called by some 'real space'. It is not, as is imaginary space, 'an accident of the mind': it is an accident of body. We can say, therefore, if we like, that there is real space. But this real space is the same as magnitude, which is itself the same as extension. Is magnitude also the same as place? Hobbes answers that it is not. Place is 'a phantasm of any body of such and such quantity and figure' and is 'nothing out of the mind'.[1] It is 'feigned extension', whereas magnitude is 'true extension',[2] which causes the phantasm that is place.

Accidents of the second type, however, do not exist in bodies in the form in which they are present to consciousness. Colour and sound, for example, as also odour and savour, are 'phantasms'; they belong to the sphere of appearance. 'The phantasm, which is made by hearing, is sound; by smell, odour; by taste, savour. . . .'[3] 'For light and colour, and heat and sound, and other qualities which are commonly called sensible, are not objects, but phantasms in the sentients.'[4] 'As for the objects of hearing, smell, taste and touch, they are not sound, odour, savour, hardness, etc., but the bodies themselves from which sound, odour, savour, hardness, etc., proceed.'[5] Bodies in motion generate motion in the organs of sense, and thence arise the phantasms which we call colour, sound, savour, odour, hardness and softness, light and so on. A contiguous and moving body effects the outermost part of the organ of sense, and pressure or motion is transmitted to the innermost part of the organ. At the same time, by reason of the natural internal motion of the organ, a reaction against this pressure takes place, an 'endeavour outwards' stimulated by the 'endeavour inwards'. And the phantasm or 'idea' arises from the final reaction to the 'endeavour inwards'. We can thus define 'sense' as 'a phantasm, made by the reaction and endeavour outwards in the organ of sense, caused by an endeavour inwards from the object, remaining for some time more or less'.[6] Colour, for instance, is our way of perceiving an external body, or, objectively, it is that in a body which causes our 'conception' of the latter. And this 'faculty' in the body is not itself colour. In the case of extension, on the contrary, it is extension itself which causes our conception of it.

---

[1] *Concerning Body*, 2, 8, 5; *E.W.*, I, p. 105.   [2] *Ibid.*
[3] *Concerning Body*, 4, 25, 10; *E.W.*, I, p. 405.
[4] *Concerning Body*, 4, 25, 3; *E.W.*, I, pp. 391–2.
[5] *Concerning Body*, 4, 25, 10; *E.W.*, I, p. 405.
[6] *Concerning Body*, 4, 25, 2; *E.W.*, I, p. 391.

The world of colour, sound, odour, savour, tactile qualities and light is thus the world of appearance. And philosophy is to a great extent the endeavour to discover the causes of these appearances, that is, the causes of our 'phantasms'. Behind appearances there are, for Hobbes, at least as far as philosophy is concerned, only extended bodies and motion.

9. Motion means for Hobbes local motion. 'Motion is a continual relinquishing of one place and acquiring of another.'[1] And a thing is said to be at rest when for any time it is in one place. It follows, therefore, from these definitions that anything which is in motion has been moved. For if it has not been moved, it is in the same place in which it formerly was. And thus it follows from the definition of rest that it is at rest. Similarly, that which is moved will yet be moved. For that which is in motion is continually changing place. Lastly, whatever is moved is not in one place during any time, however brief. If it were, it would, by definition, be at rest.

Any thing which is at rest will always be at rest, unless some other body 'by endeavouring to get into its place by motion suffers it no longer to remain at rest'.[2] Similarly, if any thing is in motion, it will be always in motion, unless some other body causes it to be at rest. For if there were no other body, 'there will be no reason why it should rest now rather than at another time'.[3] Again, the cause of motion can only be a contiguous and already moving body.

If motion is reduced to local motion, change is also reducible to local motion. 'Mutation can be nothing else but motion of the parts of that body which is changed.'[4] We do not say that any thing is changed unless it appears to our senses otherwise than it did before. But these appearances are effects produced in us by motion.

10. In animals there are two kinds of motion which are peculiar to them. The first is vital motion. This is 'the motion of the blood, perpetually circulating (as hath been shown from many infallible signs and marks by Doctor Harvey, the first observer of it) in the veins and arteries'.[5] Elsewhere Hobbes describes it as 'the course of the blood, the pulse, the breathing, the concoction, nutrition, excretion, etc., to which motions there needs no help of

---

[1] *Concerning Body*, 2, 8, 10; *E.W.*, 1, p. 109.
[2] *Concerning Body*, 2, 8, 18; *E.W.*, 1, p. 115.
[3] *Ibid.*
[4] *Concerning Body*, 2, 9, 9; *E.W.*, 1, p. 126.
[5] *Concerning Body*, 4, 25, 12; *E.W.*, 1, p. 407.

imagination'.[1] In other words, vital motions are those vital processes in the animal organism which take place without any deliberation or conscious effort, such as circulation of the blood, digestion and respiration.

The second kind of motion which is peculiar to animals is 'animal motion, otherwise called voluntary motion'.[2] As examples Hobbes gives, going, speaking, moving the limbs, when such actions are 'first fancied in our minds'.[3] The first internal beginning of all voluntary motions is imagination, while the 'small beginnings of motion within the body of man, before they appear in walking, speaking, striking, and other visible actions are commonly called endeavour'.[4] Here we have the notion of *conatus*, which plays a prominent part in the philosophy of Spinoza.

This endeavour, directed towards something which causes it, is called *appetite* or *desire*. When it is directed away from something ('fromward something', as Hobbes puts it) it is called *aversion*. The fundamental forms of endeavour are thus appetite or desire and aversion, both being motions. They are objectively the same as love and hate respectively; but when we talk of desire and aversion, we think of the objects as absent, whereas in talking of love and hate we think of the objects as present.

11. Some appetites are innate or born with men, such as the appetite for food. Others proceed from experience. But in any case 'whatsoever is the object of any man's appetite or desire, that is it which he for his part calleth *good*: and the object of his hate and aversion, *evil*; and of his contempt, *vile* and *inconsiderable*'.[5]

Good and evil are, therefore, relative notions. There is no absolute good and no absolute evil; and there is no common objective norm, taken from the objects themselves, to distinguish between good and evil. The words 'are ever used with relation to the person that useth them'.[6] The rule for distinguishing good and evil depends on the individual; that is, on his 'voluntary motions', if we consider man as he is apart from the commonwealth or State. In the commonwealth, however, it is the person who represents it; that is, the sovereign, who determines what is good and what is evil.

12. The different passions are different forms of appetite and aversion, with the exception of pure pleasure and pain, which are 'a certain fruition of good or evil'.[7] Consequently, as appetite and

---

[1] *Leviathan*, 1, 6; *E.W.*, III, p. 31.   [2] *Ibid.*   [3] *Ibid.*   [4] *Ibid.*
[5] *Ibid.*, p. 4.   [6] *Ibid.*   [7] *Concerning Body*, 4, 25, 13; *E.W.*, I, pp. 409-10.

aversion are motions, so are the different passions. External objects affect the organs of sense and there arises 'that motion and agitation of the brain which we call conception'.[1] This motion of the brain is continued to the heart, 'there to be called passion'.[2]

Hobbes finds a number of simple passions, namely, appetite, desire, love, aversion, hate, joy and grief.[3] These take different forms; or at least they are given different names according to different considerations. Thus if we consider the opinion which men have of attaining what they desire, we can distinguish hope and despair. The former is appetite with an opinion of attaining the desired object, while the latter is appetite without this opinion. Secondly, we can consider the object loved or hated. And then we can distinguish, for example, between covetousness, which is the desire of riches, and ambition, which is the desire of office or precedence. Thirdly, the consideration of a number of passions together may lead us to use a special name. Thus 'love of one singularly, with desire to be singularly beloved, is called *the passion of love*', whereas 'the same, with fear that the love is not mutual, (is called) *jealousy*'.[4] Finally, we can name a passion from the motion itself. We can speak, for instance, of 'sudden dejection', 'the passion that causeth weeping', and which is caused by events which suddenly take away some vehement hope or some 'prop of power'.[5]

But however many the passions of man may be, they are all motions. And Hobbes speaks in an oft-quoted sentence of delight or pleasure as being 'nothing really but motion about the heart, as conception is nothing but motion in the head'.[6]

13. Hobbes does not overlook the fact that human beings perform some actions with deliberation. But he defines deliberation in terms of the passions. Let us suppose that in a man's mind desire to acquire some object alternates with aversion and that thoughts of the good consequences of acquiring it alternate with thoughts of the evil consequences (that is, undesirable consequences). 'The whole sum of desires, aversions, hopes and fears continued till the thing be either done, or thought impossible, is that we call deliberation.'[7] And Hobbes draws the conclusion that

---

[1] *Human Nature*, 8, 1; *E.W.*, IV, p. 34.   [2] *Ibid.*
[3] Hobbes distinguishes between pleasures and displeasures of sense and pleasures and displeasures of the mind. The latter arise from expectation of an end or of consequences. Pleasures of the mind are called *joy*, while displeasures of the mind are called *grief* (in distinction from displeasures of sense, which are called *pain*).
[4] *Leviathan*, 1, 6; *E.W.*, III, p. 44.   [5] *Ibid.*, p. 46.
[6] *Human Nature*, 7, 1; *E.W.*, IV, p. 31.   [7] *Leviathan*, 1, 6; *E.W.*, III, p. 48.

beasts also must be said to deliberate, inasmuch as this alternate succession of appetites, aversions, hopes and fears is found in them as well as in man.

Now, in deliberation the last appetite or aversion is called *will*; that is, the act of willing. '*Will* therefore is the last appetite in deliberating';[1] and the action depends on this final inclination or appetite. From this Hobbes again concludes that since the beasts have deliberation they must necessarily also have will.

It follows that the freedom of willing or not willing is no greater in man than in the beasts. 'And therefore such a liberty as is free from necessity is not to be found in the will either of men or beasts. But if by liberty we understand the faculty or power, not of willing, but of doing what they will, then certainly that liberty is to be allowed to both and both may equally have it, whensoever it is to be had.'[2]

14. When treating of the 'intellectual virtues' Hobbes distinguishes between natural and acquired mental capacity or 'wit'. Some men are naturally quick, others slow. And the principal cause of these differences is 'the difference of men's passions'.[3] Those, for example, whose end is sensual pleasure, are necessarily less delighted with the 'imaginations' which do not conduce to this end, and they pay less attention than others to the means of acquiring knowledge. They suffer from dullness of mind, which 'proceedeth from the appetite of sensual or bodily delight. And it may well be conjectured, that such passion hath its beginning from a *grossness* and *difficulty* of the *motion* of the *spirit* about the heart.'[4] Differences in natural mental capacity are therefore ultimately caused by differences in motion. As for differences in acquired 'wit', which is reason, there are other causal factors, such as education, which have to be taken into consideration.

'The passions that most of all cause the difference of wit are principally the more or less desire of power, of riches, of knowledge, and of honour. All which may be reduced to the first, that is, desire of power. For riches, knowledge and honour are but several sorts of power.'[5] The desire for power is thus the fundamental factor in causing a man to develop his mental capacities.

---

[1] *Leviathan*, 1, 6; *E.W.*, III, p. 48.
[2] *Concerning Body*, 4, 25, 13; *E.W.*, I. p. 409.
[3] *Leviathan*, 1, 8; *E.W.*, I. p. 57.
[4] *Human Nature*, 10, 3; *E.W.*, IV, p. 55.
[5] *Leviathan*, 1, 8; *E.W.*, III, p. 61.

15. We are presented, therefore, with a multiplicity of individual human beings, each of whom is driven by his passions, which themselves are forms of motion. And it is the appetites and aversions of the individual which determine for him what is good and what is evil. In the next chapter we shall consider the consequences of this state of affairs and the transition from this atomic individualism to the construction of that artificial body, the commonwealth or State.

CHAPTER II

HOBBES (2)

The natural state of war—The laws of nature—The generation of a commonwealth and the theory of the covenant—The rights of the sovereign—The liberty of subjects—Reflections on Hobbes's political theory.

1. MEN are by nature equal in bodily and mental capacities; not, indeed, in the sense that all possess the same degree of physical strength and of quickness of mind, but in the sense that, by and large, an individual's deficiencies in one respect can be compensated by other qualities. The physically weak can master the physically strong by craft or by conspiracy; and experience enables all men to acquire prudence in the things to which they apply themselves. And this natural equality produces in men an equal hope of attaining their ends. Every individual seeks and pursues his own conservation, and some set their hearts on delectation or pleasure. Nobody resigns himself to making no effort to attain the end to which he is naturally impelled, on the ground that he is not equal to others.

Now, this fact that every individual seeks his own conservation and his own delectation leads to competition and mistrust of others. Further, every man desires that others should value him as he values himself; and he is quick to resent every slight and all signs of contempt. 'So that in the nature of man we find three principal causes of quarrel. First, competition; secondly, diffidence (that is, mistrust); thirdly, glory.'[1]

From this Hobbes draws the conclusion that until such time as men live under a common power, they are in a state of war with one another. 'For *war* consisteth not in battle only, or the act of fighting; but in a tract of time, wherein the will to contend by battle is sufficiently known: and therefore the notion of *time* is to be considered in the nature of war; as it is in the nature of weather. For as the nature of foul weather lieth not in a shower or two of rain; but in an inclination thereto of many days together: so the nature of war consisteth not in actual fighting; but in the known disposition thereto, during all the time there is no assurance to the contrary. All other time is peace.'[2]

[1] *Leviathan*, I, 13; *E.W.*, III, p. 112.

[2] *Ibid.*, p. 113.

The natural state of war, therefore, is the state of affairs in which the individual is dependent for his security on his own strength and his own wits. 'In such condition there is no place for industry; because the fruit thereof is uncertain: and consequently no culture of the earth; no navigation, nor use of the commodities that may be imported by sea; no commodious building; no instruments of moving and removing such things as require much force; no knowledge of the face of the earth; no account of time; no arts; no letters; no society; and, which is worst of all, continual fear and danger of violent death; and the life of man, solitary, poor, nasty, brutish, and short.'[1] In this frequently quoted passage Hobbes depicts the natural state of war as a condition in which civilization and its benefits are absent. The conclusion is obvious, namely, that it is only through the organization of society and the establishment of the commonwealth that peace and civilization can be attained.

The natural state of war is a deduction from consideration of the nature of man and his passions. But if anyone doubts the objective validity of the conclusion, he has only to observe what happens even in a state of organized society. Everyone carries arms when he takes a journey; bars his door at night; he locks up his valuables. And this shows clearly enough what he thinks of his fellow men. 'Does he not there as much accuse mankind by his actions, as I do by my words? But neither of us accuse man's nature in it. The desires and other passions of man are themselves no sin. No more are the actions that proceed from those passions, till they know a law that forbids them; which till laws be made they cannot know: nor can any law be made, till they have agreed upon the person that shall make it.'[2]

This quotation suggests that in the natural state of war there are no objective moral distinctions. And this is precisely Hobbes's view. In this state 'the notions of right and wrong, justice and injustice, have no place. Where there is no common power, there is no law, where no law, no injustice. Force and fraud are in war the two cardinal virtues.'[3] Further, there is 'no dominion, no *mine* and *thine* distinct; but only that to be every man's, that he can get: and for so long as he can keep it'.[4]

Does Hobbes mean that this state of war was an historical fact, in the sense that it universally preceded the organization of

---

[1] *Leviathan*, I, 13; *E.W.*, III, p. 113.
[2] *Ibid.*, p. 114.
[3] *Ibid.*, p. 115.
[4] *Ibid.*

society? Or does he mean that it precedes the organization of society only logically, in the sense that if we prescind from what man owes to the commonwealth or State, we arrive by abstraction at this layer, as it were, of atomic individualism, which is rooted in the human passions and which would obtain, were it not for other factors which naturally impel men from the beginning to organize societies and subject themselves to a common power? He means, of course, at least the latter. The state of war was never, in his opinion, universal 'over all the world'; but the idea of this condition of affairs represents the condition which would obtain, were it not for the foundation of commonwealths. There is plenty of empirical evidence for this, apart from *a priori* deduction from the analysis of the passions. We have only to look at the behaviour of kings and sovereigns. They fortify their territories against possible invaders, and even in peace-time they send spies into their neighbours' realms. They are, in fine, in a constant 'posture of war'. Again, we have only to look at what happens when peaceful government breaks down and civil war occurs. This shows clearly 'what manner of life there would be, where there were no common power to fear'.[1] At the same time, the natural state of war is, according to Hobbes, an historical fact in many places, as can be seen in America, where the savages 'live at this day in that brutish manner', if we except the internal government of small families, the harmony of which depends on 'natural lust'.

2. It is obviously in man's interest to emerge from this natural state of war; and the possibility of doing so is provided by nature itself. For by nature men have their passions and their reason. It is, indeed, their passions which bring about the state of war. But at the same time fear of death, desire of such things as are necessary to 'commodious' living, and hope of obtaining these things by industry are passions which incline men to seek for peace. It is not that the passions simply lead to war, whereas reason counsels peace. Some passions incline men to peace; and what reason does is to show how the fundamental desire of self-conservation can be made effective. It suggests first of all 'convenient articles of peace, upon which men may be drawn to agreement. These articles are they, which otherwise are called the Laws of Nature.'[2]

---

[1] *Leviathan*, 1, 13; *E.W.*, III, p. 114.
[2] *Leviathan*, 1, 14; *E.W.*, III, p. 116.

Hobbes defines a law of nature as 'the dictate of right reason,[1] conversant about those things which are either to be done or omitted for the constant preservation of life and member, as much as in us lies'.[2] Again, 'a law of nature, *lex naturalis*, is a precept, or general rule, found out by reason, by which a man is forbidden to do that which is destructive of his life or taketh away the means of preserving the same; and to omit that, by which he thinketh it may be best preserved'.[3] In interpreting these definitions we have, of course, to avoid attaching to the word 'law' any theological or metaphysical significance or reference. A law of nature in this context is for Hobbes a dictate of egoistic prudence. Every man instinctively pursues self-preservation and security. But man is not merely a creature of instinct and blind impulse; and there is such a thing as rational self-preservation. The so-called laws of nature state the conditions of this rational self-preservation. And as Hobbes goes on to argue that the rational pursuit of self-preservation is what leads men to form commonwealths or states, the laws of nature give the conditions for the establishment of society and stable government. They are the rules a reasonable being would observe in pursuing his own advantage, if he were conscious of man's predicament in a condition in which impulse and passion alone ruled and if he himself were not governed simply by momentary impulse and by prejudices arising from passion. Furthermore, Hobbes believed that by and large man, who is essentially egoistic and self-regarding, does in fact act according to these rules. For in point of fact men do form organized societies and subject themselves to governments. Hence they do in fact observe the dictates of enlightened egoism. It follows that these laws are analogous to the physical laws of nature and state the way in which enlightened egoists do in fact behave, the way in which their psychological make-up determines them to behave. Certainly, Hobbes frequently speaks as though these rules were teleological principles, and as though they were what Kant would call hypothetical imperatives; that is, assertoric hypothetical imperatives, since every individual necessarily seeks his own preservation and security. Indeed, Hobbes could hardly avoid speaking in this way. But he is dealing

---

[1] Right reason, Hobbes explains, means here 'the peculiar and true ratiocination of every man concerning those actions of his, which may either redound to the damage or benefit of his neighbours'. 'Peculiar', because in the 'state of nature' the individual's reason is for him the only rule of action.

[2] *Philosophical Elements of a True Citizen*, 2, 1; *E.W.*, II, p. 16.

[3] *Leviathan*, 1, 14; *E.W.*, III, pp. 116–17.

with the interplay of motions and forces which lead to the creation of that artificial body, the commonwealth; and the tendency of his thought is to assimilate the operation of the 'laws of nature' to the operation of efficient causality. The State itself is the resultant of the interplay of forces; and human reason, displayed in the conduct expressed by these rules, is one of these determining forces. Or, if we wish to look at the matter from the point of view of the philosophical deduction of society and government, the laws of nature can be said to represent axioms or postulates which render this deduction possible. They answer the question, what are the conditions under which the transition from the natural state of war to the state of men living in organized societies becomes intelligible. And these conditions are rooted in the dynamics of human nature itself. They are not a system of God-given laws (except, indeed, in the sense that God created man and all that is in him). Nor do they state absolute values; for, according to Hobbes, there are no absolute values.

The list of the laws of nature is given differently by Hobbes in different places. Here I confine myself to the *Leviathan*, where we are told that the fundamental law of nature is the general rule of reason that 'every man ought to endeavour peace, as far as he has hope of obtaining it; and when he cannot obtain it, that he may seek, and use, all helps and advantages of war'.[1] The first part, he asserts, contains the fundamental law of nature, namely, to seek peace and follow it, while the second part contains the sum of natural right, namely, to defend ourselves by all means that we can.

The second law of nature is 'that a man be willing, when others are so too, as far-forth, as for peace and defence of himself he shall think it necessary, to lay down this right to all things; and be contented with so much liberty against other men, as he would allow other men against himself'.[2] To lay down one's right to anything is to divest oneself of the liberty of hindering another from enjoying his own right to the same thing. But if a man lays down his right in this sense, he does so with a view to his own advantage. And it follows from this that there are 'some rights which no man can be understood by any words, or other signs, to have abandoned or transferred'.[3] For example, a man cannot lay down the right to defend his own life, 'because he cannot be understood to aim thereby at any good to himself'.[4]

Hobbes proceeds, in accordance with his declared method, to

[1] *Leviathan*, 1, 14; *E.W.*, III, p. 117.   [2] *Ibid.*, p. 118.   [3] *Ibid.*, p. 120.   [4] *Ibid.*

lay down some definitions. First a contract is defined as 'the mutual transferring of right'.[1] But 'one of the contractors may deliver the thing contracted for on his part, and leave the other to perform his part at some determinate time after, and in the meantime be trusted; and then the contract on his part is called *pact* or *covenant*'.[2] This definition is of importance because, as will be seen presently, Hobbes founds the commonwealth on a social covenant.

The third law of nature is 'that men perform their covenant made'.[3] Without this law of nature 'covenants are in vain, and but empty words; and the right of all men to all things remaining, we are still in the condition of war'.[4] Further, this law is the fountain of justice. When there has been no covenant, no action can be unjust. But when a covenant has been made, to break it is unjust. Indeed, injustice can be defined as 'the not performance of covenant. And whatsoever is not unjust, is *just*.'[5]

It may appear to be an instance of gross inconsistency on Hobbes's part if he now talks about justice and injustice when earlier he has asserted that such distinctions do not obtain in the state of war. But if we read carefully what he says, we shall see that on this point at least he is not guilty of contradicting himself. For he adds that covenants of mutual trust are invalid when there is fear of non-performance on either part, and that in the natural condition of war this fear is always present. It follows, therefore, that there are no valid covenants, and hence no justice and injustice, until the commonwealth is established; that is, until a coercive power has been established which will compel men to perform their covenants.

In the *Leviathan* Hobbes states nineteen laws of nature in all; and I omit the rest of them. But it is worth noting that after completing his list he asserts that these laws, and any others which there may be, bind in conscience. And if we take this statement in a moral sense, we can only conclude that Hobbes has suddenly adopted a point of view very different from the one which he has hitherto expressed. In point of fact, however, he appears to mean simply that reason, considering man's desire for security, dictates that he should (that is, if he is to act rationally) desire that the laws should be observed. The laws are only improperly called 'laws', Hobbes tells us; 'for they are but

---

[1] *Leviathan*, I, 14; *E.W.*, III, p. 120.   [2] *Ibid.*, p. 121.
[3] *Leviathan*, I, 15; *E.W.*, III, p. 130.   [4] *Ibid.*   [5] *Ibid.*, p. 131.

conclusions or theorems concerning what conduceth to the conservation and defence of themselves (men); whereas law, properly, is the word of him, that by right hath command over them'.[1] Reason sees that the observance of these 'theorems' conduces to man's self-preservation and defence; and it is therefore rational for man to desire their observance. In this sense, and in this sense alone, they have an 'obligatory' character. 'The laws of nature oblige *in foro interno*; that is to say, they bind to a desire they should take place: but *in foro externo*; that is, to the putting them in act, not always. For he that should be modest, and tractable, and perform all he promises, in such time and place where no man else should do so, should but make himself a prey to others, and procure his own certain ruin, contrary to the ground of all laws of nature, which tend to nature's preservation.'[2] It is clear that there is no question of a categorical imperative in the Kantian sense. Study of the laws of nature is, indeed, declared by Hobbes to be 'the true moral philosophy',[3] which is the science of good and evil. But, as we have already seen, 'private appetite is the measure of good and evil';[4] and the only reason why the laws of nature are to be called good or, as Hobbes puts it, 'moral virtues', is that men's private appetites happen to agree in desiring security. 'All men agree on this, that peace is good; and therefore also the way or means of peace.'[5]

3. Philosophy deals with generative causes. Hence it includes a study of the causes which generate the artificial body which is known as the 'commonwealth'. We have already considered the remote generative causes. Man seeks self-preservation and security, but he is unable to attain this end in the natural condition of war. The laws of nature are unable to achieve the desired end by themselves alone, that is, unless there is coercive power able to enforce their observance by sanctions. For these laws, though dictates of reason, are contrary to man's natural passions. 'And covenants, without the sword, are but words, and of no strength to secure a man at all.'[6] It is necessary, therefore, that there should be a common power or government backed by force and able to punish.

This means that a plurality of individuals 'should confer all their power and strength upon one man, or upon one assembly of men, that may reduce all their wills, by plurality of voices, unto

---

[1] *Leviathan*, I, 15; *E.W.*, III, p. 147.   [2] *Leviathan*, III, 15; *E.W.*, I, p. 145.
[3] *Ibid.*, p. 146.   [4] *Ibid.*   [5] *Ibid.*   [6] *Leviathan*, 2, 17; *E.W.*, III, p. 154.

one will'.[1] That is to say, they must appoint one man, or assembly of men, to bear their person. This done, they will form a real unity in one person, a person being defined as 'he whose words or actions are considered, either as his own, or as representing the words or actions of another man, or of any other thing, to whom they are attributed, whether truly or by fiction'.[2] If the words and actions are considered as the person's own words and actions, we have a 'natural person'. If, however, they are considered as representing the words or actions of another man or of other men, we have a 'feigned or artificial person'. In the present context we are concerned, of course, with an artificial person, with a representer. And it is 'the unity of the representer, not the unity of the represented, that maketh the person one'.[3]

How does this transfer of rights take place? It takes place 'by covenant of every man with every man, in such manner, as if every man should say to every man, *I authorize and give up my right of governing myself, to this man, or to this assembly of men, on this condition that thou give up thy right to him, and authorize all his actions in like manner.* This done, the multitude so united in one person, is called a Commonwealth, in Latin *Civitas*. This is the generation of that great Leviathan, or rather, to speak more reverently, of that *mortal god*, to which we owe under the *immortal God*, our peace and defence.'[4]

It is to be noted that when Hobbes speaks of the multitude being united in one person he does not mean that the multitude constitute this person. He means that the multitude are united in the person, whether individual or assembly, to whom they transfer their rights. He therefore defines the essence of the commonwealth as 'one person, of whose acts a great multitude, by mutual covenants one with another, have made themselves every one the author, to the end he may use the strength and means of them all, as he should think expedient, for their peace and common defence'.[5] This person is called the *sovereign*. Everyone else is his subject.

The proximate cause, therefore, of the generation of the commonwealth is the covenants made with one another by the individuals who on the establishment of the commonwealth become the subjects of the sovereign. This is an important point. For it follows that the sovereign is not himself a party to the

[1] *Leviathan*, 2, 17; *E.W.*, III, p. 157.   [2] *Leviathan*, 1, 16; *E.W.*, III, p. 147.
[3] *Ibid.*, p. 151.   [4] *Leviathan*, 2, 17; *E.W.*, III, p. 158.
[5] *Ibid.*

covenant. And Hobbes says as much in explicit terms. 'Because the right of bearing the person of them all is given to him they make sovereign, by covenant only of one to another, and not of him to any of them; there can happen no breach of covenant on the part of the sovereign.'[1] The commonwealth is certainly instituted for a specific purpose, namely, for the peaceful security of those who are party to the social covenant. And this point, too, has its importance, as will be seen later. But Hobbes's insistence that the covenants are made between the subjects, or more accurately future subjects, and not between the subjects and the sovereign, enables him to emphasize more easily the undivided nature of sovereign power. In his opinion it is by the centralization of authority in the person of the sovereign that the evil which he particularly dreaded, namely, civil war, can be avoided.

Further, this view of the matter enables Hobbes to avoid, at least in part, a difficulty which would inevitably arise if he made the sovereign a party to the covenant. For he has already said that covenants without the sword are but words. And if the sovereign were himself a party to the covenant and at the same time possessed all the authority and power which Hobbes proceeds to attribute to him, it would be difficult to see how the covenant could be valid and effective on his part. As it is, however, the parties to the covenant are simply the individuals who, on making the covenant, immediately become subjects. It is not that they first make a covenant setting up a society and then afterwards choose a sovereign. For in this case a similar difficulty would arise. The covenant would be but words: it would be a covenant within the natural condition of war. It is rather that on the covenant being made sovereign and society come into existence together. From the abstract and theoretical point of view, therefore, we can say that no period of time elapses between the making of the covenant and the setting up of sovereign authority. The covenant, therefore, cannot be made without there immediately coming into existence a power capable of enforcing the covenant.

Although, however, the sovereign is not himself a party to the covenant, his sovereignty derives from the covenant. Hobbes's doctrine lends no support to the theory of the divine right of kings; and he was in fact attacked by those who favoured this theory. In the statement of the covenant he mentions indifferently 'this man' and 'this assembly of men'. He was, as we have seen, a

[1] *Leviathan*, I, 18; *E.W.*, III, p. 161.

royalist; and he favoured monarchy as conducing to greater unity, and for certain other reasons. But as far as the origin of sovereignty is concerned, the covenant may establish monarchy, democracy or aristocracy. The main point is not what form of constitution is set up, but that wherever sovereignty lies, it must be entire and indivisible. 'The difference between these three kinds of commonwealth consisteth not in the difference of power; but in the difference of convenience or aptitude to produce the peace and security of the people; for which end they were instituted.'[1] But the sovereign's power is absolute, whether the sovereign be an individual or an assembly.

One obvious objection to the covenant theory of the generation of the State is that it bears little relation to historical fact. But, of course, it is not at all necessary to suppose that Hobbes thought that, as a matter of historical facts, States originated through an explicit covenant. He is concerned with a logical or philosophical deduction of the State, not with tracing the historical developments of States. And the theory of the covenant enables him to make the transition from the condition of atomic individualism to organized society. I do not mean to imply that for Hobbes men are less individualistic after the covenant, if one may so speak, than before. Self-interest, according to him, lies at the basis of organized society; and self-interest, in an egoistic sense, rules in organized society just as much as it did in the hypothetical state of war. But in organized society the centrifugal tendencies of individuals and their proneness to self-destructive mutual enmity and war are checked by fear of the sovereign's power. The theory of the covenant is, in part at least, a device to exhibit the rational character of subjection to the sovereign and of his exercise of power. Hobbes is a utilitarian in the sense that the basis of the commonwealth is for him utility; and the covenant-theory is an explicit recognition of this utility. The theory is doubtless open to serious objections; but any fundamental criticism of Hobbes must be directed against his account of human nature rather than against the details of the theory of the covenant.

Hobbes makes a distinction between a commonwealth 'by institution' and a commonwealth 'by acquisition'. A commonwealth is said to exist by institution when it has been established in the manner mentioned above, namely, through the covenant of every member of a multitude with every other member. A

---

[1] *Leviathan*, 2, 19; *E.W.*, III, p. 173.

commonwealth is said to exist by acquisition when the sovereign power has been acquired by force; that is to say, when men 'for fear of death or bonds do authorize all the actions of that man or assembly that hath their lives and liberty in his power'.[1]

In the case of a commonwealth by institution a multitude of men subject themselves to a chosen sovereign from fear of one another. In the case of a commonwealth by acquisition they subject themselves to him of whom they are afraid. Thus 'in both cases they do it for fear'.[2] Hobbes is quite explicit in his statement that sovereign power is based on fear. There is no question of deriving the commonwealth and the legitimacy of sovereign power from either theological or metaphysical principles. Of course, the fear, whether of men for one another or of subjects for their sovereign, is rational, in the sense that it is well-grounded. And the commonwealth by acquisition can be defended for the same utilitarian reasons as the commonwealth by institution. Thus when Hobbes says that all commonwealths are founded on fear, he does not mean to say anything in depreciation of the commonwealth. Given human nature as Hobbes describes it, the commonwealth must in any case be founded on fear. The theory of the covenant glosses over this fact to some extent, and it is perhaps designed to impart some show of legality to an institution which does not rest on legality. In this sense it does not fit in well with the rest of Hobbes's political theory. But at the same time he is quite frank about the part played by fear in politics.

4. This distinction between two kinds of commonwealth does not affect the rights of the sovereign. 'The rights and consequences of sovereignty are the same in both.'[3] Hence in examining these rights we can disregard the distinction.

Sovereignty, Hobbes insists, is not and cannot be conferred conditionally. Hence the subjects of a sovereign cannot either change the form of government or repudiate the authority of the sovereign and return to the condition of a disunited multitude: sovereignty is inalienable. This does not mean, for example, that a monarch cannot legitimately confer executive power or consultative rights on other individuals or on assemblies; but if the sovereign is a monarch, he cannot alienate part of his sovereignty. An assembly, such as a parliament, can have no rights independent of the monarch, if we suppose that the monarch is sovereign. It does not follow, therefore, from Hobbes's position that a monarch

---

[1] *Leviathan*, I, 20; *E.W.*, III, p. 185.   [2] *Ibid.*   [3] *Ibid.*, p. 186.

cannot make use of a parliament in governing a nation; but it does follow that the parliament does not enjoy part of the sovereignty and that in the exercise of its delegated powers it is necessarily subordinate to the monarch. Similarly, if an assembly which is not coextensive with the people is sovereign, the people do not and cannot enjoy part of the sovereignty. For they must be considered as having conferred unlimited and inalienable sovereignty on that assembly. Hence sovereign power cannot be forfeited. 'There can happen no breach of covenant on the part of the sovereign; and consequently none of his subjects, by any pretence of forfeiture, can be freed from his subjection.'[1]

By the very institution of sovereignty every subject becomes the author of all the sovereign's actions; and 'it follows that whatsoever he (the sovereign) doth, it can be no injury to any of his subjects; nor ought he to be by any of them accused of injustice'.[2] No sovereign can justly be put to death or in any way punished by his subjects. For, inasmuch as every subject is author of all the sovereign's actions, to punish the sovereign would be to punish another for one's own actions.

Among the prerogatives of the sovereign which are enumerated by Hobbes is that of judging what doctrines are fit to be taught. 'It belongeth therefore to him that hath the sovereign power, to be judge or constitute all judges of opinions and doctrines, as a thing necessary to peace; thereby to prevent discord and civil war.'[3] And among the diseases of the commonwealth he lists the doctrines that 'every private man is judge of good and evil actions'[4] and that 'whatsoever a man does against his conscience, is sin'.[5] In the state of nature, it is true, the individual is judge of what is good and what is evil, and he has to follow his own reason or conscience, because he has no other rule to follow. But this is not the case in the commonwealth. For there the civil law is the public conscience, the measure of good and evil.

It is no matter for surprise, therefore, if in the third and fourth parts of the *Leviathan* Hobbes defends a thoroughgoing Erastianism. To be sure, he does not deny Christian revelation or the validity of the idea of a Christian commonwealth, wherein 'there dependeth much upon supernatural revelations of the will of God'.[6] But he completely subordinates Church to State. He makes it abundantly clear that he interprets the struggle between

[1] *Leviathan*, 2, 18; *E.W.*, III, p. 161.   [2] *Ibid.*, p. 163.
[3] *Ibid.*, p. 165.   [4] *Leviathan*, 2, 29; *E.W.*, III, p. 310.
[5] *Ibid.*, p. 311.   [6] *Leviathan*, 3, 32; *E.W.*, III, p. 359.

Church and State simply in terms of power. The Church has tried to arrogate to itself an authority which belongs to the civil sovereign; and Hobbes, in a famous passage, likens the Papacy to the ghost of the Roman empire. 'And if a man consider the original of this great ecclesiastical dominion, he will easily perceive that the Papacy is no other than the *ghost* of the deceased *Roman empire*, sitting crowned upon the grave thereof. For so did the Papacy start up on a sudden out of the ruins of that heathen power.'[1] But though Hobbes regards the Catholic Church as providing the chief example in the religious sphere of an attempt to steal from the sovereign his rightful authority, he makes it clear that his primary concern is not with anti-Catholic polemics. He is concerned to reject any claim, whether by pope, bishop, priest or presbyter, to possess spiritual authority and jurisdiction independently of the sovereign. Similarly, he rejects any claim on the part of private individuals to be independent channels of divine revelations or of divinely inspired messages.

A Church is defined as 'a company of men professing Christian religion, united in the person of one sovereign, at whose command they ought to assemble'.[2] There is no such thing as a universal Church; and within the national Church the Christian sovereign is the fount, under God, of all authority and jurisdiction, and he alone is the final judge of the interpretation of the Scriptures. In his answer to Bishop Bramhall, Hobbes asks, 'If it be not from the king's authority that the Scripture is law, what other authority makes it law?'[3] And he remarks that 'there is no doubt but by what authority the Scripture or any other writing is made a law, by the same authority the Scriptures are to be interpreted or else they are made in vain'.[4] Again, when Bramhall remarks that on Hobbes's Erastian principles the authority of all general councils is destroyed, Hobbes admits that this is the case. If Anglican prelates pretend that general councils possess authority independently of the sovereign, they to this extent detract from the latter's inalienable authority and power.

5. The power of the sovereign being thus to all intents and purposes unlimited, the question arises, what freedom, if any, is possessed by the subjects or ought to be possessed by them. And in discussing this question we have to presuppose Hobbes's theory of 'natural liberty'. As we have already seen, natural liberty

---

[1] *Leviathan*, 4, 47; *E.W.*, III, pp. 697–8.
[2] *Leviathan*, 3, 39; *E.W.*, III, p. 459.
[3] *E.W.*, IV, p. 339. [4] *Ibid.*

means for him simply the absence of external hindrances to motion; and it is perfectly consistent with necessity, that is, with determinism. A man's volitions, desires and inclinations are necessary in the sense that they are the results of a chain of determining causes; but when he acts in accordance with these desires and inclinations, there being no external impediment to prevent him from so acting, he is said to act freely. A free man is thus 'he that in those things which by his strength and wit he is able to do, is not hindered to do what he has a will to do'.[1] This general conception of liberty being presupposed, Hobbes inquires what is the liberty of subjects with regard to the artificial bonds or chains which men have forged for themselves by the mutual covenants which they have made with one another in handing over their rights to the sovereign.

It is scarcely necessary to say that Hobbes has no sympathy with any demand for freedom from law. For law, backed by sanctions, is the very means which protects a man from the caprice and violence of other men. And to demand exemption from law would be a demand for a return to the state of nature. The liberty which is exalted in the histories and philosophies of the ancient Greeks and Romans is, he says, the liberty of the commonwealth, not of particular men. 'The Athenians and Romans were free; that is, free commonwealths: not that any particular men had the liberty to resist their own representative; but that their representative had the liberty to resist or invade other people.'[2] It is true that many people have found in the writings of the ancients an excuse for favouring tumults and 'licentious controlling the actions of their sovereigns . . . with the effusion of so much blood, as I think I may truly say, there was never any thing so dearly bought, as these western parts have bought the learning of the Greek and Latin tongues'.[3] But this comes from failure to distinguish between the rights of individuals and the rights of sovereigns.

At the same time it is clear that in no commonwealth are all actions regulated by law; nor can they be. Hence subjects enjoy liberty in these matters. 'The liberty of a subject lieth therefore only in those things which, in regulating their actions, the sovereign hath praetermitted: such as is the liberty to buy and sell, and otherwise contract with one another; to choose their own

---

[1] *Leviathan*, 2, 21; *E.W.*, III, pp. 196–7.
[2] *Ibid.*, p. 201.   [3] *Ibid.*, p. 203.

abode, their own diet, their own trade of life, and institute their children as they themselves think fit, and the like.'[1]

So far as Hobbes is not simply making the tautological pronouncement that actions unregulated by law are unregulated by law, he is here drawing attention to the actual state of affairs, namely, that in a very wide field of human activity subjects can, as far as the law is concerned, act according to their will and inclination. And such liberty is found, he tells us, in all forms of commonwealth. The further question arises, however, whether there are any cases in which the subject is entitled to resist the sovereign.

The answer to this question can be obtained by considering the purpose of the social covenant and what rights cannot be transferred by the covenant. The covenant is made with a view to peace and security, the protection of life and limb. It follows, therefore, that a man does not and cannot transfer or lay down his right to save himself from death, wounds and imprisonment. And from this it follows that if the sovereign commands a man kill or maim himself, or to abstain from air or food, or not to to resist those who assault him, 'yet hath that man the liberty to disobey'.[2] Nor is a man obliged to confess his own crimes. Nor is a subject obliged to kill any other man at command or to take up arms, unless refusal to obey frustrates the end for which sovereignty was instituted. Hobbes does not mean, of course, that the sovereign may not punish a subject for refusing to obey: he means that subjects, having made mutual covenants with one another, and having thus instituted sovereignty with a view to self-protection, cannot legitimately be considered as having bound themselves by covenant to injure themselves or others simply because the sovereign commands it. 'It is one thing to say, *Kill me, or my fellow, if you please*; another thing to say, *I will kill myself or my fellow.*'[3]

A point of greater importance is that subjects are absolved from their duty of obedience to the sovereign, not only if the latter relinquishes his sovereignty, but also if he has, indeed, the will to retain his power but cannot in fact protect his subjects any longer. 'The obligation of subjects to the sovereign is understood to last as long, and no longer, than the power lasteth, by which he is able to protect them.'[4] According to the intention of those who

---

[1] *Leviathan*, 2, 21; *E.W.*, III, p. 199. [2] *Ibid.*, p. 142.
[3] *Ibid.*, p. 204. [4] *Ibid.*, p. 208.

institute it, sovereignty may be immortal; but in actual fact it has in itself 'many seeds of a natural mortality'.[1] If the sovereign is conquered in war and surrenders to the victor, his subjects become subjects of the latter. If the commonwealth is torn asunder by internal discord and the sovereign no longer possesses effective power, the subjects return to the state of nature, and a new sovereign can be set up.

6. A good deal has been written about the significance of Hobbes's political theory and about the comparative importance of the various points which he makes. And different estimates are possible.

The point which is most likely to strike modern readers of the *Leviathan* is, very naturally, the power and authority attributed to the sovereign. This emphasis on the sovereign's position was, in part, a necessary counterbalance in Hobbes's political theory to his theory of atomic individualism. If according to Marxists the State, the capitalist State at least, is the means of binding together conflicting economic interests and classes, the State for Hobbes is the means of uniting warring individuals; and the State cannot perform this function unless the sovereign enjoys complete and unlimited authority. If men are naturally egoistic and always remain so, the only factor which can hold them together effectively is centralized power, vested in the sovereign.

This is not to say that Hobbes's insistence on the power of the sovereign was simply and solely the result of an inference from an aprioristic theory of human nature. He was also undoubtedly influenced by contemporary events. In the civil war he saw a revelation of man's character and of the centrifugal forces operative in human society. And he saw in strong and centralized power the only remedy for this state of affairs. 'If there had not first been an opinion received of the greatest part of England, that these powers (of legislating, administering justice, raising taxes, controlling doctrines and so on) were divided between the King, and the Lords, and the House of Commons, the people had never been divided and fallen into this civil war; first between those that disagreed in politics; and after between the dissenters about the liberty of religion. . . .'[2] Hobbes's absolutism and his Erastianism were greatly strengthened by his reflections on concrete political and religious dissensions.

[1] *Leviathan*, 2, 21; *E.W.*, III, p. 202.   [2] *Leviathan*, 2, 18; *E.W.*, III, p. 168.

At this point it may be advisable to remark that it is authoritarianism rather than 'totalitarianism' in a modern sense which is characteristic of Hobbes's political theory. Of course, there are certainly obvious elements of what we call totalitarianism in his theory. For example, it is the State, or more precisely the sovereign, that determines good and evil. In this sense the State is the fount of morality. Against this interpretation it has been objected that Hobbes admits 'natural laws' and that he allows also that the sovereign is responsible to God. But even if we are prepared to concede that he accepts the notion of natural law in any sense which is relevant to the matter under discussion, it remains true that for him it is the sovereign who interprets the natural law, just as it is the Christian sovereign who interprets the Scriptures. On the other hand, Hobbes did not envisage the sovereign as controlling all human activities; he thought of him as legislating and controlling with a view to the maintenance of peace and security. He was not concerned with exalting the State as such and in subordinating individuals to the State because it is the State; he was concerned, first and last, with the interests of individuals. And if he advocated centralized power and authority, this was because he saw no other way of promoting and preserving the peace and security of human beings, which constitute the purpose of organized society.

But though authoritarianism is certainly a prominent feature of Hobbes's political philosophy it should be emphasized that this authoritarianism has no essential connection with the theory of the divine right of kings and with the principle of legitimacy. Hobbes certainly speaks as though the sovereign is in some sense the representative of God; but in the first place monarchy is not for him the only proper form of government. For the word 'sovereign' in Hobbes's political writings we are not entitled simply to substitute the word 'monarch'; but the principle on which he insists is that sovereignty is indivisible, not that it should necessarily be vested in one man. And in the second place sovereignty, whether vested in one man or in an assembly of men, is derived from the social covenant, not from appointment by God. Further, this fiction of the social covenant would justify any *de facto* government. It would justify, for example, the Commonwealth no less than the rule of Charles I, as long, that is to say, as the latter possessed the power to rule. It is therefore easy to understand the charge brought against Hobbes that he wrote the *Leviathan* when he had a mind to go home and that he wished to win the favour of Cromwell. Thus Dr. John Wallis declared that the *Leviathan* 'was written in defence of Oliver's title, or whoever, by whatsoever means, can get to be upmost; placing the whole right of government merely in strength and absolving all his Majesty's subjects from their allegiance, whenever he is not in a present capacity to force obedience'.[1] Hobbes roundly denied that he had published his *Leviathan* 'to flatter Oliver, who was not made Protector till three or four years after, on purpose to make way for his return',[2] adding 'it is true that Mr. Hobbes came home, but it was because he would not trust his safety with the French clergy'.[3] But though Hobbes was justified in saying that he had not written his work to flatter Oliver Cromwell and that he had not intended to defend rebellion against the monarch, it remains true that his political theory is favourable neither to the idea of the divine right of kings nor to the Stuart principle of legitimacy. And commentators are right in drawing attention to the 'revolutionary' character of his theory of sovereignty, an aspect of his thought which is apt to be overlooked precisely because of his authoritarian conception of government and his personal predilection for monarchy.

If one had to find an analogy to Hobbes's theory of the State in mediaeval philosophy, it might perhaps be suggested that it is provided by St. Augustine much more than by St. Thomas Aquinas.[4] For St. Augustine regarded the State, or at least tended to do so, as a consequence of original sin; that is, as a necessary means of restraining man's evil impulses which are a result of original sin. And this view bears at any rate some likeness to Hobbes's conception of the State as the remedy for the evils consequent on man's natural condition, the war of all against all. Aquinas, on the other hand, adhering to the Greek tradition, regarded the State as a natural institution, the primary function of which is to promote the common good and which would be necessary even if man had not sinned and possessed no evil impulses.

This analogy is, of course, only partial, and it should not be pressed. St. Augustine certainly did not believe, for instance, that the sovereign determines moral distinctions. For him there is an

---

[1] *E.W.*, IV, p. 413. [2] *Ibid.*, p. 415. [3] *Ibid.*
[4] For the political theories of St. Augustine and St. Thomas Aquinas, Chapters VIII and XL of vol. II of this *History* may be consulted.

objective moral law, with transcendent foundations, which is independent of the State and to which all sovereigns and subjects are morally obliged to conform their conduct. For Hobbes, however, there is no such moral law. It is true that he allowed that the sovereign is responsible to God and that he did not admit that he had eliminated any idea of objective morality apart from the sovereign's legislation. But at the same time philosophy, according to his own assertion, is not concerned with God, and he explicitly asserted that it is the sovereign who determines what is good and what is evil. In the state of nature good and evil are simply relative to the desires of individuals. On this point Hobbes gets rid of all metaphysical and transcendental theories and ideas.

He acts in a similar way with regard to the State considered as an institution. For Aquinas the State was demanded by the natural law, which was itself a reflection of the eternal law of God. It was therefore divinely willed, irrespective of man's sin and of his evil impulses. But this transcendent foundation of the State disappears in Hobbes's theory. In so far as we can speak of him as deducing the State, he deduces it simply from the passions of man, without reference to metaphysical and transcendental considerations. In this sense his theory is thoroughly naturalistic in character. If Hobbes devotes a considerable part of the *Leviathan* to religious and ecclesiastical questions and problems, he does so in the interests of a defence of Erastianism, not in order to supply a metaphysical theory of the State. A great deal of the importance of Hobbes's theory is due to the fact that he tries to set political philosophy on its own feet, so to speak, connecting it, indeed, with human psychology and, in intention at least, with his general mechanistic philosophy, but cutting it adrift from metaphysics and theology. Whether this was a profitable step is open to dispute; but it was certainly a step of considerable importance.

Hobbes's deduction of the State from a consideration of the passions of man goes a long way towards explaining his authoritarianism and his insistence on the power of the sovereign. But we have seen that his authoritarian ideas were not simply the result of a philosophical deduction; for they were greatly strengthened by his reflections on concrete historical events in his own country and by his fear and hatred of civil war. And, in general, he can be regarded as having discerned the great part played by power in the dynamics of political life and history. In this respect he can be called a 'realist'. And we can link him up with the Renaissance writer, Machiavelli.[1] But whereas the latter had been primarily concerned with political mechanics, with the means of attaining and preserving power, Hobbes provides a general political theory in which the concept of power and its function plays a supremely important part. Much in this theory is dated, historically conditioned, as is indeed inevitable in any political theory which goes beyond principles which can be considered 'eternal', that is, of lasting applicability, precisely because they are too general and abstract to be intrinsically related to a given epoch. But his conception of the role of power in human affairs is of lasting significance. To say this is not to subscribe to his theory of human nature (which, in its nominalistic aspects, connects him with fourteenth-century nominalism) or to pronounce adequate his account of the function of the State and of sovereignty. It is simply to say that Hobbes recognized very clearly factors which have undoubtedly helped to determine the course of human history as we know it up to date. In my opinion, Hobbes's political philosophy is one-sided and inadequate. But precisely because it is one-sided and inadequate it throws into clear relief features of social and political life of which it is important to take account.

[1] For Machiavelli, pp. 315–20 of vol. III of this *History* may be consulted.

CHAPTER III

THE CAMBRIDGE PLATONISTS

Introductory remarks—Lord Herbert of Cherbury and his theory of natural religion — The Cambridge Platonists — Richard Cumberland.

1. FRANCIS BACON[1] had admitted a philosophical or natural theology, which treats of God's existence and of His nature, so far as this is manifested in creatures. Hobbes, however, excluded from philosophy all consideration of God, since he regarded philosophy as concerned with bodies in motion. Indeed, if by the term 'God' we mean an infinite spiritual or immaterial Being, reason can tell us nothing at all about Him; for terms such as 'spiritual' and 'immaterial' are not intelligible, unless they are used to connote invisible body. But this attitude was not common among the seventeenth-century British philosophers. The general tendency was rather to hold that reason can attain to some knowledge of God, and at the same time to maintain that reason is the judge of revelation and of revealed truth. Associated with this outlook we find in a number of writers the tendency to play down dogmatic differences and to belittle their importance in comparison with the general truths which are attainable by reason alone. And those who thought in this way were obviously more inclined towards a certain broadness of outlook and towards the promotion of toleration in the field of dogmatic religion than were the theologians of the diverse schools and traditions.

This general point of view may be said to have been characteristic of John Locke and his associates. But in this chapter I intend to treat of the group of writers who are known as the Cambridge Platonists. They fit in well enough at this point because, though some of them refer little or not at all to Hobbes, Ralph Cudworth regarded the latter as the principal enemy of true religion and of a spiritualist philosophy and consciously endeavoured to combat his influence. To say this is not to say, however, that the Cambridge Platonists should be estimated simply in terms of a reaction to Hobbes. For they represent a

---

[1] The philosophy of Francis Bacon is discussed in Chapter XIX of vol. III of this *History*.

positive and independent current of thought which is not without interest, even though none of them were philosophers of the first rank.

But before treating of the Cambridge Platonists I wish to say something about an earlier writer, Lord Herbert of Cherbury. He is, indeed, generally regarded as the predecessor of the eighteenth-century deists, who will be mentioned in a later chapter; but his philosophy of religion can be dealt with briefly here. On certain points his philosophical ideas have an affinity with those of the Cambridge Platonists.

2. Lord Herbert of Cherbury (1583–1648) was the author of *Tractatus de Veritate* (1624), *De causis errorum* (1645) and *De religione gentilium* (1645; complete version 1663). In his view in addition to the human cognitive faculties we must postulate a number of 'common notions' (*notitiae communes*). These 'common notions', to use the Stoic term employed by Lord Herbert, are in some sense at least innate truths, characterized by 'apriority' (*prioritas*), independence, universality, certainty, necessity (that is, necessity for life) and immediacy. They are implanted by God and are apprehended by 'natural instinct', being the pre-suppositions, not the products, of experience. The human mind is not a *tabula rasa*; rather does it resemble a closed book which is opened on the presentation of sense-experience. And experience would not be possible without these 'common notions'.

On this last point Lord Herbert, as commentators have pointed out, anticipated in some degree a conviction which at a much later date was defended by Kant. But Lord Herbert does not provide any systematic deduction of these *a priori* notions or truths; nor does he attempt to tell us what they all are. That he does not attempt to give any exhaustive list of them is not, however, surprising if we bear in mind the fact that in his view there are impediments (for example, lack of talent) which prevent men from recognizing more than a fraction of them. In other words, to say that these truths are implanted by God or by nature is not to say that they are all consciously and reflectively apprehended from the start. When recognized, they win universal consent; so that universal consent is a mark of a recognized 'common notion'. But there can be growth in insight into these virtually innate ideas or truths; and many of them come to light only in the process of discursive thought. Hence one cannot give a complete list of them *a priori*. If men follow the path of reason alone, unhampered by prejudice and passion, they will come to a fuller reflective apprehension of the ideas implanted by God.

Another reason why Lord Herbert does not attempt to list the 'common notions' is that he is primarily interested in those which are involved in religious and moral knowledge. According to him there are five fundamental truths of natural religion; that there is a supreme Being, that this supreme Being ought to be worshipped, that a moral life has always been the principal part of divine worship, that vices and crimes should be expiated by repentance, and that in the next life our deeds on earth are rewarded or punished. In his *De religione gentilium* Lord Herbert tried to show how these five truths are recognized in all religions and form their real essence, in spite of all accretions due to superstition and fantasy. He does not deny that revelation is capable of supplementing natural religion; but he insists that alleged revelation must be judged at the bar of reason. And his reserved attitude towards dogma is evident. His interest, however, lies in defending the rationality of religion and of a religious outlook rather than in purely negative criticism of the different positive religions.

3. The first word in the name 'Cambridge Platonists' is due to the fact that the group of men to whom it is applied were all associated with the University of Cambridge. Benjamin Whichcote (1609–83), John Smith (1616–52), Ralph Cudworth (1617–88), Nathaniel Culverwel (*c*. 1618–*c*. 1651) and Peter Sterry (1613–72) were all graduates of Emmanuel College, while Henry More (1614–87) was a graduate of Christ's College. Some of them were also Fellows of their college; and all were Anglican clergymen.

In what sense were these men 'Platonists'? The answer is, I think, that they were influenced by and drew inspiration from Platonism as being a spiritualist and religious interpretation of reality. But Platonism did not mean for them simply the philosophy of the historic Plato: it meant rather the whole tradition of spiritualist metaphysics from Plato to Plotinus. Moreover, though they utilized Platonism in this sense and referred to philosophers such as Plato and Plotinus, and though they regarded themselves as continuing the Platonic tradition in contemporary thought, they were concerned to expound a religious and Christian philosophy in opposition to materialistic and atheistic currents of thought rather than to propound the philosophy of Plato or that of Plotinus, between which, indeed, they made no clear distinction. Cudworth in particular was a determined opponent of

Hobbes. But though Hobbes was the chief enemy, the Cambridge Platonists also rejected Descartes' mechanistic view of nature. They did not perhaps give sufficient weight to the fact that Cartesianism possesses another and different aspect; but his views of nature seemed to them to be incompatible with a spiritual interpretation of the world and to pave the way for the more radical philosophy of Hobbes.

Emmanuel College was, in effect, a Puritan foundation and a stronghold of Calvinism. The Cambridge Platonists, however, reacted against this narrow Protestant dogmatism. Whichcote, for example, rejected the Calvinist (and, one might add, Hobbesian) view of man. For man is an image of God, gifted with reason, which is 'the candle of the Lord, lighted by God, and leading us to God'; and he should not be belittled or denigrated. Again, Cudworth rejected the doctrine that some men are predestined to hell and eternal torment antecedently to any fault of their own. His study of the ancient philosophers and of ethics liberated him from the Calvinism in which he had been educated and which he had brought with him to the university. It would, indeed, be inaccurate if one asserted that all the Cambridge Platonists rejected Calvinism and liberated themselves from its influence. Culverwel certainly did not do so. While agreeing with Whichcote in extolling reason, he at the same time emphasized the diminution of its light and the weakness of the human mind in a way which shows the influence of the Calvinist theology. None the less one can say in general that the Cambridge Platonists disliked the Calvinist denigration of human nature and its subordination of reason to faith. In fact, they were not concerned with supporting any one dogmatic system. They aimed rather at revealing the essential elements of Christianity; and they regarded a good deal in the Protestant systems as being little more than matter of opinion. With regard to dogmatic differences they thus tended to adopt a tolerant and 'broad' outlook and were known as 'Latitudinarians'. This is not to say that they rejected the idea of revealed truth or that they refused to admit 'mysteries'. They were not rationalists in the modern sense. But they strongly objected to insistence on obscure doctrines, the relevance of which to the moral life was not clear. The essence of Christianity, and indeed of all religion, they found in the moral life. Doctrinal disputes and disputes about ecclesiastical government and institution they regarded as being of secondary importance in comparison with a sincerely moral and Christian life. Religious truth is of value if it reacts on life and produces practical fruit.

By saying this I do not mean to imply that the Cambridge Platonists were pragmatists. They believed in the power of the human reason to attain to objective truth about God and to give us insight into absolute and universal moral laws. But they insisted on two points; first, that a sincere attempt to lead a moral life is a necessary condition for obtaining insight into truth about God and, secondly, that the truths which are of most importance are those which form the clearest basis for a Christian life. In their dislike for sectarian wrangling and bitter controversy about obscure theoretical problems they bear some resemblance to those fourteenth-century writers who had deplored the wrangling of the schools and all preoccupation with logical subtleties to the neglect of the 'one thing necessary'.

At the same time the Cambridge Platonists emphasized the contemplative attitude. That is to say, although they stressed the close connection between moral purity and the attainment of truth, they emphasized the understanding of reality, the personal appropriation and contemplation of truth, rather than the manipulation of reality. In other words, their attitude was different from the attitude insisted on by Francis Bacon and summed up in the aphorism 'Knowledge is power'. They had little sympathy with the subordination of knowledge to its scientific and practical exploitation. For one thing, they believed, whereas Bacon had not, that rational knowledge of supersensible reality is attainable; and this knowledge cannot be exploited scientifically. Nor, for the matter of that, had they much sympathy with the Puritan subordination of knowledge of religious truth to 'practical' purposes. They emphasized rather the Plotinian idea of the conversion of the mind to the contemplation of divine reality and of the world in its relation to God. As historians have pointed out, they were not in tune with either the empiricist or the religious movements of their time and country. It may very well be true that, as Ernst Cassirer has argued,[1] there is a historical connection between the Platonism of the Italian renaissance and the Platonism of the Cambridge divines; but as Cassirer also argues, this Cambridge Platonism stood apart from the dominant movements in con-

---

[1] *The Platonic Renaissance in England*, translated by James P. Pettegrove (Edinburgh, Nelson, 1953).

temporary British philosophical and theological thought. The Cambridge men were neither empiricists nor Puritans.

The Cambridge Platonists, therefore, were concerned with defending a spiritualist interpretation of the universe as a foundation for the Christian moral life. And the most elaborate defence of such an interpretation of the universe is given by Ralph Cudworth in his work *The True Intellectual System of the Universe* (1678). It is a tedious piece of writing, because the author discusses at length the views of different ancient philosophers to the detriment of a clear statement of his own position. But behind the welter of quotations and of expositions of Greek philosophers there appears clearly enough the figure of Hobbes, whom Cudworth interprets as a sheer atheist. In answer to Hobbes he argues that we do in fact possess an idea of God. He reduces materialism to sensationalism and then observes that sense-perception is not knowledge, thus reaffirming the position of Plato in the *Theaetetus*. Moreover, it is evident that we have ideas of many things which are not perceptible by the senses. It follows, therefore, that we cannot legitimately deny the existence of a being simply because it cannot be perceived by the senses; nor are we entitled to say that a name which purports to connote an incorporeal object is necessarily devoid of significance. 'Were existence to be allowed to nothing, that doth not fall under corporeal sense, then must we deny the existence of soul and mind in ourselves and others, because we can neither feel nor see any such thing. Whereas we are certain of the existence of our own souls, partly from an inward consciousness of our own cogitations, and partly from that principle of reason, that nothing cannot act. And the existence of other souls is manifest to us, from their effects upon their respective bodies, their motions, actions, and discourse. Wherefore since the Atheists cannot deny the existence of soul or mind in men, though no such thing fall under external sense, they have as little reason to deny the existence of a perfect mind, presiding over the universe, without which it cannot be conceived whence our imperfect ones should be derived. The existence of that God, whom no eye hath seen nor can see, is plainly proved by reason from his effects, in the visible phenomena of the universe, and from what we are conscious of within ourselves.'[1] Nor can we

---

[1] *The True Intellectual System of the Universe*, I, 5, 1; edit. Harrison, 1845, vol. II, p. 515. All quotations from this work of Cudworth are taken from Harrison's edition.

argue validly from the fact that even the theists admit the incomprehensibility of God to the conclusion that God is altogether inconceivable and that the term 'God' has no meaning. For the statement that God is incomprehensible means that the finite mind cannot have an adequate idea of Him, not that it can have no idea of Him at all. We cannot comprehend the divine perfection; but we can have an idea of absolutely perfect Being. This can be shown in various ways. For example, 'that we have an idea or conception of perfection, or a perfect Being, is evident from the notion that we have of imperfection, so familiar to us; perfection being the rule and measure of imperfection, and not imperfection of perfection . . .: so that perfection is first conceivable, in order of nature, as light before darkness, a positive before the privative or defect'.[1] And the same applies to the idea of the infinite. Further, it is useless to assert that the idea of God is a construction of the imagination, like the idea of a centaur, or that it is implanted in the mind by lawgivers and politicians for their own ends. For a finite and imperfect mind could not have constructed the idea of an infinitely perfect Being. 'Were there no God, the idea of an absolutely or infinitely perfect Being could never have been made or feigned, neither by politicians, nor by poets, nor philosophers, nor any other.'[2] 'The generality of mankind in all ages have had a prolepsis or anticipation in their minds concerning the real and actual existence of such a being.'[3] And it is possible to demonstrate the existence of God by means of the idea of God. For example, 'because we have an idea of God, or a perfect Being, implying no manner of contradiction in it, therefore must it needs have some kind of entity or other, either an actual or possible one; but God, if he be not, is possible to be, therefore he doth actually exist'.[4]

The influence of Descartes on Cudworth's mind is evident from what has just been said about the idea of the perfect. Cudworth does, indeed, give other lines of argument. For example, he argues that from nothing there can come nothing, so that 'if once there had been nothing, there could never have been any thing'.[5] There must, therefore, be something which existed from all eternity, itself unmade; and this something must exist by the necessity of its own nature. But there is nothing which exists necessarily and eternally save an absolutely perfect Being. Hence either God

[1] *The True Intellectual System of the Universe*, I, 5, I; II, pp. 537–8.
[2] *Ibid.*, p. 635.   [3] *Ibid.*, p. 509.
[4] *Ibid.*, III, pp. 49–50.   [5] *Ibid.*, p. 54.

exists or nothing at all exists. But though Cudworth gives a variety of arguments, the influence of Descartes is undeniable. Nor does Cudworth attempt to deny it. He criticizes Descartes' use of our knowledge of God's existence on the ground that it involves us in a scepticism from which we can never escape. Interpreting Descartes as saying that we cannot be sure of anything, even of the trustworthiness of our reason, until we have proved that God exists, he argues that the attainment of such a proof is rendered impossible, because it presupposes the very fact which it is afterwards used to establish, namely, that we can trust our reason and the first principles of reason. But this does not alter the fact that Cudworth drew inspiration from the writings of Descartes.

However, though Cudworth was certainly influenced by Descartes, he viewed with sharp disfavour the latter's mechanistic theory of the material world. Descartes belongs to the class of those who have 'an undiscerned tang of the mechanic Atheism hanging about them', because of 'their so confident rejecting of all final and intending causality in nature, and admitting of no other causes of things, as philosophical, save the material and mechanical only'.[1] Cudworth calls the Cartesians 'mechanic Theists' and rejects Descartes' contention that we should not claim the power of discerning God's purposes in nature. That eyes were made for seeing and ears for hearing is so plain that 'nothing but sottish stupidity or atheistic incredulity can make any doubt thereof'.[2] Cudworth argues also against the notion that animals are machines and favours attributing to them sensitive souls. 'If it be evident from the phenomena that brutes are not mere senseless machines or automata, and only like clocks or watches, then ought not popular opinion and vulgar prejudice so far to prevail with us, as to hinder our assent to that which sound reason and philosophy clearly dictate, that therefore they must have something more than matter in them.'[3]

Cudworth thus rejects altogether the sharp dichotomy made by Descartes between the spiritual and material worlds. I do not mean by this that he postulated an evolutionary continuity between inanimate matter, plants, sensitive life and rational life. On the contrary, he denied that life can proceed from inanimate matter, and he denounced Hobbes's account of consciousness and thought in materialist terms. 'There is nothing in body or matter,

---

[1] *The True Intellectual System of the Universe*, 3, 37; I, p. 217.
[2] *Ibid.*, 5, I; II, p. 616. [3] *Ibid.*, 5, 4; III, p. 441.

but magnitude, figure, site, and motion or rest: now it is mathematically certain, that these, however combined together, can never possibly compound, or make up life or cogitation.'[1] Moreover the rational soul of man is naturally immortal, whereas the sensitive souls of brutes are not. There are, therefore, essential differences of degree in nature. 'There is a scale, or ladder of entities and perfections in the universe, one above another, and the production of things cannot possibly be in way of ascent from lower to higher, but must of necessity be in way of descent from higher to lower.'[2] But precisely because there are these various degrees of perfection in nature we cannot make a simple division between the spiritual sphere on the one hand and, on the other, the material sphere, from which final causality is banished and where vital phenomena are interpreted in purely mechanistic terms.

A more pronounced hostility towards the Cartesian dualism was shown by Henry More. In his younger days he had been an enthusiastic admirer of Descartes. Thus in a letter to Clerselier, written in 1655, he remarks not only that Cartesianism is useful for promoting the highest end of all philosophy, namely, religion, but also that the reasoning and method of demonstration concerning God and man is soundest if it is based on Cartesian principles. Indeed, if exception is made perhaps for Platonism, there is no system of philosophy besides Cartesianism, properly understood, which so stoutly bars the way to atheism.[3] But in his *Enchiridion metaphysicum* (1671) More depicted the Cartesian philosophy as an enemy of religious belief. Inclined as he was to mysticism and theosophy he found Descartes' intellectualism repugnant. The notion of a material world sharply separated from spiritual reality and consisting of extension which can be adequately treated in terms of mathematics was unacceptable to a man who regarded nature as permeated by vitality, by soul. In nature we see the creative activity of the world-soul, a vital dynamic principle, not to be identified with God but operating as the divine instrument. Cudworth, too, speaks of 'Plastic Nature', which, as the instrument of God, is the immediate agent in producing natural effects. In other words, Cudworth and More turned their backs on the Cartesian interpretation of nature and on its developments and attempted to reinstate a philosophy of nature of the type which was popular at the time of the Renaissance.

---

[1] *The True Intellectual System of the Universe*, 5, 4; III, p. 440.
[2] *Ibid.*   [3] *Œuvres de Descartes*, A.T., v, pp. 249f.

What has been said about Cudworth's theory of the idea of the perfect as being prior to the idea of imperfection indicates clearly enough his opposition to empiricism. Indeed, he does not hesitate to declare that the statement that the human mind is originally 'a mere blank or white sheet of paper that hath nothing at all in it, but what was scribbled upon it by the objects of sense',[1] implies that the human soul is generated from matter or that it is 'nothing but a higher modification of matter'.[2] He is, of course, interpreting the statement as meaning that the mind is merely the passive recipient of sense-impressions. But in his writings he makes it clear that he intends to reject the empiricist principle even when it is not interpreted in this narrow sense. Thus in the *Treatise concerning eternal and immutable Morality*[3] he states that there are two kinds of 'perceptive cogitations' in the soul. The first kind consists of passive perceptions of the soul, which may be either sensations or images (or phantasms). The other kind consists of 'active perceptions which rise from the mind itself without the body'.[4] And these are called 'conceptions of the mind' or νοήματα. They include not only ideas such as those of justice, truth, knowledge, virtue and vice but also propositions such as 'Nothing can be and not be at the same time' or 'Out of nothing there can come nothing'. These conceptions of the mind are not abstracted from phantasms by any active intellect (a view which, according to Cudworth, has been erroneously attributed to Aristotle). The idea that they are so abstracted is due to the fact that they are 'most commonly excited and awakened occasionally from the appulse of outward objects knocking at the door of our senses',[5] and men have failed to distinguish between the outward occasion of these conceptions and their active, productive cause. In reality 'they must needs arise from the innate vigour and activity of the mind itself',[6] which is a created image of the divine mind. These virtually innate ideas are imprinted on the human mind by God. And by them we know not only immaterial objects and eternal truths but also material things. This is not to deny that sense and imagination have a part to play in our knowledge of material things. But sensation cannot give us knowledge of the essence of any thing or of any scientific truth. We cannot have scientific knowledge of the

---

[1] *The True Intellectual System of the Universe*, 5, 4; III, p. 438.   [2] *Ibid.*
[3] This treatise is included in vol. III of Harrison's edition of *The True Intellectual System of the Universe*. And references are given according to pagination in this edition.
[4] 4, I, 7; III, p. 582.   [5] *Ibid.*, 4, 2, 2; III, p. 587.   [6] *Ibid.*, 4, 3, I; III, pp. 601-2.

material world save by the activity of the mind producing 'conceptions' from within itself by virtue of its God-given power.

The criterion of theoretical truth is 'the clearness of the apprehensions themselves'.[1] 'Clear intellectual conceptions must of necessity be truths, because they are real entities.'[2] Cudworth accepts, therefore, the Cartesian criterion of truth, clarity and distinction of idea; but he rejects the use of the hypothesis of the 'evil genius' and Descartes' device to escape from the possibility of error and deception. Men are, indeed, sometimes deceived and imagine that they clearly understand what they do not clearly understand. But, says Cudworth, it does not follow that they can never be certain that they do clearly comprehend some thing. We might just as well argue that 'because in our dreams we think we have clear sensations we cannot therefore be ever sure, when we are awake, that we see things that really are'.[3] Cudworth evidently thought that it was absurd to suggest that waking life might be a dream.

The mind, therefore, can perceive eternal essences and immutable truths. And it can do this, as has already been mentioned, because it derives from and depends on the eternal mind 'which comprehends within itself the steady and immutable *rationes* of all things and their verities'.[4] It can therefore discern eternal moral principles and values. Good and evil, just and unjust, are not relative conceptions, as Hobbes imagined. Even if it is possible to have varying degrees of insight into moral values and principles, these are none the less absolute. Cudworth had therefore no sympathy with the view, which he ascribes to Descartes, that moral and other eternal truths are subject to the divine omnipotence and therefore, in principle, variable. Indeed, he goes so far as to say that 'if any one did desire to persuade the world, that Cartesius, notwithstanding all his pretences to demonstrate a Deity, was indeed but an hypocritical Theist, or personated and disguised Atheist, he could not have a fairer pretence for it out of all his writings than from hence; this being plainly to destroy the Deity, by making one attribute thereof to devour and swallow up another; infinite will and power, infinite understanding and wisdom'.[5]

This belief in the mind's power of discerning immutable truths, which bear the evidence of their truth within themselves and which

---

[1] *The True Intellectual System of the Universe*, 4, 5, 9; III, p. 637.
[2] *Ibid.*   [3] *Ibid.*, 4, 5, 12; III, pp. 638–9.   [4] *Ibid.*, 4, 6, 2; III, p. 639.
[5] *Ibid.*, 5, 1; II, p. 533.

are in some sense imprinted on the mind, was shared by other Cambridge Platonists. Whichcote, for example, spoke of 'truths of first inscription', of which we have knowledge 'by the light of first impression'. 'For God made man to them (moral truths of first inscription), and did write them upon the heart of man, before he did declare them upon Mount Sinai, before he engraved them upon the tables of stone, or before they were writ in our Bibles: God made man to them, and wrought his law upon men's hearts; and as it were, interwove it into the principles of our reason. . . . (We possess) principles that are *concreated*. . . . Things of natural knowledge, or of first impression in the heart of man by God, these are known to be true as soon as ever they are proposed. . . .'[1] Such are, for example, the principles of reverence for the Deity and the fundamental principles of justice.

Similarly, Henry More, in his *Enchiridion ethicum* (1668) enumerates twenty-three moral principles which he calls *Noemata moralia*. According to him, they are 'the fruit of that faculty which is properly called *Nous*',[2] and their truth is immediately evident. The first of them is that 'good is that which is pleasing, agreeable and fitting to some perceptive life, or to a degree of this life, and which is conjoined with the conservation of the per-cipient'.[3] Another is that 'what is good should be chosen; but evil should be avoided. The greater good should be chosen in preference to the latter, while a lesser evil should be tolerated lest we undergo a greater.'[4] But More evidently did not think that his list of twenty-three fundamental moral principles was exhaustive; for he speaks of 'these propositions and their like'.[5] This laying-down of a large number of 'undeniable' principles links More with Lord Herbert of Cherbury and anticipates the procedure of the later 'Scottish School'.

The Cambridge Platonists, as we have seen, were not much in sympathy with the prevailing philosophical and religious move-ments of their country and time. Though they certainly did not deny the part played by experience in human knowledge, they were not in sympathy with the restricted and narrow concept of experience which was becoming characteristic of what we call 'empiricism'. And though they were far from denouncing science, they showed little understanding of the development and method of contemporary mathematical physics. They tended to look back to 'Platonic' philosophies of nature rather than to attempt a

---

[1] *Selected sermons*, 1773, pp. 6-7. [2] I, 4, 2. [3] *Ibid.* [4] *Ibid.* [5] *Ibid.*, I, 4, 4.

forward-looking synthesis or harmonization of physics with meta-physics. Further, their devotion to a Platonic and Christian humanism led them to hold aloof from, and to adopt a critical attitude towards, the theological controversy of the time. It is understandable, therefore, that their influence was comparatively slight, particularly if one bears in mind the unattractive literary presentation of their ideas. This is not to say, of course, that they exercised no influence at all. For example, in his *Enchiridion metaphysicum* Henry More argued that the Cartesian geometrical interpretation of nature leads us to the idea of absolute space, indestructible, infinite and eternal. These attributes cannot, how-ever, be the attributes of material things. Absolute space must be, therefore, an intelligible reality which is a kind of shadow or symbol of the divine presence and immensity. More was primarily concerned with arguing that the mathematical interpretation of nature, which separated the corporeal from the spiritual, ought logically to lead to the linking of the one to the other; in other words, he was concerned with developing an *argumentum ad hominem* against Descartes. But his argument appears to have exercised an influence on the Newtonian conception of space. Again, Shaftesbury, who will be considered in connection with ethics, was certainly influenced by Cambridge Platonists such as Cudworth, More and Whichcote. Yet though Cambridge Platon-ism did exercise some influence, it obviously stands apart from what is generally considered to be the chief development in British philosophy of the period, namely, empiricism.

4. The theory of innate ideas and principles was criticized by Richard Cumberland (1632–1718), who died as bishop of Peter-borough. In the introduction to his *De legibus naturae* (1672) he makes it clear that in his opinion it is an unjustifiable short-cut if in order to defend the moral order one simply postulates innate ideas. To build natural religion and morality on a hypothesis which has been rejected by the majority of philosophers and which can never be proved is, he says, an ill-advised procedure.

But though Cumberland rejected the Cambridge Platonists' hypothesis of innate ideas, he was at one with Cudworth in his zeal to refute the philosophy of Hobbes. Laws of nature, in the moral sense, were for him 'propositions of unchangeable truth, which direct our voluntary actions about choosing good and evil; and impose an obligation to external actions even without civil laws, and laying aside all consideration of those compacts which constitute civil government'.[1] The moral law does not depend, therefore, on civil law or on the sovereign's will. And the word 'good' has an objective meaning, signifying that which preserves, develops and perfects the faculties of one or more things. But the point which Cumberland especially emphasizes is that the good of the individual is inseparable from that of others. For man is not, as Hobbes depicted him, a human atom, entirely and incurably egoistic: he is a social being, and he possesses altruistic and benevolent, as well as egoistic, inclinations. There is, therefore, no contradiction between the promotion of one's own good and the promotion of the common good. Indeed, the common good comprises within itself the good of the individual. It follows, therefore, that 'the common good is the supreme law'.[2] And the laws of nature prescribe those actions which will promote the common good, 'and by which only the entire happiness of particular persons can be obtained'.[3]

Cumberland does not work out his ideas in any very precise way. But because he lays down the promotion of the common good as the supreme law, in relation to which all other moral rules should be determined, he has been called the precursor of utilitarianism. It should be noted, however, that promotion of the common good includes for him not only promotion of benevolence and love of other men but also love of God. For perfection of our faculties, even if Cumberland does not define 'perfection', certainly involves for him the conscious appropriation and expression of our relationship to God. Moreover, the law of benevolence is itself an expression of the divine will and is furnished with sanctions, even though disinterested love of God and man provides a higher motive for obedience to the law than is provided by a self-regarding consideration of sanctions.

In view of the emphasis which is customarily, and rightly, placed on the development of empiricism in British philosophy, it is as well not to forget the existence of men such as the Cambridge Platonists and Richard Cumberland. For they represent what Professor J. H. Muirhead called 'the Platonic tradition in Anglo-Saxon Philosophy'. If we wish to use the term 'idealism' in the very wide sense in which the Marxists are accustomed to use the word, we can speak of the Cambridge Platonists and kindred thinkers as representing one phase of the idealist tradition in British philosophy, the tradition which found an eminent expression

---

[1] *De legibus naturae*, 1.   [2] *Ibid.*   [3] *Ibid.*, 5.

(combined with empiricism) in the writings of Berkeley and which flourished in the latter part of the nineteenth century and in the first two decades of the twentieth. On the Continent British philosophy is often supposed to be inherently and constantly empiricist and even naturalistic in character. The existence of another tradition needs, therefore, to be emphasized if we are to form a balanced view of the development of British thought.

CHAPTER IV

LOCKE (1)

Life and writings—Locke's moderation and common sense— The purpose of the Essay—*The attack on innate ideas—The empiricist principle.*

1. JOHN LOCKE was born at Wrington, near Bristol, in 1632. His father was a country attorney, and he was educated at home until he went in 1646 to Westminster School, where he remained until 1652. In that year he entered the university of Oxford as a junior student of Christ Church. After taking in due course the B.A. and M.A. degrees, he was elected in 1659 to a senior studentship at Christ Church. In the following year he was made a lecturer in Greek, and later he was appointed Reader in rhetoric and Censor of Moral Philosophy.

When Locke started studying philosophy at Oxford, he found there a debased and rather petrified form of Scholasticism for which he conceived a great distaste, regarding it as 'perplexed' with obscure terms and useless questions. No doubt, like some other Renaissance and modern philosophers who revolted against Aristotelian Scholasticism, he was more influenced by it than he himself was aware; but his interest in philosophy was aroused by his private reading of Descartes rather than by what was then being taught at Oxford. This is not to say that Locke was ever a Cartesian. But on certain points he was influenced by Descartes, and in any case the latter's writings showed him that clear and orderly thinking is as possible inside as it is outside the sphere of philosophy.

Locke's studies at Oxford were not confined to philosophy. As a friend of Sir Robert Boyle and his circle, he interested himself in chemistry and physics, and he also pursued studies in medicine, though it was not until a later date (1674) that he obtained his medical degree and a licence to practise. He did not, however, take up the practice of medicine as a regular career, nor did he continue his academic life at Oxford. Instead he became involved, in a minor way, in public affairs.

In 1665 Locke left England as secretary to a diplomatic mission, headed by Sir Walter Vane, to the Elector of Brandenburg. Two years later, after his return to England, he entered the service of Lord Ashley, afterwards the first earl of Shaftesbury, acting as medical adviser to his patron and as tutor to the latter's son. But Shaftesbury evidently held a higher opinion of Locke's abilities; for when he became Lord Chancellor in 1672, he appointed his friend to the post of secretary for the presentation of ecclesiastical benefices. In 1673 Locke was made secretary to the council of trade and plantations; but Shaftesbury's political fortunes suffered a reverse, and Locke retired to Oxford, where he still held his studentship at Christ Church. Ill-health, however, led him to go to France in 1675, and he remained there until 1680. During this period he met Cartesians and anti-Cartesians and was influenced by the thought of Gassendi.

On his return to England Locke re-entered the service of Shaftesbury. But the latter was engaged in intrigue against King James II, then Duke of York, and he was finally forced to take refuge in Holland, where he died in the January of 1683. Locke, believing that his own safety also was menaced, fled to Holland in the autumn of the same year. Charles II died in 1685, and Locke's name was placed on a list of people wanted by the new government in connection with Monmouth's rebellion. He therefore lived under an assumed name and did not return to England even when his name had been removed from the list of wanted persons. However, as Locke was aware, plans were afoot for placing William of Orange on the throne of England, and shortly after the revolution of 1688 Locke returned to his own country, the Dutchman having been safely installed in London.

For reasons of health Locke declined the proffered post of ambassador to the Elector of Brandenburg; but he retained a minor office in London until in 1691 he retired to Oates in Essex, where he lived as guest of the Masham family, though from 1696 until 1700 his duties as Commissioner of Trade forced him to spend part of the year in the capital. He died in October 1704, while Lady Masham was reading the Psalms to him. Incidentally, this lady was the daughter of Ralph Cudworth, the Cambridge Platonist, with whom Locke had been acquainted and with some of whose views he was in sympathy.

Locke's principal work is his *Essay concerning Human Understanding*.[1] In 1671 he was engaged in philosophical discussion with five or six friends when it occurred to him that they could not

---

[1] References to this work by volume and page are to the edition by A. C. Fraser.

make further progress until they had examined the mind's capacities and seen 'what objects our understandings were, or were not, fitted to deal with'.[1] Locke prepared a paper on the subject, and this formed the nucleus of the two early drafts of the *Essay*. He continued work on the treatise during the following years, and the first edition was published in 1690 (preceded in 1688 by a French abstract for Le Clerc's *Bibliothèque universelle*). Three further editions were published during Locke's lifetime.

In 1690 there also appeared Locke's *Two Treatises of Civil Government*. In the first he attacked the theory of the divine right of kings as expounded by Sir Robert Filmer, while in the second he developed his own political theory. According to Locke in his preface to the *Treatises* his motive in writing was to justify the revolution of 1688 and make good the title of William of Orange to occupy the throne of England. But this does not mean that his political principles had been hurriedly conceived with a view to achieving this practical purpose. Moreover, his expression of his political theory remains one of the most important documents in the history of liberal thought, just as the *Essay* remains one of the most important documents in the history of empiricism.

In 1693 Locke published *Some Thoughts concerning Education* and in 1695 *The Reasonableness of Christianity*. In 1689 he published in Latin, and anonymously, his first *Letter on Toleration*; and this was followed, in 1690 and 1693, by two other letters on the same subject. An incomplete fourth letter appeared posthumously in 1706, together with his discourse on miracles, his examination of Malebranche's opinion about seeing all things in God, the uncompleted work on *The Conduct of the Understanding*, his memoirs of Shaftesbury, and some letters. Other material has been subsequently published.

2. Locke, as is evident from his writings, was very much a man of moderation. He was an empiricist, in the sense that he believed that all the material of our knowledge is supplied by sense-perception and introspection. But he was not an empiricist in the sense that he thought that we can know only sense-presentations. In his own modest fashion he was a metaphysician. He was a rationalist in the sense that he believed in bringing all opinions and beliefs before the tribunal of reason and disliked the substitution of expressions of emotion and feeling for rationally grounded judgments. But he was not a rationalist in the sense of

[1] *Essay*, 'Epistle to the Reader'.

one who denies spiritual reality or the supernatural order or the possibility of divine revelation of truths which, while not contrary to reason, are above reason, in the sense that they cannot be discovered by reason alone and may not be fully understandable even when revealed. He disliked authoritarianism, whether in the intellectual or in the political field. And he was one of the earlier exponents of the principle of toleration. But he was far from being a friend of anarchy; and there were limits to the extent to which he was willing to apply the principle of toleration. He was a religious man; but he had no sympathy with fanaticism or with intemperate zeal. One does not look to him for brilliant extravaganzas or for flashes of genius; but one finds in him an absence of extremes and the presence of common sense.

One or two commentators have objected against over-emphasizing Locke's 'common sense'. And it is true, for example, that his theory of an occult substrate in material things is not a common-sense view, if by this one means a view spontaneously held by a man who is innocent of all philosophy. But when one speaks of Locke's common sense, one does not mean to imply that his philosophy is no more than an expression of the spontaneously held views of the ordinary man. One means rather that he endeavoured to reflect on and analyse common experience, that he did not strive after originality by producing far-fetched theories and one-sided, if brilliant, interpretations of reality, and that the theories which he did produce were, in his opinion, required by rational reflection on common experience. To those who expect from a philosopher startling paradoxes and novel 'discoveries' he inevitably appears as pedestrian and unexciting. But he gives throughout the impression of being an honest thinker. In reading him one is not forced to ask oneself constantly whether he can possibly have believed what he was saying.

In his writings Locke employs ordinary English, apart from a few technical terms; and he is to this extent easy to follow. But, as far as the *Essay* at any rate is concerned, terms are not always employed in the same sense; and he is to this extent difficult to follow. In his 'Epistle to the Reader' Locke makes open acknowledgement of the fact that the *Essay* was 'written by incoherent parcels; and after long intervals of neglect, resumed again, as my humour or occasions permitted'. This serves to explain defects in arrangement and a certain repetitiveness; 'the way it has been writ in, by catches, and many long intervals of interruption, being apt to cause some repetitions'. The reason for leaving the results as they are is provided by Locke himself. 'But to confess the truth, I am too lazy, or too busy to make it shorter.' He might, however, have profitably cleared up some major inconsistencies and fixed more definitely the meaning of certain terms. For example, sometimes he speaks as though what we know is our ideas and the relations between ideas, and, indeed, he defines the idea as the object of the understanding when a man thinks. But at other times he implies that we know at least some things directly. In other words, he sometimes implies a representationist view of knowledge, while on other occasions he implies the opposite. Again, in what he has to say about universal ideas there are several different strands or tendencies of thought. Sometimes he speaks in a nominalist fashion, but at other times he implies what the Scholastics call 'moderate realism'. And the result of all this is that under the *prima facie* simplicity and clarity of Locke's writing there is a certain amount of ambiguity and confusion. It is not that Locke was incapable of clearing up these obscurities of thought: he has himself provided what is doubtless the true explanation, namely, that he was either too lazy or too busy to do so.

3. We have seen that Locke undertook to institute an inquiry concerning human knowledge. Other philosophers before him had, of course, reflected on and written about human knowledge. In the Greek world both Plato and Aristotle had done so and, from a very different point of view, the sceptics. St. Augustine had reflected on this subject, and the leading mediaeval philosophers all considered it in one connection or another. In post-Renaissance philosophy Descartes had treated the problem of certainty, and in England both Francis Bacon and Hobbes had written about human knowledge. But Locke was really the first philosopher to devote his main work to an inquiry into human understanding, its scope and its limits. And we can say that the prominent place occupied in modern philosophy by the theory of knowledge is in large measure due to him, even though it was the influence of Kant which subsequently led to this branch of philosophical inquiry usurping to all intents and purposes the whole field of philosophy; that is to say, among those thinkers who adhered more or less closely to the position of Kant himself. The mere fact, therefore, that Locke devoted a large-scale treatise to an inquiry into human understanding and knowledge has a peculiar importance of its own.

Now it has already been mentioned that in his 'Epistle to the Reader', prefaced to the *Essay*, Locke says that he considered it necessary to inquire, with what objects are our understandings fitted to deal, with what objects are they not fitted to deal. That he asked such a question is understandable. For he thought that men not infrequently wasted their energies on problems which could not be solved by the human mind. And he also considered that this procedure is an occasion for scepticism in others. If we confined our attention to matters which fall within the scope of the human intellect, we should make progress in knowledge, and less occasion would be given for scepticism. But though it is understandable that he asked the question, its formulation, as given above, is unfortunate. For how, it may be asked, can we distinguish between the objects with which the mind is capable of dealing and those with which it is incapable of dealing without passing beyond the scope of the mind? Or the objection can be expressed in this way. If we can mention any object with which the human mind is incapable of dealing, have we not implicitly stated that the mind is capable of saying something about it and so 'dealing' with it to a certain extent?

Further, Locke defines an idea as 'whatever is meant by phantasm, notion, species, or whatever it is which the mind can be employed about in thinking'.[1] Here he tells us that the objects of the mind are ideas. And it would appear that the mind is fitted to deal with all its ideas. We could not say, with what objects the mind is not fitted to deal. For if we could say this, we should have ideas of these objects. And in this case we could deal with them, since an idea is defined as that about which the mind can be employed in thinking.

In his introduction to the *Essay* Locke says that his purpose is 'to inquire into the original, certainty, and extent of human knowledge; together with the grounds and degrees of belief, opinion, and assent'.[2] He thus makes no clear distinction between the psychological question concerning the origin of our ideas and epistemological questions such as the nature of certain knowledge and the sufficient grounds for 'opinion'. But this could hardly be expected at the time. Before speaking of the method which he proposes to employ, he remarks that it is worth while 'to search out the bounds between opinion and knowledge; and examine by what measures, in things, whereof we have no certain knowledge,

[1] *E.*, Introduction, 8; 1, p. 32.   [2] *Ibid.*, 2; 1, p. 26.

we ought to regulate our assent, and moderate our persuasions'.[1] Here we have a more or less epistemological programme. But the first point of the method of inquiry which Locke then gives is to inquire 'into the origin of those ideas, notions, or whatever else you please to call them, which a man observes, and is conscious to himself he has in his mind; and the ways, whereby the understanding comes to be furnished with them'.[2] Here we have a psychological inquiry.

This inquiry into our ideas covers the first and second books of the *Essay*. In the first book Locke argues against the theory of innate ideas, while in the second he gives his own theories about our ideas, their origin and nature. But, as one might expect when an idea is defined as whatever is the object of the understanding when a man thinks, discussion of ideas is sometimes discussion of our ideas of things and sometimes of the things of which we have ideas.

The third book treats of words. It is closely connected with the preceding book, because 'words in their primary or immediate signification stand for nothing but the ideas in the mind of him that uses them'.[3] Ideas represent things, and words stand for ideas.

The second and third points in Locke's method are 'to show what knowledge the understanding hath by those ideas; and the certainty, evidence, and extent of it' and to inquire 'into the nature and grounds of faith, or opinion'.[4] These subjects, knowledge and opinion, are dealt with in the fourth book.

4. With a view to clearing the ground in preparation for laying the empiricist foundations of knowledge Locke first disposes of the theory of innate ideas. He understands this theory as being the doctrine that 'there are in the understanding certain innate principles; some primary notions, κοιναὶ ἔννοιαι, characters, as it were stamped upon the mind of man, which the soul receives in its very first being; and brings into the world with it'.[5] Some of these principles are speculative. Locke gives as examples 'whatsoever is, is' and 'it is impossible for the same thing to be and not to be'. Others are practical, that is to say general moral, principles. In the course of his discussion of this theory Locke makes explicit mention of Lord Herbert of Cherbury's theory of 'common notions'.[6] But he says that he consulted the latter's *De veritate*

---

[1] *E.*, Introduction, 3; I, p. 27.   [2] *Ibid.*, p. 28.   [3] *E.*, 3, 2, 2; II, p. 9.
[4] *E.*, Introduction, 3; I, p. 28.   [5] *E.*, I, I, I; I, p. 37.   [6] *E.*, I, 2, 15f.; I, p. 80.

'when I had writ this' (the foregoing part of the discussion). Hence he did not set out to attack Lord Herbert specifically; and he does not tell us which philosopher or philosophers he had in mind when he started to attack the theory of innate ideas. His remarks about this theory being 'an established opinion amongst some men' and about there being 'nothing more commonly taken for granted' suggest perhaps that he was simply writing in general against the theory, without intending to direct his criticism against any individual in particular, Descartes, for example, or against a particular group, such as the Cambridge Platonists. He includes in a global fashion all the upholders of the theory.

The chief argument, according to Locke, which is customarily adduced in favour of the theory is universal consent. Because all men agree about the validity of certain speculative and practical principles, it needs must be, it is argued, that these principles are originally imprinted on men's minds and that they brought them into the world with them 'as necessarily and really as they do any of their inherent faculties'.[1]

Against this theory Locke argues in the first place that even if it were true that all men agree about certain principles this would not prove that these principles are innate, provided that some other explanation can be given of this universal agreement. In other words, if the agreement of all mankind about the truth of these principles can be explained without introducing the hypothesis of innate ideas, the hypothesis is superfluous, and the principle of economy should be applied. Locke was, of course, convinced that the origin of all our ideas can easily be explained without postulating innate ideas. And for this reason alone he was prepared to exclude the theory.

Secondly, Locke argues that the argument which is brought in favour of the theory of innate ideas is worthless. For there is no universal consent about the truth of any principle. Children and idiots have minds, but they have no knowledge of the principle that it is impossible for the same thing to be and not to be. Yet if this principle were really innate, it must be known. 'No proposition can be said to be in the mind, which it never yet knew, which it was never yet conscious of.'[2] Moreover, 'a great part of illiterate people, and savages, pass many years, even of their rational age, without ever thinking on this and the like general propositions'.[3] The general principles of the speculative order are 'seldom

[1] *E.*, I, I, 2; I, p. 39.   [2] *E.*, I, I, 5; I, p. 40.   [3] *E.*, I, I, 12; I, p. 45.

mentioned in the huts of Indians, much less are they to be found
in the thoughts of children, or any impression of them on the
minds of naturals'.[1] As for the practical or moral principles, 'it
will be hard to instance any one moral rule, which can pretend to
so general and ready an assent as, "What is, is" or to be so manifest
a truth as this, that "it is impossible for the same thing to be, and
not to be"'.[2] Where is the moral rule to which all men assent? The
general principles of justice and of observing contracts seem to be
the most generally received. But it is difficult to believe that those
who habitually infringe these rules have received them at birth as
innate principles. It may be urged that these people assent in their
minds to rules which they contradict in practice. But 'I have
always thought the actions of men the best interpreters of their
thoughts'.[3] And 'it is very strange and unreasonable to suppose
innate practical principles, that terminate only in contemplation'.[4]
We have, indeed, natural tendencies; but natural tendencies are
not the same thing as innate principles. If moral principles were
really innate, we should not find those differences in moral outlook and practice in different societies and in different epochs
which we do in fact find.

It may be objected that all this presupposes that principles, to
be innate, must be consciously apprehended from the beginning of
life, and that this presupposition is unwarranted. For they may be
innate, not in the sense that infants in arms consciously apprehend
them, but in the sense that they are apprehended when people
come to the use of reason. They may even be innate simply in the
sense that if and when a man comes to understand the meaning
of the relevant terms, he necessarily sees the truth of the proposition in question.

If to apprehend the truth of a principle when one reaches the
age of reason means apprehending its truth when one reaches
a certain determinate age, Locke did not believe that there are
any principles which a man necessarily apprehends when he has
passed a certain time in this world. Indeed, he thought, as we
have seen, that there are men who apprehend no general abstract
principles at all. As for the view that those principles are innate
the truth of which is seen when the meaning of the terms is known,
Locke did not deny that there are principles of this kind, but he
refused to admit that there is any adequate reason for calling them

---

[1] *E.*, I, I, 27; I, p. 62.   [2] *E.*, I, 2, 1; I, p. 64.
[3] *E.*, I, 2, 3; I, pp. 66–7.   [4] *Ibid.*, p. 67.

'innate'. If immediate assent to a proposition once the terms are understood is a certain sign that the proposition is an innate principle, people 'will find themselves plentifully stored with innate principles'.[1] There will be 'legions of innate propositions'.[2] Moreover, the fact that the meanings of the terms have to be learned and that we have to acquire the relevant ideas is a sure sign that the propositions in question are not in fact innate.

If, therefore, we take 'innate' to mean explicitly innate, Locke objects that all the available evidence goes to show that there are no explicitly innate principles. If, however, 'innate' is taken to mean implicitly or virtually innate, Locke asks what is really signified by the statement that there are innate principles in this sense. 'It will be hard to conceive what is meant by a principle imprinted on the understanding implicitly; unless it be this, that the mind is capable of understanding and assenting firmly to such propositions.'[3] And nobody denies that the mind is capable of understanding and assenting firmly to, for example, mathematical propositions. Why, then, call them innate? By the addition of this epithet nothing is explained and nothing further is said.

In view of the facts that the theory of innate ideas is not a theory which counts in contemporary thought and that in any case the Kantian theory of the *a priori* superseded the older theory of innate ideas, it may seem that I have given too much space to an outline of Locke's treatment of the subject. But his discussion of the theory serves at least to illustrate Locke's common-sense attitude and his constant recourse to the available empirical evidence. Moreover, the purpose of a history of philosophy is not simply that of mentioning theories which have an importance also today. And in Locke's time the theory of innate ideas was influential. To a certain extent he may have been tilting at a windmill; for it is hard to think of anyone who believed that infants in arms apprehend explicitly any innate propositions. But, as we have seen, Locke also attacked the theory of implicitly or virtually innate ideas and principles; the theory in this form was held by men of the calibre of Descartes and Leibniz.

5. Setting aside, therefore, the hypothesis of innate ideas, how does the mind come to be furnished with ideas? 'Whence has it all the materials of reason and knowledge? To this I answer, in one word, from *experience*. In that all our knowledge is founded, and

[1] *E.*, I, I, 18; I, p. 51.   [2] *Ibid.*, p. 53.   [3] *E.*, I, I, 22; I, p. 56.

from that it ultimately derives itself.'[1] But what does Locke *Sensation*[1] understand by experience? His theory is that all our ideas are ultimately derived from sensation or from reflection; and that these two make up experience. 'Our senses, conversant about particular sensible objects, do convey into the mind several distinct perceptions of things, according to the ways wherein those objects do affect them . . . when I say the senses convey into the mind, I mean, they from external objects convey into the mind what produces there those perceptions.'[2] This is sensation. The other *reflection*[2] source of ideas is the perception of the operations of our own minds, such as perceiving, thinking, doubting, believing and willing. This source is reflection, 'the ideas it affords being such only as the mind gets by reflecting on its own operations within itself.'[3] All our ideas come from one or other of these sources.

Attention may be drawn in passing to the ambiguous use of the term 'idea' to which allusion has already been made. Locke frequently speaks, for example, of our ideas of sensible qualities, while at other times the sensible qualities are spoken of as ideas. Further, as will be shown later, he uses the term 'idea' not only for sense-data but also for concepts and universal ideas. And though it is doubtless possible to make out what Locke really wishes to say on a given occasion, this careless use of the term 'idea' scarcely serves the cause of clarity.

In any case, however, Locke is convinced that experience is the fountain of all ideas. If we observe children, we see how their ideas are formed, develop and increase in number together with their experience. The human being's attention is primarily directed outwards, and sensation is thus the chief source of ideas. 'Growing up in a constant attention to outward sensation, (men) seldom make any considerable reflection on what passes within them till they come to be of riper years; and some scarce ever at all.'[4] But though reflection or introspection is not generally developed to the same extent as sensation, we have no ideas of psychical activities such as thinking and willing save by actual experience of these activities. If the words are used when we have had no experience at all of the corresponding activities, we do not know what the words mean. Locke's conclusion is, therefore, that 'all those sublime thoughts which tower above the clouds, reach as high as heaven itself, take their rise and footing here: in all that good

[1] E., 2, 1, 2; 1, pp. 121-2.   [2] E., 2, 1, 3; 1, pp. 122-3.
[3] E., 2, 1, 4; 1, p. 124.   [4] E., 2, 1, 8; 1, p. 127.

extent wherein the mind wanders, in those remote speculations, it may seem to be elevated with, it stirs not one jot beyond those ideas which sense or reflection have offered for its contemplation'.[1]

Locke's general principle, that all our ideas are grounded in experience and depend on it, was basic in classical British empiricism. And in view of the fact that rationalist philosophers such as Descartes and Leibniz believed in virtually innate ideas, we can speak of it as the 'empiricist principle'. But this should not be taken to mean that Locke invented it. To take but one example, St. Thomas Aquinas in the thirteenth century maintained that all our natural ideas and knowledge are grounded in experience, and that there are no innate ideas. Moreover, Aquinas admitted sense-perception and introspection or reflection as 'fountains' of ideas, to use Locke's way of talking, though he subordinated the latter to the former, in the sense that attention is directed first to external material objects. Aquinas was not, of course, what is generally called an 'empiricist'. Nor, for the matter of that, was Locke himself a pure 'empiricist', if by pure empiricism we mean a philosophy which excludes all metaphysics. But I do not wish to institute any comparison between Aquinas and Locke. My object in mentioning the former is simply to point out that it is a mistake to suppose that Locke invented the theory that our ideas originate in experience and to speak as though the doctrine of innate ideas had held undisputed sway in the Middle Ages. Quite apart from the fourteenth-century philosophers of the Ockhamist current of thought, a metaphysician of the thirteenth century such as Aquinas, who adhered more closely than did philosophers such as St. Bonaventure to the Aristotelian way of thinking, had no belief in the hypothesis of innate ideas. Locke's assertion of the empiricist principle was of great historical importance, but it was not a novelty in the sense that nobody before him had maintained anything of the kind.

[1] *E.*, 2, 1, 24; 1, p. 142.

CHAPTER V

LOCKE (2)

Simple and complex ideas—Simple modes; space, duration, infinity—Mixed modes—Primary and secondary qualities—Substance—Relations—Causality—Identity in relation to inorganic and organic bodies and to man—Language—Universal ideas—Real and nominal essences.

1. WHAT was said in the final section of the last chapter about the origin of our ideas may suggest that in Locke's view the mind is purely passive; that is, that ideas are 'conveyed into the mind' and lodged there, and that in the formation of ideas the mind plays no active part at all. But this would be an erroneous interpretation of Locke's theory, if it were taken to be an adequate account. For he made a distinction between simple and complex ideas. And while the mind receives the former passively, it exercises an activity in the production of the latter.

As examples of simple ideas Locke first gives the coldness and hardness of a piece of ice, the scent and whiteness of a lily, the taste of sugar. Each of these 'ideas' comes to us through one sense only. Thus the idea of whiteness comes to us only through the sense of sight, while the idea of the scent of a rose comes to us only through the sense of smell. Locke calls them, therefore, 'ideas of one sense'. But there are other ideas which we receive by more than one sense. Such are 'space or extension, figure, rest, and motion. For these make perceivable impressions, both on the eyes and touch; and we can receive and convey into our minds the ideas of the extension, figure, motion and rest of bodies, both by seeing and feeling.'[1]

Both these classes of simple ideas are ideas of sensation. But there are also simple ideas of reflection, the two principal ones being the ideas of 'perception or thinking, and volition or willing'.[2] Further, there are other simple ideas 'which convey themselves into the mind by all the ways of sensation and reflection, viz. pleasure or delight, and its opposite, pain or uneasiness; power; existence; unity'.[3] Thus pleasure or pain, delight or uneasiness, accompanies almost all our ideas, both of sensation and reflection,

---

[1] *E.*, 2, 5; 1, p. 158.   [2] *E.*, 2, 6; 1, p. 159.   [3] *E.*, 2, 7, 1; 1, p. 160.

while 'existence and unity are two other ideas that are suggested
to the understanding by every object without, and every idea
within'.[1] So also we obtain the idea of power both by observing
the effects which natural bodies produce on one another and by
observing in ourselves our own power of moving the members of
our bodies at will.

power

We have, therefore, four classes of simple ideas. And a common
characteristic of all these ideas is that they are passively received.
'For the objects of our senses do, many of them, obtrude their
particular ideas upon our minds whether we will or not; and the
operations of our minds will not let us be without at least some
obscure notions of them. No man can be wholly ignorant of what
he does when he thinks.'[2] Moreover, once the mind has these
simple ideas it cannot alter or destroy them or substitute new ones
at will. 'It is not in the power of the most exalted wit, or enlarged
understanding, by any quickness or variety of thought, to invent
or frame one new simple idea in the mind, not taken in by the
ways aforementioned: nor can any force of the understanding
destroy those that are there.'[3]

On the other hand the mind can actively frame complex ideas,
using simple ideas as its material. A man can combine two or more
simple ideas into one complex idea. He is not confined to bare
observation and introspection, but he can voluntarily combine the
data of sensation and reflection to form new ideas, each of which
can be considered as one thing and given one name. Such are, for
example, 'beauty, gratitude, a man, an army, the universe'.[4]

Locke's general notion of a complex idea presents no great
difficulty. For example, we combine the simple ideas of whiteness,
sweetness and hardness to form the complex idea of a lump of
sugar. In what sense Locke's simple ideas can properly be called
'simple' is doubtless disputable, just as it is open to question in
what sense they can properly be termed 'ideas'. Still, the general
notion is clear enough, as long as we do not scrutinize it too closely.
But Locke complicates matters by giving two classifications of
complex ideas. In the original draft of the *Essay* he divided complex ideas into ideas of substances (for example, the idea of a man
or of a rose or of gold), of collective substances (for example, of an
army), of modes or modifications (of figure, for example, or of
thinking or running) and of relations, 'the considering of one idea

---

[1] *E.*, 2, 7, 7; I, p. 163.   [2] *E.*, 2, I, 25; I, p. 142.
[3] *E.*, 2, 2, 2; I, p. 145.   [4] *E.*, 2, 12, I; I, p. 214.

with relation to another'.[1] And this classification reappears in the published *Essay*, being reduced for convenience to the three heads of modes, substances and relations. It is a classification in terms of objects. But he includes another threefold classification in the published *Essay*, and puts it in the first place. This is a classification according to the mind's activities. The mind may combine simple ideas into one compound one, 'and thus all complex ideas are made',[2] a remark which seems at first sight to restrict complex ideas to ideas of this type. Secondly, the mind can bring together two ideas, whether simple or complex, and compare them with one another without uniting them into one. And thus it obtains its ideas of relations. Thirdly, it can separate ideas 'from all other ideas that accompany them in their real existence; this is called abstraction: and thus all its general ideas are made'.[3] Having given this classification in the fourth edition of the *Essay*, Locke then proceeds to give his original classification. In the ensuing chapters he follows the latter, treating first of modes, then of substances, and afterwards of relations.

Once given the general theory of simple and complex ideas, it is incumbent on Locke to justify it. It is his business to show how abstract ideas which seem to be extremely remote from the immediate data of sensation and reflection are in fact explicable in terms of the compounding or comparing of simple ideas. 'This I shall endeavour to show in the ideas we have of space, time and infinity, and some few others, that seem the most remote from those originals.'[4]

2. We have seen that complex ideas are divided by Locke into the ideas of modes, substances and relations. Modes are defined as 'complex ideas which, however compounded, contain not in them the supposition of subsisting by themselves, but are considered as dependencies on or affections of substances; such as are ideas signified by the words triangle, gratitude, murder, etc.'.[5] And there are two kinds of modes, namely, simple and mixed. Simple modes are 'variations or different combinations of the same simple idea, without the mixture of any other, (while mixed modes are) compounded of simple ideas of several kinds, put together to make one complex one'.[6] For example, if we suppose that we have the simple idea of one, we can repeat this idea or combine three ideas of the same kind to form the complex idea of three, which is a

---

[1] Edit. Rand, p. 120. [2] *E.*, 2, 12, 1; I, p. 213. [3] *Ibid.*, p. 214.
[4] *E.*, 2, 12, 8; I, p. 217. [5] *E.*, 2, 12, 4; I, p. 215. [6] *E.*, 2, 12, 5; I, pp. 215-16.

simple mode of one. According to Locke's definition it is a simple mode, because it is the result of combining ideas 'of the same kind'. The idea of beauty, however, is the idea of a mixed mode. It is the idea of a mode and not of a substance, because beauty does not subsist of itself but is an affection or mode of things. It is the idea of a mixed mode, because it consists 'of a certain composition of colour and figure, causing delight in the beholder',[1] that is to say, it consists of ideas of different kinds.

Examples of simple modes discussed by Locke are space, duration, number, infinity, modes of motion and modes of sound, colour, taste and smell. Thus 'to slide, roll, tumble, walk, creep, run, dance, leap, skip' and so on are 'all but the different modifications of motion'.[2] Similarly, blue, red and green are variations or modifications of colour. And some indication has been given above of the way in which Locke regarded distinct numbers as simple modes of number. But it is not so easy to see how he could think of space, duration and infinity as simple modes, and a brief explanation must be given here.

The simple idea of space comes to us through two senses, sight and touch. 'This space considered barely in length between any two beings, without considering anything else between them, is called distance; if considered in length, breadth and thickness, I think it may be called capacity. The term extension[3] is usually applied to it in what manner soever considered.'[4] Now, 'each different distance is a different modification of space; and each idea of any different distance or space is a simple mode of this idea'.[5] And we can repeat or add to or expand a simple idea of space until we come to the idea of a common space, for which Locke suggests the name of 'expansion'. The complex idea of this common space, in which the universe is thought of as extended, is thus due to combining or repeating or enlarging simple ideas of space.

The ultimate foundation of our idea of time is our observation of the train of ideas succeeding one another in our minds. 'Reflection on these appearances of several ideas, one after another, in our minds, is that which furnishes us with the idea of succession; and the distance between any parts of that succession, or between

---

[1] E., 2, 12, 5; I, p. 216.   [2] E., 2, 18, 2; I, p. 294.
[3] Locke insists, against Descartes and his followers, that extension and body are not the same thing. The idea of body involves, for example, the idea of solidity, but the idea of extension does not.
[4] E., 2, 13, 3; I, p. 220.   [5] E., 2, 13, 4; I, p. 220.

the appearances of any two ideas in our minds, is that we call duration.'[1] We thus obtain the ideas of succession and duration. And by observing certain phenomena occurring at regular and apparently equidistant periods we get the ideas of lengths or measures of duration, such as minutes, hours, days and years. We are then able to repeat ideas of any length of time, adding one to another without ever coming to the end of such addition; and so we form the idea of eternity. Lastly, 'by considering any part of infinite duration, as set out by periodical measures, we come by the idea of what we call time in general'.[2] That is to say, time in general, in one of the possible meanings of the term, is 'so much of infinite duration as is measured by and coexistent with the existence and motions of the great bodies of the universe, so far as we know anything of them: and in this sense time begins and ends with the frame of this sensible world'.[3]

Finite and infinite, says Locke, seem to be modes of 'quantity'. It is true that God is infinite; but He is at the same time 'infinitely beyond the reach of our narrow capacities'.[4] For present purposes, therefore, the terms 'finite' and 'infinite' are attributed only to things which are capable of increase or diminution by addition or subtraction; 'and such are the ideas of space, duration and number'.[5] And the question is, how the mind obtains the ideas of finite and infinite as modifications of space, duration and number. Or, rather, the question is, how the idea of infinity arises, since the idea of the finite is easily explicable in terms of experience.

Locke's answer is what we would expect from the foregoing paragraphs. We can continue adding to any idea of a finite space, and, however long we go on adding, we are no nearer the limit beyond which no addition is possible. We thus obtain the idea of infinite space. It does not follow that there is such a thing as infinite space; for 'our ideas are not always proofs of the existence of things';[6] but we are concerned simply with the origin of the idea. Similarly, by repeating the idea of any finite length of duration, we arrive, as has already been seen, at the idea of eternity. Again, in the addition or increase of number we can set no bound or limit.

An obvious objection to the foregoing account of the origin of the idea of the infinite is that Locke slurs over the gap between, say, the ideas of progressively larger finite spaces and the idea of

[1] E., 2, 14, 3; I, p. 239. [2] E., 2, 14, 31; I, p. 256. [3] E., 2, 15, 6; I, p. 262.
[4] E., 2, 17, 1; I, p. 277. [5] Ibid., p. 276. [6] E., 2, 17, 4; I, p. 278.

infinite space. But it should be noted that he does not claim that we have or can have a positive idea of the infinite. 'Whatsoever positive ideas we have in our minds of any space, duration or number, let them be ever so great, they are still finite; but when we suppose an inexhaustible remainder, from which we remove all bounds, and wherein we allow the mind an endless progression of thoughts, without ever completing the idea, there we have our idea of infinity.'[1] He can say, therefore, with regard to number, that 'the clearest idea it (the mind) can get of infinity is the confused incomprehensible remainder of endless addible numbers, which affords no prospect of stop or boundary'.[2] In an idea of the infinite there is, of course, a positive element, namely, the idea of 'so much' space or duration of 'so great' a number; but there is also an indefinite or negative element, namely, the indefinite ideas of what lies beyond, conceived as boundless.

Commentators have drawn attention to the crudeness and inadequacy of Locke's description of the genesis of our idea of the infinite and to the fact that his account of infinite number would certainly not satisfy the modern mathematician. But whatever may be the defects of Locke's analysis, whether from the psychological or from the mathematical point of view, his main endeavour, of course, is to show that even those ideas, such as the ideas of immensity or boundless space, of eternity and of infinite number, which seem to be very remote from the immediate data of experience, can nevertheless be explained on empiricist principles without recourse to the theory of innate ideas. And on this point many, who criticize his analysis on other grounds, would agree with him.

3. Mixed modes, says Locke, consist of combinations of simple ideas of different kinds. These ideas must be compatible, of course; but, apart from this condition, any simple ideas of different kinds can be combined to form a complex idea of a mixed mode. This complex idea will then owe its unity to the mind's activity in effecting the combination. There may, indeed, be something in nature corresponding to the idea, but this is by no means necessarily the case.

As examples of mixed modes Locke gives, for instance, obligation, drunkenness, hypocrisy, sacrilege and murder. No one of these is a substance. And each one (or, more accurately, the idea of each one) is a combination of simple ideas of different kinds.

---

[1] *E.*, 2, 17, 8; 1, pp. 281–2.   [2] *E.*, 2, 17, 9; 1, p. 283.

Can they be said to exist, and, if so, where? Murder, for example, can be said to exist externally only in the act of murder. Hence its external existence is transient. It has, however, a more lasting existence in men's minds, that is, as an idea. But 'there too they (mixed modes) have no longer any existence than whilst they are thought on'.[1]

They appear to have their most lasting existence in their names; that is, in the words which are used as signs for the relevant ideas. In the case of mixed modes, indeed, we are very prone, according to Locke, to take the name for the idea itself. The name plays an important role. Because we have the word 'parricide', we tend to have the corresponding complex idea of a mixed mode. But because we have no one name for the killing of an old man (who is not the murderer's father) as distinct from the killing of a young man, we do not combine the relevant simple ideas into a complex idea, nor do we regard the killing of an old man, as distinct from a young man, as a specifically different type of action. Locke was well aware, of course, that we could choose to form this complex idea as a distinct idea and attach a separate name to it. But, as will be seen presently, he believed that one of the principal ways in which we come to have complex ideas of mixed modes is through the explanation of names. And where there is no name, we are apt not to have the corresponding idea.

There are three ways in which we come to have complex ideas of mixed modes. First, 'by experience and observation of things themselves. Thus, by seeing two men wrestle or fence, we get the idea of wrestling or fencing.'[2] Secondly, by voluntarily putting together several simple ideas of different kinds: 'so he that first invented printing, or etching, had an idea of it in his mind, before it ever existed'.[3] Thirdly, 'which is the most usual way, by explaining the names of actions we never saw, or notions we cannot see'.[4] What Locke means is clear enough. A child, for example, learns the meanings of many words not by actual experience of the things signified but by having the meanings explained to him by others. He may never have witnessed sacrilege or murder, but he can obtain the complex ideas of these mixed modes if someone explains the meanings of the words in terms of ideas with which he is already familiar. In Locke's terminology, the complex idea can be conveyed to the child's mind by resolving it into simple ideas and then combining these ideas, provided, of course, that the child

[1] E., 2, 22, 8; 1, p. 385.   [2] E., 2, 22, 9; 1, p. 385.   [3] Ibid.   [4] Ibid.

already has these simple ideas or, if he has not got them, that they can be conveyed to him. As a child has the idea of man and most probably also possesses the idea of killing, the complex idea of murder can easily be conveyed to him, even though he has never witnessed a murder. Indeed, the majority of people have never witnessed a murder, but they none the less have the complex idea of it.

4. It will be remembered that Locke divides complex ideas into the ideas of modes, of substances and of relations. And after treating of his distinction between simple and complex ideas I have gone on to deal with the complex ideas of simple and mixed modes, in order to illustrate more easily the application of his theory that all our ideas are derived ultimately from sensation and reflection; that is, from experience, without there being any need to postulate the hypothesis of innate ideas. But before proceeding to discuss the ideas of substance and of relation I wish to say something about his theory of primary and secondary qualities. He treats of this matter in a chapter entitled 'Some farther considerations concerning our simple ideas', before, that is to say, proceeding to speak of complex ideas.

Locke makes a distinction between ideas and qualities. 'Whatsoever the mind perceives in itself or is the immediate object of perception, thought or understanding, that I call idea; and the power to produce any idea in our mind I call quality of the subject wherein that power is.'[1] Taking the example of a snowball, he explains that the snowball's powers of producing in us the ideas of white, cold and round are called by him 'qualities', while the corresponding 'sensations or perceptions' are called 'ideas'.

A further distinction must now be made. Some qualities are inseparable from a body, whatever changes it undergoes. A grain of wheat has solidity, extension, figure and mobility. If it is divided, each part retains these qualities. 'These I call original or primary qualities of body, which I think we may observe to produce simple ideas in us, viz. solidity, extension, figure, motion or rest, and number.'[2] Besides these primary qualities there are also secondary qualities. The latter are 'nothing in the objects themselves but powers to produce various sensations in us by their primary qualities'.[3] Such are colours, sounds, tastes and odours. Locke also mentions tertiary qualities, namely, the powers in bodies of producing, not ideas in us, but changes of bulk, figure,

[1] E., 2, 8, 8; 1, p. 169.   [2] E., 2, 8, 9; 1, p. 170.   [3] E., 2, 8, 10; 1, p. 170.

texture and motion in other bodies, so that the latter operate on
our senses in a different way from the way in which they previously operated. 'Thus the sun has a power to make wax white,
and fire to make lead fluid.'[1] But we can confine our attention to
primary and secondary qualities.

Locke supposes that in the production of our ideas both of
primary and of secondary qualities 'insensible particles' or
'imperceptible bodies' emanate from objects and act on our senses.
But there is this great difference between our ideas of primary and
those of secondary qualities. The former are resemblances of
bodies, 'and their patterns do really exist in the bodies themselves; but the ideas produced in us by these secondary qualities
have no resemblance of them at all. There is nothing like our ideas
existing in the bodies themselves. They are, in the bodies we
denominate from them, only a power to produce those sensations
in us; and what is sweet, blue or warm in idea is but the certain
bulk, figure and motion of the insensible parts in the bodies themselves, which we call so.'[2] Thus our idea of figure, for example,
resembles the object itself which causes the idea in us: the object
really has figure. But our idea of, say, red does not resemble the
rose considered in itself. What corresponds in the rose to our idea
of red is its power of producing in us the idea of red through the
action of imperceptible particles on our eyes. (In modern terminology we would speak, of course, of the action of light-waves.)

It is not terminologically accurate to say that according to
Locke secondary qualities are 'subjective'. For, as we have seen,
what he calls secondary qualities are powers in objects of producing
certain simple ideas in us. And these powers are really in the
objects. Otherwise, of course, the effect would not be produced.
But the ideas of secondary qualities, that is to say, the simple
ideas of colours, sounds and so on, which are produced in us are
not copies, as it were, of colours and sounds in the objects themselves. Obviously, we can say that the ideas of secondary qualities
are subjective; but then so are the ideas of primary qualities, if
we mean by 'subjective' existing in the percipient subject. Locke's
point is, however, that the latter resemble what is in the object,
whereas the former do not. 'The particular bulk, number, figure and
motion of the parts of fire or snow are really in them, whether any
one's senses perceive them or no; and therefore they may be called
real qualities, because they really exist in those bodies. But light,

[1] *E.*, 2, 8, 23; 1, p. 179.   [2] *E.*, 2, 8, 15; 1, p. 173.

heat, whiteness or coldness are no more really in them than sickness or pain is in manna.'[1] 'Why are whiteness and coldness in snow, and pain not, when it produces the one and the other idea in us; and can do neither, but by the bulk, figure, number and motion of its solid parts?'[2] 'Let us consider the red and white colours in porphyry: hinder light from striking on it, and its colours vanish, it no longer produces any such ideas in us; upon the return of light, it produces these appearances on us again.'[3] Again, 'Pound an almond, and the clear white colour will be altered into a dirty one, and the sweet taste into an oily one. What real alteration can the beating of the pestle make in any body, but an alteration of the texture of it?'[4] Such considerations show us that our ideas of secondary qualities have no resembling counterparts in bodies.

This theory about secondary, as distinct from primary, qualities was not Locke's invention. It had been held by Galileo[5] and Descartes, and something of the kind had been maintained by Democritus[6] many centuries before. And at first sight at least it may appear to be a perfectly reasonable conclusion, perhaps the only reasonable conclusion, to be drawn from the available scientific data. Nobody, for instance, would wish to question the fact that our sensations of colour depend on certain differences in the wave-lengths of the light rays which affect our eyes. But it is possible to maintain that there is no necessary connection at all between admitting the scientific data which are more or less established and saying that it is improper to speak, for instance, of an object as crimson or blue. If two men argue about the physical events involved in sensation, the argument is a scientific and not a philosophical argument. If they are in agreement about the scientific data, they can dispute about the propriety or impropriety of speaking of roses as white or red, and of sugar as sweet and of tables as hard. And it might well be maintained that the scientific data provide no cogent reasons for saying anything else but what we are accustomed to say. But it would not be appropriate to discuss the problem here for its own sake. I wish instead to point out the very difficult position in which Locke places himself.

That Locke's way of expressing himself is confused and careless is scarcely open to denial. Sometimes he speaks of 'the ideas' of

[1] E., 2, 8, 17; I, p. 174.
[2] E., 2, 8, 16; I, p. 174.
[3] E., 2, 8, 19; I, p. 176.
[4] E., 2, 8, 20; I, p. 176.
[5] See vol. III of this History, p. 287.
[6] See vol. I of this History, pp. 124-5.

white and black. And it is clear enough that if the term 'idea' were
taken in the ordinary sense, these ideas can only be in the mind.
If an idea can be said to be somewhere, where else can it be said
to be but in the mind? True, he tells that what he here calls 'ideas'
are sensations or perceptions. But, again, that our sensations are
our sensations and not the object's which produces them is an
obvious truism. And Locke does not raise the question whether,
if the object is not crimson or sweet, the sensation is to be spoken
of as crimson or sweet. He simply says that we have an idea or
sensation of crimson or sweet. However, these questions left aside,
the main difficulty which arises on Locke's premises arises from the
fact that for him an idea is 'the immediate object of perception,
thought or understanding'.[1] We do not know things immediately
but mediately, by means of ideas. And these ideas (in the present
context we can substitute sense-data, if we like) are regarded as
representing things, as signs of them. Ideas of primary qualities
really resemble things; ideas of secondary qualities do not. But if
what we know immediately are ideas, how can we ever know
whether these ideas do or do not resemble things? How, for the
matter of that, can we be certain that things other than our ideas
even exist? For if we know only ideas immediately, we are in no
position to compare ideas with things and ascertain whether the
former resemble the latter or not, or even to establish whether
there are any things other than ideas. On Locke's representative
theory of perception he has no means of establishing the validity
of his distinction between primary and secondary qualities.

Locke was not unaware of this difficulty. As will be seen later
on, he fell back on the notion of causality to show that there are
things which correspond to our ideas. When we observe constantly recurring collections of simple ideas, which are conveyed
to us without choice on our part (except, of course, for the choice
not to shut one's eyes and stop one's ears), it is at least highly
probable that there are external things which cause these ideas,
at least during the time when the latter are being passively received
by our minds. And from the common-sense point of view this
inference is reliable. But, apart from any intrinsic difficulties in
this theory, it would scarcely be sufficient to warrant his distinction between primary and secondary qualities. For this seems to
require further knowledge than the knowledge that there is 'something out there'.

[1] *E.*, 2, 8, 8; 1, p. 169.

Berkeley

Berkeley, as will be shown later in connection with the latter's philosophy, maintained that Locke's arguments to show that colour, taste, odour and so on are ideas in our minds and not real qualities of objects, could just as well be employed to show that the so-called primary qualities are ideas in our minds and not real qualities of objects. And there is obviously a great deal to be said in favour of this point of view. According to Locke, primary qualities are inseparable from bodies. But this is true only if he is speaking of determinable and not of determinate primary qualities. To take one of his own examples, the two parts of a divided grain of wheat certainly possess extension and figure; but they do not possess the determinate extension and figure of the whole grain of wheat. One can also say, however, of a pounded almond that even if, as Locke asserts, it has not the same colour as the unpounded almond, it still possesses colour. And do not the perceived size and shape of an object vary with the position of the percipient subject and with other physical conditions just as much as secondary qualities vary?

The foregoing considerations are not, of course, intended to express doubt concerning the scientific data which can be used to support Locke's position. They are intended to show some of the difficulties which arise on Locke's theory when this is presented as a philosophical theory and thus as something more than an account of scientific data. His representationist theory of perception is a particular source of difficulty. To be sure, he sometimes forgets this theory and speaks in common-sense terms, implying that we know objects immediately; but his prevalent and, so to speak, official position is that ideas are, in Scholastic language, the *media quae*, or immediate objects, of knowledge. And matters are further complicated because, as has already been noted, he uses the term 'idea' in different senses on different occasions.

5. Mention has been made above of 'collections' of simple ideas. We find certain groups of similar sense-data constantly recurring or tending to recur. For example, a certain colour and a certain shape may be associated with a certain scent and with a certain softness or hardness. This is a matter of common experience. If I go into the garden on a summer day I see certain patches of colour (say, the petals of a red rose) of definite shapes and I perceive a certain scent. I can also have certain experiences through the sense of touch, by performing the action which we call touching the rose. There is thus a given constellation or cluster or collection

of qualities which appear to accompany one another and which are
associated together in my mind. If I go into the same garden in
the dark, I do not see the colour patches, but I perceive the scent
and I can have similar experiences of touch to those which I had
in the daylight. And I am confident that if there were sufficient
light I should see the colours which appear to go with the scent
and texture. Again, certain sounds may be associated in my
experience with certain colours and with a certain shape. For
instance, what we call the song of the blackbird is a succession of
sounds which appear to go together with the presence of certain
colours and with a certain figure or shape.

There are, therefore, collections or clusters of qualities or, as
Locke puts it, 'ideas'. And 'not imagining how these simple ideas
can subsist by themselves, we accustom ourselves to suppose some
substratum wherein they do subsist and from which they do
result; which therefore we call substance'.[1] This is the idea of
substance in general, namely, 'a supposition of he knows not what
support of such qualities, which are capable of producing simple
ideas in us; which qualities are commonly called accidents'.[2] The
mind supplies the idea of a substratum, a support for qualities.
More accurately, the mind supplies the idea of a substratum or
support in which the primary qualities inhere and which has the
power of producing in us, by means of the primary qualities,
simple ideas of secondary qualities. The general idea of substance
is 'nothing but the supposed but unknown support of those
qualities we find existing, which we imagine cannot subsist *sine re
substante*, without something to support them, (and) we call that
support *substantia*, which, according to the true import of the
word, is in plain English "standing under" or "upholding"'.[3]

It is important to understand that Locke is talking about the
origin of our idea of substance. Bishop Stillingfleet of Worcester
at first understood him to mean that substance is nothing but the
figment of men's fancies. To this Locke replied that he was discussing the idea of substance, not its existence. To say that the
idea is grounded in our custom of supposing or postulating some
support for qualities is not to say that this supposition or postulate
is unwarranted and that there is no such thing as substance. In
Locke's view the inference to substance is justified; but this does
not alter the fact that it is an inference. We do not perceive substances; we infer substance as the support of 'accidents', qualities

[1] *E.*, 2, 23, 1; I, pp. 390–1.   [2] *E.*, 2, 23, 2; I, p. 391.   [3] *Ibid.*, p. 392.

or modes, because we cannot conceive the latter as subsisting by themselves. And to say that the general idea of substance is the idea of an unknown substratum is to say that the only characteristic note of the idea in our minds is that of supporting accidents; that is, of being the substratum in which the primary qualities inhere and which possesses the power of causing simple ideas in us. It is not to say that substance is a mere figment of the imagination.

This general idea of substance, which is not clear and distinct, must be distinguished from our distinct ideas of particular substances. These are 'nothing but several combinations of simple ideas. . . . It is by such combinations of simple ideas, and nothing else, that we represent particular sorts of substances to ourselves.'[1] For example, we have a number of simple ideas (of red or white, of a certain odour, a certain figure or shape, and so on) which go together in experience, and we call the combination of them by one name, 'rose'. Similarly, 'the idea of the sun, what is it but an aggregate of those several simple ideas, bright, hot, roundish, having a constant regular motion, at a certain distance from us, and perhaps some other?'[2] In fine, 'all our ideas of the several sorts of substances are nothing but collections of simple ideas, with a supposition of something to which they belong, and in which they subsist; though of this supposed something we have no clear distinct idea at all'.[3]

The simple ideas which we unite to form the complex idea of a particular substance are obtained through sensation or reflection. Thus our idea of the spiritual substance of the soul is obtained by combining together simple ideas of thinking, doubting and so on, which are obtained by reflection, with the vague and obscure notion of a substratum in which these psychical operations inhere.

It may be as well to remark at once that by 'spiritual substance' in this connection Locke means simply a substance which thinks. In the fourth book of the *Essay*, when discussing the extent of our knowledge he declares that 'we have the ideas of matter and thinking, but possibly shall never be able to know, whether any mere material being thinks or no'.[4] For all we know, divine omnipotence might be able to confer the faculty of thinking on a material thing. Dr. Stillingfleet, bishop of Worcester, objected that in this case it is impossible to prove that there is in us a spiritual substance. To this Locke replied that the concept of

---

[1] *E.*, 2, 23, 6; 1, p. 396. [2] *Ibid.*, p. 397.
[3] *E.*, 2, 23, 37; 1, p. 422. [4] *E.*, 4, 3, 6; II, p. 192.

substance is vague and indeterminate, and that the addition of thinking makes it a spiritual substance. That there is a spiritual substance in us can thus be shown. But if Dr. Stillingfleet means by 'spiritual substance' an immaterial substance, the existence of such a substance in us cannot be strictly proved by reason. Locke does not say that God can confer the faculty of thinking on a material thing, but rather that he does not see that it is inconceivable that God should do so. As for the implications with regard to immortality, to which the bishop draws attention, our certainty on this matter is derived from faith in revelation rather than from strict philosophical demonstration.

Further, 'if we examine the idea we have of the incomprehensible Supreme Being, we shall find that we come by it in the same way, and that the complex ideas we have both of God and separate spirits are made up of the simple ideas we receive from reflection'.[1] When we frame the idea of God we enlarge to infinity the ideas of those qualities 'which it is better to have than to be without'[2] and combine them to form one complex idea. In Himself God is simple and not 'compounded'; but our idea of Him is complex.

Our distinct ideas of corporeal substances are made up of the ideas of primary qualities, those of secondary qualities (the powers in things of producing different simple ideas in us through the senses), and those of the powers of things to cause in other bodies or to receive in themselves such alterations of primary qualities as will produce different ideas in us from the ideas formerly produced. Indeed, 'most of the simple ideas that make up our complex ideas of substances, when truly considered, are only powers, however we are apt to take them for positive qualities'.[3] For example, the greater part of our idea of gold is made up of ideas of qualities (such as yellowness, fusibility and solubility in *aqua regia*) which, as they exist in the gold itself, are only active or passive powers.

Now, in so far as our distinct complex ideas of particular substances are simply combinations of simple ideas received through sensation and reflection, their formation can be explained in terms of Locke's empiricist premisses. For he expressly allowed for the formation of complex ideas by combining simple ideas. But it seems to be doubtful whether his premisses permit of his explaining the formation of the general idea of substance as an occult substratum. Dr. Stillingfleet thought at first that Locke meant that substance is nothing but a combination of qualities. And in

---

[1] *E.*, 2, 23, 33; I, p. 418.   [2] *Ibid.*   [3] *E.*, 2, 23, 37; I, p. 422.

Problem w/ general substance idea

his reply Locke distinguished between our complex ideas of particular substances and the general idea of substance. The former are obtained by combining simple ideas, but the latter is not. How, then, is it obtained? By 'abstraction', Locke tells us. But earlier on he has described the process of abstraction as 'separating them (ideas) from all other ideas that accompany them in their real existence'.[1] And in the formation of the general idea of substance it is not a question of fixing the attention on one particular member of a cluster of ideas and omitting or abstracting from the rest, but rather of inferring a substratum. And in this case a novel idea seems to make its appearance which is not obtained by sensation or reflection, or by combining simple ideas, or by abstraction in the sense mentioned above. True, Locke speaks of the general idea of substance as being neither clear nor distinct. But he nevertheless speaks of this 'idea'. And if it is an idea at all, it seems difficult to explain, on Locke's premises, how it arises. He certainly attributed to the mind an active power. But the difficulty of explaining the origin of the general idea of substance remains, unless Locke is willing to revise or re-state his premises.

Locke's idea of substance obviously derives from Scholasticism. But it is not, as is sometimes supposed, the same as that of Aquinas. The explicit distinction between substance and accident was for Aquinas, as for Locke, the work of the reflective mind; but for the former it was a distinction made within the total datum of experience, the modified or 'accidentified' thing or substance, whereas for Locke substance lies beyond experience and is an unknown substratum. Again, on Aquinas's view substance is not an unchanging substratum, even though we can distinguish between accidental and substantial change. (Locke, however, speaks as though substance were an unchanging substratum hidden beneath the changing phenomena.) In other words, Aquinas's conception of substance stands nearer to the point of view of common sense than does that of Locke.

Locke's distinction between the general idea of substance and our ideas of particular substances is connected with his distinction between real and nominal essences. But he does not discuss this topic before the third book of the *Essay*, and I leave it aside for the moment to consider his account of the origin of our idea of causality.

6. It has already been pointed out that in the first draft of the

[1] *E.*, 2, 12, 1; I, pp. 213–14.

Essay Locke classified relations, together with substances and modes, under the general heading of complex ideas. But though this classification reappears in the fourth edition, Locke gives us another as well, in which relations stand in a class by themselves. This juxtaposition of two methods of classification is obviously unsatisfactory. However, we are told that relations arise from the act of comparing one thing with another. If I consider Caius as such, merely by himself, I do not compare him with any other thing. And the same is true when I say that Caius is white. 'But when I give Caius the name *husband*, I intimate some other person; and when I give him the name *whiter*, I intimate some other thing: in both cases my thought is led to something beyond Caius, and there are two things brought into consideration.'[1] Terms like 'husband', 'father', 'son', and so on, are obviously relative terms. But there are other terms which appear at first sight to be absolute but which 'conceal a tacit, though less observable relation'.[2] Such, for example, is the term 'imperfect'.

Any idea, whether simple or complex, can be compared with another idea and thus give rise to the idea of a relation. But all our ideas of relations can in the long run be reduced to simple ideas. This is one of the points which Locke is most concerned to make. For if he wishes to show that his empiricist account of the origin of our ideas is justified, he has to show that all ideas of relations are ultimately made up of ideas obtained through sensation or reflection. And he proceeds to argue that this is true by applying his theory to certain selected relations, such as causality.

But before we consider Locke's analysis of causality it is worth while drawing attention to the ambiguous way in which he speaks about relations. Primarily, indeed, he is concerned to show how the mind acquires its ideas of relations; that is to say, he is primarily concerned with a psychological question rather than with the ontological question, what is the nature of relations. However, as he has described an idea as whatever is the object of the mind when it thinks, it follows that relations, as thought about, are ideas. And some of his pronouncements can hardly be understood as meaning anything else but that relations are purely mental. For example, we are told that 'the nature of relation consists in the referring or comparing two things one to another'.[3] Again, 'relation is a way of comparing or considering two things

[1] *E.*, 2, 25, 1; I, p. 427.   [2] *E.*, 2, 25, 3; I, p. 428.   [3] *E.*, 2, 25. 5; I, p. 428.

together, and giving one or both of them some appellation from that comparison; and sometimes giving even the relation itself a name'.[1] Moreover, he states explicitly that a relation is 'not contained in the real existence of things, but (is) something extraneous and superinduced'.[2] And when treating later on of the abuse of words he remarks that we cannot have ideas of relations which disagree with things themselves, because relation is only a way of considering together or comparing two things and so 'an idea of my own making'.[3] At the same time Locke speaks freely about ideas of relations; and he does not make it clear what he means to imply by this. Suppose that I do not consider John simply by himself but 'compare' him with Peter, his son. I can then think of John as father, which is a relative term. Now, as we have seen, Locke says that a relation is the comparing of one thing with another. The relationship in the case in point should be the act of 'comparing' John with Peter. And the idea of the relation should be the idea of the act of comparing. But it would be odd to say that the relationship of fatherhood is the act of comparing one man with another; and it would be still more odd to say that the idea of the relationship of fatherhood is the idea of the act of comparing. Moreover, when in the fourth book of the *Essay* Locke speaks about our knowledge of the existence of God, he clearly implies that all finite things really depend on God as their cause, that is to say, that they have a real relation of dependence on God. The truth of the matter seems to be that he did not work out his theory of relations in any clear and precise way. When speaking of relations in general, he seems to say that they are all mental; but this does not prevent him from speaking about some particular relations as though they were not purely mental. This can be seen, I think, in his treatment of causality.

7. According to Locke, 'that which produces any simple or complex idea we denote by the general name *cause*; and that which is produced, *effect*'.[4] We receive our ideas of cause and effect, therefore, from observing that particular things, qualities or substances, begin to exist. Observing, for instance, that fluidity, a 'simple idea', is produced in wax by the application of a certain degree of heat, 'we call the simple idea of heat, in relation to fluidity in wax, the cause of it, and fluidity the effect'.[5] Similarly, observing that wood, a 'complex idea', is reduced to ashes, another

[1] *E.*, 2, 25, 7; I, pp. 429–30. [2] *E.*, 2, 25, 8; I, p. 430.
[3] *E.*, 3, 10, 33; II, p. 145. [4] *E.*, 2, 26, 1; I, p. 433. [5] *Ibid.*, p. 434.

'complex idea', by the application of fire, we call the fire, in relation to the ashes, *cause* and the ashes *effect*. The notions of cause and effect arise, therefore, from ideas received through sensation or reflection. And 'to have the idea of cause and effect it suffices to consider any simple idea, or substance, as beginning to exist by the operation of some other, without knowing the manner of that operation'.[1] We can discriminate between different kinds of production. Thus when a new substance is produced from pre-existing material we speak of 'generation'. When a new 'simple idea' (quality) is produced in a pre-existent thing we speak of 'alteration'. When anything begins to exist without there being any pre-existent material out of which it is constituted we speak of 'creation'. But our ideas of all these different forms of production are said to be derived from ideas received through sensation and reflection, though Locke does not offer any explanation how this general proposition covers the case of our idea of creation.

In so far as causality is a relation between ideas, it is a mental construction. But it has a real foundation, and this is power; the powers, that is to say, which substances have of affecting other substances and of producing ideas in us. The idea of power is classified by Locke as a simple idea, though 'I confess power includes in it some kind of relation, a relation to action or change'.[2] And powers are divided, as we have already seen, into active and passive. We can ask, therefore, whence we derive our idea of active power and causal efficacy. The answer, according to Locke, is that our clearest idea of active power is derived from reflection or introspection. If we observe a moving ball which hits a ball at rest and sets it in motion, we do not observe any active power in the first ball; for 'it only communicates the motion it had received from another and loses in itself so much as the other received: which gives us but a very obscure idea of an active power moving in body, whilst we observe it only to transfer, but not produce any motion. For it is but a very obscure idea of power which reaches not the production of the action, but the continuation of the passion.'[3] If, however, we turn to introspection, 'we find in ourselves a power to begin or forbear, continue or end several actions of our minds and motions of our bodies, barely by a thought or preference of the mind ordering or, as it were, commanding the doing or not doing such or such a particular action'.[4] It is the

[1] *E.*, 2, 26, 2; I, p. 435.   [2] *E.*, 2, 21, 3; I, p. 310.
[3] *E.*, 2, 21, 4; I, p. 312.   [4] *E.*, 2, 21, 5; I, p. 313.

exercise of volition, therefore, which gives us our clearest idea of power and causal efficacy.

Locke thus establishes to his own satisfaction the empirical foundations of our ideas of cause and effect and of causal efficacy or the exercise of active power. But he does not give any real analysis of the causal relation. However, he makes it clear, both in his arguments for the existence of God and when writing to Stillingfleet, that he was convinced that the proposition 'everything which has a beginning must have a cause' is an indubitable proposition. It has been made a charge against him that he does not explain how this proposition is established by experience. But, as the fourth book of the *Essay* makes abundantly clear, Locke believed that there is such a thing as intuitive certainty and that the mind can apprehend a necessary connection between ideas. In the case of the proposition in question Locke would doubtless say that we obtain through experience our ideas of a thing beginning to be and of cause, and that then we perceive the necessary connection between the ideas, which is expressed in the statement that everything which begins to be has a cause. Presumably he thought that this account of the matter satisfied the demands of his empiricist theory of the foundations of all our ideas and knowledge. Whether it fits in with his remarks about relations as mental constructions is another question.

8. In connection with relations Locke devotes a chapter to the ideas of identity and diversity. When we see a thing existing in a certain place at a certain instant of time we are sure that it is itself and not another thing which exists at the same time in another place, even though the two things may be alike in other respects. For we are certain that one and the same thing cannot exist simultaneously in more than one place. Locke here refers to common linguistic usage. If we observe body A existing at time t in place x and if we observe body B existing at time t in place y, we speak of them as two different bodies, however much they may resemble one another. But if A and B both existed at time t in place x, they would be indistinguishable; and we would speak of one and the same body, not of two bodies. I do not mean that Locke thought that this view was 'simply a matter of words': I mean that he adopts the common-sense point of view which finds expression in ordinary linguistic usage. As God is eternal, immutable and omnipresent, there can be, Locke tells us, no doubt about His constant self-identity. But finite things begin to exist

in time and space; and the identity of each thing will be determined, as long as it exists, by its relation to the time at which and the place in which it begins to exist. And we can therefore solve the problem of individuation by saying that the principle of individuation is 'existence itself, which determines a being of any sort to a particular time and place, incommunicable to two beings of the same kind'.[1] The last part of this definition is included because two substances of different kinds may occupy the same place at the same time. Presumably Locke is thinking primarily of God's eternity and omnipresence.

But though Locke defines identity in general in relation to the temporal and spatial co-ordinates of a thing's existence, he sees that the matter is rather more complicated than is allowed for by this formula. If two atoms are joined to form one 'mass of matter', we speak of the mass as being the same, as long as the same two atoms are conjoined. But if one atom is taken away and another added, the result is a different mass or body. In organic things, however, we are accustomed to speak of the organism as being the same organic body, even though obvious changes in the matter have taken place. A plant continues to be the same plant 'as long as it partakes of the same life, though that life be communicated to new particles of matter vitally united to the living plant, in a like continued organization conformable to that sort of plant'.[2] The case of animals is similar. The continued identity of an animal is in some ways similar to that of a machine. For we speak of a machine as being the same, even if parts of it have been repaired or renewed, because of the continued organization of all the parts with a view to the attainment of a certain end or purpose. An animal differs from a machine, however, in that in the case of the latter the motion comes from without whereas in the case of the animal the motion comes from within.

The identity of a 'simple' inorganic thing can be defined, therefore, in terms of time and place (though Locke does not mention continuity of the thing's spatio-temporal history as one of the criteria of persisting self-identity). The continued identity of a compound inorganic thing demands the continuous identity (in relation to space and time) of its constituent parts. The continuous identity of an organic body, however, is defined in relation to the organization of parts informed by a common life rather than in relation to the continued identity of the parts themselves. In fact,

[1] E., 2, 27, 4; I, pp. 441–2.   [2] E., 2, 27, 5; I, p. 443.

'in these two cases, a mass of matter and a living body, identity is not applied to the same thing'.[1] Inorganic and organic bodies are different in kind, and the criteria of identity differ in the two cases, though in both there must be a continuous existence which has some relation to spatio-temporal co-ordinates.

How far can we apply to man the criteria of identity which are applicable to other organic bodies? Locke answers that a man's continued self-identity consists 'in nothing but a participation of the same continued life by constantly fleeting particles of matter in succession vitally united to the same organized body'.[2] He does not explain in exact terms the precise meaning of this statement, but he makes it clear that in his opinion we are accustomed, and justifiably accustomed, to speak of 'the same man' when there is bodily continuity. Whatever psychological changes may take place in a man, we still call him the same man provided that his bodily existence is continuous. If, however, we take identity of soul as the one and only criterion of sameness, strange results follow. For example, if we assume for the sake of argument the hypothesis of reincarnation, we should have to say that X, living in ancient Greece, was the same man as Y, living in mediaeval Europe, simply because the soul was the same. But this way of speaking would be very strange. 'I think nobody, could he be sure that the soul of Heliogabalus were in one of his hogs, would yet say that hog were a man or Heliogabalus.'[3] In other words, Locke appeals here to ordinary linguistic usage. We speak of a man as being the same man when there is bodily continuity. And we have here an empirical criterion of sameness. But, in Locke's opinion, there would be no way of controlling our use of the word 'same' if we said that it is identity of soul that makes a man the same man.

But though we are ordinarily accustomed to speak of a man as the same man when there is bodily continuity, we can still raise the question in what does personal identity consist, meaning by 'person' 'a thinking, intelligent being, that has reason and reflection and can consider itself as itself, the same thinking thing in different times and places'.[4] The answer to this question is consciousness, which Locke declares to be inseparable from thinking and essential to it, 'it being impossible for anyone to perceive without perceiving that he does perceive'.[5] 'As far as this

---

[1] *E.*, 2, 27, 4; I, p. 442. [2] *E.*, 2, 27, 7; I, p. 444. [3] *Ibid.*, p. 445.
[4] *E.*, 2, 27, 11; I, p. 448. [5] *Ibid.*, p. 449.

consciousness can be extended backwards to any past action or thought, so far reaches the identity of that person.'[1]

Locke draws the logical conclusion that if it is possible for the same man (that is, a man who is the same man in the sense that there is bodily continuity) to have at time t^1 one distinct and incommunicable consciousness and at time t^2 another distinct and incommunicable consciousness, we could not speak of the man as being the same 'person' at time t^2 as he was at time t^1. This is 'the sense of mankind in the solemnest declaration of their opinions, human laws not punishing the madman for the sober man's actions, nor the sober man for what the madman did, thereby making them two persons; which is somewhat explained by our way of speaking in English, when we say such an one is not himself, or is beside himself; in which phrases it is insinuated as if those who now, or at least first used them, thought that self was changed, the self-same person was no longer in that man'.[2]

9. At the end of the second book of the *Essay* Locke tells us that having given an account of the source and kinds of our ideas he at first proposed to proceed immediately to consider the use which the mind makes of these ideas and the knowledge which we obtain through them. But reflection convinced him that it was necessary to treat of language before going on to discuss knowledge. For ideas and words are clearly closely connected, and our knowledge, as he puts it, consists in propositions. He therefore devoted the third book to the subject of words or language.

3rd Book— language

God made man a social being by nature. And language was to be 'the great instrument and common tie of society'.[3] Language consists of words, and words are signs of ideas. 'The use of words is to be sensible marks of ideas; and the ideas they stand for are their proper and immediate signification.'[4] It is true that we take our words to be signs of ideas in other men's minds as well of ideas in our own minds, when, that is to say, we and they are speaking a common language. And we often suppose words to stand for things. None the less a man's words signify primarily and immediately the ideas in his own mind. Words can, of course, be used without meaning. A child can learn and use a word in parrot-fashion, without having the idea which is normally signified by it. But in this case the word is nothing but a non-significant noise.

[1] *E.*, 2, 27, 11; I, p. 449.   [2] *E.*, 2, 27, 20; I, p. 461.
[3] *E.*, 3, 1, 1; II, p. 3.   [4] *E.*, 3, 2, 1; II, p. 9.

Although Locke insists tenaciously that words are signs of ideas, he does not give any thorough explanation of the meaning of this statement. However, his general position is clear enough, if we do not pry into it too closely. Ideas, according to Locke's representationist theory, are the immediate objects of thought; and ideas, or some of them rather, stand for things or are signs of things. But ideas are private. And to communicate our ideas to others and to learn others' ideas we stand in need of 'sensible' and public signs. This need is fulfilled by words. But there is this difference between ideas, which are signs of things, and words. Those ideas which signify things or represent things are natural signs. Some of them at least, that is to say, are produced by things, though others are mental constructions. Words, however, are all conventional signs: their signification is fixed by choice or convention. Thus while the idea of man is the same in the minds of a Frenchman and an Englishman, the sign of this idea is *homme* in French and *man* in English. It is clear that Locke assumed that thought in itself is really distinct from the use of words and symbols, and that the possibility of expressing the same thought in different linguistic forms and in different language is a proof of this distinction.

There is, however, a qualification to be added to the statement that words are signs of ideas. 'Besides words which are names of ideas in the mind there are a great many others that are made use of to signify the connection that the mind gives to ideas or propositions one with another.'[1] The mind needs not only signs of the ideas 'before it' but also signs to show or intimate some action of its own in relation to these ideas. For example, 'is' and 'is not' show or intimate or express the mind's acts of affirming and denying. Locke calls words of this kind 'particles', and he includes under this heading not only the copula in propositions but also prepositions and conjunctions. These all mark or express some action of the mind in relation to its ideas.

Although Locke does not give any thorough explanation of his theory of signification, he saw clearly enough that to say that words are signs of ideas and that language, composed of conventional signs, is a means of communicating ideas, constitutes an over-simplification. 'To make words serviceable to the end of communication, it is necessary that they excite in the hearer exactly the same idea they stand for in the mind of the speaker.'[2]

[1] *E.*, 3, 7, 1; II, p. 98.   [2] *E.*, 3, 9, 6; II, p. 106.

But this end is not always attained. For example, a word may stand for a very complex idea; and in this case it is very difficult to ensure that the word always stands for precisely the same idea in common use. 'Hence it comes to pass that men's names of very compound ideas, such as for the most part are moral words, have seldom, in two different men, the same precise signification; since one man's complex idea seldom agrees with another's, and often differs from his own, from that which he had yesterday or will have tomorrow.'[1] Again, as mixed modes are mental constructions, collections of ideas put together by the mind, it is difficult to find any fixed standard of meaning. The meaning of a word such as 'murder' depends simply on choice. And although 'common use regulates the meaning of words pretty well for common conversation',[2] there is no recognized authority which can determine the precise meaning of such words. Hence it is one thing to say that names stand for ideas and another thing to say precisely for what ideas they stand.

This 'imperfection' of language is scarcely avoidable. But there is also such a thing as an avoidable 'abuse' of words. In the first place, men not infrequently coin words which do not stand for any clear and distinct ideas. 'I shall not need here to heap up instances; every man's reading and conversation will sufficiently furnish him; or if he wants to be better stored, the great mint-masters of this kind of terms, I mean the Schoolmen and metaphysicians (under which, I think, the disputing natural and moral philosophers of these latter ages may be comprehended) have wherewithal abundantly to content him.'[3] Secondly, words are often abused in controversy through being used by the same man in different senses. Another abuse consists in taking words for things and supposing that the structure of reality must correspond to one's ways of talking about it. Locke also mentions figurative speech as one abuse of language. He would have done better perhaps to have cited it as a source of or occasion for the abuse of language. Indeed, he feels this himself to some extent. For he remarks that 'eloquence, like the fair sex, has too prevailing beauties in it to suffer itself ever to be spoken against'.[4] But his point is that 'eloquence' and rhetoric are used to move the passions and mislead the judgment, as indeed they not infrequently are; and he is too much of a rationalist to attempt to distinguish clearly

[1] E., 3, 9, 6; II, p. 107.   [2] E., 3, 9, 8; II, p. 108.
[3] E., 3, 10, 2; II, p. 123.   [4] E., 3, 10, 34; II, p. 147.

between the proper and improper use of emotive and evocative language.

The misuse of words is thus a prolific source of error, and Locke evidently considered this a subject of considerable importance. For at the end of the *Essay* he insists on the need for studying the science of signs. 'The consideration, then, of ideas and words as the great instruments of knowledge makes no despicable part of their contemplation who would take a view of human knowledge in the whole extent of it. And perhaps if they were distinctly weighed and duly considered, they would afford us another sort of logic and critic than what we have been hitherto acquainted with.'[1] But it is only in very recent times that Locke's suggestion has been taken with any great seriousness.

10. As general terms play such a prominent part in discourse, it is necessary to pay special attention to their origin, meaning and use. We must have general terms; for a language made up exclusively of proper names could not be memorized, and, even if it could, it would be useless for purposes of communication. If, for example, a man was unable to refer to cows in general but had to have a proper name for every particular cow which he had seen, the names would have no meaning for another man who was unacquainted with these particular animals. But although it is obviously necessary that there should be general names, the question arises how we come to have them. 'For since all things that exist are only particulars, how come we by general terms or where find we those general natures they are supposed to stand for?'[2]

Locke replies that words become general by being made signs of general ideas, and that general ideas are formed by abstraction. 'Ideas become general by separating from them the circumstances of time and place and any other ideas that may determine them to this or that particular existence. By this way of abstraction they are made capable of representing more individuals than one; each of which having in it a conformity to that abstract idea is (as we call it) of that sort.'[3] A child, let us suppose, is acquainted first of all with one man. It later becomes acquainted with other men. And it frames an idea of the common characteristics, leaving out the characteristics peculiar to this or that individual. It thus comes to have a general idea, which is itself signified by the general term 'man'. And with the growth of experience it can go on to

---

[1] *E.*, 4, 21, 4; II, p. 462. [2] *E.*, 3, 3, 6; II, p. 16. [3] *Ibid.*, pp. 16–17.

form other wider and more abstract ideas, each of which will be signified by a general term.

It follows that universality and generality are not attributes of things, which are all individual or particular, but of ideas and words: they are 'the inventions and creatures of the understanding, made by it for its own use, and concern only signs, whether words or ideas'.[1] Of course, any idea or any word is also particular; it is this particular idea or this particular word. But what we call general or universal words and ideas are universal in their signification. That is to say, a universal or general idea signifies a sort of thing, like cow or sheep or man; and the general term stands for the idea as signifying a sort of thing. 'That, then, which general words signify is a *sort* of things; and each of them does that by being a sign of an abstract idea in the mind, to which idea, as things existing are found to agree, so they come to be ranked under that name; or, which is all one, be of that sort.'[2]

To say, however, that universality belongs only to words and ideas is not to say that there is no objective foundation for the universal idea. 'I would not here be thought to forget, much less to deny, that nature in the production of things makes several of them alike: there is nothing more obvious, especially in the races of animals and all things propagated by seed.'[3] But it is the mind which observes these likenesses among particular things and uses them as the occasion to form general ideas. And when a general idea has been formed, say the idea of gold, a particular thing is said to be or not to be gold in so far as it conforms or does not conform to this idea.

Locke occasionally speaks in a manner which suggested to Berkeley that the general idea was a composite image consisting of incompatible elements. For instance, he speaks of the general idea of a triangle, which 'must be neither oblique nor rectangle, neither equilateral, equicrural, nor scalenon; but all and none of these at once. . . . It is an idea wherein some parts of several different and inconsistent ideas are put together.'[4] But this statement must be understood in the light of what Locke says elsewhere about 'abstraction'. He does not say that the general idea of a triangle is an image; nor does he say that it is composed of mutually inconsistent or incompatible ideas. He says that it is composed of 'parts' of different and inconsistent ideas. That is to

[1] *E.*, 3, 3, 11; II, p. 21. [2] *E.*, 3, 3, 12; II, p. 22.
[3] *E.*, 3, 3, 13; II, p. 23. [4] *E.*, 4, 7, 9; II, p. 274.

say, the mind omits the notes peculiar to this or that kind of triangle and puts together the common characteristics of different kinds of triangle to form the general idea of triangularity. Abstraction is thus depicted as a process of elimination or leaving out and of putting together what remains, common characteristics. This may, indeed, be unfortunately vague; but there is no need to make Locke talk absolute nonsense by ascribing to him the view that general ideas are composed of mutually incompatible elements.

11. It is important not to understand the word 'abstraction' in the present context as meaning the abstraction of the real essence of a thing. Locke distinguishes two senses of the term 'real essence'. 'The one is of those who, using the word essence for they know not what, suppose a certain number of those essences, according to which all natural things are made, and wherein they do exactly every one of them partake, and so become of this or that species.'[1] This theory is, says Locke, an untenable hypothesis, as is shown by the production of monsters. For the theory presupposes fixed and stable specific essences, and it cannot explain the fact of borderline cases and of variations in type. In other words, it is incompatible with the available empirical data. Further, the hypothesis of stable but unknown specific essences is so useless that it might well be discarded even if it were not contradicted by the empirical data. 'The other and more rational opinion (about real essences) is of those who look on all natural things to have a real but unknown constitution of their insensible parts, from which flow those sensible qualities which serve us to distinguish them one from another, according as we have occasion to rank them into sorts under common denominations.'[2] But though this opinion is 'more rational', there can obviously be no question of abstracting unknown essences. Every collection of simple ideas depends on some 'real constitution' of a thing; but this real constitution is unknown by us. Hence it cannot be abstracted.

From real essences Locke distinguishes nominal essences. We are accustomed to decide whether a given thing is gold or not by observing whether it possesses those common characteristics, possession of which is regarded as necessary and sufficient for a thing to be classed as gold. And the complex idea of these characteristics is the nominal essence of gold. This is why Locke can say that 'the abstract idea for which the (general) name stands and

[1] E., 3, 3, 17; II, p. 27.   [2] Ibid., pp. 27–8.

the essence of the species is one and the same',[1] and that 'every distinct abstract idea is a distinct essence'.[2] It is the nominal essence, therefore, which is abstracted, by leaving out characteristics peculiar to individual things as individuals and retaining their common characteristics.]

Locke adds that in the case of simple ideas and modes the real and nominal essences are the same. 'Thus a figure including a space between three lines is the real as well as nominal essence of a triangle.'[3] But in the case of substances they are different. The nominal essence of gold is the abstract idea of the observable characteristics common to the things which are classed as gold; but its real essence, or substance, is 'the real constitution of its insensible parts, on which depend all those properties of colour, weight, fusibility, fixedness, etc., which are to be found in it'.[4] And this real essence, the particular substance of gold, is unknown by us. Locke's way of speaking is certainly open to criticism. For in the case of the universal idea of triangularity it is inappropriate to speak about 'real essence' at all, if the latter is defined as the real but unknown constitution of the insensible parts of a material substance. But his general meaning is sufficiently clear, namely, that in the case of material substances it makes sense to speak of a real essence distinct from the nominal essence or abstract idea, whereas in the case of triangularity it does not.)

[1] *E.*, 3, 3, 12; II, p. 23. [2] *E.*, 3, 3, 14; II, 9, 25.
[3] *E.*, 3, 3, 18; II, p. 29. [4] *Ibid.*, p. 29.

CHAPTER VI

LOCKE (3)

Knowledge in general—The degrees of knowledge—The extent and reality of our knowledge—Knowledge of the existence of God —Knowledge of other things—Judgment and probability— Reason and faith.

1. IN the draft of the *Essay* Locke remarks that 'it remains now to enquire what kind of knowledge it is we have of or by these ideas, the proper object of knowledge being truth, which lies wholly in affirmation or negation, or propositions either mental or verbal, which is no more but apprehending things to be as really as they are and do exist, or expressing our apprehensions by words fitted to make others apprehend as we do'.[1] But in the published *Essay* he starts the fourth book with the unequivocally representationist statement, 'Seeing the mind in all its thoughts and reasonings hath no other immediate object but its own ideas, which it alone does or can contemplate, it is evident that our knowledge is only conversant about them'.[2] And he goes on to say that knowledge consists exclusively in the perception of the connection and agreement or disagreement and repugnance of any of our ideas. When we see that the three angles of a triangle are equal to two right angles, we perceive a necessary connection between ideas. And therefore we can legitimately be said to know that the three angles of a triangle are equal to two right angles.

But what is meant by 'agreement' and 'disagreement' of ideas? The primary form of agreement or disagreement is what Locke calls 'identity or diversity'. The mind, for example, knows immediately and infallibly that the ideas of white and round (when he has received them through sense-experience, needless to say) are what they are and not the other ideas which we call red and square. A man may, indeed, be in error about the right terms for these ideas; but he cannot possess them without seeing that each agrees with itself and disagrees with other and different ideas. The second form mentioned by Locke is called 'relative'. He is here thinking of the perception of relations between ideas, which may

---

[1] Rand, p. 85.   [2] *E.*, 4, 1, 1; 11, p. 167.

be relations of agreement or of disagreement. Mathematical propositions provide the chief, though not the only, example of relational knowledge. Thirdly, there is agreement or disagreement of coexistence. Thus our knowledge of the truth that a substance remains unconsumed by fire is a knowledge that the power of remaining unconsumed by fire coexists with or always accompanies the other characteristics which together form our complex idea of the substance in question. Finally, there is agreement or disagreement 'of real existence'. Locke gives as an example the statement 'God is'. That is to say, we know that the idea of God 'agrees with' or corresponds to a really existent being.

Two points in this classification of forms of knowledge are immediately evident. In the first place knowledge of identity and knowledge of coexistence are both relational. Locke, indeed, explicitly admits this. 'Identity and coexistence are truly nothing but relations.'[1] But he goes on to claim that they have peculiar features of their own which justify their consideration under separate headings, though he does not explain what these peculiar features are. In the second place knowledge of real existence should evidently cause Locke considerable difficulty. For if an idea is defined as whatever is the object of the mind when it thinks, it is not easy to see how we can ever know that our ideas correspond to real existents, in so far as these latter are not our ideas. However, leaving this point aside for the moment, we can say that knowledge consists for Locke either in perceiving the agreement or disagreement between ideas or in perceiving the agreement or disagreement of ideas with things which are not themselves ideas.

2. Locke proceeds to examine the degrees of our knowledge. And here he shows a decidedly rationalistic turn of mind. For he exalts intuition and demonstration, which is characteristic of, though not confined to, mathematical knowledge, at the expense of what he calls 'sensitive knowledge'. He does not, of course, recant his general empiricist theory that all our ideas come from experience, from sensation or reflection. But, presupposing this theory, he then clearly takes mathematical knowledge as the paradigm of knowledge. And on this point at least he shows an affinity with Descartes.

'If we reflect on our own ways of thinking, we shall find that sometimes the mind perceives the agreement or disagreement of two ideas immediately by themselves, without the intervention of

[1] *E.*, 4, 1, 7; II, p. 171.

any other: and this, I think, we may call intuitive knowledge.'[1] Thus the mind perceives immediately by intuition that white is not black and that three are more than two.[2] This is the clearest and most certain kind of knowledge which the human mind can attain. There is no room for doubt, and 'it is on this intuition that depends all the certainty and evidence of all our knowledge'.[3]

The second degree of knowledge is demonstrative knowledge, where the mind does not perceive immediately the agreement or disagreement of ideas but needs intervening ideas to be able to do so. Locke is thinking primarily of mathematical reasoning, where a proposition is proved or demonstrated. We do not, he says, have immediate intuitive knowledge that the three angles of a triangle are equal to two right angles: we need 'intervening ideas' with the aid of which the agreement in question is proved. Demonstrative knowledge of this kind lacks, we are told, the facility and clarity of intuition. At the same time each step in the reasoning has intuitive certainty. But if Locke had paid more attention to syllogistic reasoning than he actually did, he might have felt some doubt about the truth of this last statement. For there can be a valid syllogistic argument containing a contingent proposition. And the truth of a contingent proposition is not known with what Locke calls intuitive certainty. There is no necessary connection between the terms; hence we cannot perceive it immediately. In other words, as commentators have pointed out, Locke's idea of demonstration inevitably restricts the range of demonstrative knowledge to a very narrow field.

Whatever comes short of intuition and demonstration is not knowledge 'but faith or opinion, at least in all general truths'.[4] However, there is sensitive knowledge of particular existence. Some people, Locke remarks, may express doubt whether there are any existent things corresponding to our ideas; 'but yet here, I think, we are provided with an evidence that puts us past doubting'.[5] When a man sees the sun by day his perception is different from his thought of the sun during the night; and there is an unmistakable difference between smelling the scent of a rose and recalling the scent of a rose. If he says that all may be a dream, he must none the less admit that there is a great difference between dreaming of being in the fire and actually being in it.

3. There are, therefore, three degrees of knowledge: intuitive,

---

[1] E., 4, 2, 1; II, p. 176.   [2] Ibid., p. 177.   [3] Ibid.
[4] E., 4, 2, 14; II, p. 185.   [5] Ibid., p. 186.

demonstrative and sensitive. But how far is our knowledge capable of extending? If knowledge consists in perceiving the agreement or disagreement between ideas, it follows that 'we can have knowledge no further than we have ideas'.[1] But according to Locke 'the extent of our knowledge comes not only short of the reality of things, but even of the extent of our own ideas'.[2] And it is necessary to examine what he means by this. We can follow him in taking one by one the four forms of knowledge mentioned in the first section and in seeing how far our knowledge extends or can extend in each of these ways of perceiving the agreement or disagreement of our ideas.

In the first place, our knowledge of 'identity and diversity' extends as far as our ideas extend. That is to say, we cannot have an idea without intuitively perceiving that it is itself and that it is different from any other idea.

But this is not the case with regard to our knowledge of 'co-existence'. 'In this our knowledge is very short, though in this consists the greatest and most material part of our knowledge concerning substances.'[3] Our idea of a particular kind of substance is a collection of simple ideas coexisting together. For example, 'our idea of a flame is a body hot, luminous and moving upward; of gold, a body heavy to a certain degree, yellow, malleable and fusible'.[4] But what we perceive is a factual coexistence or togetherness of simple ideas: we do not perceive any necessary connection between them. Our complex ideas of substances are made up of ideas of their secondary qualities, and these depend upon 'the primary qualities of their minute and insensible parts; or if not upon them, upon something yet more remote from our comprehension'.[5] And if we do not know the root from which they spring, we cannot know what qualities necessarily result from or are necessarily incompatible with the insensible constitution of the substance. Hence we cannot know what secondary qualities must always coexist with the complex idea which we have of the substance in question or what qualities are incompatible with this complex idea. 'Our knowledge in all these inquiries reaches very little farther than our experience.'[6] Again, we cannot discern any necessary connection between the powers of a substance to effect sensible changes in other bodies and any of those ideas which together form our notion of the substance in question. 'Experience

[1] E., 4, 3, 1; II, p. 190.   [2] E., 4, 3, 6; II, p. 191.   [3] E., 4, 3, 9; II, p. 199.
[4] Ibid.   [5] E., 4, 3, 11; II, p. 200. [6] E., 4, 3, 14; II, p. 203.

is that which in this part we must depend on. And it were to be wished that it were more improved.'[1] And if we turn from bodies to spirits, we find ourselves even more in the dark.

The reason which Locke gives for saying that our knowledge of 'coexistence' does not extend very far is of considerable interest. It is clear that he has in his mind an ideal standard of knowledge. To have a 'real knowledge' of the coexistence of the ideas which together form the nominal essence of a thing would mean seeing their necessary connections with one another, in a manner analogous to that in which we perceive necessary connections between ideas in mathematical propositions. But we do not perceive these necessary connections. We see that the complex idea of gold comprises the idea of yellowness as a matter of fact; but we do not perceive a necessary connection between yellowness and the other qualities which together form a complex idea of gold. Hence our knowledge is judged to be deficient; it is simply a knowledge based on experience, on *de facto* connections. We cannot demonstrate propositions in natural science or 'experimental philosophy': 'certainty and demonstration are things we must not, in these matters, pretend to'.[2] We cannot attain 'general, instructive, unquestionable truths'[3] concerning bodies. In all this Locke's attitude seems to be that of a 'rationalist', who takes mathematical knowledge as the ideal standard, rather than that of an 'empiricist'.

At the same time I do not think that this point of view should be over-emphasized. Locke does, indeed, imply that natural science is deficient precisely because it is empirical; but he also attributes its shortcomings simply to contemporary ignorance. 'Though we are not without ideas of these primary qualities of bodies in general, yet not knowing what is the particular bulk, figure and motion of the greatest part of the bodies of the universe, we are ignorant of the several powers, efficacies and ways of operation whereby the effects which we daily see are produced.'[4] Here it is a question simply of ignorance. Our senses are not acute enough to perceive the 'minute particles' of bodies and discover their operations. Our experiments and researches do not carry us very far, though 'whether they will succeed again another time, we cannot be certain. This hinders our certain knowledge of universal truths concerning natural bodies; and our reason carries

[1] *E.*, 4, 3, 16; II, p. 206.   [2] *E.*, 4, 3, 26; II, p. 218.
[3] *Ibid.*   [4] *E.*, 4, 3, 24; II, p. 215.

us herein very little beyond particular matter of fact.'[1] Locke does, indeed, strike a pessimistic note. For he is 'apt to doubt that how far soever human industry may advance useful and experimental philosophy in physical things, scientifical (knowledge) will still be out of reach'.[2] And he asserts that though our ideas of bodies will serve us for ordinary practical purposes, 'we are not capable of scientifical knowledge; nor shall ever be able to discover general, instructive and unquestionable truths concerning them. Certainty and demonstration are things we must not, in these matters, pretend to.'[3] We have here, as was remarked in the last paragraph, a depreciation of natural science because it falls short of an ideal knowledge: we have a clear statement that natural science can never become 'science'. At the same time, however, Locke's pessimistic remarks about natural science are due in large part simply to contemporary ignorance and lack of the technical equipment required for startling advances and discoveries. Hence, while it is necessary to note the rationalistic attitude which is apparent in the fourth book of the *Essay*, I think that we should be careful not to over-emphasize it in this particular context.

As for the third kind of knowledge, relational knowledge, it is difficult to say how far it is capable of extending, 'because the advances that are made in this part of knowledge, depending on our sagacity in finding intermediate ideas that may show the relations and habitudes of ideas whose coexistence is not considered, it is a hard matter to tell when we are at the end of such discoveries'.[4] Locke is thinking primarily of mathematics. Those who are ignorant of algebra, he says, cannot imagine its potentialities, and we cannot determine in advance the further resources and utility of mathematics. But he is not thinking exclusively of mathematics, and he suggests that ethics might be made a demonstrative science. Locke's ideas about ethics, however, will be left to the next chapter.

Finally, there is knowledge of the actual existence of things. Locke's position here is easily summarized. 'We have an intuitive knowledge of our own existence; and a demonstrative knowledge of the existence of a God; of the existence of any thing else we have no other but a sensitive knowledge, which extends not beyond the objects present to our senses.'[5] As for knowledge of our own existence, we perceive it so plainly and with such certainty that

[1] *E.*, 4, 3, 25; II, p. 217.   [2] *E.*, 4, 3, 26; II, pp. 217–18.
[3] *Ibid.*   [4] *E.*, 4, 3, 18; II, p. 207.   [5] *E.*, 4, 3, 21; II, p. 212.

it neither needs nor is capable of proof. 'If I doubt of all other things, that very doubt makes me perceive my own existence and will not suffer me to doubt of that.'[1] As we have seen in the last chapter, Locke does not mean that I have intuitive certainty of the existence of an immaterial soul in myself. But I perceive clearly that I am a thinking self, though precisely what is intuited Locke does not explain. Our knowledge of God and of things other than God and ourselves will be considered in the following sections of this chapter. Meanwhile, I raise a question which Locke treats under the heading 'the reality of our knowledge'.

We have just seen that according to Locke we can know that things exist. And we can know something about them. But how can we do this if the immediate object of knowledge is an idea? 'It is evident that the mind knows not things immediately, but only by the intervention of the ideas it has of them. Our knowledge therefore is real only so far as there is a conformity between our ideas and the reality of things. But what shall be here the criterion? How shall the mind, when it perceives nothing but its own ideas, know that they agree with things themselves?'[2] The question is clear enough. What is Locke's answer?

We can put mathematical and moral knowledge on one side. Pure mathematics gives us certain and real knowledge, but it is knowledge 'only of our own ideas'.[3] That is to say, pure mathematics is formal: it makes statements about the properties of 'ideas', such as the idea of a triangle or circle, and about the relations between ideas, but not about the world of things. And the truth of mathematical propositions is not affected by the presence or absence of things corresponding to the ideas which the mathematician employs in his reasoning. If he makes a statement about the triangle or the circle, the existence or non-existence of a corresponding triangle or circle in the world is entirely irrelevant to the truth of his statement. If the latter is true, it remains true even though there may be no existent triangle or circle which corresponds to the mathematician's ideas of triangles or circles. For the truth of his statement follows simply from his definitions and axioms. 'In the same manner the truth and certainty of moral discourses abstracts from the lives of men and the existence of those virtues in the world whereof they treat. Nor are Tully's Offices (Cicero's *De officiis*) less true because there is nobody in the world that exactly practises his rules and lives up to that pattern

[1] *E.*, 4, 9, 3; II, p. 305.   [2] *E.*, 4, 4, 3; II, p. 228.   [3] *E.*, 4, 4, 6; II, p. 231.

of a virtuous man which he has given us and which existed
nowhere, when he writ, but in idea.'[1]

The situation is different, however, with regard to simple ideas.
For these are not fabricated by the mind, as is the idea of a perfect
circle; they are imposed on the mind. Hence they must be the
product of things operating on the mind, and they must have a
conformity with things. In view of the fact that colours, for
example, bear little resemblance to the powers in objects which
produce in us the relevant simple ideas, one might expect Locke
to explain more precisely the nature of this 'conformity'. However,
he is satisfied with remarking that 'the idea of whiteness, or bitter-
ness, as it is in the mind, exactly answering that power which is
in any body to produce it there, has all the real conformity it can,
or ought to have, with things without us. And this conformity
between our simple ideas and the existence of things is sufficient
for real knowledge.'[2] It may be sufficient; but this is not the point
at issue. The question is, how do we know, or rather how can we
know on Locke's premises, that there is any conformity at all?

Simple ideas, therefore, are said to have a conformity with
external objects. What, then, of complex ideas? This question
concerns our ideas of substances. For as other complex ideas are
'archetypes of the mind's own making, not intended to be the
copies of any thing',[3] the problem of their conformity is not so
pressing. They can give us 'real' knowledge as in mathematics,
even if nothing corresponds to them outside the mind. But ideas of
substances are referred, to use Locke's language, to archetypes
outside us; that is to say, they are thought to correspond to
external reality. And the question arises, how can we know that
they correspond supposing that they do in fact correspond in some
way to external reality? This question refers, of course, to
nominal essences; for according to Locke we do not know the real
essences of things. His answer is that our complex ideas of substances are formed of simple ideas, and that 'whatever simple
ideas have been found to coexist in any substance, these we may
with confidence join together again, and so make abstract ideas of
substances. For whatever have once had an union in nature may
be united again.'[4]

Of course, if qualities are simple *ideas*, and if we know immediately only ideas, we can never compare the collections of

[1] *E.*, 4, 4, 8; II, p. 233.   [2] *E.*, 4, 4, 4; II, p. 230.
[3] *E.*, 4, 4, 5; II, p. 230.   [4] *E.*, 4, 4, 12; II, p. 237.

qualities in our minds with the clusters of qualities outside our minds. And Locke's answer certainly does not clear up this difficulty. But though he talks about 'simple ideas' he also talks about our ideas of qualities and of substances. In other words, he oscillates between a representationist view, according to which ideas are the object of knowledge, and the view that ideas are simply psychic modifications by means of which we know things directly. Or, more accurately, he oscillates, not between two 'views' (since his declared view is that the object of knowledge is ideas), but between two ways of talking, speaking sometimes as though the idea is the *medium quod* of knowledge (his declared view) and sometimes as though it is the *medium quo* of knowledge. And this ambiguity may be partly responsible for his failure to deal seriously with the difficulty which arises out of his representationism.

However, let us assume that we can know the correspondence between our complex ideas of substances and existent sets of compresent qualities. As we have seen, Locke will not allow that any necessary connections are perceived between these qualities. Hence our knowledge, though real, does not extend beyond the actual experience which we have had, and if we express this knowledge in the form of general or universal propositions we cannot legitimately claim for the latter that they are more than probably true.

4. In the preceding section mention was made of Locke's view that we have, or rather can have, demonstrative knowledge of the existence of God. By this he means that we can deduce the existence of God 'from some part of our intuitive knowledge'.[1] And the intuitively known truth from which he starts is our knowledge of our own existence. More accurately perhaps, the individual's demonstrative knowledge of God's existence is based on his intuitive knowledge of his own existence. But knowledge of one's own existence does not by itself prove God's existence. We need other intuitively known truths. And the first of these is the proposition that 'bare nothing can no more produce any real being than it can be equal to two right angles'.[2] Intuitive knowledge of my own existence shows me that at least one thing exists. Now, I know that I did not exist from eternity but had a beginning. But that which had a beginning must have been produced by something else; it cannot have produced itself. There must, therefore,

[1] <i>E.</i>, 4, 10, 1; II, p. 306.   [2] <i>E.</i>, 4, 10, 3; II, p. 307.

says Locke, be something which existed from eternity. He does not make the steps of the argument very clear. But what he evidently means is that for anything at all to exist at any time there must be a being which itself had no beginning; for, if this were not the case, some being would have produced itself or have 'simply happened', and this is inconceivable. That anything which begins to be does so through the efficacy of an already existent extrinsic cause is obviously taken by Locke to be a self-evident proposition. But he does not explain whether he intends to rule out an infinite regress in the temporal order (an infinite regress, that is to say, going back into the past) or an infinite regress in the order of existential dependence here and now, without reference to the past. However, from various remarks which he makes it seems to follow that he is thinking of an infinite regress going back into the past. If this is the case, his line of argument differs from that of Aquinas, for example, who tried to develop a proof of God's existence which would be independent of the question whether or not there is a series of temporal events reaching back indefinitely into the past. In fact, Locke's argument is carelessly constructed and lacks precision. Some would rule it out altogether on the ground that what Locke regards as self-evident truths are not self-evidently true. But even if we are not prepared to do this, it is difficult to say very much about it, because Locke does not state it clearly.

If we assume, however, that there is a being which existed from eternity, the question arises, what is its nature? Here Locke uses the principle that 'what had its being and beginning from another must also have all that which is in and belongs to its being from another too'.[1] As, therefore, man finds in himself powers, and as he also enjoys perception and knowledge, the eternal being on which he depends must also be powerful and intelligent. For a thing which is itself void of knowledge cannot produce a knowing being. And from this Locke concludes that 'there is an eternal, most powerful and most knowing being; which whether anyone will please to call God, it matters not. The thing is evident, and from this idea duly considered will easily be deduced all those other attributes which we ought to ascribe to this eternal being.'[2]

5. A man knows his own existence by intuition and that of God by demonstration. 'The knowledge of the existence of any other thing we can have only by sensation.'[3] For there is no necessary

<hr />

[1] *E.*, 4, 10, 4; 11, p. 308. [2] *E.*, 4, 10, 6; 11, p. 309. [3] *E.*, 4, 11, 1; 11, p. 325.

connection between the idea which a man has of anything other than God and the existence of the thing. The fact that we have an idea of a thing does not prove that it exists. We know that it exists only when it is operating upon us. 'It is therefore the actual receiving of ideas from without that gives us notice of the existence of other things and makes us know that something doth exist at that time without us.'[1] The receiving of ideas from without is sensation, and we know the existence of things which affect our sense-organs only while they are doing so. When I open my eyes, it does not depend on my choice what I see; I am acted upon. Further, if I put my hand too near the fire, I feel pain, whereas when I have the mere idea of putting my hand too near the fire I do not suffer pain. Such considerations show us that our confidence in the existence of other things is not ill-grounded. True, our knowledge of the existence of external things extends only as far as the present testimony of our senses; but it is probable that the table which I saw a moment ago is still existing; and it is folly to look for demonstrative knowledge before we are prepared to assent to an existential proposition. 'He that in the ordinary affairs of life would admit of nothing but direct plain demonstration would be sure of nothing in this world but of perishing quickly. The wholesomeness of his meat or drink would not give him reason to venture on it: and I would fain know what it is he could do upon such grounds as are capable of no doubt, no objection.'[2]

6. The mind is said to 'know' when 'it certainly perceives and is undoubtedly satisfied of the agreement or disagreement of any ideas'.[3] We know that X is Y when we clearly perceive a necessary connection between them. But the mind has what Locke calls another 'faculty', namely, judgment, which is 'the putting ideas together or separating them from one another in the mind when their certain agreement or disagreement is not perceived but presumed to be so. . . . And if it so unites or separates them as in reality things are, it is right judgment.'[4] Judgment is therefore concerned with probability and yields 'opinion'.

Probability is defined by Locke as 'the appearance of agreement upon fallible proofs'.[5] That is to say, when we judge that a proposition is probably true, that which moves us to give assent to the proposition as probably true is not its self-evident character (for in this case we would know it to be certainly true) but extrinsic

---

[1] *E.*, 4, 11, 2; 11, p. 326.   [2] *E.*, 4, 11, 10; 11, pp. 335–6.
[3] *E.*, 4, 14, 4; 11, p. 362.   [4] *Ibid.*   [5] *E.*, 4, 15, 1; 11, p. 363.

grounds or reasons which are not sufficient to demonstrate its truth. There are two main extrinsic grounds for believing a proposition to be true though it is not self-evidently true. The first of these is 'the conformity of anything with our own knowledge, observation and experience'.[1] For instance, so far as my experience goes, iron sinks in water. If I have often and always seen this happen, the probability that it will happen on future occasions is proportionately greater than if I had only seen it happen once. In fact, when consistent experiences give rise to judgment and this judgment is constantly verified in further experience, probability rises so high that it influences our expectations and actions in practically the same way that the evidence of demonstration influences them. The second ground for believing a proposition to be probably true is testimony. And here again there can be degrees of probability. If, for example, there are a large number of reliable witnesses to some events, and if their testimonies agree, there is a much higher degree of probability than if the witnesses are few· and unskilful or if the accounts given disagree with one another.

Locke divides 'the propositions we receive upon inducements of probability'[2] into two classes. The first class consists of propositions concerning 'matters of fact' which fall under observation and can be the object of human testimony. That it froze in England last winter would be an example. The second class consists of propositions concerning matters which cannot be the object of human testimony because they are incapable of empirical investigation. That there are angels would be one example, and that heat consists in 'a violent agitation of the imperceptible minute parts of the burning matter'[3] would be another. In such cases it is from analogy that we draw the grounds of probability. Observing the different stages in the hierarchy of levels of being below man (animals, plants, inorganic things), we can judge it probable that between man and God there are finite immaterial spirits. Again, observing that the rubbing of two bodies together produces heat, we can argue by analogy that heat probably consists in the violent motion of imperceptible particles of matter.

It is clear, therefore, that for Locke the propositions of the natural sciences can enjoy at best only a very high degree of probability. This view is closely connected, of course, with his conviction that we know only the nominal essences of things and not their 'real essences', in the sense explained in the last chapter.

[1] *E.*, 4, 15, 4; II, p. 365. [2] *E.*, 4, 16, 5; II, p. 374. [3] *E.*, 4, 16, 12; II, p. 380.

Historical propositions too, which rest on human testimony, can enjoy only varying degrees of probability. And Locke reminds his readers that the degree of probability which is enjoyed by a historical statement depends on the value of the relevant testimony and not on the number of people who may have repeated the statement.

7. It might be expected perhaps that Locke would have included all statements accepted by faith in the class of probable propositions. But he did not do so. For he admitted a divine revelation which gives us certainty about the truth of the doctrines revealed, since the testimony of God admits of no doubt. 'We may as well doubt of our own being, as we can whether any revelation from God be true. So that faith is a settled and sure principle of assent and assurance, and leaves no manner of room for doubt or hesitation.'[1] This does not mean, of course, that all truths about God are accepted on faith. For Locke, as we have seen, asserted the demonstrative character of our knowledge of God's existence. Revealed truths are those which are above, though not contrary to, reason, and the truth of which we know on the testimony of God. In other words, Locke continued the mediaeval distinction between truths about God which can be discovered by the unaided human reason and those which cannot be known unless God reveals them.

At the same time Locke had a great dislike of what he called 'enthusiasm'. He was thinking of the attitude of those people who are prone to assume that some idea which comes into their heads constitutes a private divine revelation, a product of divine inspiration. They do not bother about objective reasons in support of the claim that their ideas are inspired by God: strong feeling is for them more persuasive than any reason. 'They are sure because they are sure; and their persuasions are right because they are strong in them.'[2] They say that they 'see' and 'feel'; but what is it they 'see'? That some proposition is evidently true or that it has been revealed by God? The two questions must be distinguished. And if the proposition is not evidently true or if it is not put forward as probably true on the basis of some objective grounds for belief, reasons must be given for thinking that it is in fact revealed by God. But for the people suffering from 'enthusiasm' a proposition 'is a revelation because they firmly believe it, and they believe it because it is a revelation'.[3] Locke insisted, therefore,

[1] *E.*, 4, 16, 14; II, p. 383.   [2] *E.*, 4, 19, 9; II, p. 434.   [3] *E.*, 4, 19, 10; II, p. 436.

that even though God can certainly reveal truths which transcend reason, in the sense that reason alone cannot establish them as true, it must be shown by reason that they are in fact revealed before we can be expected to accept them by faith. 'If strength of persuasion be the light which must guide us, I ask how shall anyone distinguish between the delusions of Satan and the inspirations of the Holy Ghost?'[1] After all, 'God, when He makes the prophet, does not unmake the man. He leaves all his faculties in the natural state, to enable him to judge of his inspirations whether they be of divine origin or no.'[2] By disposing of reason to make room for revelation 'enthusiasm' does away with both. In his treatment of enthusiasm Locke's strong common sense is very much in evidence.

Locke did not question, therefore, the possibility of divine revelation. In fact he believed in doctrines such as that of the immortality of the soul and the resurrection of the body on the testimony of God's word. But he insisted that propositions which are contrary to reason cannot have been revealed by God. And it is clear, I think, that when he talks in this way he is thinking very largely of Catholic dogmas such as that of transubstantiation to which he explicitly refers in his chapter on wrong assent or error.[3] The retort might obviously be made that if there is good reason for thinking that a proposition is revealed by God, it cannot be contrary to reason even though it is above reason.[4] But Locke, having made up his mind that certain doctrines were contrary to reason, concluded that they cannot have been revealed and that there cannot be any adequate reason for thinking that they have been revealed. To discuss controversial questions of this kind here would be out of place. But it is worth while drawing attention to the fact that Locke continued the point of view of the Cambridge Platonists or 'latitudinarians'. While rejecting on the one hand what he regarded as the misguided enthusiasm of self-appointed prophets and preachers, he rejected also what would appear to be the logical consequences of a belief in the possibility of divine revelation, namely, that if there are good reasons for thinking that God has revealed truth through a certain mouthpiece no proposition taught by the accredited authority can be contrary to reason. Locke would doubtless reply that the only criterion for deciding

---

[1] *E.*, 4, 19, 13; II, p. 438.   [2] *E.*, 4, 19, 14; II, p. 438.   [3] *E.*, 4, 20, 10; II, p. 450.
[4] Catholic theologians would not deny that reason is capable *in principle* of distinguishing between propositions which are contrary to reason and propositions, the truth or falsity of which cannot be decided by reason without the aid of revelation. But in particular cases we may, when left to our own devices, confuse the latter with the former.

whether a doctrine is contrary to reason or simply 'above reason' is reason itself. But he makes his position easier to maintain by admitting, sincerely enough, the possibility of divine revelation without embarking upon the question where this revelation is to be found and through what particular organ or organs it has been made.

Locke's general attitude of moderation and his dislike of extremes, together with his conviction that the reach of certainty is very limited whereas the field of probability, in its various degrees, is very large, led him to espouse, within limits, the cause of toleration. I say 'within limits' because in his *Letter concerning Toleration* he says that toleration should not be extended to atheists, to those whose religion involves allegiance to a foreign power, and to those whose religious faith does not permit them to extend to others the toleration which they claim for themselves. Atheism, in his opinion, necessarily involves lack of moral principles and disregard of the binding character of oaths, covenants and promises. As for the other two classes, he is evidently thinking primarily of Catholics, even if he mentions the Mohammedans. On this matter Locke shared the common attitude of his fellow-countrymen at the time towards Catholics, though it would be interesting to know what he really thought, if he gave any real attention to the matter, of the methods employed in the courts by Lord Chief Justice Scroggs in the trials arising from the 'Popish Plot'. Presumably he sympathized with the ulterior political aims of Shaftesbury and his faction. However, if one takes into consideration the contemporary attitude both in his own country and elsewhere, the remarkable thing is that he advocated toleration at all. He was evidently well aware of this, since he published his writings on the matter anonymously.

CHAPTER VII

LOCKE (4)

Locke's ethical theory—The state of nature and the natural moral law—The right of private property—The origins of political society; the social compact—Civil government—The dissolution of government—General remarks—Locke's influence.

1. IN the first chapter on Locke's philosophy we saw that in rejecting the theory of innate ideas he denied both that there are innate speculative principles and that there are innate practical or moral principles. Our moral ideas must, therefore, be derived from experience, in the sense that they must, as Locke puts it, 'terminate in simple ideas'; that is to say, at least the elements from which they are composed must be derived from sensation or reflection. But Locke did not think that this empiricist account of the origin of our moral ideas is any bar to our recognizing moral principles which are known with certainty. For once we have obtained our ideas, we can examine and compare them and discern relations of agreement and disagreement. This enables us to enunciate moral rules, and if they express necessary relations of agreement or disagreement between ideas they are certain and knowable as certain. We have to distinguish between the ideas or terms which occur in an ethical proposition and the relation asserted in the proposition. In a moral rule the ideas must be severally derivable, ultimately at least, from experience; but the truth or validity of a moral rule is independent of its observance. If I say, for example, that truth-telling is morally good, the ideas of telling truth and of moral goodness must be ultimately derivable from experience; but the relation asserted between these ideas holds even if most people tell lies.

If we bear in mind this point of view, it is not so surprising as it might otherwise appear that in the third and fourth books of the *Essay* Locke proposes a 'rationalistic' ideal of ethics. He there remarks that 'morality is capable of demonstration, as well as mathematics'.[1] The reason is that ethics is concerned with ideas which are real essences. In natural science we do not know the

---

[1] *E.*, 4, 12, 8; II, p. 347.

real, but only the nominal, essences of things. In mathematics, however, this distinction between nominal essence and real essence falls away; and it is the same with ethics. Our idea of justice is derived ultimately from experience, in the sense that the elements of which it is composed are so derived, but there is no entity 'out there' called justice, the real essence of which could be unknown to us. There is, therefore, no reason why ethics should not be made a demonstrative science, 'For certainty being but the perception of the agreement or disagreement of our ideas and demonstration nothing but the perception of such agreement by the intervention of other ideas or mediums; our moral ideas, as well as mathematical, being archetypes themselves and so adequate and complete ideas; all the agreement or disagreement which we shall find in them will produce real knowledge, as well as in mathematical figure.'[1] By saying that our moral ideas are themselves archetypes Locke means, for example, that the idea of justice is itself the standard by which we discriminate between just and unjust actions; justice is not a subsistent entity with which an idea of justice must agree in order to be a true idea. If, therefore, we take the trouble to define our moral terms clearly and precisely, 'moral knowledge may be brought to so great clearness and certainty'[2] as our mathematical knowledge.

These suggestions of Locke may seem to imply that for him ethics is no more than an analysis of ideas in the sense that there is no one set of moral rules which men ought to obey. If we frame this set of ideas, we shall enunciate these rules: if we frame that set of ideas, we shall enunciate those rules. And which set is adopted is a matter of choice. But this was not at all Locke's view of the matter. At least it is certainly not the view which finds expression in the second book of the *Essay* where Locke talks about moral good and evil and about moral rules or laws.

It has already been mentioned that Locke defined good and evil with reference to pleasure and pain. Good is that which is apt to cause or increase pleasure in mind or body, or to diminish pain, while evil is that which is apt to cause or increase any pain or to diminish pleasure.[3] Moral good, however, is the conformity of our voluntary actions to some law, whereby good (that is, 'pleasure') accrues to us according to the will of the law-giver; and moral evil consists in the disagreement' of our voluntary actions with some law, whereby evil (that is, 'pain') 'is drawn on us from the will and

[1] *E.*, 4, 4, 7; II, p. 232.   [2] *E.*, 3, 11, 17; II, p. 157.   [3] *E.*, 2, 20, 2; I, p. 303.

power of the law-maker'.[1] Locke does not say that moral good and evil are pleasure and pain. Nor is he logically committed to saying this. For he defined good and evil not as pleasure and pain (though he does sometimes carelessly speak in this way), but as that which procures pleasure and that which brings pain. Moral good is the conformity of our voluntary actions to a law backed by sanctions; he does not say that it is the same thing as the reward for conformity.

What sort of a law has Locke in mind? He distinguishes three kinds: the divine law, the civil law and 'the law of opinion or reputation'.[2] By the third type of law he means the approval or disapproval, praise or blame, 'which by a secret and tacit consent establishes itself in the several societies, tribes and clubs of men in the world, whereby several actions come to find credit or disgrace amongst them, according to the judgments, maxims or fashion of that place'.[3] In relation to divine law actions are judged to be duties or sins; in relation to the civil law, innocent or criminal; and in relation to the law of opinion or reputation, virtues or vices. Now, it is obvious that these laws might be at variance with one another. As Locke observes, in a given society men may approve of actions which are contrary to the divine law. And he certainly did not think that the civil law is the ultimate criterion of right and wrong. It follows, therefore, that the divine law is the ultimate criterion, in relation to which voluntary actions are called morally good or morally evil. 'That God has given a rule whereby men should govern themselves, I think there is nobody so brutish as to deny. He has a right to do it, we are his creatures: he has goodness and wisdom to direct our actions to that which is best; and he has power to enforce it by rewards and punishments, of infinite weight and duration in another life: for nobody can take us out of his hands. This is the only true touchstone of moral rectitude.'[4]

Now, if we had to understand Locke as meaning that the criterion of moral good and evil, of right and wrong actions, is the arbitrary law of God, there would be a flagrant contradiction between what he says in the second book of the *Essay* and what he says in the fourth. For if the divine law were arbitrarily imposed by God, we could know it only by revelation. And in this case the comparison between ethics and mathematics, which we

---

[1] *E.*, 2, 28, 5; I, p. 474.   [2] *E.*, 2, 28, 7; I, p. 475.
[3] *E.*, 2, 28, 10; I, p. 477.   [4] *E.*, 2, 28, 8; I, p. 475.

find in the fourth book, would be entirely misplaced. But when speaking of the divine law in the second book Locke explains that 'I mean that law which God has set to the actions of men, whether promulgated to them by the light of nature, or the voice of revelation'.[1] By the light of nature he means reason; and he evidently thought that we can discover something of the law of God by reason alone, even if Christian revelation gives us further light. And when we turn to the fourth book we find him saying that 'the idea of a supreme being infinite in power, goodness and wisdom, whose workmanship we are and on whom we depend, and the idea of ourselves as understanding rational beings, being such as are clear in us, would, I suppose, if duly considered and pursued, afford such foundations of our duty and rules of actions, as might place morality amongst the sciences capable of demonstration; wherein I doubt not but from self-evident principles, by necessary consequences, as incontestable as those in mathematics, the measures of right and wrong might be made out to anyone that will apply himself with the same indifferency and attention to the one as he does to the other of those sciences'.[2] Clearly, Locke thought that by considering the nature of God and that of man and the relation between them we could arrive at self-evident moral principles from which other more particular moral rules could be deduced. And the system of deducible rules would constitute the law of God as known by the light of nature. Whether he thought of the revealed moral law as supplementary or as forming part of the premises, he does not make clear. Nor did he himself make any attempt to demonstrate an ethical system on the lines proposed. The examples he gives of self-evident propositions are not very illuminating: 'where there is no property, there is no injustice' and 'no government allows absolute liberty'.[3] (The second proposition is given as a factual statement, but Locke's explanation shows that he did not intend it to be understood in this way.)

I am not disposed, therefore, to subscribe to the verdict of those historians who say that Locke gives us two moral theories which he made no attempt to reconcile. For it seems to me that he does make some attempt to show how the lines of thought given in the second and fourth books of the *Essay* hang together. At the same time it can hardly be denied that what he has to say is sketchy and muddled and that it represents a conflation of different

---

[1] *E.*, 2, 28, 8; I, p. 475.   [2] *E.*, 4, 3, 18; II, p. 208.   [3] *Ibid.*

elements. Although, as we have seen, he cannot simply be dubbed a hedonist, even in the second book, there is an element of hedonistic utilitarianism, partly inspired perhaps by Gassendi. Again, there is an element of authoritarianism, based on the idea of the rights of the Creator. Finally, Locke's distinction between the light of nature and revelation recalls Aquinas's distinction between the natural law, known by reason, and the divine positive law; and this distinction was doubtless inspired largely by Hooker, who had taken over a good deal from mediaeval philosophy.[1] The influence of Hooker, and of mediaeval theory through Hooker, on Locke's thought can be seen in the latter's notion of natural rights, which will be considered presently in connection with his political theory.

2. In his preface to the *Treatises of Civil Government*[2] Locke expresses his hope that what he has written is sufficient 'to establish the throne of our great restorer, our present king William (and) to make good his title in the consent of the people'. Hume, as will be seen later, thought that Locke's political theory was unable to fulfil this function. But in any case it would be a mistake to think that Locke developed his political theory simply with a view to establishing William's title to the throne; for he was in possession of the principles of the theory well before 1688. Further, his theory is of lasting historical importance as a systematic expression of the liberal thought of the day, and his treatises are much more than a Whig pamphlet.

The first *Treatise of Civil Government* need not detain us. In it Locke argues against the theory of the divine right of kings as upheld in Sir Robert Filmer's *Patriarcha* (1680). The patriarchal theory of the transmission of royal authority is held up to ridicule. There is no evidence that Adam possessed a divinely granted royal authority. If he had it, there is no evidence that his heirs had it. If they did, the right of succession was not determined, and even if there were a divinely determined order of succession, all knowledge of it has long since perished. In point of fact Filmer was not such an ass as Locke makes him out to be; for he had already published works of greater merit than the *Patriarcha*. But the work was recently published and had raised discussion, and it is quite understandable that Locke selected it for attack in his first treatise.

[1] For Hooker, vol. III of this *History* may be consulted, pp. 322–4.
[2] Unless otherwise indicated, '*T.*' in references signifies the second *Treatise*.

In the first *Treatise*[1] Locke asserts that 'Sir Robert Filmer's great position is that "men are not naturally free". This is the foundation on which his absolute monarchy stands.' This theory of the natural subjection of men was flatly rejected by Locke, who maintains in the second *Treatise* that in the state of nature men were naturally free and equal. 'This equality of men by nature the judicious Hooker looks upon as so evident in itself and beyond all question that he makes it the foundation of that obligation to mutual love amongst men on which he builds the duties we owe one another and from whence he derives the great maxims of justice and charity.'[2]

Locke starts, therefore, as did Hobbes, with the idea of the state of nature; and in his view 'all men are naturally in that state and remain so till by their own consents they make themselves members of some politic society'.[3] But his idea of the state of nature is very different from that of Hobbes. Indeed, Hobbes is evidently the chief opponent whom he has in mind in the second *Treatise*, though he does not say so explicitly. There is a radical difference, according to Locke, between the state of nature and the state of war. 'Men living together according to reason, without a common superior on earth with authority to judge between them, is properly the state of nature.'[4] Force, exercised without right, creates a state of war; but this is not to be identified with the state of nature, since it constitutes a violation of the state of nature; that is, of what it ought to be.

Locke can speak of what the state of nature ought to be because he admits a natural moral law which is discoverable by reason. The state of nature is a state of liberty but not of licence. 'The state of nature has a law of nature to govern it, which obliges everyone; and reason, which is that law, teaches all mankind who will but consult it that, being all equal and independent, no one ought to harm another in his life, health, liberty or possessions.'[5] For all men are the creatures of God. And though a man may defend himself against attack and punish aggressors on his private initiative, since, as is supposed, there is no common temporal sovereign or judge, his conscience is bound by the natural moral law which obliges all independently of civil society and its legal enactments. Natural law, therefore, means something quite different for Locke from what it meant for Hobbes. For the latter it meant the law of power and force and fraud, whereas for Locke

[1] 2, 6.   [2] *T.*, 2, 5.   [3] *T.*, 2, 15.   [4] *T.*, 3, 19.   [5] *T.*, 2, 6.

it meant a universally obligatory moral law promulgated by the human reason as it reflects on God and His rights, on man's relation to God and on the fundamental equality of all men as rational creatures. Hooker has already been mentioned as one of the sources of Locke's theory of the natural moral law. We can also mention the Cambridge Platonists in England and, on the Continent, writers such as Grotius[1] and Pufendorf.

Believing, as he did, in a natural moral law which binds in conscience independently of the State and its legislation, Locke also believed in natural rights. Every man has, for example, the right to preserve himself and to defend his life, and he has a right to his freedom. There are, too, of course, correlative duties. In fact, because a man has a duty to preserve and defend his life, he has a right to do so. And because he is morally obliged to take the means at his disposal to preserve his life, he has not the right either to take it himself or, by subjecting himself to slavery in the fullest sense of the word, to give to another the power of taking it.

3. The natural right to which Locke paid most attention was, however, the right of property. As man has the duty and the right to preserve himself, he has a right to those things which are required for this purpose. God has given to men the earth and all that is in it for their support and well-being. But though God has not divided up the earth and the things on it, reason shows that it is in accordance with God's will that there should be private property, not only with regard to the fruits of the earth and the things on and in it, but also with regard to the earth itself.

What constitutes the primary title to private property? In Locke's view it is labour. In the state of nature a man's labour is his own, and whatever he removes from its original condition by mixing his labour with it becomes his. 'Though the water running in the fountain be everyone's, yet who can doubt but that in the pitcher is his only who drew it out? His labour hath taken it out of the hands of nature, where it was common and belonged equally to all her children, and hath thereby appropriated it to himself.'[2] Suppose that a man picks up apples for his nourishment under a tree in a wood. Nobody will dispute his ownership of them and his right to eat them. But when did they begin to be his? When he had digested them? When he was eating them? When he cooked them? When he brought them home? It is clear that they became his when he picked them up; that is to say, when he 'mixed his

---

[1] For Grotius, vol. III of this *History* may be consulted, pp. 328–34.   [2] *T.*, 5, 29.

labour' with them and so removed them from the state of being common property. And landed property is acquired in the same way. If a man fells the trees in a forest and makes a clearing, ploughs and sows, the land and its produce are his; for they are the fruit of his labour. The land would not bear the corn unless he had prepared it for doing so.

Locke's theory of labour as the primary title to property was eventually to be incorporated in the labour theory of value and to be used in a way that its author never envisaged. But it would be irrelevant to treat of these developments here. It is more to the point if attention is drawn to the frequently asserted view that in stressing so much the right of private property Locke was expressing the mentality of the Whig landowners who were his patrons. No doubt, there is some truth in this assertion. At least it is not unreasonable to think that the attention which Locke devoted to private property was due in part to the influence of the outlook of the section of society in which he moved. At the same time it should be remembered that the doctrine that there is a right of private property independently of the laws of civil societies was not a novel invention on Locke's part. It should also be noted that he did not say that any man is entitled to amass property without limit to the detriment of others. He himself raises the objection that if gathering the fruits of the earth confers a right to them, anyone may amass as much as he likes, and he answers, 'Not so. The same law of nature that doth by this means give us property does also bound that property too.'[1] The fruits of the earth are given for use and enjoyment; and 'as much as anyone can make use of to any advantage of life before it spoils, so much he may by his labour fix a property in: whatever is beyond this is more than his share and belongs to others'.[2] As for land, the doctrine that labour is the title to property sets a limit to property. For 'as much land as man tills, plants, improves, cultivates and can use the product of, so much is his property'.[3] It is clear that Locke presupposes a state of affairs in which there is plenty of land for everybody, as in the America of his day. 'In the beginning all the world was America, and more so than it is now; for no such thing as money was anywhere known.'[4]

It is clear that Locke assumes that there is a natural right to inherit property. In fact he expressly says that 'every man is born with a double right: first, a right of freedom to his own person . . .

[1] *T.*, 5, 31.   [2] *Ibid.*   [3] *T.*, 5, 32.   [4] *T.*, 5, 49.

secondly, a right, before any other man, to inherit with his brethren his father's goods'.[1] The family is a natural society, and fathers have the duty of providing for their offspring. Still, Locke devotes more attention to explaining how property is acquired than to justifying the right of inheritance, a point which he leaves obscure.

4. Although the state of nature is a condition of affairs in which men have no common authority over them, God 'put him (man) under strong obligations of necessity, convenience and inclination to drive him into society'.[2] We cannot say, therefore, that society is unnatural to man. The family, the primary form of human society, is natural to man, and civil or political society is natural in the sense that it fulfils human needs. For although men, considered in the state of nature, are independent of one another, it is difficult for them to preserve their liberties and rights in actual practice. For from the fact that in the state of nature all are bound in conscience to obey a common moral law it does not follow that all actually obey this law. And from the fact that all enjoy equal rights and are morally bound to respect the rights of others it does not follow that all actually respect the rights of others. It is in man's interest, therefore, to form an organized society for the more effectual preservation of their liberties and rights.

Although, therefore, Locke painted a different picture of the state of nature from that painted by Hobbes, he did not look on this state as an ideal condition of affairs. In the first place, 'though the law of nature be plain and intelligible to all rational creatures, yet men being biased by their interest, as well as ignorant for want of studying it, are not apt to allow of it as a law binding to them in the application of it to their particular cases'.[3] It is desirable, therefore, that there should be a written law to define the natural law and decide controversies. In the second place, though a man in the state of nature enjoys the right to punish transgressions, men are only too apt to be over-zealous in their own cause and too remiss in the cause of others. It is desirable, therefore, that there should be an established and commonly recognized judicial system. In the third place, in the state of nature men may often lack the power to punish crimes, even when their sentence is just. 'Thus mankind, notwithstanding all the privileges of the state of nature, being but in an ill condition while they remain in it, are quickly driven into society.'[4]

[1] *T.*, 16, 190.   [2] *T.*, 7, 77.   [3] *T.*, 9, 124.   [4] *T.*, 9, 127.

According to Locke, 'The great and chief end of men's uniting into commonwealths and putting themselves under government is the preservation of their property'.[1] But this assertion is misinterpreted if we take the word 'property' in the ordinary restricted sense. For Locke has already explained that he is using the word in a wider sense. Men join together in society 'for the mutual preservation of their lives, liberties and estates, which I call by the general name, property'.[2]

Now, Locke is concerned to show that political society and government rest on a rational foundation. And the only way he can see of showing this is to maintain that they rest on consent. It is not enough to explain the disadvantages of the state of nature and the advantage of political society, even though this explanation shows that this society is rational in the sense that it fulfils a useful purpose. For the complete freedom of the state of nature is necessarily curtailed to some extent by the institution of political society and government, and this curtailment can be justified only if it proceeds from the consent of those who are incorporated, or, rather, of those who incorporate themselves, into political society and subject themselves to government. A political society arises 'wherever any number of men in the state of nature enter into society to make one people, one body politic, under one supreme government; or else when anyone joins himself to, and incorporates with any government already made. . . .'[3] 'Men being, as has been said, by nature all free, equal and independent, no one can be put out of this estate and subjected to the political power of another without his own consent. The only way whereby anyone divests himself of his natural liberty and puts on the bonds of civil society is by agreeing with other men to join and unite into a community for their comfortable, safe and peaceable living one amongst another, in a secure enjoyment of their properties and a great security against any that are not of it.'[4]

What, then, do men give up when they join together to form a political community? And to what do they give their consent? In the first place, men do not give up their liberty to enter a state of servitude. Each does, indeed, give up his legislative and executive powers in the form in which they belong to him in the state of nature. For he authorizes society, or rather the legislative, to make such laws as are required for the common good, and he relinquishes to society the power to enforce these laws and exact

---

[1] T., 9, 124.   [2] T., 9, 123.   [3] T., 7, 89.   [4] T., 8, 95.

punishment for their infringement. And to this extent the liberty
of the state of nature is curtailed. But men relinquish these powers
in order to enjoy their liberties more securely. 'For no rational
creature can be supposed to change his condition with an intention
to be worse.'[1] In the second place, 'whosoever out of a state of
nature unite into a community must be understood to give up all
the power necessary to the ends for which they unite into society
to the majority of the community, unless they expressly agreed
in any number greater than the majority'.[2] In Locke's view, therefore, the 'original compact' must be understood as involving the
individual's consent to submit to the will of the majority. 'It is
necessary the body should move that way whither the greater
force carries it, which is the consent of the majority.'[3] Either the
unanimous and explicit consent of every individual is required for
every measure to be enacted, and this is in most cases im-
practicable; or the will of the majority must prevail. Locke
evidently considered that the right of the majority to represent
the community was practically self-evident; but he apparently did
not realize that a majority might act tyrannically with regard to
the minority. At any rate his main concern was to show that
absolute monarchy was contrary to the original social compact,
and he doubtless thought that the danger to liberty from majority
rule was much less than the danger to liberty which comes from
absolute monarchy. And having included consent to majority
rule in his 'original compact' he was able to say that 'absolute
monarchy, which by some men is counted the only government in
the world, is indeed inconsistent with civil society and so can be
no form of civil government at all'.[4]

One obvious objection to the theory of the social compact or
contract is the difficulty in finding historical instances of it. The
question arises, therefore, whether Locke thought of the social
compact as an historical event. He himself raises the objection that
there are no instances of man in the state of nature meeting
together and making an explicit agreement to form a political
society. He then proceeds to argue that some instances can in fact
be found, such as the beginnings of Rome and Venice and of
certain political communities in America. And even if we had no
records of any such instances, silence would be no disproof of the
hypothesis of a social compact. For 'government is everywhere
antecedent to records, and letters seldom come in amongst a

---

[1] T., 9, 131.   [2] T., 8, 99.   [3] T., 8, 96.   [4] T., 7, 90.

people till a long continuation of civil society has, by other more necessary arts, provided for their safety, ease and plenty'.[1] All this suggests that Locke did in fact regard the social compact as an historic event. But he insists at the same time that even if it can be shown that civil society grew out of the family and tribe and that civil government is a development of patriarchal rule, this does not alter the fact that the rational foundation of civil society and government is consent.

A second objection arises, however. Even if it could be shown that political societies originated in a social compact, in the consent of the men who voluntarily created these societies, how would this justify political society as we know it? For it is evident that the citizens of Great Britain, for example, give no explicit consent to being members of their political society and subjects of its government, whatever their remote ancestors may have done. Indeed, Locke himself, who is quite aware of the difficulty, underlines it by maintaining that a father 'cannot, by any compact whatsoever, bind his children or posterity'.[2] A man may lay down conditions in his will so that his son cannot inherit and continue to enjoy his property without being and remaining a member of the same political society as his father. But the latter cannot bind his son to accept the property in question. If his son does not like the conditions, he can renounce his inheritance.

In order to meet the objection Locke has to have recourse to a distinction between explicit and tacit consent. If a man grows up in a certain political society, inherits property in accordance with the laws of the State and enjoys the privileges of a citizen, he must be supposed to have given at least a tacit consent to membership of that society. For it would be utterly unreasonable to enjoy the privilege of a citizen and at the same time to maintain that one was still in the state of nature. In other words, a man who avails himself of the rights and privileges of a citizen of a certain State must be supposed to have voluntarily undertaken, at any rate tacitly, the duties of a citizen of that State. And in answer to the objection that a man who is born as an Englishman or a Frenchman has no choice but to submit himself to the obligations of a citizen, Locke answers that he can in point of fact withdraw from the State, either by going to another State or by retiring to some remote part of the world where he can live in the state of nature. This answer must be understood, of course, in the light of the

[1] *T.*, 8, 101.   [2] *T.*, 8, 116.

circumstances prevailing in Locke's day, when passport regula-
tions, emigration laws, universal military conscription and so on
were unknown, and when it was at least physically possible for a
man to go off and live in the wilds of America or Africa if he so
chose. But all the same, Locke's remarks help to show the artificial
and unreal character of the social compact theory. In Locke's
account of the origins of political society we find a conflation of
two elements; the mediaeval idea, coming from Greek philosophy,
of the 'natural' character of political society and the rationalist
attempt to find a justification for the limitations of liberty in
organized society when a state of nature has been presupposed in
which unlimited liberty (except, in Locke's case, for the moral
obligation to obey the natural moral law) is enjoyed.

5. Hobbes, as we saw, asserted that there is one covenant by
which a number of men hand over to a sovereign the 'rights' which
they enjoyed in the state of nature. Thus political society and
government are created at the same time by the one consent. It
has been argued, however, that Locke's political theory allows
for two covenants or compacts or contracts, one whereby political
society is formed, the other whereby a government is set up.
There is, indeed, no explicit mention of two compacts; but, it has
been argued, Locke tacitly assumes that there are two. By the
first compact a man becomes a member of a definite political
society and obliges himself to accept the decisions of the majority,
while by the second compact the majority (or all) of the members
of the new-formed society agree either to carry on the government
themselves or to set up an oligarchy or a monarchy, hereditary or
elective. While, therefore, on the theory of Hobbes the overthrow
of the sovereign logically involves the dissolution of the political
society in question, on Locke's theory this is not the case, because
political society was formed by a distinct compact and can be
dissolved only by agreement of its members.

There is certainly a good deal to be said in favour of this interpretation. But at the same time Locke appears to think of the
relation between citizen and government in terms of the idea of
trusteeship rather than in terms of a compact. The people set up a
government and entrust it with a definite task; and the government is under an obligation to fulfil this trust. 'The first and fundamental positive law of all commonwealths is the establishing of the
legislative power.'[1] And 'the community put the legislative power

[1] *T.*, 11, 134.

into such hands as they think fit with this trust, that they shall be governed by declared laws, or else their peace, quiet and property will still be at the same uncertainty as it was in the state of nature'.[1]

Locke speaks of the legislature as the 'supreme power' in the commonwealth.[2] And 'all other powers, in any members or parts of the society, (must be) derived from and subordinate to it'.[3] When there is a monarch who possesses supreme executive power he can, in ordinary language, be called the supreme power, especially if acts need his consent to become law and the legislative is not always sitting; but this does not mean that he has in himself all the power of law-making, and it is the whole legislative which is the supreme power in the technical sense. Locke emphasized the desirability of a division of powers in the commonwealth. For example, it is highly undesirable that the persons who make the laws should themselves execute them. For 'they may exempt themselves from obedience to the laws they make, and suit the law, both in its making and execution, to their own private advantage and thereby come to have a distinct interest from the rest of the community'.[4] The executive should, therefore, be distinct from the legislative. And because Locke so emphasized the desirability of a separation of power in the commonwealth it has been argued that he has nothing corresponding to Hobbes's sovereign. This is, of course, true if we attach to the word 'sovereign' the entire meaning which Hobbes attached to it; but, as we have seen, Locke recognizes a supreme power, namely, the legislative. And in so far as it is the supreme power in the commonwealth, to that extent it may perhaps be said to correspond to Hobbes's sovereign.

Though, however, 'there can be but one supreme power, which is the legislative, to which all the rest are and must be subordinate, yet the legislative being only a fiduciary power to act for certain ends, there remains still in the people a supreme power to remove or alter the legislative when they find the legislative act contrary to the trust reposed in them'.[5] Thus the power of the legislative is certainly not absolute: it has a trust to fulfil. And it is, of course, subject to the moral law. Locke accordingly lays down 'the bounds which the trust that is put in them (the members of the legislative) by the society and the law of God and nature have set to the legislative power of every commonwealth in all forms

[1] *T.*, 11, 136.   [2] *T.*, 11, 134.   [3] *T.*, 13, 150.   [4] *T.*, 12, 143.   [5] *T.*, 13, 149.

of government'.[1] First, the legislative must govern by promulgated laws which are the same for all and are not varied in particular cases. Secondly, these laws must be designed for no other end than for the good of the people. Thirdly, the legislative must not raise taxes without the consent of the people, given by themselves or their deputies. For the principal purpose for which society is formed is for the presentation and protection of property. Fourthly, the legislative is not entitled to transfer the power of making laws to any person or assembly to which the people has not entrusted this power, nor can it do so validly.

When we speak of the separation of powers, we generally refer to the threefold distinction of the legislative, executive and judicial powers. But Locke's triad is different, consisting of the legislative, the executive and what he calls the 'federative'. This federative power comprises the power to make war and peace, alliances and treaties 'and all the transactions with all persons and communities without the commonwealth'.[2] Locke regarded it as distinct power, though he remarks that it can hardly be separated from the executive in the sense of being entrusted to a different person or to different persons, as this would be apt to cause 'disorder and ruin'.[3] As for the judicial power, Locke seems to have regarded it as part of the executive. In any case the two points on which he insists are that the legislative must be supreme and that every power, including the legislative, has a trust to fulfil.

6. 'Whenever the society is dissolved, it is certain the government of that society cannot remain.'[4] If a conqueror 'mangles societies to pieces'[5] it is obvious that their governments are dissolved. This dissolution by force is called by Locke 'overturning from without'. But there can also take place a dissolution 'from within', and it is to this theme that he devotes most of the last chapter of the second *Treatise*.

The government may be dissolved from within by the legislative being altered. Let us suppose, says Locke, who is evidently thinking of the British constitution, that the legislative power is vested in an assembly of representatives chosen by the people, in an assembly of hereditary nobility, and in a single hereditary person, the prince, who possesses the supreme executive power and also the right to convoke and dissolve the two assemblies. If the prince substitutes his arbitrary will for the laws, or if he hinders the legislative (that is, the assemblies, particularly the representative

[1] *T.*, 11, 142.   [2] *T.*, 12, 146.   [3] *T.*, 12, 148.   [4] *T.*, 19, 211.   [5] *Ibid.*

assembly) from coming together at the proper time or from acting freely; or if he arbitrarily changes the method of election without the people's consent and contrary to the interest of the people; in all such cases the legislative is altered. Again, if the holder of supreme executive power abandons or neglects his charge so that the laws cannot be enforced, government is effectually dissolved. Further, governments are dissolved when the prince or the legislative act in a manner contrary to their trust, as when either of them invades the property of citizens or tries to obtain arbitrary dominion over their lives, liberties or property.

When government is 'dissolved' in any of these ways, rebellion is justified. To say that this doctrine encourages frequent rebellion is no sound argument. For if the citizens are subjected to the arbitrary caprice of tyrannical power, they will be ready to seize the opportunity to rebel however much the sacred character of the rulers may have been extolled. Moreover, rebellions do not occur in point of fact 'upon every little mismanagement in public affairs'.[1] And though we speak of 'rebellion' and 'rebels' when speaking of subjects and their acts, we might more properly speak of the rulers as rebels when they turn themselves into tyrants and act in a manner contrary to the will and interest of the people. True, there can be unjustified insurrections and rebellions, and these are crimes, but the possibility of misuse does not take away the right to rebel. And if it is asked who is to judge when circumstances render rebellion legitimate, 'I reply, the people shall be judge'.[2] For it is only they, under God, who can decide whether the trustee has abused his trust or not.

7. Locke's political theory is obviously open to criticism on several grounds. Together with other political theories which are more than the enunciation of very general principles, so general that they can be called 'perennial', it shares the defect of being too closely related to contemporary historical circumstances. This is, of course, inevitable in the case of a theory which enters more or less into detail. And there is nothing surprising in the fact that Locke's *Treatise on Civil Government* reflects to some extent the contemporary historical circumstances and its author's private political convictions as a Whig and as an opponent of the Stuarts. For unless the political philosopher wishes to confine himself to enunciating propositions such as 'government should be carried on with a view to the common good', he cannot help taking as the

---

[1] *T.*, 19, 225.   [2] *T.*, 19, 240.

material for his reflection the political data of his time. In political theories we see a certain outlook and spirit and movement of political life attaining reflective expression; and in varying degrees political theories are inevitably dated. This is obviously true of Plato's political theory. It is also true of the Marxist political theory. And it is only natural that it should be true of Locke's theory as well.

It may be said that what is practically speaking inevitable, cannot properly be called a 'defect'. But if a political philosopher puts forward his theory as *the* theory, it would be idle, I think, to cavil at the use of this word. In any case Locke's political theory suffers from other defects as well. Attention has already been drawn to the artificiality of the social compact theory. And we may also note Locke's failure to give any thorough analysis of the concept of the common good. He tends to assume without more ado that the preservation of private property and the promotion of the common good are to all intents and purposes synonymous terms. It may be said that this criticism is made from the point of view of one who looks back on a development of economic, social and political life which Locke could not have foreseen, a development which necessitated a revision of the liberalism of his time. And this is partly true. But it does not follow that even within the framework of his own historical circumstances Locke could not have given a more adequate account of the function of political society and of government. There is something wanting from his account which was present both in Greek and in mediaeval political thought, even if in a rudimentary form.

To say, however, that Locke's political theory is open to criticism is not to say that it does not possess some lasting value. And to say that the principles which can be considered of perennial validity are principles which transcend limitation and restriction to a particular epoch or set of circumstances precisely because of their generality is not the same thing as to say that these principles are worthless. A principle is not rendered worthless because it has to be applied in different ways at different times. Locke's principle that the government, in the wide sense of the State organization and not merely in the narrow sense in which the term 'the government' is generally used today, has a trust to fulfil and that it exists to promote the common good is as true now as it was when he enunciated it. It was not, of course, a novelty. Aquinas would have said the same. But the point is that the principle needs constant reiteration. To be operative, it has to be applied in different ways at different times; and Locke tried to show how, in his opinion, it should be applied in the circumstances of his time, which were not those of the Middle Ages.

The responsibility of government to the people and its function of promoting the common good would be generally admitted. But I should wish to add, as a position of lasting validity, a position which Locke himself constantly adopted but which has been called in question. I refer to the doctrine that there are natural rights and that there is a natural moral law which obliges in conscience both governors and governed. This doctrine is not bound up inextricably with the theories of the state of nature and of the social compact; and it is a lasting safeguard against tyranny when it is sincerely accepted.

Quite apart, however, from its intrinsic merits and demerits, Locke's political theory is of great historical importance. Despite some criticism it obtained general acceptance in his own country in the eighteenth century. And even when writers such as Hume attacked the theory of the social compact Locke's general notions about government were none the less accepted. Later on, of course, different lines of thought made their appearance, with Benthamism on the one hand and the theories of Burke on the other. But much of what Locke had said remained common property. Meanwhile his political theory became known on the Continent, in Holland, of course, where he had lived in exile, and also in France, where he influenced writers of the Enlightenment such as Montesquieu. Further, there can be no doubt of his great influence in America, even if it is difficult to assess the precise degree of his influence on individual leaders of the revolution such as Jefferson. In fine, the widespread and lasting effects of Locke's *Treatise of Civil Government* is a standing disproof of the notion that philosophers are ineffectual. It is doubtless true that Locke himself brought to articulate expression an already existing movement of thought; but this articulate expression was itself a powerful influence in the consolidation and dissemination of the movement of thought and drift of political life which it expressed.

8. According to d'Alembert, the French Encyclopaedist, Locke created metaphysics in much the same way that Newton created physics. By metaphysics in this connection d'Alembert meant the theory of knowledge as conceived by Locke, as, that is to say, the determination of the extent, powers and limitations of the human

understanding. And the impetus given by Locke to the development of the theory of knowledge and to a treatment of metaphysics in function of an analysis of the human understanding was, indeed, one of the principal ways in which he exercised a powerful influence on philosophical thought. But his influence was also powerful in ethics, through hedonistic elements in his ethical theory, and, as we saw in the last section, in political theory. It may be added that economic liberalism of the *laissez-faire* type, such as is found in the writings of the French 'physiocrats' (for instance, François Quesnay, 1694–1774) and in Adam Smith's *Wealth of Nations* (1776), has at least a remote connection with Locke's economic and political theories.

The influence of Locke's empiricism is best seen in the philosophies of Berkeley and Hume, which will be considered later. In the course of this development of thought his empiricist principle was applied in ways which he had not himself envisaged. But there is nothing surprising in this. Locke was a moderate and balanced thinker. He could appeal, therefore, to a man like Samuel Clarke, who evidently had a considerable respect for him. But it is only natural that different aspects of Locke's thought should have been developed by others in a way which he himself would have considered to be exaggerated. For example, his remarks about reason as the judge of revelation exercised an influence on the deists, who will be considered later, and we find Bolingbroke extolling Locke as the one leading philosopher for whom he had any respect. Again, Locke's observations in the *Essay* about the association of ideas bore fruit later on in the associationist psychology of David Hartley (1705–57) and Joseph Priestley (1733–1804). Both these men emphasized the connection between physical and psychical events, and the latter at any rate adopted a materialist position. Locke himself was not, of course, a materialist; nor did he regard thoughts and ideas as being simply transformed sensations. At the same time he made statements which could be used as a basis for sensationalism. He said, for example, that for all we know God might give the power of thinking to a purely material thing. And these elements of sensationalism influenced, for instance, Peter Browne (d. 1735), bishop of Cork, and the French philosopher, Condillac (1715–80). Indeed, the elements of sensationalism in Locke's philosophy exercised a considerable influence, direct or indirect, on the thinkers of the French Enlightenment, such as the Encyclopaedists.

In brief, Locke was one of the outstanding figures of the period of the Enlightenment in general, representing in himself and in his writings the spirit of free inquiry, of 'rationalism' and of dislike of all authoritarianism which was characteristic of the age. It must be added, however, that he possessed qualities of moderation, of piety and of a serious sense of responsibility which were sometimes lacking in the continental thinkers who came under his influence.

But if Locke was one of the master-thinkers of his age, Newton was another. And d'Alembert was not unjustified in mentioning them together. Hence, although this work is certainly not intended to be a history of physical science, something at least must be said about the great mathematician and physicist who exercised such a profound influence on men's thought.

CHAPTER VIII

NEWTON

Robert Boyle—Sir Isaac Newton.

1. LOCKE's circle of friends included Robert Boyle (1627–91). As a chemist and physicist, Boyle was interested in particular analyses of sensible data rather than in framing wide and far-reaching hypotheses about Nature in general; and in his conception of scientific method he laid stress on experimental research. He thus carried on the work of men such as Gilbert and Harvey. In the emphasis which he laid on experiment he shows an affinity, of course, with Francis Bacon; but in his earlier years he purposely avoided serious study of the works of those whom he subsequently acknowledged as his chief predecessors, namely, Bacon, Descartes and Gassendi, in order to escape premature indoctrination with theories and hypotheses. And he is rightly regarded as one of the leading promoters of experimental science and as a man who contributed to making clear by his own work the inadequacy of theorizing which is unaccompanied by controlled experimental verification or confirmation. Thus his experiments on air and the vacuum by means of an air-pump, an account of which was given in his *New Experiments Physico-Mechanical* (1660), disposed of Hobbes's *a priori* theorizing and dealt a fatal blow to opponents of the experimental method. Again, in his *Sceptical Chymist* (1661) he criticized with effect not only the doctrine of four elements but also the current theory of salt, sulphur and mercury as the three constituent principles of material things. (A chemical element, according to his definition, is a substance which cannot be decomposed into simpler constituents, though he was unable himself to supply a list of these elements.) In 1662 he achieved the generalization which is known as Boyle's Law, namely, the statement that the pressure and volume of a gas are inversely proportional. He himself believed in alchemy, but his own insistence on and use of the experimental method constituted a most effective means of putting an end to alchemy.

To say that Boyle insisted on and used the experimental method in physics and chemistry is not, of course, to say that he was merely an 'experimenter' and that he eschewed all hypotheses.

Had he done this, he would scarcely have achieved eminence as a scientist. What he objected to was not the formation of hypotheses as such but the hasty assertion of theories without the controlling use of the experimental method and the confident assertion of the truth of theories and hypotheses which enjoy only varying degrees of probability. It is preferable to accumulate a little knowledge which is securely based on experiment than to construct sweeping philosophical systems which cannot be verified. But this does not mean that hypotheses should not be formed. For the scientist endeavours to interpret and explain the facts which he has ascertained. At the same time, even when it is possible to show that a given explanatory hypothesis is more probable than any other hypothesis which purports to explain the same facts, there is no guarantee that it will not be superseded in the future. Boyle, it may be noted, embraced the hypothesis of ether; that is to say, of a subtle ethereal substance diffused throughout space. The hypothesis of ether had been postulated to avoid the notion of a vacuum and to explain the propagation of motion without any apparent medium. But there were also phenomena such as magnetism of which no satisfactory explanation had been given in terms of the mechanical conception of the world. Boyle accordingly suggested that the ether might be composed of two kinds of particles or corpuscles, by the aid of one of which we might explain phenomena such as magnetism. He was thus able to avoid Henry More's theory of a spirit of Nature or soul of the world, which the Cambridge Platonist offered as an explanation of phenomena such as magnetism and gravity.[1] In other words, Boyle suggested a more naturalistic and 'scientific' hypothesis. But he was well aware that his own hypothesis was no more than probable and that it might have to be discarded. He did not claim for his own scientific theories a final truth which he would not allow to the theories of others. He was acutely conscious of the limitations of human knowledge in general and of the hypothetical and provisional character of scientific explanation in particular.

Further, to say that Boyle insisted on the experimental method in science is not to say that he was blind to the rôle of mathematics in physics. Although he was not himself a great mathematician, he was in full sympathy with Galileo and Descartes in their views about the mathematical structure of Nature, considered as a

[1] To explain gravity mechanically, Descartes had postulated that the ethereal medium forms vortices

system of bodies in motion; and he even looked on mathematical principles as transcendent truths which are the foundation and instrument of all our knowledge. And, with a qualification which will be mentioned shortly, he accepted the mechanical interpretation of Nature. He postulated a theory of atoms, endowed with primary qualities of size and shape, and he argued that the natural phenomena of the material world can be explained mechanically if we also postulate motion. Motion is not an inherent quality of matter and does not pertain to its essence; hence it has to be postulated in addition to matter. It is, so to speak, super-added by God, and the laws of motion are determined by God. Boyle would not accept Descartes' metaphysical proof of the conservation of the same sum-total of motion or energy, namely, the proof from the divine immutability. This metaphysical argument does not constitute a proof, and we do not know that the sum-total of motion must always remain constant. However, given matter and motion, the system of Nature is a cosmic mechanism, though we must reject the view of Hobbes that motion must necessarily be communicated to a body by another contiguous body. For if we accept this view, we involve ourselves in an infinite regress and we rule out the causal activity of a spiritual God.

But though Boyle shared to a large extent the Cartesian interpretation of the mechanical system of Nature, he considered that this interpretation was exaggerated and stood in need of a qualification. He saw, indeed, and explicitly stated that an explanation of events in terms of final causality is not an answer to the question how these events occur, and any slick substitution of a teleological explanation for an answer to a question about efficient causality was as foreign to his mind as it was to that of Descartes. At the same time he insisted on the validity of the notion of final causality and on the possibility of teleological explanation, even if it is not the business of the physicist or of the chemist as such to concern himself with such matters. Descartes, it is true, had not denied that there are final causes when he excluded teleological explanations from physics or experimental philosophy. And Boyle's insistence on the relevance of final causality to metaphysics should not be described as a counterblast to Descartes. But what he has to say on the subject shows his dissatisfaction with the mechanical interpretation of the world, as maintained by Descartes and Hobbes, when it is taken as an adequate interpretation. It may be adequate for certain purposes or within a restricted field; but as a general philosophy of the world it is inadequate. Boyle was convinced that no satisfactory interpretation or general account of creation can be given without reference to an intelligent Author and Disposer of things, who adapts means to ends.

Boyle was strongly opposed to the materialism of Hobbes. But he was also opposed to what he regarded as the tendency of Galileo and Descartes to depreciate man's importance in the world and to relegate him to the condition of a spectator. He evidently considered it paradoxical that those who had contributed so much to the rise of a new natural philosophy and of a new outlook on the world should tend to push out of the picture, as it were, the very being who had evolved this new philosophy. If one may be permitted to employ a later way of speaking, he thought it odd that the subject should be eager to depreciate its own importance in favour of the object, when the new conceptions of the object were themselves due to the subject.

An expression of Boyle's point of view can be seen in his insistence that though our perception of secondary qualities can be explained mechanically, this is no sufficient ground for saying that secondary qualities are unreal. To say this is to forget man's factual presence in the world. For, given this factual presence, secondary qualities are as real as the primary.

However, though Boyle insisted on the importance of man's position within the cosmos, his interpretation of man's nature was sufficiently Cartesian in character to compel him to draw attention to the great difficulty encountered in solving the problem of interaction. For he thought of the spiritual soul as residing in some mysterious way in the conarion, shut away, as it were, within the brain where it awaits messages from the organs of sense. Further, he inferred from the soul's situation that the mind's power is necessarily very limited and restricted. And this inference has a close connection with Boyle's views about the hypothetical and provisional character of our theories and about the need for experimental verification, though the latter can never prove the absolute truth of an hypothesis.

One conclusion which Boyle drew from the restricted reach of our minds is that we ought to attach all the more value to the Christian religion, which enlarges our knowledge. He was in fact a deeply religious man. He regarded his experimental work in science as a service of God, and he founded the series of Boyle lectures with a view to answers being provided to difficulties about Christianity which might arise out of the scientific and philosophical developments of the time. In his writings he insisted that consideration of the cosmic system in general and of the faculties and operations of the human soul in particular affords sure evidence of the existence of a supremely powerful, wise and good Creator, who has also revealed Himself in the Scriptures. This does not mean that Boyle postulated God simply as the originator of the universe and of motion. He spoke frequently of the divine conservation of the world and of God's 'concurrence' with all its operations. He may not have attempted any systematic harmonization of this doctrine with his view of Nature as a mechanical system; but it was perhaps necessary to do so if he held, as he did, that the laws of Nature have no intrinsic necessity. Further, he insisted that God is by no means bound to His ordinary and general concurrence; that is, to maintaining the system of Nature precisely as we know it in normal experience. Miracles are possible and have occurred.

In Boyle, therefore, we see an interesting combination of an insistence on the experimental method in science and on the hypothetical character of scientific theories with a Cartesian view of the relation of soul to body and with theological convictions which came, indirectly, from mediaeval and Renaissance Scholasticism. His theory of the divine concurrence and his theory that God sees all that He knows intuitively in Himself illustrate the last-mentioned element in his thought.

2. Another of Locke's friends was Sir Isaac Newton (1642–1727), who has already been mentioned in the third volume of this *History*.[1] It is scarcely necessary to add that we have here a greater name than that of Boyle. For it was Newton's genius which achieved the completion of the world-view prepared by men such as Copernicus, Galileo and Kepler,[2] and his name dominated science up to recent times. We are still accustomed to speak of modern physics up to the coming of the quantum mechanics as the Newtonian physics.

Born at Woolsthorpe in Lincolnshire, Newton went to Trinity College, Cambridge, in June 1661 and took his degree in January 1665. After spending the intervening period at Woolsthorpe,

[1] p. 284.
[2] For these Renaissance scientists Chapter XVIII of vol. III of this *History* may be consulted.

where he gave his attention to the problem of gravitation and also discovered the integral calculus and the binomial theorem, he was elected a Fellow of Trinity in 1667, and in 1669 he became Lucasian professor of mathematics. In 1687 he published his *Philosophiae naturalis principia mathematica*, commonly known as Newton's *Principia*, the cost of printing being defrayed by his friend, the astronomer Halley. He twice represented the University of Cambridge in Parliament, from 1689 to 1690 and from 1701 to 1705. In 1703 he was elected president of the Royal Society, of which he had become a member in 1672. He was knighted by Queen Anne in 1705. The second and third editions of the *Principia* appeared in 1713 and 1726. Newton was buried in Westminster Abbey.

Newton's genius as a mathematical physicist and his power of co-ordination, unification and simplification are, of course, unquestioned. For example, using Kepler's laws he was able to show that the motion of the planets round the sun can be explained if it is supposed that the sun exerts a force on each planet which varies in inverse proportion to the square of the distance of that planet from the sun. He then asked whether, if we suppose that the earth's attraction extends to the moon, the moon's retention in its orbit can be explained in a manner consonant with this basis. And eventually he was able to enunciate a universal law of gravitation, determining the mutual attraction of masses. Any body of mass M and any other body of mass m attract one another along the line between them with a force F, this force being equivalent to GMm/d^2, when d is the distance between the bodies and G is a universal constant. Newton was thus able to bring under a single mathematical law such major phenomena as the motions of the planets, the comets, the moon and the sea. He was able to show that the movements of terrestrial bodies follow the same laws of motion as celestial ones; and he thus completed the destruction of the Aristotelian theory that terrestrial and celestial bodies obey essentially different laws.

In general, Newton suggested that all the phenomena of motion in Nature might also be derived mathematically from mechanical principles. For instance, in his work *Opticks* (1704) he maintained that, given the relevant theorems relating to the refraction and composition of light, the phenomena of colours could be explained in mathematical-mechanical terms. In other words, he expressed the hope that in the long run all natural phenomena might prove to be explicable in terms of mathematical mechanics. And his own outstanding successes in the solution of particular problems obviously tended to confer authority on his general view. His achievement thus gave a powerful impetus to the mechanical interpretation of the world. At the same time it must be noted that his theory was generally regarded as weakening the extreme mechanism of Descartes, because his 'gravitational force' did not seem to be reducible to the mere motion of material particles. Some eighteenth-century apologists used the existence of gravity, as something inexplicable on a purely mechanistic theory, as an argument for the existence of God.

It is to be noted that for Newton natural philosophy studies the phenomena of motions. Its object is 'from the phenomena of motions to investigate the forces of nature, and then from these forces to demonstrate the other phenomena'.[1] What are these 'forces of nature'? They are defined as the causes of changes in motion. But we have to be careful not to misunderstand the meaning of the word 'cause' in this context. Needless to say, Newton is not referring to the efficient, metaphysical cause of phenomena, namely, God. Nor is he referring to the hypothetical, physical causes which are postulated either to explain those phenomena that have not been successfully reduced to the operation of mechanical laws or to explain the factual conformity of actual motions to these laws. He is referring to the mechanical laws themselves. These descriptive laws are not, of course, physical agents; they do not exercise efficient causality. They are 'mechanical principles'.

The passage quoted from the *Principia mathematica* indicates Newton's conception of scientific method. It comprises two main elements, the inductive discovery of mechanical laws from a study of the phenomena of motions and the deductive explanation of phenomena in the light of these laws. In other words, the method consists of analysis and of synthesis or composition. Analysis consists in making experiments and observations and in deriving general conclusions from them by induction. Synthesis consists in assuming the established laws or principles or 'causes' and in explaining phenomena by deducing consequences from these laws. Mathematics is the mind's tool or instrument in the whole process. It is needed from the start, in the sense that the motions to be studied must be measured and reduced to mathematical formulation. And the scope of the method and of natural philosophy is

[1] *Principia mathematica*, preface to first edition.

thereby restricted. But mathematics is regarded by Newton as an instrument or tool which the mind is forced to use rather than, as with Galileo, an infallible key to reality.

This is, indeed, a point of some importance. That Newton attributed to mathematics an indispensable role in natural philosophy is indicated by the very title of his great work, the *Mathematical Principles of Natural Philosophy*. The great instrument in the demonstrations of natural philosophy is mathematics. And this may suggest that for Newton mathematical physics, proceeding in a purely deductive manner, gives us the key to reality, and that he stands closer to Galileo and Descartes than to English scientists such as Gilbert, Harvey and Boyle. This, however, would be a misconception. It is doubtless right to stress the importance which Newton attached to mathematics; but one must also emphasize the empiricist aspect of his thought. Galileo and Descartes believed that the structure of the cosmos is mathematical in the sense that by the use of the mathematical method we can discover its secrets. But Newton was unwilling to make any such presupposition. We cannot legitimately assume in advance that mathematics gives us the key to reality. If we start with abstract mathematical principles and deduce conclusions, we do not know that these conclusions provide information about the world until we have verified them. We start with phenomena and discover laws or 'causes' by induction. We can then derive consequences from these laws. But the results of our deductions stand in need of experimental verification, so far as this is possible. The use of mathematics is necessary, but it is not by itself a guarantee of scientific knowledge about the world.

True, Newton himself makes certain assumptions. Thus in the third book of the *Principia mathematica* he lays down some rules for philosophizing or rules of reasoning in natural philosophy. The first of these is the principle of simplicity, which states that we ought not to admit more causes of natural things than such as are both true and sufficient to explain their appearances. The second rule states that to the same natural effects we must, as far as possible, assign the same causes. And the third states that those qualities of bodies which admit of neither intension nor remission of degrees, and which are found to belong to all bodies within the reach of experiment, are to be accounted the universal qualities of all bodies whatsoever. The question arises, therefore, whether Newton regarded the first two rules, which state the simplicity and uniformity of nature, as *a priori* truths or as methodological assumptions suggested by experience. Newton does not provide us with any clear answer to this question. He does, indeed, speak of the analogy of nature, which tends to simplicity and uniformity. But he seems to have thought that Nature observes simplicity and uniformity because it has been so created by God, and this may suggest that the first two rules have for him a metaphysical basis. The fourth rule, however, suggests that the first two should be regarded as methodological postulates or assumptions. It states that in experimental philosophy we ought to look on propositions which are the result of induction from phenomena as being accurately or very nearly true, in spite of any contrary hypotheses which may be imagined, until such time as other phenomena occur which may make the propositions either more accurate or liable to exceptions. And this seems to imply that experimental verification is the ultimate criterion in natural philosophy and that the first two rules are, even if Newton does not say so, methodological postulates.

Now, Newton says of this fourth rule that we ought to follow it 'that the argument of induction may not be evaded by hypotheses'. And in the *Opticks* he states roundly that 'hypotheses are not to be regarded in experimental philosophy'.[1] Again, in the *Principia mathematica* he states that he has been unable to discover the cause of the properties of gravity from phenomena, adding 'and I frame no hypotheses'.[2] And these statements obviously stand in need of some comment.

When Newton rejected hypotheses in natural philosophy, he was thinking primarily, of course, of unverifiable speculations. Thus when he says that the fourth rule should be followed in order that arguments from induction may not be evaded by hypotheses, he was thinking of theories for which no experimental evidence is offered. Propositions which have been arrived at by induction should be accepted until experiment shows that they are not accurate, and unverifiable contrary theories should be disregarded. When he says that he has been unable to discover the causes of the properties of gravity inductively and that he frames no hypotheses, he means that he is concerned only with the descriptive laws which state how gravity acts and not with the nature or essence of gravity. This is made clear by a statement in the *Principia mathematica*. 'Whatever is not deduced from the

---

[1] Third edition, 1721, p. 380. [2] II, p. 314, translation by A. Motte.

phenomena is to be called a hypothesis; and hypotheses, whether metaphysical or physical, whether of occult qualities or mechanical, have no place in experimental philosophy. In this philosophy particular propositions are inferred from the phenomena, and afterwards rendered general by induction. Thus it was that the impenetrability, the mobility, and the impulsive force of bodies, and the laws of motion and of gravitation, were discovered.'[1]

Of course, if we understand the word 'hypothesis' in the sense in which it is used in physical science today, we shall have to say that Newton's exclusion of hypotheses constitutes an exaggeration. Further, it is clear that Newton himself framed hypotheses. For example, his atomistic theory, namely, that there are extended, hard, impenetrable, indestructible, mobile particles, endowed with the *vis inertiae*, was an hypothesis. So was his theory of an ethereal medium. Neither of these hypotheses was gratuitous. The theory of the ether was postulated primarily to account for the propagation of light. And the theory of particles was not unverifiable in principle. Newton himself suggested that we might be able to perceive the largest of these particles or atoms if we possessed more powerful microscopes. But the theories were none the less hypotheses.

We must, however, allow for the fact that Newton made a distinction between experimental laws and speculative hypotheses which were, as he recognized, merely plausibly or possibly true. And from the start he refused to look on the latter as *a priori* assumptions which constituted an integral part of the scientific explanation of natural phenomena. As, however, he found it difficult to make people grasp this distinction, he came to make pronouncements about the necessity of excluding from physics or experimental philosophy all 'hypotheses', whether metaphysical or physical. The occult qualities of the Aristotelians, he tells us, constitute a hindrance to progress in science, and to say that a specific type of thing is endowed with a specific occult quality in virtue of which it acts and produces its observable effects is to say nothing at all. 'But to derive two or three general principles of motion from phenomena and afterwards to tell us how the properties and actions of all corporeal things follow from those manifest principles would be a very great step in philosophy, though the causes of those principles were not yet discovered.'[2] Newton may have spoken sometimes in an exaggerated way, and

[1] II, p. 314. [2] *Opticks*, 3rd edition, 1721, p. 377.

he may not have done justice to the part which has been played by speculative hypotheses in the development of science. But his fundamental intention is clear enough, to rule out useless and unverifiable hypotheses and to warn people against questioning the results of inductively ascertained principles or laws in the name of 'hypotheses' in the sense of unverified speculative assumptions. We are to admit no objections against inductively ascertained 'conclusions' apart from those objections which are based on experiments or on truths which are certain. This is what he means by saying that hypotheses are not to be regarded in experimental philosophy.

The tendency of Newton's thought, therefore, was to continue the purification of physical science from metaphysics and to exclude from science the search for 'causes', whether ultimate efficient causes or what the Scholastics called 'formal causes', namely, natures or essences. Science for him consisted in laws, formulated mathematically when possible, which are inferred from phenomena, which state how things act and which are empirically verified by consequences derived from them. But to say this is not to say that he eschewed all speculation in actual practice. Mention has already been made of his theory of ether, which he postulated to account for the propagation of light. He also believed that it served the purpose of providing for the conservation and increase, when needed, of the decaying motion in the world. He evidently thought that the conservation of energy could not be explained without introducing this additional factor which contains active principles. The ether is not, as Descartes imagined, a kind of dense, pervasive fluid; it is somewhat like air, though much rarer, and Newton sometimes spoke of it as 'spirit'. But he did not really attempt to describe its nature in any precise manner. He does not appear to have felt any doubt about the existence of an ethereal medium; but he recognized that his speculations about its character were only tentative hypotheses, and his general policy of abstaining from descriptions of unobserved entities prevented him from making dogmatic pronouncements about its precise nature.

Newton's theories of absolute space and time provide further examples of speculative hypotheses. Absolute time, as distinct from relative, apparent and common time, is said to flow equably without regard to anything external, and 'by another name (it) is called duration'.[1] Absolute space, as distinct from relative space,

[1] *Principia mathematica*, I, p. 6.

'remains always similar and immovable'.[1] Newton did, indeed, make some attempt to justify his postulating absolute space and time, not, of course, by suggesting that they are observable entities, but by arguing that they are presuppositions of experimentally measurable motion. In so far, however, as he tends to speak of them as entities in which things move, he certainly transcends the sphere of that experimental philosophy from which hypotheses are banished. Further, there are internal difficulties in Newton's conception of the triad, absolute motion, absolute space and absolute time. For instance, relative motion is a change in a body's distance from some other particular body or the translation of a body from one relative place into another. Absolute motion, therefore, will be the translation of a body from one absolute place into another. And this seems to demand absolute space in order to provide absolute, and not relative, points of reference. But it is difficult to see how absolute, infinite and homogeneous space can provide any such points of reference.

So far we have a mechanical description of the world, with the introduction of certain hypotheses, such as that of ether, to account for phenomena when these apparently cannot be explained in purely mechanical terms. Newton defined bodies as masses, meaning that in addition to its geometrical properties each possesses a *vis inertiae* or force of inertia, measurable by the acceleration which a given external force imparts to the body. We have, therefore, the conception of masses moving in absolute space and time according to the mechanical laws of motion. And in this world of the scientist there are only primary qualities. In things, colours, for instance, are 'nothing but a disposition to reflect this or that sort of rays more copiously than the rest, (while) in the rays they are nothing but their dispositions to propagate this or that motion into the sensorium, and in the sensorium they are sensations of those motions under the forms of colours'.[2] If we prescind, therefore, from man and his sensations we are left with a system of masses, possessing the primary qualities, moving in absclute space and time and pervaded by the ethereal medium.

Yet this picture conveys a very inadequate idea of Newton's total outlook on the world. For he was a religious man and a firm believer in God. He wrote a number of theological treatises, and though these are somewhat unorthodox, particularly on the subject of the Trinity, he certainly looked on himself as a good

---

[1] *Principia mathematica*, I, p. 6.   [2] *Opticks*, pp. 108f.

Christian. Further, even though a distinction can be made between his scientific and his religious beliefs, he did not think that science is in no way relevant to religion. He was convinced that the cosmic order provides evidence for the existence of God, and that it appears 'from phenomena that there is a being, incorporeal, living, intelligent, omnipresent'.[1] Indeed, he seems to have thought that the motion of the planets round the sun was an argument for God's existence. Moreover, God exercises the function of maintaining the stars at their proper distances from one another, so that they do not collide, and of 'reforming' irregularities in the universe. In Newton's opinion, therefore, God does not simply conserve His creation in a general sense of the word, but He also actively intervenes to keep the machine going.

Furthermore, Newton gave a theological interpretation to his theory of absolute space and time. In the *General Scholium* to the second edition of the *Principia mathematica* he speaks of God as constituting duration and space by existing always and everywhere. Indeed, infinite space is described as the divine *sensorium* or 'sensory' in which God perceives and comprehends all things. Things move and are known 'within His boundless uniform sensorium'.[2] This may appear at first sight to lead to pantheism, but Newton did not maintain that God is to be identified with absolute space and time. Rather does He constitute absolute space and time through His omnipresence and eternity; and He is said to know things in infinite space as it were in His sensorium, because through His omnipresence everything is immediately present to Him.

It is clear that Newton was a philosopher as well as a mathematician and physicist. But it is not so clear how his metaphysics fits in with his views of the nature and function of physical science. In the *Opticks* he does, indeed, say that 'the main business of natural philosophy is to argue from phenomena without feigning hypotheses, and to deduce causes from effects, till we come to the very first cause, which certainly is not mechanical'.[3] And he goes on to argue that reflection on phenomena shows us that there is a spiritual, intelligent Being, who sees all things in infinite space, as it were in His sensory. Thus he obviously thought that his philosophical theology followed from his scientific ideas. But it can hardly be maintained, I think, that there is a perfect harmony between his metaphysics and his more 'positivistic' pronouncements

[1] *Opticks*, p. 344.   [2] *Ibid.*, p. 379.   [3] p. 344.

about the nature of science. Nor does Newton seem to have made it very clear which functions are fulfilled by the ether and which by God. Further, Newton's philosophical theology labours under an obvious disadvantage from the point of view of the theist, as Berkeley saw and noted. If, for example, we argue to God's existence from 'irregularities' in Nature and from the need of putting the machine right from time to time, so to speak, such arguments will be deprived of all cogency if the supposed irregularities turn out to be empirically explicable and if phenomena which once appeared to be incapable of mechanical explanation are eventually found to fit without difficulty into a mechanical account of Nature. Again, the concepts of absolute space and time provide weak foundations for a proof of God's existence. It was not without reason that Berkeley feared that Newton's way of arguing to the existence of God would bring philosophical theism into disrepute. In any case, of course, arguments based on physical hypotheses can have no greater validity than the hypotheses themselves. There cannot be a certain *a posteriori* proof of God's existence unless it is based on propositions the truth of which is certain independently of scientific developments, so that it remains unaffected by progress in science.

It is not, however, Newton's philosophical theology which constitutes the chief reason why he should be mentioned in any history of modern philosophy. Nor is it even his philosophy of science, in the sense of his account of scientific method and of the nature of natural or experimental philosophy, an account which was not elaborated in altogether clear, consistent and precise terms. The chief reason is his great importance as one of the outstanding makers of the modern mind, of the scientific conception of the world. He carried on the work which had been developed by men such as Galileo and Descartes, and by giving to the mechanical interpretation of the material cosmos a comprehensive scientific foundation he exercised a vast influence on succeeding generations. It is not necessary to accept the views of those who rejected Newton's theological ideas and who regarded the world as a self-sustaining mechanism in order to recognize his importance. Within the scientific sphere he gave a powerful impetus to the development of empirical science, as distinct from *a priori* theorizing, and by developing the scientific interpretation of the world he helped to provide subsequent philosophical thought with one of the most important data for its reflections.

CHAPTER IX

RELIGIOUS PROBLEMS

Samuel Clarke—The deists—Bishop Butler.

1. AMONG Newton's fervent admirers was Samuel Clarke (1675–1729). In 1697 he published a Latin translation of Jacques Rohault's *Traité de physique*, with notes designed to facilitate the transition to Newton's system. Becoming an Anglican clergyman, he published a number of theological and exegetical works, and he delivered two series of Boyle lectures, the first in 1704 on the being and attributes of God, the second in 1705 on the evidences of natural and revealed religion. In 1706 he wrote against Henry Dodwell's view that the soul is naturally mortal but that God confers immortality on it through His grace with a view to punishment or reward in the next life. He also published a translation of Newton's *Opticks*. In the years 1715 and 1716 he was engaged in controversy with Leibniz about the principles of religion and natural philosophy. At the time of his death he was rector of St. James's, Westminster, a benefice which had been conferred upon him by Queen Anne in 1709.

In his Boyle lectures,[1] which were directed against 'Mr. Hobbes, Spinoza, the author of the *Oracles of Reason* and other deniers of natural and revealed religion', Clarke develops at length an *a posteriori* argument for God's existence. He declares his intention of urging 'such propositions only as cannot be denied without departing from that reason which all atheists pretend to be the foundation of their unbelief'.[2] He then proceeds to enunciate and prove a number of propositions, designed to exhibit in a logical and systematic way the rational character of belief in God.

The propositions are as follows. First, 'it is absolutely and undeniably certain that something has existed from all eternity'.[3] For there are things which exist now; and they cannot have arisen out of nothing. If anything now exists, something existed from eternity. Secondly, 'there has existed from eternity some one

---

[1] The two series of Boyle lectures mentioned above were subsequently published together in one volume with the title *A Discourse concerning the Being and Attributes of God, the Obligations of Natural Religion, and the Truth and Certainty of the Christian Revelation.* References are to the 1719 edition of this work.

[2] *A Discourse*, I, p. 9.   [3] *Ibid.*

unchangeable and independent being'.[1] There are dependent beings, and so there must be a non-dependent being. Otherwise there is no adequate cause for the existence of any dependent thing. Thirdly, 'that unchangeable and independent being, which has existed from eternity, without any external cause of its existence, must be self-existing, that is, necessarily-existing'.[2] Clarke then argues that this necessary being must be simple and infinite, and that it cannot be the world or any material thing. For a necessary being is necessarily all that it is and is thus unchangeable. But though we can know what this being is not, we cannot comprehend its substance. Hence the fourth proposition states that 'what the substance or essence of that being, which is self-existent or necessarily-existing, is, we have no idea, neither is it at all possible for us to comprehend it'.[3] We do not comprehend the essence or substance of anything; much less of God. Nevertheless, says the fifth proposition, 'though the substance or essence of the self-existent being is itself absolutely incomprehensible to us, yet many of the essential attributes of His nature are strictly demonstrable, as well as His existence. Thus, in the first place, the self-existent being must of necessity be eternal.'[4] The sixth proposition[5] states that the self-existent being must be infinite and omnipresent, the seventh[6] that this being must be one and one only, the eighth[7] that God must be intelligent, the ninth[8] that He must be endowed with liberty, the tenth[9] that He must be infinitely powerful, the eleventh[10] that the supreme cause must be infinitely wise, and the twelfth that the supreme cause must be a being 'of infinite goodness, justice and truth and all other moral perfections such as become the supreme governor and judge of the world'.[11]

In the course of his reflections and arguments Clarke passes some more or less conventional criticism on the Scholastics; for example, that they used meaningless terms. Apart, however, from the fact that he lays himself open to the same type of criticism by using technical terms, it is obvious to any reader who knows anything of the Scholastic tradition that Clarke makes copious use of it. This is not to say, however, that there is nothing in Clarke except what comes from the Scholastics. For example, when he tries to defend his sixth proposition (that the self-existent being is necessarily infinite and omnipresent) against the objection that

---

[1] *A Discourse*, I, p. 12. [2] *Ibid.*, p. 15. [3] *Ibid.*, p. 38. [4] *Ibid.*, pp. 41–2.
[5] *Ibid.*, p. 44. [6] *Ibid.*, p. 48. [7] *Ibid.*, p. 51. [8] *Ibid.*, p. 64.
[9] *Ibid.*, p. 76. [10] *Ibid.*, p. 113. [11] *Ibid.*, p. 119.

ubiquity or omnipresence does not necessarily pertain to the notion of a self-existent being, he argues that space and duration (that is, absolute and infinite space and duration) are properties of God.[1] 'Space is a property of the self-existent substance, but not of any other substance. All other substances are *in* space and are penetrated by it, but the self-existent substance is not in space, nor penetrated by it, but is itself (if I may so speak) the substratum of space, the ground of the existence of space and duration itself. Which space and duration being evidently necessary and yet themselves not substances but properties, show evidently that the substance without which these properties could not subsist is itself much more (if that were possible) necessary.'[2] In answer to further objections Clarke admits that to say that 'the self-existent substance is the substratum of space, or space a property of the self-existent substance, are not perhaps very proper expressions'.[3] But he goes on to indicate that he regards infinite space and duration as being in some sense realities which are independent of finite things. They are not, however, substances. Clarke does not prove God's existence in the first place from space and duration. As we have seen, he proves the existence of a self-existent substance before he arrives at his sixth proposition. But, having proved God's existence, he argues that infinite space and duration must be properties of God. There seems, however, to be an important ambiguity in his account of the matter, which he does not clarify. For to say that space and duration are properties of God and to say that God in some sense grounds space and time are not the same thing. It may be said that for Clarke infinite space and infinite duration are the divine omnipresence and eternity. But if this is the case, an explanation is needed of how we can know them without already knowing God.

Clarke's views on this matter bear such a marked resemblance to Newton's that it has sometimes been maintained that he took them from the latter's writings. But historians have rightly pointed out that Clarke had first expounded his ideas some nine years before Newton published the *General Scholium* to the second edition of the *Principia*. But even though Clarke did not borrow his ideas from Newton, it is perfectly understandable that in his correspondence with Leibniz he undertook to defend Newton's theory against the criticism passed by the latter, who evidently

---

[1] Cf. the letters printed at the end of *A Discourse*, p. 16.
[2] *Ibid.*, pp. 21–2.   [3] *Ibid.*, p. 27.

considered it to be absurd. He also takes the opportunity of developing his own ideas. Thus 'space is not a being, an eternal and infinite being, but a property or consequence of a being infinite and eternal. Infinite space is immensity; but immensity is not God; and therefore infinite space is not God'.[1] Leibniz objected that absolute or pure space is imaginary, a construction of the imagination; but Clarke answered that 'extra-mundane space (if the material world be finite in its dimensions) is not imaginary but real'.[2] The precise relation of this space to God is, however, left obscure. To say that it is not God but a property of God is not very illuminating, and confusion is simply increased if it is also spoken of as a 'consequence' of God. According to Clarke, 'if no creatures existed, yet the ubiquity of God and the continuance of His existence would make space and time to be exactly the same as they are now'.[3] Leibniz, however, contended that 'if there were no creatures, space and time would be only in the ideas of God'.[4]

Leaving aside Clarke's rather obscure theory about space and time, we can say in general that in his eyes the existence of God is or ought to be plain to anyone who gives careful consideration to the implications of the existence of any one finite thing. So also does he consider that anyone can discern without difficulty the objective distinctions between right and wrong. 'There are certain necessary and eternal differences of things, and certain consequent fitnesses or unfitnesses of the application of different things or different relations one to another; not depending on any positive constitutions, but founded unchangeably in the nature and reason of things, and unavoidably arising from the differences of the things themselves.'[5] For example, man's relation to God makes it unchangeably fitting that he should honour, worship and obey his Creator. 'In like manner, in men's dealing and conversing one with another it is undeniably more fit, absolutely and in the nature of the thing itself, that all men should endeavour to promote the universal good and welfare of all than that all men should be continually contriving the ruin and destruction of all.'[6]

Clarke insists against Hobbes that these relations of fitness and unfitness are independent of any social compact or covenant, and that they give rise to obligations quite apart from any legal enactment and from the application of sanctions, present or future. In

[1] A Collection of Papers which passed between the late learned Mr. Leibniz and Dr. Clarke, 1717, p. 77.   [2] Ibid., p. 125.   [3] Ibid., p. 149.   [4] Ibid., p. 113.
[5] A Discourse, 2, p. 47.   [6] Ibid., 2, p. 38.

fact, moral principles are so 'plain and self-evident that nothing but the extremest stupidity of mind, corruption of manners or perverseness of spirit can possibly make any man entertain the least doubt concerning them'.[1] These 'eternal moral obligations are indeed of themselves incumbent on all rational beings, even antecedent to the consideration of their being the positive will and command of God'.[2] But their fulfilment is in fact positively willed by God, and He rewards and punishes men according to their fulfilment or infringement of the moral law. We can thus speak of a 'secondary and additional obligation', but 'the original obligation of all . . . is the eternal reason of things'.[3] There is, in other words, a natural moral law, the main principles of which at least are discerned by the minds of all who are neither idiots nor thoroughly corrupted. And 'that state which Mr. Hobbes calls the state of nature is not in any sense a natural state but a state of the greatest, most unnatural and most intolerable corruption that can be imagined'.[4]

Though, however, the fundamental principles of the moral law are self-evident to the unclouded and unperverted mind, and though more particular rules can be deduced from these, the actual condition of man is such that instruction in moral truth is necessary to him. This means in the end that revelation is morally necessary; and the true divine revelation is the Christian religion. Christianity comprises not only truths which reason can, in principle, find out for itself but also truths which transcend reason, though they are not contrary to it. But 'every one of these doctrines has a natural tendency and a direct and powerful influence to reform men's lives and correct their manners. This is the great end and ultimate design of all true religion.'[5] And the truth of the Christian religion is confirmed by miracle and prophecy.

2. Like the Cambridge Platonists or Latitudinarians, Clarke was a 'rationalist' in the sense that he appealed to reason and maintained that Christianity has a rational foundation. He was not the man to appeal to faith without any reference to the rational grounds for believing. And we can even find in his writings a tendency to rationalize Christianity and to play down the concept of 'mystery'. At the same time he distinguished himself sharply from the deists. In the second series of his Boyle lectures he divides the so-called deists into four sorts or groups. The first group consists of those who acknowledge that God created the

---

[1] A Discourse, 2, p. 39.   [2] Ibid., p. 5.   [3] Ibid., p. 54.
[4] Ibid., p. 107.   [5] Ibid., p. 284.

world but who deny that He plays any part in governing it. The second group consists of those who believe that all natural events depend on the divine activity but who at the same time assert that God takes no notice of man's moral behaviour, on the ground that moral distinctions depend simply on human positive law. The third group consists of those who think indeed that God expects moral behaviour from His rational creatures but who do not believe in the immortality of the soul. The fourth group consists of those who believe that there is a future life in which God rewards and punishes but who accept only those truths which can be discovered by reason alone. And 'these, I say, are the only true Deists'.[1] In Clarke's opinion these 'only true Deists' are to be found exclusively among those philosophers who lived without any knowledge of divine revelation but who recognized and lived up to the principles and obligations of natural religion and natural morality. In others words, he recognizes as 'true' deists those pagan philosophers, if any, who fulfilled the necessary qualifications, and not the contemporary deists.

Clarke's observations about the deists are highly polemical in tone; but his classification, even if over-schematized, is useful in that it draws attention both to common ground and to differences. The word 'deism' was first used in the sixteenth century, and it is employed for a number of writers belonging, for the most part, to the last part of the seventeenth and the early part of the eighteenth century, who rejected the idea of supernatural revelation and of revealed mysteries. Locke himself did not reject the idea of revelation, but, as we have seen, he insisted that reason is the judge of revelation, and his book on the *Reasonableness of Christianity* (1695) acted as a powerful impetus in the direction of the rationalization of the Christian religion. The deists applied his ideas in a more radical manner and tended to reduce Christianity to a purely natural religion, discarding the idea of a unique revelation and trying to find the rational essence at the heart of the different historical religions. They had in common a belief in God, which differentiated them from the atheists, together with a disbelief in any unique revelation and supernatural scheme of salvation, which differentiated them from the orthodox Christians. In other words, they were rationalists who believed in God. At the same time they differed very much among themselves, and there is no such thing as a school of deism. Some were hostile to

[1] *A Discourse*, 2, p. 19.

Christianity while others were not hostile, though they tended to reduce the Christian religion to a natural religion. Some believed in the immortality of the soul, others did not. Some spoke as though God created the world and then left it to proceed on its way according to natural laws. These were obviously strongly influenced by the new mechanical conception of the cosmic system. Others had some belief at least in divine providence. Finally, some tended to identify God and nature, while others believed in a personal God. But in the course of time the word 'theist' was used to designate the latter as distinct from the naturalistic pantheists and from those who denied all divine providential government. In fine, eighteenth-century deism meant the de-supernaturalizing of religion and the refusal to accept any religious propositions on authority. For the deists reason, and reason alone, was the judge of truth in religion as elsewhere. They were therefore also called 'free-thinkers', the word indicating that for them the activity of reason should be restricted by no tradition and by no authority, whether of the Scriptures or of the Church.

This appeal to reason as the one and only arbiter of religious truth is represented by such books as *Christianity Not Mysterious* (1696) by John Toland (1670–1722) and *Christianity as Old as the Creation; or, the Gospel a Republication of the Religion of Nature* (1730) by Matthew Tindal (*c.* 1656–1733). The last-named work was regarded as a kind of deistic Bible and elicited a number of replies, such as the *Defence of Revealed Religion* (1732) by John Conybeare. Butler's *Analogy of Religion* was also directed in large measure against Tindal's work. Other deistic writings of the same kind are *The Religion of Nature Delineated* (1722) by William Wollaston (1659–1724) and *The True Gospel of Jesus Christ* (1739) by Thomas Chubb (1679–1747). The rights of 'free-thinking' were proclaimed by Anthony Collins (1676–1729) in his work *A Discourse of Free-thinking, occasioned by the Rise and Growth of a Sect called Free-thinkers* (1713).

Some of the deists, such as Tindal, were doubtless concerned simply with expounding what they considered to be the common essence of true, natural religion. And the essence of Christianity consisted for them principally in its ethical teaching. They had no sympathy with the dogmatic disputes of different Christian bodies, but they were not radically hostile to Christianity. Other deists, however, were more radical thinkers. John Toland, who was for a short time a convert to Catholicism before he returned to

Protestantism, ended as a pantheist, this phase of his thought being represented by his *Pantheisticon* (1720). He blamed Spinoza for not seeing that motion is an essential attribute of body, but he approximated to the former's position, with the qualification that he was much more of a materialist than was Spinoza. For Toland the mind was simply a function or epiphenomenon of the brain. Again, Anthony Collins put forward a frankly deterministic theory in his *Inquiry concerning Human Liberty* (1715). And Thomas Woolston (1669–1733), under cover of allegorizing the Bible, called in question the historicity of Christ's miracles and of the Resurrection. *The Trial of the Witnesses of the Resurrection of Jesus* (1729) by Thomas Sherlock was an answer to Woolston's *Discourses* so far as they concerned the Resurrection.

Notable among the deists by reason of his prominence in political life was Henry St. John, Viscount Bolingbroke (1678–1751). Bolingbroke acknowledged Locke as his master, but his way of interpreting Locke's empiricism was hardly consonant with the latter's spirit. For he tended to develop it in a positivistic direction. Plato and 'Platonists', including St. Augustine, Malebranche, Berkeley, the Cambridge Platonists and Samuel Clarke, were anathema to him. Metaphysics was in his eyes a creature of the imagination. This did not prevent him, indeed, from maintaining that the existence of an omnipotent and all-wise Creator can be proved by means of reflection on the cosmic system. But he stressed the divine transcendence and rejected the 'Platonist' idea of 'participation'. It is nonsense to speak of God loving man: such talk merely ministers to man's desire to exaggerate his importance. This means, of course, that Bolingbroke had to eviscerate Christianity of its characteristic elements and reduce it to what he regarded as natural religion. He did not explicitly deny that Christ was the Messiah or that He performed miracles: indeed he affirms both propositions. But the work of St. Paul and his successors was the object of bitter attack. The purpose of Christ's coming and of His activity was simply to confirm the truth of natural religion. The theology of redemption and salvation is a worthless accretion. In spite of all his esteem for Locke, Bolingbroke was entirely lacking in Locke's genuine Christian piety, and his outlook was contaminated by a cynicism which was conspicuously absent from the mind of the father of British empiricism. In Bolingbroke's opinion the masses should be left to adhere to the dominant and prevailing religion and not be disturbed by free-thinkers. Free-thought should be a prerogative of the aristocratic and educated.

The English deists were by no means profound philosophers; but the movement exercised a certain considerable influence. In France, for example, Voltaire was an admirer of Bolingbroke, and Diderot was, for a time at least, a deist. The American statesman, Benjamin Franklin, who had once written from an irreligious point of view against Wollaston's *Religion of Nature Delineated*, also confessed himself a deist. But there was, of course, a considerable difference between the French and the American deists. The former were inclined to bitter scoffing and attack against orthodox Christianity, whereas the latter were more akin to the English deists in their positive concern for natural religion and morality.

3. The most eminent among the opponents of the deists was Joseph Butler (1692–1752), bishop of Durham. In 1736 appeared his chief work, *The Analogy of Religion, Natural and Revealed, to the Constitution and Course of Nature*.[1] In the preface or 'advertisement' to this book Butler remarks that 'it is come, I know not how, to be taken for granted by many persons that Christianity is not so much as a subject of inquiry, but that it is now at length discovered to be fictitious. And accordingly they treat it as if, in the present age, this were an agreed point among all people of discernment, and nothing remained but to set it up as a principal subject of mirth and ridicule, as it were by way of reprisal for its having so long interrupted the pleasures of the world.'[2] At the time at which Butler was writing religion was at a very low ebb in England, and his chief concern was to show that belief in Christianity is not unreasonable. So far as he was concerned with the deists in particular, he looked on them as symptomatic of the general decline of religion. But that he was concerned with them is clear from the fact that he presupposes the existence of God and does not undertake to prove it.

The purpose of *The Analogy of Religion* is not to prove that there is a future life, that God rewards and punishes after death, and that Christianity is true. The scope of the work is more limited, being that of showing that the acceptance of such truths is not unreasonable, unless the deists are prepared to say that all their beliefs about the system and course of nature are unreasonable.

---

[1] Page references are given to Gladstone's edition of Butler's works in two volumes (Oxford, 1896).   [2] I, pp. 1-2.

Our knowledge of nature is probable. True, probability can vary much in degree; but the knowledge which we possess of nature is based on experience and, even when it attains a very high degree of probability, it is still only probable. And there is much that we do not understand. Yet in spite of the limitations of our knowledge the deists do not question the reasonableness and legitimacy of our beliefs about nature simply because much is obscure to us. We can argue by analogy, therefore, that if in the sphere of religious truth we encounter difficulties similar to those encountered in our knowledge of nature, which is admittedly God's creation, these difficulties are no reason for rejecting religious doctrines out of hand. In other words, the deists advance difficulties against certain truths of natural religion, such as the immortality of the soul, and against the truths of revealed religion; but the existence of such difficulties does not constitute a disproof of the propositions in question if the former are analogous to or have their counterpart in our knowledge of the constitution and course of nature, the author of which is admitted by the deists themselves to be God. In his introduction Butler cites Origen to the effect that a man who believes the Scriptures to be the work of Him who is the Author of nature may well expect to find the same sort of difficulties in them as are found in nature. 'And in a like way of reflection it may be added that he who denies the Scriptures to have been from God upon account of these difficulties may, for the very same reason, deny the world to have been formed by Him.'[1]

Butler does not, of course, confine himself to arguing that difficulties in the sphere of religious truth do not constitute a disproof of religious propositions when they are analogous to difficulties encountered in our knowledge of nature. He argues further that natural facts provide a ground for inferring the probable truth of natural and revealed religion. And since it is a question of propositions which are of vital concern to us in the practical order, and not simply of propositions the truth or falsehood of which is a matter of indifference to us, we ought to act according to the balance of probability. For example, there is no natural fact which forces us to say that immortality is impossible; and, further, analogies drawn from our present life make it positively probable that there is a future life. We see caterpillars turning eventually into butterflies, birds breaking their shells and

[1] Introduction, 8; I, pp. 9–10.

entering upon a fuller life, human beings developing from an embryonic to a mature state; and 'therefore that we are to exist hereafter in a state as different (suppose) from our present as this is from our former, is but according to the analogy of nature'.[1] True, we see the dissolution of the body, but while death deprives us of any 'sensible proof' that a man's powers survive, it does not mean that he does not survive, and the unity of consciousness in this life suggests that he can do so. Again, even in this life our actions meet with natural consequences, happiness and unhappiness depending upon our behaviour. The analogy of nature suggests, therefore, that our actions here meet with reward and punishment in the future life. As for Christianity, it is not true to say that it is merely a 'republication' of natural religion. For it teaches us much that we could not have known otherwise. And if our natural knowledge is deficient and limited, as it is, there is no *a priori* reason why we should not acquire fresh light through revelation. Further, 'analogy of nature shows that we are not to expect any benefits without making use of the appointed means for obtaining or enjoying them. Now reason shows us nothing of the particular immediate means of obtaining either temporal or spiritual benefits. This therefore we must learn either from experience or revelation. And experience the present case does not admit of.'[2] It is folly, therefore, to treat Christian revelation and teaching as light and trivial matters. For we cannot obtain the end and reward proposed by God without using the means appointed by Him, means which are known through revelation.

If Butler's arguments are interpreted as proofs of the truths of natural and revealed religion, they seem to be often extremely weak. But he was aware of this himself. He says, for instance, that 'it is most readily acknowledged that the foregoing treatise is by no means satisfactory; very far indeed from it'.[3] And he considers the objection that 'it is a poor thing to solve difficulties in revelation by saying that there are the same in natural religion, when what is wanting is to clear both of them of these their common, as well as other their respective, difficulties. . . .'[4] At the same time he points out that he has been concerned with a particular line of objection brought against religion, namely, that there are difficulties and doubtful points in it, and that if it were true, it would be free from these. But this objection presupposes that there are no

[1] 1, 1, 3; 1, p. 22.   [2] 2, 1, 24; 1, p. 201.
[3] 2, 8, 17; 1, pp. 362–3.   [4] 2, 8, 2; 1, p. 354.

difficulties and doubts in natural non-religious knowledge; and this is not the case. Yet in their temporal concerns people do not hesitate to act upon evidence of the same kind that is available in religious matters. 'And as the force of this answer lies merely in the parallel which there is between the evidence for religion and for our temporal conduct, the answer is equally just and conclusive whether the parallel be made out by showing the evidence of the former to be higher or the evidence of the latter to be lower.'[1] The object of the treatise is not to clear up all difficulties and justify divine providence but to show what we ought to do. It may be said that we ought not to act without evidence. But for the truth of Christianity we have historical evidence, especially miracles and prophecies.

The *Analogy of Religion* is obviously very deficient if it is considered as a philosophy of religion. But it was not intended to be this, and it should not be judged as such. It is also deficient if considered as a book of systematic apologetics, though it is interesting to observe that Butler outlines the notion of a cumulative argument for Christianity amounting to a proof. 'But the truth of our religion, like the truths of common matters, is to be judged by all the evidence taken together. And unless the whole series of things which may be alleged in this argument, and every particular thing in it, can reasonably be supposed to have been by accident (for here the stress of the argument for Christianity lies) then is the truth of it proved.'[2] This is a valuable line of thought in apologetics. Still, the work was not intended to be a work of systematic apologetics in the modern sense. It was meant to be an answer to the deists' line of objection against revealed religion, an answer based on the analogy of nature in the sense described above. It must be admitted, I think, that some of Butler's analogies are not convincing. There are, for example, obvious objections against arguing from the fact that temporal happiness and unhappiness depend upon our conduct in this life to the probability that happiness and unhappiness in the next life also depend on our behaviour in *this* life. At the same time the great strength of the work seems to lie in Butler's awareness of the role of probability in our interpretation of Nature and in our conduct in temporal concerns, and in his argument that in this case we ought to act according to the balance of probability also in religious affairs, without demanding that all difficulties and obscurities

[1] 2, 8, 9; I, p. 359.   [2] 2, 7, 62; I, p. 352.

should first be cleared up. This line of argument may be an *argumentum ad hominem*, namely, against the deists; but it is an effective line of argument in this connection. For the contemporary deists were not, like Lord Herbert of Cherbury, upholders of the theory of innate ideas, but stood rather in the empiricist tradition. And Butler places himself on the same ground, though how this may affect our knowledge of the existence of God he does not explain.

Butler's ethical theory will be considered in the next chapter. But it is not inappropriate to say something here of his views on personal identity, which are given in the first dissertation appended to *The Analogy of Religion*.

In the first place, says Butler, personal identity cannot be defined. Yet to say this is not to say that we are not aware of personal identity or that we have no notion of it. We cannot define similarity or equality, but we know what they are. And we know what they are by viewing, for example, the similarity of two triangles or the equality between twice two and four. In other words, we come to have the notions of similarity and equality by acquaintance with instances. And so it is with personal identity. 'Upon comparing the consciousness of oneself or one's own existence in any two moments there immediately arises to the mind the idea of personal identity.'[1]

Butler does not intend to say that consciousness makes personal identity. Indeed, he criticizes Locke for defining personal identity in terms of consciousness. 'One should really think it self-evident that consciousness of personal identity presupposes, and therefore cannot constitute, personal identity, any more than knowledge in any other case can constitute truth, which it presupposes.'[2] Butler admits that to be endowed with consciousness is inseparable from our idea of a person or intelligent being. But it does not follow that present consciousness of past actions or feelings is necessary to our being the same persons who performed those actions or had those feelings. True, the successive consciousnesses which we have of our own existence are distinct. But 'the person of whose existence the consciousness is felt now, and was felt an hour or a year ago, is discerned to be, not two persons, but one and the same person; and therefore is one and the same'.[3] To attempt to prove the truth of what we perceive in this way is futile; for we could only do so by means of the perceptions themselves.

[1] 2; I, p. 388.　　　[2] 3; I, p. 388.　　　[3] 5; I, p. 392.

In the same way we cannot prove the ability of our faculties to know truth; for to do so we should have to rely on these very faculties. Butler evidently thinks that the fault lies, not with the person who cannot demonstrate what is evident, but with him who demands a demonstration of what cannot be demonstrated and what does not need to be demonstrated. The reason why he discusses the problem of personal identity is its connection with the problem of immortality. And though he can hardly be said to have treated the question very thoroughly, he certainly makes a good point against Locke.

CHAPTER X

PROBLEMS OF ETHICS

Shaftesbury — Mandeville — Hutcheson — Butler — Hartley —
Tucker—Paley—General remarks.

1. In the seventeenth century Hobbes had defended an interpretation of man as essentially egoistic and an authoritarian conception of morality, in the sense that according to him the obligatory character of moral laws, as we normally conceive them, depends on the will either of God or of the political sovereign. And as it is the latter who interprets the law of God, we can say that for Hobbes the source of obligation in social morality is the authority of the sovereign.

Locke, as we have seen, was in important respects strongly opposed to Hobbes. He did not share the latter's pessimistic views about human nature when considered in abstraction from the constraining influence of society and government; nor did he think that the obligatory character of moral laws depends on the authority and will of the political sovereign. But in some of his pronouncements on ethics he certainly implied that moral obligation depends on the divine will. Indeed, he sometimes implied that moral distinctions depend on this will. Thus he did not hesitate to state that moral good and evil are the agreement or disagreement of our voluntary actions with a law whereby good or evil is 'drawn on us' by the will and power of the law-maker, this law-maker being God. Again, he asserted that if a Christian is asked why a man ought to keep his word, he will answer that God, who has the power of eternal life and death, requires it of us. To be sure, this authoritarian element represents only one part or aspect of Locke's reflections on morality. But it is none the less an element.

In the first half of the eighteenth century, however, there was a group of moralists who opposed not only Hobbes's interpretation of man as essentially egoistic but also all authoritarian conceptions of the moral law and of moral obligation. As against Hobbes's idea of man they insisted on man's social nature; and as against ethical authoritarianism they insisted on man's possession of a moral sense by which he discerns moral values and moral distinctions independently of the expressed will of God, and still more of the law of the State. They tended, therefore, to set ethics on its own feet, so to speak; and for this reason alone they are of considerable importance in the history of British moral theory. They also gave a social interpretation of morality, in terms of a social rather than of a private end. And in eighteenth-century moral philosophy we can see the beginnings of the utilitarianism which is associated above all with the name of J. S. Mill in the nineteenth century. At the same time we should not allow an interest in the development of utilitarianism to lead us to overlook the peculiar characteristics of moralists of the eighteenth century such as Shaftesbury and Hutcheson.

The first philosopher of the group to be considered here was a pupil of Locke. Anthony Ashley (1671–1713), third earl of Shaftesbury and grandson of Locke's patron, was associated with Locke for three years (1686–9). But though he retained respect for his tutor, he was never a disciple of Locke, in the sense of accepting all the latter's ideas. Shaftesbury was an admirer of what he regarded as the Greek ideal of balance and harmony, and in his opinion Locke would have rendered better service to moral and political philosophy if he had possessed a profounder knowledge and appreciation of Greek thought. For one thing, he would then have been in a position to see more clearly the truth of Aristotle's view that man is by nature a social being. As it was, his dislike of Scholastic Aristotelianism prevented him from appreciating the historic Aristotle and the truths presented in the *Ethics* and *Politics*. The human end, which sets a standard for the distinctions between good and evil, right and wrong, is a social end, and in virtue of his nature man has a natural feeling for these distinctions. To say this is not incompatible with Locke's rejection of innate ideas. The salient question is not about the time at which moral ideas enter the mind but rather whether man's nature is such that in due course moral ideas or ideas of moral values inevitably arise in him. They do not arise because they are innate in the sense in which Locke understood and rejected innate ideas, but because man is what he is, a social being with a moral end which is social in character. Moral ideas are 'connatural' rather than innate.

Shaftesbury had no intention of denying that the individual naturally seeks his own good. 'We know that every creature has a private good and interest of his own, which nature has compelled him to seek.'[1] But man is part of a system, and 'to deserve the name of *good* or *virtuous* a creature must have all his inclinations and affections, his dispositions of mind and temper, suitable and agreeing with the good of his kind or of that system in which he is included and of which he constitutes a part'.[2] A man's individual or private good consists in the harmony or balance of his appetites, passions and affections under the control of reason. But because man is part of a system, that is, because he is by nature a social being, his affections cannot be perfectly harmonized and balanced unless they are in harmony with respect to society. We are not forced to choose between self-love and altruism, between concern for one's own good and concern for the public good as though they are of necessity mutually exclusive. True, 'if there be found in any creature a more than ordinary self-concernment or regard to private good, which is inconsistent with the interest of the species or public, this must in every respect be esteemed an ill and vicious affection. And this is what we commonly call *selfishness*.'[3] But if a man's regard for his private good is not only consistent with the public good but contributes to it, it is in no way blameworthy. For example, though concern for one's own preservation is to be esteemed vicious if it renders one incapable of any generous or benevolent action, a well-ordered concern for their own preservation on the part of individuals contributes to the common good. Thus Shaftesbury does not answer Hobbes by condemning all 'egoism': he maintains that in the moral man the self-regarding impulses and the altruistic or benevolent impulses are harmonized. Benevolence is an integral part of morality, and it is rooted in man's nature as part of a system; but it is not the entire content of morality.

Shaftesbury conceives, therefore, the good of man as something objective, in the sense that it is that which satisfies man as man and in the sense that its nature can be determined by reflection on human nature. 'There is that in which the nature of man is satisfied, and which alone must be his good.'[4] 'Thus is philosophy established. For everyone, of necessity, must reason concerning his own happiness, what his good is and what his ill. The question is only, who reasons best.'[5] This good is not pleasure. To say without

---

[1] *Characteristics*, II, p. 15. References to Shaftesbury's writings will be given according to volume and page of the 1773 edition of the *Characteristics of Men, Manners, Opinions, Times*, which contains a number of treatises and pieces on ethical matters.   [2] *Characteristics*, II, p. 77.   [3] *Ibid.*, p. 23.
[4] *Ibid.*, p. 436.   [5] *Ibid.*, p. 442.

qualification or discrimination that pleasure is our good 'has as little meaning as to say, "We choose what we think eligible" and "We are pleased with what delights or pleases us". The question is whether we are rightly pleased and choose as we should do.'[1] Shaftesbury does not describe the nature of the good very precisely. On the one hand he speaks of it as virtue. Thus he writes of 'that quality to which we give the name of goodness or virtue'.[2] The emphasis is placed on the affections or passions. 'Since it is therefore by affection merely that a creature is esteemed good or ill, natural or unnatural, our business will be to examine which are the good and natural, and which the ill and unnatural affections.'[3] When a man's affections and passions are in a proper state of harmony and balance, with regard both to himself and to society, 'this is rectitude, integrity or virtue'.[4] Here the emphasis is laid on character rather than on actions or on any extrinsic end to be achieved by action. On the other hand, Shaftesbury speaks about the affections as directed towards the good, and of the good as 'interest'. 'It has already been shown that in the passions and affections of particular creatures, there is a constant relation to the interest of a species or common nature.'[5] And this may seem to imply that the good is something other than virtue or moral integrity. Shaftesbury had a low opinion of academic, pedantic philosophy, and it is perhaps not surprising that he did not express his ethical ideas in unambiguous terms. But we can say at any rate that the emphasis is consistently laid on virtue and character. For example, a man is not to be esteemed good merely because he happens to do something which is advantageous to mankind; for he may perform such actions under the impulse of a purely selfish affection or through unworthy motives. In actual fact, a man will contribute to his own interest or good or happiness and to the public or common interest or good or happiness in proportion as he is virtuous. Virtue and interest thus go together; and to show that this is so is one of Shaftesbury's main concerns. He can thus say that 'virtue is the good, and vice the ill of everyone'.[6]

Every man, Shaftesbury considered, is capable, to some degree at least, of perceiving moral values, of discriminating between virtue and vice. For all men possess conscience or the moral sense, a faculty which is analogous to that whereby men perceive

---

[1] *Characteristics*, II, p. 227.   [2] *Ibid.*, p. 16.   [3] *Ibid.*, p. 22.
[4] *Ibid.*, p. 77.   [5] *Ibid.*, p. 78.   [6] *Ibid.*, p. 176.

differences between harmonies and discords, proportion and lack of proportion. 'Is there a natural beauty of figures? And is there not as natural a one of actions? . . . No sooner are actions viewed, no sooner the human affections and passions discerned (and they are most of them as soon discerned as felt) than straight an inward eye distinguishes and sees the fair and shapely, the amiable and admirable, apart from the deformed, the foul, the odious or the despicable. How is it possible therefore not to own that as these distinctions have their foundation in nature, the discernment itself is natural and from nature alone?'[1] It may be that there are wicked and depraved persons who lack any real antipathy towards what is wrong and any real love for what is right for its own sake; but even the wickedest man has some moral sense, to the extent at least that he can distinguish to some degree between meritorious conduct and conduct which is deserving of punishment.[2] The sense of right and wrong is natural to man, though custom and education may lead people to have false ideas of what is right and what is wrong. In other words, there is in all men a fundamental moral sense or conscience, though it may be darkened or perverted through bad customs, through erroneous religious ideas, and so on.

We find, therefore, in Shaftesbury the assimilation of the moral to the aesthetic 'sense' or faculty. The mind 'feels the soft and harsh, the agreeable and disagreeable, in the affections, and finds a foul and a fair, a harmonious and a dissonant, as really and truly here as in any musical numbers or in the outward forms or representations of sensible things. Nor can it withhold its admiration and ecstasy, its aversion and scorn, any more in what relates to the one than to the other of these subjects.'[3] This does not mean that there are innate ideas of moral values. We know, for example, the affections and actions of pity and gratitude by experience. But then 'there arises another kind of affection towards those very affections themselves, which have been already felt and are now become the subject of a new liking or dislike'.[4] The moral sense is innate, but moral concepts are not innate.

A point on which Shaftesbury insists is that virtue should be sought for its own sake. Rewards and punishments can, indeed, be profitably used for educational purposes. But the object of this education is to produce a disinterested love of virtue. It is only when a man comes to love it 'for its own sake, as good and amiable

---

[1] *Characteristics*, II, pp. 414–15. [2] *Ibid.*, pp. 42–3.
[3] *Ibid.*, p. 29. [4] *Ibid.*, p. 28.

in itself'[1] that he can properly be called virtuous. To make virtue dependent on the will of God or to define it in relation to divine rewards is to begin at the wrong end. 'For how can Supreme Goodness be intelligible to those who know not what goodness itself is? Or how can virtue be understood to deserve reward, when as yet its merit and excellence is unknown? We begin surely at the wrong end, when we would prove merit by favour and order by a Deity.'[2] Ethics, in other words, possesses a certain independence: we ought not to start with the ideas of God, of divine providence and of eternal reward and punishment and base moral concepts on these ideas. At the same time virtue is not complete unless it comprises piety towards God; and piety reacts on the virtuous affections, giving them firmness and constancy. 'And thus the perfection and height of virtue must be owing to the belief of a God.'[3]

Given this point of view, it is scarcely necessary to add that Shaftesbury does not define obligation in terms of obedience to divine will and authority. One might perhaps expect him to say that the moral sense or conscience discerns obligations and to leave the matter there. But in considering obligation he tries to show that concern for one's own interest and concern for the public interest or common good are inseparable, and that virtue, to which benevolence is essential, is to the advantage of the individual. To indulge in selfishness is to be miserable, whereas to be completely virtuous is to be supremely happy. This answer to the problem of obligation is influenced by the way in which he states the question. 'It remains to inquire, what obligation there is to virtue; or what reason to embrace it.'[4] The reason which he gives is that virtue is necessary for happiness, and that vice spells misery. Probably one can see here the influence of Greek ethical thought.

Shaftesbury's ethical writings had a considerable effect on the minds of other philosophers, both in Great Britain and abroad. Hutcheson, whose moral philosophy will be considered presently, owed a great deal to him, and through Hutcheson Shaftesbury influenced later thinkers such as Hume and Adam Smith. He was also appreciated by Voltaire and Diderot in France, and by German literary figures such as Herder. But the next section will be devoted to one of Shaftesbury's critics.

[1] *Characteristics*, II, p. 66.   [2] *Ibid.*, p. 267.
[3] *Ibid.*, p. 76.   [4] *Ibid.*, p. 77.

2. Bernard de Mandeville (1670–1733) subjected Shaftesbury's ethical theory to criticism in his work *The Fable of the Bees or Private Vices Public Benefits* (1714; 2nd edition, 1723), which was a development of *The grumbling Hive or Knaves turned Honest* (1705). Shaftesbury, says Mandeville, called every action which is performed with regard to the public good a virtuous action, and he stigmatizes as vice all selfishness which excludes regard for the common good. This view supposes that it is a man's good qualities which make him sociable and that he is naturally gifted with altruistic inclinations. But daily experience teaches us the contrary. We have no empirical evidence that man is naturally an altruistic being. Nor have we any cogent evidence that society benefits only by what Shaftesbury called virtuous actions. On the contrary, it is vice (that is, self-regarding affections and actions) which benefits society. A society which was endowed with all the 'virtues' would be a static and stagnant society. It is when individuals, seeking their own enjoyment and comfort, contrive or promote new inventions and when, by luxurious living, they circulate capital, that society progresses and flourishes. In this sense private vices are public benefits. Further, Shaftesbury's notion that there are objective standards of morality and objective moral values is incompatible with the empirical evidence. We cannot make objectively grounded distinctions between virtue and vice and between higher and lower pleasures. Exalted notions of social virtues are the result partly of a selfish desire for self-preservation on the part of those who combine together in society to secure this end, partly of an equally selfish desire to assert man's superiority over the brutes, and partly of the activity of politicians playing on man's vanity and pride.

Mandeville's ideas, which were criticized by Berkeley in *Alciphron*, naturally give the impression of being the fruit of a thorough-going moral cynicism. He continued Hobbes's egoistic interpretation of human nature, but at the same time, whereas Hobbes considered that man can and in some sense ought to be constrained by external power to pursue social morality, Mandeville maintained that society is best served by the flourishing of private vices. And this view, so described, necessarily appears to be the expression of moral cynicism. But we have to bear in mind what Mandeville meant by 'vices'. The search for 'luxury', that is, for material amenities which are more than what is necessary, was stigmatized by him as 'vicious'. And seeing the impetus given by this search to the development of material civilization, he asserted that private vice can be a public benefit. But it is obviously by no means everyone who would be willing to call this search for luxury 'vicious'; and to do so is in part an expression of a certain puritanical rigorism rather than of moral cynicism. However, the view that altruistic and disinterested conduct is secured by the ability of statesmen to play on human vanity and pride can legitimately be called cynical; and it was this sort of notion which appeared fashionable to some of his contemporaries and monstrous and hateful to others. Mandeville can certainly not be reckoned a great moral philosopher; but his general idea that private egoism and the public good are not at all inconsistent is of some importance. It is an idea which is implicit in the *laissez-faire* type of political and economic theory.

3. Shaftesbury was neither a systematic nor a particularly clear and precise thinker. His ideas were, however, to a certain extent systematized and developed by Francis Hutcheson (1694–1746), who was for some time professor of moral philosophy at Glasgow. I say 'to some extent' because Shaftesbury was by no means the only influence on Hutcheson's mind and on the formation of his ideas. In the first edition of his first work, *An Inquiry into the Original of our Ideas of Beauty and Virtue* (1725), Hutcheson explicitly set out to explain and defend the principles of Shaftesbury as against those of Mandeville. But his *Essay on the Nature and Conduct of the Passions and Affections, with Illustrations on the Moral Sense* (1728) shows evidence of Butler's influence. Further modifications are observable in his *System of Moral Philosophy*, which was edited by William Leechman and appeared posthumously in 1755, though Hutcheson had completed it by 1737. Finally, the *Philosophiae moralis institutio compendiaria libris tribus ethices et jurisprudentiae naturalis principia continens* (1742) shows the influence, in a minor degree, of Marcus Aurelius, the greater part of whose *Meditations* had been translated by Hutcheson about the time that he was writing his Latin work. It is not possible, however, to note all the successive modifications, changes and developments in his moral philosophy in the brief account which is all that can be given in the present section.

Hutcheson takes up again the subject of the moral sense. He is aware, of course, that the word 'sense' is ordinarily used with reference to vision, touch, and so on. But in his opinion the extended use of the word is justified. For the mind can be passively affected not only by objects of sense in the ordinary meaning of the term but also by objects in the aesthetic and moral orders. He makes a distinction, therefore, between the external and internal senses. By external sense the mind receives, in Locke's terminology, simple ideas of single qualities of objects. 'Those ideas which are raised in the mind upon the presence of external objects and their acting upon our bodies are called sensations.'[1] By internal sense we perceive relations which give rise to a feeling or feelings which are different from the seeing or hearing or touching of separate related objects. And internal sense in general is divided into the sense of beauty and the moral sense. The object of the former is 'uniformity amidst variety',[2] a term which Hutcheson substituted for Shaftesbury's 'harmony'. By the moral sense 'we perceive pleasure, in the contemplation of such (good) actions in others, and are determined to love the agent (and much more do we perceive pleasure in being conscious of having done such actions ourselves) without any view of further natural advantage from them'.[3]

In his account of our reception of simple ideas Hutcheson is obviously dependent to a great extent on Locke. The idea of the moral sense comes, of course, from Shaftesbury, not from Locke. To postulate a moral sense would hardly fit in well with the latter's pronouncements on ethics. But the passivity of external sense, which is found in Locke's theory of our reception of simple ideas, is reflected in Hutcheson's account of the passivity of the moral sense. Moreover, Hutcheson is sufficiently influenced by Locke's empiricism to emphasize the difference between the theory of the moral sense and the theory of innate ideas. In exercising the moral sense we do not contemplate innate ideas, nor do we draw ideas out of ourselves. The sense itself is natural and inborn; but by it we perceive moral qualities as by the external sense we perceive sensible qualities.

What precisely is it that we perceive by the moral sense? Hutcheson does not seem to be very clear on this point. Sometimes he speaks of perceiving the moral qualities of actions; but his considered view seems to be rather that we perceive qualities of character. Of course, the whole matter is complicated, at least in the *Inquiry*, by the hedonistic colouring of his way of describing the activity of the moral sense. Thus in the passage quoted above he speaks of perceiving *pleasure* in the contemplation of good

---

[1] *Inquiry*, I, I.   [2] *Ibid*. I, 2.   [3] *Ibid*., II, Introduction.

actions, whether in ourselves or in others. But in the *System of Moral Philosophy* he describes the moral sense as 'the faculty of perceiving moral excellence and its supreme objects'.[1] The 'primary objects of the moral sense are the affections of the will'.[2] Which affections? Primarily those which Hutcheson calls the 'kind affections', namely, affections of benevolence. We have, he tells us, a distinct perception of beauty or excellence in the kind affections of rational agents. In the *Inquiry* he speaks of the perception of excellence 'in every appearance or evidence of benevolence',[3] and a similar emphasis on benevolence is clear in his later writings. But there is an obvious difficulty in claiming that the primary object of the moral sense consists in affections, as far as other people at least are concerned. For it may be asked how we can be said to perceive affections other than our own. According to Hutcheson, 'the object of the moral sense is not any external motion or action, but the inward affections and dispositions which by reasoning we infer from the actions observed'.[4] Perhaps we can conclude that the primary object of the moral sense is benevolence as manifested in action. The moral sense tends to become a capacity for a particular type of approbation of a particular type of action (or, rather, of affection or disposition in the agent) rather than a perception of 'pleasure'. The hedonistic element in Hutcheson's theory tends to retreat into the background, as far as the actual activity of the moral sense is concerned, though it by no means disappears.

Given the emphasis which Hutcheson lays on benevolence, what is the place of self-love? We experience a great number of particular self-regarding desires, and they cannot all be satisfied; for the satisfaction of one desire frequently interferes with or prevents the satisfaction of another. But we can reduce them to harmony, in accordance with the principle of calm self-love. In Hutcheson's opinion this calm self-love is morally indifferent. That is to say, actions which spring from self-love are not bad unless they injure others and are incompatible with benevolence; but at the same time they are not morally good. It is only benevolent actions which are morally good. Or, more precisely, it is only the kind or benevolent affections (which are the primary object of the moral sense and which, in the case of persons other than the subject of the moral sense, are inferred from their actions) that are morally good. Thus Hutcheson tends to make virtue synonymous

[1] *System,* I, I, 4.   [2] *Ibid.*   [3] *Inquiry,* II, 7.   [4] *System,* I, I, 5.

with benevolence. In the *Essay on the Passions* calm, universal benevolence, as the desire of universal happiness, becomes the dominating principle in morality.

By concentrating on the idea of the beauty of virtue and the ugliness or deformity of vice, Shaftesbury had already given to morality a strongly aesthetic colouring. And Hutcheson continued this tendency to speak of the activity of the moral sense in aesthetic terms. But it is not, I think, true to say simply that he reduces ethics to aesthetics. He does, indeed, speak about a moral sense of beauty; but what he means is a sense of moral beauty. The aesthetic sense and the moral sense are different functions or faculties of internal sense in general; and though they have some characteristics in common, they are distinguishable from one another. The object of the feeling for beauty or of the aesthetic sense may be a single object, considered with reference to the proportion and disposition of its parts and qualities. We then have what Hutcheson calls 'absolute beauty'. Or it may be a relation or set of relations between different objects. And then we have 'relative beauty'. In a case of relative beauty it is not required that each object, taken separately, should be beautiful. For example, a painting of a family group can be beautiful, exhibiting 'uniformity in variety', even though we would not say of any individual person depicted in the group that he or she is beautiful. The primary object of the moral sense is, as we have seen, benevolent affections, giving rise to a feeling of approbation. Therefore, even though Hutcheson, like Shaftesbury, tends to assimilate ethics to aesthetics, the moral sense has an assignable object of its own; and he can speak of two internal senses.[1]

It must be added, however, that Hutcheson is very uncertain about the number of the internal senses or about the divisions of internal sense. In the *Essay on the Passions* he gives a fivefold division of sense in general. Besides external sense and the internal sense of beauty (the aesthetic sense) there are public sense or benevolence, the moral sense, and the sense of honour, which makes approbation or gratitude on the part of others for any good action that we have done a necessary source of pleasure. In the *System of Moral Philosophy* we find various subdivisions of the sense of beauty or aesthetic sense, and we also read of the sense of

---

[1] It is worth noting that a number of Hutcheson's ideas about aesthetic appreciation (for example, about its disinterested character) reappear in Kant's account of the judgment of taste.

sympathy, the moral sense or faculty of perceiving moral excellence, the sense of honour and the sense of decency or decorum. In the Latin *Compendiaria* Hutcheson adds the senses of the ridiculous and of veracity. Obviously, once we begin to distinguish senses and faculties according to distinguishable objects and aspects of objects, there is hardly any limit to the number of senses and faculties which we can postulate.

In Hutcheson's ethical theory, in which virtue as a quasi-aesthetic excellence of character is the chief theme, we would hardly expect to find much attention devoted to the subject of obligation, especially when he practically reduces liberty to spontaneity. But he offers a criterion for judging between different possible courses of action. 'In comparing the moral quality of actions in order to regulate our elections among various actions proposed, or to find which of them has the greatest moral excellence, we are led by our moral sense of virtue to judge thus: that in equal degrees of happiness, expected to proceed from the action, the virtue is in proportion to the number of persons to whom the happiness shall extend . . . so that that action is best which procures the greatest happiness for the greatest numbers, and that worst which in like manner occasions misery.'[1] Here we have a clear anticipation of utilitarianism. Indeed, Hutcheson is one of the sources of the utilitarian moral philosophy.

Now, the idea of a moral sense, considered as the perception of pleasure in contemplating good actions, suggests feeling rather than a rational process of judging. But the sentence quoted in the last paragraph, which is taken from the same early work in which Hutcheson speaks of the moral sense in hedonistic terms, describes this sense as passing a judgment about the consequences of actions. And in later writings he attempts to bring together these two points of view in a systematic manner. Thus in the *System of Moral Philosophy* he distinguishes between the material and formal goodness of actions. An action is materially good when it tends towards the interest of the system; that is, towards the common interest or happiness, whatever the affections or motives of the agent may be. An action is formally good when it proceeds from good affections in a just proportion. Both the material and formal goodness are objects of the moral sense. Hutcheson borrows Butler's word 'conscience' and distinguishes between antecedent and subsequent conscience. Antecedent conscience is the faculty

[1] *Inquiry*, II, 3.

of moral decision or judgment and prefers that which appears most conducive to the virtue and happiness of mankind. Subsequent conscience has as its object past actions in relation to the motives or affections from which they sprang.

In the *Inquiry* obligation is described as 'a determination, without regard to our own interest, to approve actions and to perform them, which determination shall also make us displeased with ourselves and uneasy upon having acted contrary to it'.[1] And Hutcheson explains that 'no mortal can secure to himself a perfect serenity, satisfaction and self-approbation but by a serious inquiry into the tendency of his actions and a perpetual study of universal good according to the justest notions of it'.[2] But such remarks scarcely touch the problem of obligation. From his description of the moral sense it would appear that it is the moral beauty of virtue rather than the obligatory character of certain actions which is immediately revealed to us. Perhaps he would say that the fitness of actions contributing to the greater good of the greatest possible number is immediately evident to anyone who enjoys the use of an unclouded moral sense. But in the *System of Moral Philosophy* and in the Latin *Compendiaria* 'right reason' makes its appearance as the source of law, as possessing authority and jurisdiction. The affections are Nature's voice, and Nature's voice echoes the voice of God. But this voice needs interpretation and right reason, as one of the functions of conscience or the moral faculty, issues commands. It is called by Hutcheson, using a Stoic phrase, τὸ ἡγεμονικόν. Here the moral sense, become the moral faculty, takes on a rationalistic colouring.

There are so many different elements in Hutcheson's ethical theory that it does not seem possible to harmonize them all. But one of the chief features of his reflections on morals, a feature which they have in common with those of Shaftesbury, is the assimilation of morals to aesthetics. And when we bear in mind the fact that both men speak of the aesthetic and moral 'senses', it may seem that intuitionism should have the last word in their theories. But both writers were concerned to refute Hobbes's theory of man as essentially egoistic. And with Hutcheson especially benevolence is brought so much to the fore that it tends to usurp the whole field of morality. The ideas of benevolence and altruism naturally foster concentration on the idea of the common good and on promoting the greater good or happiness of the

---

[1] *Inquiry*, II, 7.   [2] *Ibid.*

greatest possible number. There is, therefore, an easy passage to a utilitarian interpretation of ethics. But utilitarianism, with its regard for the consequences of actions, involves judgment and reasoning, so that the moral sense must be something more than a 'sense'. And if one wishes, as Hutcheson did, to link up morality with metaphysics and theology, the decisions of the moral faculty or conscience become a reflection of the voice of God, not in the sense that morality depends on the divine choice, but in the sense that the moral faculty's approval of moral excellence reflects or mirrors God's approval of this excellence. This line of thought, however, which was doubtless influenced to some extent by Hutcheson's reading of Butler, is not the line of thought which we immediately associate with the former's name. In the history of moral theory Hutcheson is remembered as a champion of the moral sense theory and as a precursor of utilitarianism.

4. Both Shaftesbury and Hutcheson endeavoured to redress the balance which had been upset by Hobbes's egoistic interpretation of man's nature. For both men, as we have seen, insisted on the social character of man and on the naturalness of altruism. But whereas Shaftesbury, by finding the essence of virtue in a harmony of the self-regarding with the altruistic affections, had included self-love within the sphere of complete virtue, Hutcheson tended to identify virtue with benevolence. And though he did not condemn 'calm self-love', he regarded it as morally indifferent. On this point Bishop Butler[1] took his stand with Shaftesbury rather than with Hutcheson.

In his *Dissertation of the Nature of Virtue*, which was published in 1736[2] as an appendix to *The Analogy of Religion*, Butler remarks that 'it may be proper to observe that benevolence and the want of it, singly considered, are in no sort the whole of virtue and vice'.[3] And though he does not mention Hutcheson by name, he is probably thinking of him when he says that 'some of great and distinguished merit have, I think, expressed themselves in a manner which may occasion some danger to careless readers of imagining the whole of virtue to consist in singly aiming, according to the best of their judgment, at promoting the happiness of mankind in the present state, and the whole of vice in doing what

---

[1] References to Butler's writings are given according to volume and page of Gladstone's edition of his works (1896).

[2] This dissertation, therefore, was published after the appearance of Hutcheson's *Inquiry* and *Essay on the Passions*.

[3] 12; I, p. 407.

they foresee, or might foresee, is likely to produce an overbalance of unhappiness in it'.[1] This is a terrible mistake, Butler observes. For it might appear on occasion that grave acts of injustice or of persecution would increase human happiness in the future. It is certainly our duty to contribute, 'within the bounds of veracity and justice',[2] to the common happiness. But to measure the morality of actions simply according to their apparent capacity or lack of it for promoting the greater happiness of the greatest possible number is to open the door to all sorts of injustice perpetrated in the name of mankind's future happiness. We cannot know with certainty what the consequences of our actions will be. Further, the object of the moral sense is action; and though intention forms part of the action considered as a total action, it is not the whole of it. We may intend good and not bad consequences; but it does not necessarily follow that the consequences will actually be what we wish or expect them to be.

Virtue, therefore, cannot be reduced simply to benevolence. Benevolence is, indeed, natural to man; but so is self-love. The term 'self-love' is, however, ambiguous, and some distinctions must be made. Everyone has a general desire for his own happiness, and this 'proceeds from or is self-love'.[3] It 'belongs to man as a reasonable creature reflecting upon his own interest or happiness'.[4] Self-love in this general sense pertains to man's nature, and though it is distinct from benevolence, it does not exclude the latter. For desire for our own happiness is a general desire, whereas benevolence is a particular affection. 'There is no peculiar contrariety between self-love and benevolence; no greater competition between these than between any other particular affection and self-love.'[5] The fact of the matter is that happiness, the object of self-love, is not identifiable with self-love. 'Happiness or satisfaction consists only in the enjoyment of those objects which are by nature suited to our several particular appetites, passions and affections.'[6] Benevolence is one particular, natural human affection. And there is no reason why its exercise should not contribute to our happiness. Indeed, if happiness consists in the gratification of our natural appetites, passions and affections, and if benevolence or love of the neighbour is one of these affections, its gratification does contribute to our happiness. Benevolence, therefore, cannot be inconsistent with self-love, which is the desire

---

[1] *Dissertation of the Nature of Virtue*, 15; I, pp. 409–10.
[2] *Ibid.*, 16; I, p. 410.   [3] *Sermons*, 11, 3; II, p. 187.   [4] *Ibid.*
[5] *Sermons*, 11, 11; II, p. 196.   [6] *Sermons*, 11, 6; II, p. 190.

of happiness. There can, however, be a clash between the gratification of a particular appetite or passion or affection, say the desire of riches, and benevolence; and we all know what the word 'selfish' means. When people say that self-love and benevolence or altruism are incompatible, this is often due to a confusion of selfishness with self-love. But this is an unfortunate way of speaking. For it disregards the fact that what we call selfishness may very well be incompatible with true self-love. 'Nothing is more common than to see men give themselves up to a passion or an affection to their known prejudice and ruin, and in direct contradiction to manifest and real interest and the loudest calls of self-love.'[1]

Butler sometimes contrasts 'reasonable self-love' or 'cool self-love' with 'immoderate self-love'.[2] He also contrasts reasonable self-love with 'supposed self-love' or 'supposed interest'; and this way of talking is possibly preferable. For he is contrasting the desire of those ends the attainment of which do in fact confer happiness with the desire of those ends which are mistakenly thought to confer happiness. The particular enjoyments which make up 'the sum total of our happiness' are sometimes 'supposed to arise from riches, honours and the gratification of sensual appetites'.[3] But it is a mistake to think that these enjoyments are the sole components of human happiness. And the people who think in this way have a wrong notion of what true self-love demands.

It may be objected, of course, that happiness is something subjective, and that each individual is the best judge of what constitutes his happiness. But Butler can meet this objection, provided that he can show that 'happiness' has some definite and objective meaning which is independent of different persons' various ideas of happiness. And this he tries to do by giving a definite objective content to the concept of nature, that is to say, human nature. In the first place he mentions two possible meanings of the word 'nature' in order to exclude them. 'By nature is often meant no more than some principle in man, without regard either to the kind or degree of it.'[4] But when we say that nature is the rule of morality, it is obvious that we are not using the word

---

[1] *Sermons*, II, 18; II, p. 203.
[2] Hutcheson was influenced by such distinctions through his acquaintance with Butler's *Sermons*. But, as we have seen, he went on to identify morality with benevolence to all intents and purposes. And it was this position that Butler criticized in his dissertation on virtue.
[3] *Sermons*, II, 13; II, p. 199.   [4] *Sermons*, II, 7; II, p. 57.

'nature' in this sense, namely, to indicate any appetite or passion or affection without regard to its character or intensity. Secondly, 'nature is frequently spoken of as consisting in those passions which are strongest and most influence the actions'.[1] But this meaning of nature must also be excluded. Otherwise we should have to say that a man in whose conduct sensual passion, for instance, was the dominating factor was a virtuous man, acting according to nature. We must look, therefore, for a third sense of the term. According to Butler, the 'principles', as he calls them, of man form a hierarchy, in which one principle is superior and possesses authority. 'There is a superior principle of reflection or conscience in every man, which distinguishes between the internal principles of his heart, as well as his external actions: which passes judgment upon himself and them; pronounces determinately some actions to be in themselves just, right, good; others to be in themselves evil, wrong, unjust. . . .'[2] In so far as conscience rules, therefore, a man acts according to his nature, while in so far as some principle other than conscience dictates his actions, these actions can be called disproportionate to his nature. And to act in accordance with nature is to attain happiness.

But what does Butler mean by conscience? The last quotation shows, of course, that in his view conscience passes judgment on goodness and badness of character, whether in oneself or others, and on the goodness and badness, rightness and wrongness of actions. But this does not tell us what is the precise nature and status of conscience. In the *Dissertation of the Nature of Virtue* he speaks of conscience as 'this moral approving and disapproving faculty'.[3] And in the next section he speaks again of this 'moral faculty, whether called conscience, moral reason, moral sense, or divine reason; whether considered as a sentiment of the understanding or as a perception of the heart, or, which seems the truth, as including both'.[4] Furthermore, Butler sometimes seems at first sight to imply that conscience and self-love are the same.

To take the last point first. Butler maintained that self-love is a superior principle in man. 'If passion prevails over self-love, the consequent action is unnatural; but if self-love prevails over passion, the action is natural: it is manifest that self-love is in human nature a superior principle to passion. This may be contradicted without violating that nature; but the former cannot. So

---

[1] *Sermons*, 11, 8; 11, p. 57.   [2] *Sermons*, 11, 10; 11, p. 59.
[3] 1; 1, p. 398.   [4] *Ibid.*, 1, p. 399.

that, if we will act conformably to the economy of man's nature, reasonable self-love must govern.'[1] But he did not maintain that self-love and conscience are identical. They generally coincide, in Butler's opinion; but to say this is to imply that they are not precisely the same thing. 'It is manifest that, in the common course of life, there is seldom any inconsistency between our duty and what is called interest: it is much seldomer that there is an inconsistency between duty and what is really our present interest; meaning by interest, happiness and satisfaction.'[2] 'Self-love, then, though confined to the interest of the present world, does in general perfectly coincide with virtue; and leads us to one and the same course of life.'[3] Again, 'conscience and self-love, if we understand our true happiness, always lead us in the same way. Duty and interest are perfectly coincident; for the most part in this world, but entirely and in every instance if we take in the future and the whole; this being implied in the notion of a good and perfect administration of things.'[4] Conscience may dictate a course of action which is not, or does not appear to be, in accordance with our temporal interest; but in the long run, if we take into account the future life, conscience always dictates that which is to our true interest, that which contributes to our complete happiness. But it does not follow from this that conscience is the same thing as self-love; for it is conscience which tells us that we should do what contributes to our complete happiness as human beings. Nor does it necessarily follow that we should do what conscience dictates from the conscious motive of serving our true interest. For to say that conscience dictates what is to our interest or that duty and interest coincide and to say that we should do our duty with the motive of securing our interest are not one and the same statement.

In his *Dissertation of the Nature of Virtue* Butler says that the object of the faculty of conscience is 'actions, comprehending under that name active or practical principles: those principles from which men would act, if occasions and circumstances gave them power; and which, when fixed and habitual in any person, we call his character'.[5] 'Acting, conduct, behaviour, abstracted from all regard to what is, in fact and event, the consequence of it, is itself the natural object of the moral discernment; as speculative truth and falsehood is of speculative reason. Intention of such and

---

[1] *Sermons*, 2, 16; II, p. 62.   [2] *Sermons*, 3, 11; II, p. 74.
[3] *Sermons*, 3, 12; II, p. 75.   [4] *Sermons*, 3, 13; II, p. 76.   [5] 4; I, p. 400.

such consequences, indeed, is always included; for it is part of the action itself.'[1] Secondly, our perception of the goodness or badness of actions involves a 'discernment of them as of good or ill desert'.[2] Thirdly, the perception of vice and 'ill desert' arises from a comparison of actions with the capacities of the agents. We do not judge the action of a madman, for example, in the same way that we judge the actions of sane men.

Conscience, therefore, is concerned with actions without regard to the consequences which occur in point of fact, though not without regard to the agent's intention. For his intention is part of his action when considered as the object of the moral sense or faculty. Actions, therefore, must have objective moral qualities to be discerned. And this was, indeed, Butler's view. The goodness or badness of actions arises simply 'from their being what they are; namely, what becomes such creatures as we are, what the state of the case requires, or the contrary'.[3] Now, this view may give rise to a misunderstanding. For Butler might be interpreted as meaning that we reason from an analysis of human nature to the goodness or badness, rightness or wrongness, of particular actions. This is not, however, quite what he means. We can, indeed, reason in this way. But to do so is more characteristic of the moral philosopher than of the ordinary moral agent. In Butler's opinion, we can generally discern the rightness or wrongness of actions by inspecting the given situation, without referring to general rules or performing any work of deduction. 'The inquiries which have been made by men of leisure after some general rule, the conformity to or disagreement from which should denominate our actions good or evil, are in many respects of great service. Yet let any plain honest man, before he engages in any course of action, ask himself, Is this I am going about right, or is it wrong? Is it good, or is it evil? I do not in the least doubt, but that this question would be answered agreeably to truth and virtue, by almost any fair man in almost any circumstance.'[4]

What, then, of obligation? Butler does not express himself very clearly on this matter. But his dominant view is that conscience, when it recognizes this action as right and that action as wrong, pronounces authoritatively that the former ought and that the latter ought not to be performed. In the Preface to the *Sermons* he says that 'the natural authority of the principle of reflection is an

[1] *Dissertation of the Nature of Virtue*, 4; I, pp. 400–1.   [2] *Ibid.*, 5; I, p. 401.
[3] Preface to *Sermons*, 33; II, p. 25.   [4] *Sermons*, 3, 4; II, p. 70.

obligation the most near and intimate, the most certain and known'.[1] Similarly, 'Take in then that authority and obligation, which is a constituent part of this reflex approbation and it will undeniably follow, though a man should doubt of everything else, yet, that he would still remain under the nearest and most certain obligation to the practice of virtue; an obligation implied in the very idea of virtue, in the very idea of reflex approbation.'[2] He seems to imply that virtue carries with it its own claim on us, and that to approve morally is to declare obligatory, in the sense that if, when faced with an actual choice, I recognize one line of action as good, the other as evil, I inevitably assert that I ought to follow the first line of action and avoid the second. Assuming that there is a law of our nature, he asks, what obligation are we under to follow it! And he replies that 'the question carries its own answer along with it. Your obligation to obey this law is its being the law of your nature. That your conscience approves of and attests to such a course of action is itself alone an obligation. Conscience does not only offer itself to show us the way we should walk in, but it likewise carries its own authority with it. . . .'[3] He does not say that the fact that an action is to our interest constitutes by itself obligation, but rather, as we have seen, that duty and interest are coincident, in the sense at least that God will see to it that doing what we recognize to be our duty will lead in the long run to our complete happiness and satisfaction.

Doubtless, Butler paid insufficient attention to varieties and differences in moral outlook and convictions. He admits, indeed, that there may be doubt about particular points; but he insists that 'in general there is in reality a universally acknowledged standard of it (of virtue). It is that which all ages and all countries have made profession of in public; it is that which every man you meet puts on the show of: it is that which the primary and fundamental laws of all civil constitutions over the face of the earth make it their business and endeavour to enforce the practice of upon mankind: namely, justice, veracity, and regard to common good.'[4] But though he does not adequately discuss the difficulties arising from the strong element of *de facto* relativism in the moral codes of humanity, the important point to notice in his ethical theory seems to me to be his assertion of an ethics which is neither purely authoritarian on the one hand nor purely utilitarian on the

[1] 21; II, p. 15.   [2] *Ibid.*, 22; II, p. 16.   [3] *Sermons*, 3, 6; II, p. 71.
[4] *Dissertation of the Nature of Virtue*, 3; I, pp. 399–400.

other. Conscience promulgates, as it were, the moral law, which does not depend on the arbitrary choice of God, and still less on the law of the State. At the same time, he neither identifies morality with benevolence nor makes self-love the unique supreme principle in morality. The moral law has reference to human nature and is founded on it; but conscience ought to be followed even when duty does not coincide with interest as far as this life is concerned. That duty and interest coincide infallibly in the long run is due to divine providence. But this does not mean that we should act simply with a view to obtaining reward and avoiding punishment. The supreme authority is conscience. 'Had it strength, as it has right; had it power, as it has manifest authority, it would absolutely govern the world.'[1] Butler's ethical theory is inadequate on any count; for there are topics of importance which are scarcely discussed. One could wish, for example, for a more exact analysis of the terms good and evil, right and wrong, and a discussion of the precise relations between the terms. Again, further analysis of obligation and a clear explanation of what is actually said about this subject would be desirable. Yet Butler's ethical theory is a remarkable piece of work, even as it stands, and it certainly provides valuable material for any more thoroughly worked-out and elaborate moral philosophy.

5. In connection with the influence of Locke mention was made of David Hartley (1705–57). Abandoning his original intention of becoming an Anglican clergyman, he devoted himself to the study of medicine and subsequently practised as a doctor. In 1749 he published his *Observations on Man*. In the first part of this work he deals with the connection between body and mind, while in the second part he treats of matters relating to morality, especially under its psychological aspect. His general position is based on that of Locke. Sensation is the prior element in cognition, and antecedently to sensation the mind is empty or blank. Hence the need of showing how man's ideas in all their diversity and complexity are formed from the data of the senses. And here Hartley makes use of Locke's notion of the association of ideas, though in his preface to the *Observations on Man* he acknowledges his debt to the *Dissertation concerning the Fundamental Principles of Virtue and Morality* which had been written by John Gay (1699–1745), a clergyman, and which had been prefixed by Bishop Law to his translation of the Latin work on the *Origin of Evil* (1731) by

[1] *Sermons*, 2, 19; 11, p. 64.

Archbishop King. But while Hartley's psychological theories were prompted by Gay's dissertation, his physical theory about the connection between body and mind was influenced by Newton's speculations about nervous action in the *Principia*. We can say, therefore, that Hartley's reflections were influenced by Locke, Newton and Gay. In turn, he himself gave an impulse to the study of the connections between body and mind and to the associationist psychology.

Hartley, while agreeing with Locke that the mind is originally devoid of content, disagreed with him about the status of reflection. The latter is not a distinct source of ideas: the only source is sensation. And sensation is the result of vibrations in the particles of the nerves, which are transmitted by means of the ether, the idea of which was suggested by Newton's hypothesis of an ether to account for the action of forces at a distance. Some vibrations are moderate, and these produce pleasure; others are violent, and these produce pain. Memory is explained by postulating faint vibrations or 'vibratiuncles', tendencies which are imprinted by vibrations on the medullary substance of the brain. Indeed, there are always vibrations in the brain, though what they are depends on a man's past experience and, of course, on present external influences. We can thus account for the cause of memories and ideas even when there is no obvious cause in present sensation. The building-up of man's complex mental life is to be explained in terms of association, which Hartley reduced to the influence of 'contiguous' elements, where 'contiguous' includes successive contiguity. When different sensations are frequently associated with one another, each of them becomes associated with the ideas produced by the others; and the ideas which correspond to associated sensations enter into a mutual association.

The principle of association was employed by Hartley in explaining the genesis of man's moral ideas and feelings. But it is important to note his insistence that the product of association can be a new idea, in the sense that it is more than the mere summation of its component elements. He also insisted that that which is prior in the order of nature is less perfect than that which is posterior. In other words, Hartley did not attempt to reduce the moral life to non-moral elements by saying that it is no more than the latter. Rather did he attempt to explain, by employing the idea of association, how the higher and new emergent is produced from lower elements, and ultimately from one original source, namely, sensation. Thus he tried to show that the moral sense and altruistic affections are not original characteristics of human nature, but that they emerge, through the operation of association, from self-regarding affections and the tendency to secure private happiness.

Hartley, in accordance with the demands of his physiological and psychological theories, embraced, if reluctantly, the determinist position. But though some critics maintained that his theories amounted to a materialistic sensationalism, he himself thought otherwise, and he tried to trace the evolution of the higher out of the lower pleasures, from the pleasures of sense and of self-interest, through the pleasures of sympathy and benevolence, up to the supreme pleasure of the pure love of God and of perfect self-denial.

6. While considering the ethical theory of Hutcheson, we noticed the element of utilitarianism which it contains. Clearer anticipations of later utilitarianism can be seen in the theories of Tucker and Paley (to omit Hume, who will be treated separately and more at length).

Abraham Tucker (1705–74), author of *The Light of Nature Pursued*, of which three volumes appeared during his lifetime, believed that the moral-sense theory was an ethical variant of the theory of innate ideas which Locke had successfully demolished. And, like Hartley, though he does not mention his debt to the latter, he tried to account for the 'moral sense' and for our ethical convictions with the aid of the principle of association, which he named 'translation'.

In the Introduction to *The Light of Nature Pursued* Tucker informs his readers that he has examined human nature and has found that satisfaction, each man's own private satisfaction, is the ultimate spring of all his actions. But he also tells his readers that he has aimed at establishing the rule of universal charity or benevolence, directed towards all men without exception, and that the fundamental rule of conduct is to labour for the common good or happiness; that is, to increase the common stock of satisfaction. He has, therefore, to show how such altruistic conduct is possible if every man is impelled by nature to seek his own satisfaction. This he does by arguing that through 'translation' that which was at first a means came to be regarded as an end. For example, the 'pleasure of benefiting' prompts us to do services to others because we like doing them. In time benevolence or service of others becomes an end in itself, in the sense that no thought is given to the securing of one's own satisfaction. By analogous processes virtue comes to be desired for its own sake and general rules of conduct are formed.

But Tucker found some difficulty in explaining the more complete acts of self-sacrifice. A man may be kind to others because he likes behaving in a kindly way and finds no satisfaction in unkindness. And he may very well come to behave in a kindly manner without adverting to his own satisfaction. But, as Tucker remarks, it is one thing to practise benevolence and take measures to increase the public happiness while one is not conscious of the tendency of such behaviour to increase one's own happiness, and it is another thing to discern clearly that the measures which one takes for the common good extinguish one's own capacity for satisfaction. The man who sacrifices his life for his country may be aware that his act is contrary to his own happiness, in the sense that it extinguishes the capacity for further enjoyment. How can such acts be explained and justified?

The problem is solved, to Tucker's satisfaction at least, by passing beyond human nature considered in itself as something empirically given and by introducing the concepts of God and of the other world. He supposes that there is a 'bank of the universe', a common stock of happiness which is administered by God. Men have really no merits, and God parcels out the common stock of happiness or pleasure in equal shares. By working to increase the public happiness I therefore inevitably increase my own; for God will certainly give me my share in due time, in the next world if not in this. If my sacrifice of myself is for the common good, I shall not be the loser in the long run. Indeed, I shall increase my ultimate satisfaction.

This ingenious argument is obviously not the most important feature of Tucker's ethical theory from the historical point of view. More important are his quantitative estimate of pleasure (pleasures differ in degree, but not in kind), his insistence on private satisfaction as the ultimate motive of conduct, his assessment of moral rules in terms of conduciveness to the general happiness or pleasure, and his attempt to show how man's fundamental egoism can be reconciled with benevolence and altruistic conduct. Here we find the elements of later utilitarianism. The difficulties common to Tucker's version and to the utilitarianism of Bentham and the Mills can best be discussed in connection with the latter.

7. William Paley (1743–1805) became fellow and tutor of Christ's College, Cambridge, where he had studied as an undergraduate. He subsequently occupied various ecclesiastical positions, though he was never given high office, because, it is said, of his latitudinarian views.

Paley is best known for his writings in defence of the credibility of natural religion and of Christianity, especially for his *View of the Evidences of Christianity* (1794) and his *Natural Theology, or Evidences of the Existence and Attributes of the Deity collected from the Appearances of Nature* (1802). In the last-named work he presented his development of the argument from design. He does not base his argument upon the phenomena of the heavens. 'My opinion of Astronomy has always been that it is *not* the best medium through which to prove the agency of an intelligent Creator; but that, this being proved, it shows, beyond all other sciences, the magnificence of his operations.'[1] He takes his stand instead on anatomy, as he puts it; that is, on evidence of design in the animal organism, particularly in the human organism. And he argues that the data are inexplicable without reference to a designing mind. 'Were there no example in the world of contrivance except that of the *eye*, it would be alone sufficient to support the conclusion which we draw from it as to the necessity of an intelligent Creator.'[2] It is not infrequently said that Paley's argument from design has been deprived of all force by the evolutionary hypothesis. If this means that the evolutionary hypothesis is incompatible with any teleological argument for the existence of God, it is a disputable opinion. But if it is meant that Paley's argument as he states it is insufficient and, in particular, that the evolutionary hypothesis and its supporting data need to be considered in any restatement of the argument, most people would, I suppose, agree. Paley was not a particularly original writer. For example, his famous analogy of the watch at the beginning of the work was not his invention. And he probably took too much for granted. But he showed very considerable skill and ability in his arrangement of his matter and in the development of his argument. And it is, in my opinion, an exaggeration to suggest, as is sometimes done, that his line of thought is worthless.

However, we are concerned here rather with Paley's work on *The Principles of Moral and Political Philosophy* (1785), a revision and enlargement of lectures delivered at Cambridge. Here again

---

[1] *N.T.*, 22; *Works*, 1821, IV, p. 297.   [2] *N.T.*, 6; IV, p. 59.

he is not particularly original; but he did not pretend to be. And in his Preface he makes a frank acknowledgement of his debt to Abraham Tucker.

Moral philosophy is defined by Paley as 'that science which teaches men their duty and the reasons of it'.[1] He does not think that we can build a moral theory on the hypothesis of a moral sense, considered as a kind of instinct. 'Upon the whole it seems to me either that there exist no such instincts as compose what is called the moral sense, or that they are not now to be distinguished from prejudices and habits; on which account they cannot be depended upon in moral reasoning.'[2] We cannot draw conclusions about the rightness or wrongness of actions without considering their 'tendency'; that is to say, without considering their end. This end is happiness. But what is meant by happiness? 'In strictness, any condition may be denominated happy, in which the amount or aggregate of pleasure exceeds that of pain; and the degree of happiness depends upon the quantity of this excess. And the greatest quantity of it ordinarily attainable in human life is what we mean by happiness, when we inquire or pronounce what human happiness consists in.'[3]

In determining what happiness is in the concrete, Paley accepts Tucker's view that 'pleasures differ in nothing but in continuance and intensity'.[4] It is impossible, he says, to lay down a universal ideal of happiness valid for all, because men differ so much from one another. But there is a presumption in favour of those conditions of life in which men generally appear to be most cheerful and contented. These include the exercise of the social affections, the exercise of our mental or bodily faculties in the pursuit of some 'engaging end' (an end which provides continuing interest and hope), prudent habits and good health.

Virtue is defined in a frankly utilitarian spirit. It is 'the doing good to mankind, in obedience to the will of God, and for the sake of everlasting happiness'.[5] The good of mankind is the subject-matter of virtue; the will of God provides the rule; and everlasting happiness provides the motive. For the most part we act, not as a result of deliberate reflection, but according to pre-established habits. Hence arises the importance of forming virtuous habits of conduct.

Given this definition of virtue, one would expect a utilitarian

[1] *Principles*, I, 1; I, p. 1.   [2] *Principles*, I, 5; I, p. 14.
[3] *Principles*, I, 6; I, pp. 16–17.   [4] *Ibid.*, p. 18.   [5] *Principles*, I, 7; I, p. 31.

interpretation of moral obligation. And this is in fact what we find. Answering the question what we mean when we say that a man is obliged to do something, Paley answers that 'a man is said to be obliged when he is urged by a violent motive resulting from the command of another'.[1] 'We can be obliged to nothing but what we ourselves are to gain or lose something by: for nothing else can be a "violent motive" to us.'[2] If the further question be asked, why I am obliged to do something, the answer that I am urged to do so by a 'violent motive' is quite sufficient. Paley admits that when he first turned his mind to moral philosophy there seemed to him to be something mysterious in the subject, especially with regard to obligation. But he came to the conclusion that moral obligation is like all other obligations. '*Obligation* is nothing more than an *inducement* of sufficient strength, and resulting, in some way, from the command of another.'[3] If it be asked what is the difference between an act of prudence and an act of duty, the answer is that the only difference is this. 'In the one case we consider what we shall gain or lose in the present world; in the other case we consider also what we shall gain or lose in the world to come.'[4] Paley can say, therefore, that 'private happiness is our motive, and the will of God our rule'.[5] He does not mean that God's will is purely arbitrary, in the sense that actions are commanded which have no relation to our happiness. God wills the happiness of men and thus wills the acts which conduce to this happiness. But by attaching eternal sanctions of reward and punishment to human conduct God imposes moral obligation by providing an inducement or violent motive which transcends the motive of prudence, in so far as prudence is concerned simply with this world.

Hume, Paley notes, in the fourth appendix to his *Enquiry concerning the Principles of Morals*, takes exception to attempts to link ethics closely with theology. But if there are eternal sanctions, Paley insists, they must be taken into consideration by the Christian moralist. What is peculiar to Christian morality is not so much the content of morality, so to speak, as the additional motive, provided by a knowledge of eternal sanctions, which operates as an inducement to perform or not to perform some action.

'So then actions are to be estimated by their tendency. Whatever

[1] *Principles*, 2, 2; I, p. 44.   [2] *Ibid.*, p. 45.   [3] *Principles*, 2, 3; I, p. 46.
[4] *Ibid.*, p. 47.   [5] *Ibid.*, p. 46.

is expedient, is right. It is the utility of any moral rule alone which constitutes the obligation of it.'[1] And in estimating the consequences of actions we should ask what the consequences would be if the same sort of action were universally permitted. The statement that whatever is expedient is right must be understood of long-term expediency or utility, taking into account collateral and remote effects, as well as those which are direct and immediate. Thus while the particular consequence of forgery is the loss of a particular sum to a particular man, the general consequence would be the destruction of the value of all currency. And moral rules can be established by estimating the consequences of actions in this general sense.

Paley is, indeed, consistently utilitarian. But it is noticeable that in treating of particular moral rules and duties and of the rightness or wrongness of particular types of actions he tends to forget his original insistence on the motive of private happiness and to take public benefit as a criterion. Moreover, by insisting on the need for developing and preserving good habits he evades to some extent the very great difficulties which arise out of the idea of calculation of consequences as a criterion of good and evil, right and wrong. But Paley is inclined to slur over or make short work of serious difficulties against his position. And he takes far too much for granted. It is not at all evident, for example, that when a man says that he is morally obliged he means that he is urged by a violent motive resulting from the command of another. It may be added that in Paley's opinion all moral systems come more or less to the same conclusions. Thus those who say that I am obliged to do X because X is agreeable to the fitness of things must mean by fitness, fitness to produce happiness. In other words, Paley assumes that all moral philosophers are implicitly asserting utilitarianism.

Paley was also, of course, a utilitarian in his political theory. From the historical point of view 'government, at first, was either patriarchal or military: that of a parent over his family, or of a commander over his fellow-warriors'.[2] But if we ask for the ground of the subject's obligation to obey the sovereign, the only true answer is 'the will of God as collected from expediency'.[3] Paley explains what he means by this. It is the will of God that human happiness should be promoted. Civil society conduces to this end.

---

[1] *Principles*, 2, 6; 1, p. 54.   [2] *Principles*, 6, 1; 1, p. 353.
[3] *Principles*, 6, 3; 1, p. 375.

Civil societies cannot be maintained unless the interest of the whole society is binding on every member. Hence it is the will of God that the established government should be obeyed as long as it 'cannot be resisted or changed without public inconveniency'.[1] Thus Paley rejects the contract-theory and substitutes the concept of public benefit or 'public expediency' as the ground (and also, of course, as indicating the limit) of political obligation. Hume had already maintained the same view.

8. In this chapter Shaftesbury and Hutcheson have been depicted as concerned to refute Hobbes's view of man by showing that the benevolent or altruistic impulses are as natural to the human being as the egoistic impulses, or that benevolence is as natural as self-love. And Mandeville was depicted as a critic and adversary of Shaftesbury and so, by implication, as a defender of Hobbes's point of view. But in one sense at least Mandeville was a critic of Hobbes. For while the latter considered that it is ultimately only through fear and constraint that human beings are led to act altruistically and with a view to the good of society, Mandeville maintained that egoism of itself serves the common good and that private 'vices' are public benefits. He thus adopted a point of view different from that of Hobbes, who regarded the natural egoism of the individual as something to be overcome through the constraints imposed by society. However, it obviously remains true that the principal opponents of Hobbes were Shaftesbury and Hutcheson.

Hobbes had, of course, other critics and opponents. An earlier chapter was devoted to the Cambridge Platonists, and in the last chapter something was said about Samuel Clarke. The Cambridge Platonists and Clarke were rationalists, in the sense that they believed that the human reason apprehends eternal and immutable moral principles. And in upholding this view they were opposed to Hobbes. But Shaftesbury and Hutcheson, who were also opposed to Hobbes, did not follow them in their rationalism. Instead, they had recourse to the theory of the moral sense. I do not mean to imply that there was no common ground at all between the rationalists and the defenders of the moral-sense theory. For in both types of ethical theory there was, for example, an element of intuitionism. But there were also important differences. For the rationalist the mind apprehends eternal and immutable moral principles, which he can use as a guide to

[1] *Principles*, 6, 3; I, p. 375.

conduct. For the adherent of the moral-sense theory a man apprehends immediately moral qualities in concrete instances rather than abstract principles.

This means that the defender of the moral-sense theory is probably more likely than the rationalist to pay attention to the way in which the ordinary man's mind works when he makes moral decisions and judgments. In other words, we would perhaps expect to find him paying more attention to what we may call the psychology of ethics. And in point of fact we find in Butler in particular a considerable psychological acumen. Further, the moral-sense theory in general reflects an apprehension of the part played by 'feeling', by immediacy, in the moral life. The analogy drawn between moral discrimination and aesthetic appreciation helps to bring out this fact.

But if we examine the ordinary moral consciousness, it will be seen that 'feeling' or immediacy is only one element. There are also, for example, moral judgment or decision and an authoritative imperative to take into account. Bishop Butler tried to do justice to this side of the matter in his analysis of conscience. And by doing so he transformed to a great extent the original moral-sense theory and helped to show the differences between moral discrimination and aesthetic appreciation.

There is another point about Butler's moral theory which should be noticed. Shaftesbury and Hutcheson had laid emphasis on 'moral excellence', on virtue as a state of character, on 'affections'. The primary object of the moral sense was for Hutcheson, as we saw, the kind or benevolent affections. But conscience and moral decision are concerned primarily with actions. So with Butler we can see a tendency to shift the emphasis from affections to actions, not, of course, actions considered merely as external actions but actions as informed by motives, as proceeding from human beings. And the more the emphasis is laid on actions, the more the assimilation of ethics to aesthetics retreats into the background.

Now, in the ethical theories of Shaftesbury and Hutcheson there were several latent potentialities. In the first place the idea of universal benevolence, when coupled with the idea of producing happiness, naturally leads to a utilitarian theory. And we have seen that there was an anticipation of utilitarianism in one aspect of Hutcheson's philosophy. This element was developed by other moralists whom we have considered. Thus, on the psychological side, Hartley and Tucker, using Locke's principle of association, tried to show how altruism and benevolence are possible, even if man seeks by nature his own satisfaction. Further, with Tucker, and still more with Paley, we find a theological utilitarianism. But when Paley emphasized, as a motive for acting altruistically, the thought of divine reward, he was adopting, of course, a point of view very different from that of Shaftesbury and Hutcheson.

In the second place we find in both Shaftesbury and Hutcheson, with their emphasis on virtue and character, a point of departure for an ethics based on the idea of the self-perfection of man or on the harmonious and complete development of human nature rather than on the principles of hedonistic utilitarianism. And in so far as Butler adumbrated the idea of a hierarchy of principles in man under the dominating authority of conscience, he helped to develop this idea. Further, Shaftesbury's idea of the correspondence between man, the microcosm, and the whole of which he forms a part was developed to some extent by Hutcheson, who linked up the idea with the idea of God. Here we have the introduction of metaphysical considerations and materials, as it were, for the development of an idealistic ethic. But it was the utilitarian element in the thinkers with whom we have dealt in this chapter[1] that was most influential. The impetus to a development of idealist ethics in the nineteenth century came from another source.

There was thus a considerable number of divergent elements and potentialities in the moral theories of the philosophers who have been mentioned in this chapter. But the overall picture is of the growth of moral philosophy as a separate subject of study, separated for the most part from theology and standing on its own feet, even though men such as Hutcheson and Butler tried, very naturally and properly, to link up their ethics with their theological beliefs. This interest in moral philosophy has remained one of the characteristic features of British thought.

[1] I do not mean to imply that Butler can properly be called a utilitarian. For the matter of that, it would be misleading to describe Hutcheson in this way.

CHAPTER XI

BERKELEY (1)

Life—Works—Spirit of Berkeley's thought—Theory of Vision.

1. GEORGE BERKELEY was born at Kilcrene near Kilkenny in Ireland on March 12th, 1685, his family being of English descent. In his eleventh year he was sent to Kilkenny College, and in March 1700 he entered Trinity College, Dublin, being then fifteen years old. After studying mathematics, languages, logic and philosophy he took his B.A. degree in 1704. In 1707 he published his *Arithmetica* and *Miscellanea mathematica*, and in June of that year he became a Fellow of the College. He had already begun to doubt the existence of matter, his interest in this subject having been stimulated by the study of Locke and Malebranche. In fulfilment of statutory requirements he was ordained deacon in 1709 and priest in 1710 in the Protestant Church and held various academic offices first as Junior Fellow and later, from 1717, as Senior Fellow. But in 1724 he obtained the post of dean of Derry and was thus compelled to resign his Fellowship. His residence at the college had not been without a break, of course. He had visited London, where he had made the acquaintance of Addison, Steele, Pope and other notables; and he had twice visited the Continent.

Soon after his installation as dean of Derry, Berkeley left for London in order to interest the Crown and government circles in his project of founding a college in the island of Bermuda for the education of the sons of English planters and of native Indians. He apparently envisaged English youths and Indians coming a very considerable distance from the mainland of America for general, and especially religious, education, after which they would return to the mainland. Berkeley succeeded in obtaining a charter and parliamentary approval of a proposed grant, and in 1728 he set sail with some companions for America and made his way to Newport in Rhode Island. Having become doubtful of the wisdom of his earlier plan, he made up his mind to apply for leave, once the grant was given, to build the projected college in Rhode Island rather than in Bermuda. But the money was not forthcoming, and Berkeley returned to England, reaching London at the end of October 1731.

After his return to England Berkeley waited in London, hoping for preferment, and in 1734 he was in fact appointed bishop of Cloyne. It is to this period of his life that there belongs his famous propaganda on behalf of the virtues of tar-water which he regarded as a panacea for human diseases. Whatever one may think of this specific remedy Berkeley's zeal for the relief of suffering is undoubted.

In 1745 Berkeley refused the offer of the more lucrative bishopric of Clogher, and in 1752 he settled at Oxford with his wife and family, where he took a house in Holywell Street. He died peacefully on January 14th, 1753, and was buried in Christ Church chapel, the cathedral of the diocese of Oxford.

2. Berkeley's most important philosophical works were written at an early period in his career, during his first years as a Fellow of Trinity College. *An Essay towards a New Theory of Vision* appeared in 1709. In this work Berkeley dealt with problems of vision, analysing, for example, the foundations of our judgments of distance, size and position. But though he was already convinced of the truth of immaterialism he did not express in the *Essay* the doctrine for which he is famous. This doctrine was put forward in *A Treatise concerning the Principles of Human Knowledge*, Part I, which was published in 1710, and in *Three Dialogues between Hylas and Philonous*, published in 1713. Preliminary work for the *Essay* and for the *Principles* was contained in Berkeley's notebooks which were written in 1707 and 1708. These were published by A. C. Fraser in 1871 under the title *Commonplace Book of occasional Metaphysical Thoughts* and by Professor A. A. Luce in 1944 under the title *Philosophical Commentaries*. In 1712 Berkeley published a pamphlet on *Passive Obedience*, in which he maintained the doctrine of passive obedience though he qualified it by admitting the right of revolt in extreme cases of tyranny.

Berkeley's Latin treatise *De motu* appeared in 1721, and in the same year he published *An Essay towards preventing the Ruin of Great Britain* which contained a call to religion, industry, frugality and public spirit in view of the calamities caused by the South Sea Bubble. While he was in America he wrote *Alciphron or the Minute Philosopher*, which he published in London in 1732. Comprising seven dialogues, it is the longest of his books and is essentially a work of Christian apologetic, directed against freethinkers. In 1733 appeared *The Theory of Vision or Visual Language showing the immediate Presence and Providence of a Deity*

Vindicated and Explained in answer to a newspaper criticism of the *Essay*; and in 1734 Berkeley published *The Analyst or a Discourse addressed to an Infidel Mathematician* in which he attacked Newton's theory of fluxions and argued that if there are mysteries in mathematics it is only reasonable to expect them in religion. A Dr. Jurin published a reply, and Berkeley retorted with *A Defence of Free-thinking in Mathematics*, published in 1735.

In 1745 Berkeley published two letters, one addressed to his own flock, the other to the Catholics in the diocese of Cloyne. In the latter he urged non-participation in the Jacobite rising. His ideas about the question of an Irish bank appeared anonymously at Dublin in three parts in 1735, 1736 and 1737 under the title of *The Querist*. Berkeley took a considerable interest in Irish affairs, and in 1749 he addressed *A Word to the Wise* to the Catholic clergy of the country, urging them to join in a movement for the promotion of better social and economic conditions. In connection with his propaganda on behalf of the virtues of tar-water, he published in 1744 *Siris*, a work which also contained a certain amount of philosophy. His last known writing was *Farther Thoughts on Tar-water*, included as the opening piece in his *Miscellany*, published in 1752.

3. Berkeley's philosophy is exciting in the sense that a brief statement of it (for instance, there exist only God, finite spirits and the ideas of spirits) makes it appear so remote from the ordinary man's view of the world that it arrests the attention. How, we may wonder, could an eminent philosopher think himself justified in denying the existence of matter? Indeed, when Berkeley published the *Principles of Human Knowledge* he not unnaturally became the target of criticism and even of ridicule. To many minds it appeared that he had denied what was most obvious, so obvious that no ordinary man would call it in question, and asserted what was by no means so obvious. Such a philosophy was nothing but a fantastic extravagance. Its author might be mentally unbalanced, as some thought, or a hunter after paradoxical novelties or a humorous Irishman perpetrating an elaborate joke. But nobody who believed or who affected to believe that houses and tables and trees and mountains were the ideas of spirits or minds could reasonably expect other men to share his opinions. Some conceded that Berkeley's arguments were ingenious and subtle and difficult to refute. At the same time there must be something wrong with arguments which led to such

paradoxical conclusions. Others thought that it was easy to refute Berkeley's position. Their reaction to his philosophy is well symbolized by Dr. Samuel Johnson's famous refutation. The learned doctor kicked a great stone, exclaiming, 'I refute him thus.'

Berkeley himself, however, was very far from regarding his philosophy as a piece of extravagant fantasy, contrary to common sense, or even as being at variance with the spontaneous convictions of the ordinary man. On the contrary, he was convinced that he was on the side of common sense, and he explicitly classed himself with 'the vulgar' as distinct from the professors and, in his opinion, misguided metaphysicians who propounded strange and bizarre doctrines. In his notebooks we read the significant entry: 'Mem: To be eternally banishing metaphysics, etc., and recalling men to common sense.'[1] One may not, indeed, be inclined to regard Berkeley's philosophy as a whole as being an example of banishing metaphysics; but his denial of Locke's theory of occult material substance was certainly for him an example of this activity. And he did not regard his doctrine that bodies or sensible objects are dependent on perceiving minds as incompatible with the views of the ordinary man. True, the latter would say that the table exists and is present in the room even when there is nobody there to perceive it. But Berkeley would reply that he has no wish to deny that the table can be said to exist in some sense when there is nobody in the room to perceive it. The question is not whether the statement is true or false, but in what sense it is true. What does it mean to say that the table is in the room when nobody is present and perceiving it? What can it mean except that if someone were to enter the room, he would have the experience which we call seeing a table? Would not the ordinary man argue that this is what he means when he says that the table is in the room even when nobody is perceiving it? I do not suggest that the matter is as simple as these questions may seem to imply. Nor do I wish to commit myself to Berkeley's view. But I wish to indicate very briefly in advance how the latter could maintain that opinions which his contemporaries were inclined to look on as fantastic were in point of fact quite consonant with common sense.

[1] *Philosophical Commentaries*, 751; 1, p. 91. References to Berkeley's writings by volume and page are to the critical edition of his Works by Professors A. A. Luce and T. E. Jessop. The *Philosophical Commentaries* will be referred to as P.C.; the *Essay towards a New Theory of Vision* as E.; the *Principles of Human Knowledge* as P.; the *Three Dialogues* as D.; the *De motu* as D.M.; *Alciphron* as A.

Mention has just been made of the question, what does it mean to say of a body or sensible thing that it exists when it is not actually perceived? Berkeley was not only one of those philosophers who are capable of writing their own language well: he was also greatly concerned with the meanings and uses of words. This is, of course, one of the principal reasons for the interest which is taken in his writings today by British philosophers. For they see in him a precursor of the movement of linguistic analysis. Berkeley insisted, for example, on the need for an accurate analysis of the term 'existence'. Thus in his notebooks he remarks that many ancient philosophers ran into absurdities because they did not know what existence was. But ''tis on the discovering of the nature and meaning and import of Existence that I chiefly insist'.[1] In Berkeley's view the conclusion, *Esse est percipi*, was the result of an accurate analysis of the term 'exist' when we say that sensible things exist. Again, Berkeley gave particular attention to the meaning and use of abstract terms, such as those occurring in the Newtonian scientific theories. And his analysis of their use enabled him to anticipate views about the status of scientific theories which have later become common coin. Scientific theories are hypotheses, and it is a mistake to think that because a scientific hypothesis 'works', it must necessarily be the expression of the human mind's natural power of penetrating the ultimate structure of reality and attaining final truth. Further, terms such as 'gravity', 'attraction', and so on, certainly have their uses; but it is one thing to say that they possess instrumentalist value and quite another thing to say that they connote occult entities or qualities. The use of abstract words, though it cannot be avoided, tends to contaminate physics with metaphysics and to give us a wrong idea of the status and function of physical theories.

But though Berkeley spoke about banishing metaphysics and recalling men to common sense, he was himself a metaphysician. He thought, for example, that, given his account of the existence and nature of material things, it follows with certainty that God exists. There is no material substance (Locke's occult and un-known substratum) to support the qualities which Berkeley called 'ideas'. Material things can therefore be reduced to clusters of ideas. But ideas cannot exist on their own apart from some mind. At the same time it is obvious that there is a difference between the ideas which we frame for ourselves, creatures of the imagination (for

---

[1] *P.C.*, 491; I, pp. 61-2.

instance, the idea of a mermaid or of a unicorn), and the phenomena or 'ideas' which a man perceives in normal circumstances
and conditions during his waking life. I can create an imaginative
world of my own; but it does not depend on me what I see when I
raise my eyes from my book and look out of the window. These
'ideas' must, therefore, be presented to me by a mind or spirit;
that is to say, by God. This is not exactly how Berkeley expresses
the matter; but it will suffice as a brief indication of the fact that
in his view phenomenalism entails theism. Whether it does or not is,
of course, another question. But Berkeley thought that it does; and
this is one reason why he considered that belief in God is a matter
of plain common sense. If we take a common-sense view of the
existence and nature of material things, we shall be led to affirm
the existence of God. Conversely, belief in material substance
promotes atheism.

This is a matter of some importance if we are considering the
spirit of Berkeley's philosophizing. For he made it quite plain that
he regarded his criticism of material substance as serving to pave
the way for an acceptance of theism in general and of Christianity
in particular. As has been said, his philosophy was looked on by
many contemporaries as a fantastic extravagance. And his willing-
ness to sacrifice a career in the Protestant Church in Ireland[1] in
order to carry out his Bermuda project was considered by some
as a symptom of madness. But his immaterialistic philosophy and
his Bermuda project reveal the same character and bent of mind
which are revealed in another way in his concern for the sufferings
of the Irish poor and in his enthusiastic propaganda for the virtues
of tar-water. Whatever value may be attached to his philosophy
and whichever elements in it may be stressed by later generations
of philosophers, his own estimate of it is admirably summarized
in the closing words of the *Principles*. 'For after all, what deserves
the first place in our studies, is the consideration of God, and our
duty; which to promote, as it was the main drift and design of my
labours, so shall I esteem them altogether useless and ineffectual,
if by what I have said I cannot inspire my readers with a pious
sense of the presence of God: and having shown the falseness or
vanity of those barren speculations, which make the chief employment of learned men, the better dispose them to reverence and

---

[1] Berkeley was not, indeed, indifferent to ecclesiastical preferment. And he had
a family to maintain. But his plans for the evangelization of America, however
abortive they may have proved, reveal him as an idealist, certainly not as a place-
hunter.

embrace the salutary truths of the Gospel, which to know and to practise is the highest perfection of human nature.'[1]

Berkeley was thus quite explicit about the practical function of his philosophy. The full title of the *Principles* is *A Treatise concerning the Principles of Human Knowledge, wherein the chief causes of error and difficulty in the Sciences, with the grounds of Scepticism, Atheism and Irreligion, are inquired into*. Similarly, the aim of the *Three Dialogues* is said to be 'plainly to demonstrate the reality and perfection of human knowledge, the incorporeal nature of the soul and the immediate providence of a Deity, in opposition to sceptics and atheists'.[2] But the conclusion should not be drawn from these and similar declarations that Berkeley's philosophy is so coloured by preconceptions and preoccupations of a religious and apologetic character that it has nothing of value to offer for philosophical reflection. He was a serious philosopher; and whether one agrees or not with the arguments which he employed and the conclusions at which he arrived, his lines of thought are well worth consideration, and the problems which he raised are of interest and importance. In general, he is remarkable as an empiricist who was also a metaphysician and a phenomenalist who did not think that phenomenalism has the last word in philosophy. His philosophy may, of course, appear to be a hybrid. It inevitably appears in this light if we regard it simply as a stepping-stone on the way from Locke to Hume. But it is, I think, of interest for its own sake.

4. It has already been mentioned that Berkeley did not give his immaterialist philosophy to the world without having made some effort to prepare men's minds for its reception. For though he was convinced of the truth of his views and of their compatibility with common sense, he was aware that his statements would appear strange and bizarre to many readers. He sought, therefore, to prepare the way for the *Principles of Human Knowledge* by publishing first his *Essay towards a New Theory of Vision*.

It would be a mistake, however, to imagine that this *Essay* was merely a device for predisposing men's minds to accord a sympathetic hearing to what Berkeley intended to say in later publications. It is a serious study of a number of problems connected with perception, and it is of interest for its own sake, quite apart from its prefatory function. The construction of optical instruments had stimulated the development of theories of optics.

---

[1] *P.*, 1, 156; 11, p. 113.   [2] *D.*, sub-title; 11, p. 147.

A number of works had already appeared, such as Barrow's
Optical Lectures (1669); and in the *Essay* Berkeley made his own
contribution to the subject. His aim, as expressed in his own
words, was 'to show the manner wherein we perceive by sight the
distance, magnitude, and situation of objects. Also to consider the
difference there is betwixt the ideas of sight and touch, and whether
there be any idea common to both senses.'[1]

Berkeley assumes as agreed that we do not immediately perceive distance of itself. 'It remains therefore that it be brought
into view by means of some other idea that is itself immediately
perceived in the act of vision.'[2] But Berkeley rejects the current
geometrical explanation by means of lines and angles. For one
thing, experience does not support the notion that we compute or
judge distance by geometrical calculation. For another thing, the
lines and angles referred to are hypotheses framed by mathematicians with a view to treating optics geometrically. Instead of
the geometrical explanation Berkeley offers suggestions on these
lines. When I am looking at a near object with both eyes, the
interval between my pupils is lessened or widened according as the
object approaches or recedes. And this alteration in the eyes is
accompanied by sensations. The result is that an association is
set up between the different sensations and different distances.
Thus the sensations act as intermediate 'ideas' in the perception of
distance. Again, if an object is placed at a certain distance from
the eye and is then made to approach, it is seen more confusedly.
And thus 'there ariseth in the mind an habitual connection between the several degrees of confusion and distance; the greater
confusion still implying the lesser distance, and the lesser confusion the greater distance of the object'.[3] But when an object,
placed at a certain distance from the eye, is brought nearer, we
can, for some time at least, prevent its appearance becoming
confused by straining the eye. And the sensation accompanying
the effort of strain helps us to judge the distance of the object. The
greater the effort of straining the eye, the nearer is the object.

As for our perception of the magnitude or size of sensible
objects, we must first distinguish between two sorts of objects
apprehended by sight. Some are properly and immediately visible;
others do not fall immediately under the sense of sight but are
rather tangible objects, and these are seen only mediately, by
means of what is directly visible. Each sort of object has its own

[1] *E.*, 1; II, p. 171.   [2] *E.*, 11; II, p. 173.   [3] *E.*, 21; II, p. 175.

distinct magnitude or extension. For example, when I look at the moon, I see directly a coloured disc. The moon, as a visible object, is greater when it is situated on the horizon than when it is situated on the meridian. But we do not think of the magnitude of the moon, when it is considered as a tangible object, as changing in this way. 'The magnitude of the object, which exists without the mind, and is at a distance, continues always invariably the same. But the visible object still changing as you approach to, or recede from, the tangible object, it hath no fixed and determinate great-ness. Whenever, therefore, we speak of the magnitude of anything, for instance a tree or a house, we must mean the tangible magni-tude, otherwise there can be nothing steady and free from ambiguity spoken of it.'[1] 'Whenever we say an object is great or small, of this or that determinate measure, I say it must be meant of the tangible, and not the visible extension which, though immediately perceived, is nevertheless taken little notice of.'[2] The magnitude of tangible objects, however, is not directly perceived; it is judged by the visible magnitude, according to the confusion or distinctness, faintness or vigour, of the visible appearances. There is, indeed, no necessary connection between visible magni-tude and tangible magnitude. For instance, a tower and a man, when situated at appropriate distances, might have more or less the same visible magnitude. But we do not on that account judge that they have the same tangible magnitude. Our judgment is affected by a variety of experimental factors. This does not, how-ever, alter the fact that before we touch an object its tangible magnitude is suggested by its visible magnitude, though the latter has no necessary connection with the former. 'As we see distance, so we see magnitude. And we see both in the same way that we see shame or anger in the looks of a man. Those passions are them-selves invisible, they are nevertheless let in by the eye along with colours and alterations of countenance, which are the immediate object of vision: and which signify them for no other reason than barely because they have been observed to accompany them. Without experience we should no more have taken blushing for a sign of shame than of gladness.'[3]

Berkeley's ideas about visual perception were by no means all original. But he utilized the ideas which he borrowed in the con-struction of a carefully worked out theory which, apart from particular points of value, possess the great merit of being the

[1] *E.*, 55; II, p. 191.   [2] *E.*, 61; II, p. 194.   [3] *E.*, 65; II, p. 195.

result of reflection, with the aid of particular examples, on the ways in which we do as a matter of fact perceive distance, magnitude and situation. He had, of course, no wish to question the utility of a mathematical theory of optics; but it was clear to him that in ordinary visual perception we do not judge distance and size by mathematical calculations. We can, indeed, employ mathematics to determine distances; but this process obviously presupposes the ordinary visual perception of which Berkeley is speaking.

It is unnecessary to enter here into further details of Berkeley's account of perception. The point to notice is the distinction which he makes between sight and touch and between their respective objects. We have already seen that he distinguishes between objects which are, properly speaking, the objects of sight or vision and objects which are only mediately objects of visual perception. Visible magnitude or extension is distinct from tangible extension. But we can go further and say, in general, that 'there is no idea common to both senses'.[1] That this is so can be easily shown. The immediate objects of sight are light and colours, and there is no other immediate object.[2] But light and colours are not perceived by touch. Hence there are no immediate objects common to both senses. It may seem perhaps that Berkeley is contradicting himself when he says that the only immediate objects of sight are light and colours, though at the same time he speaks of visible extension. But what we see are colour-patches, as it were extended colours. And visible extension, visible as patches of colour, is, Berkeley insists, entirely distinct from tangible extension.

It may be said that to assert the heterogeneity of the objects of sight and touch is to assert a truism. Everyone knows, for example, that we perceive colours by sight and not by touch. We say, for instance, that a thing looks green, and not that it feels green. All of us are just as much aware that light and colours are the proper objects of sight as we are that sounds are heard and not smelt. But in insisting on the heterogeneity of the objects of sight and touch Berkeley has an ulterior aim. For he wishes to maintain that visual objects, the 'ideas of sight', are symbols or signs which suggest to us tangible ideas. There is no necessary connection between the two; but 'these signs are constant and universal, (and) their connection with tangible ideas has been learnt at our first entrance into the world'.[3] 'Upon the whole, I think we may fairly conclude that the proper objects of vision constitute an

---

[1] E., 129; II, p. 223.   [2] Ibid.   [3] E., 144; II, p. 229.

universal language of the Author of nature, whereby we are instructed how to regulate our actions in order to attain those things that are necessary to the preservation and well-being of our bodies, as also to avoid whatever may be hurtful and destructive of them. . . . And the manner wherein they signify and mark unto us the objects which are at a distance is the same with that of languages and signs of human appointment, which do not suggest the things signified by any likeness or identity of nature, but only by an habitual connection that experience has made us to observe between them.'[1]

The words 'signify and mark unto us the objects which are at a distance' should be noted. The implication is that the objects of sight or vision are not at a distance. That is to say, they are in some sense within the mind, not 'out there'. Berkeley has already implied this by remarking that 'the magnitude of the object which exists without the mind and is at a distance, continues always the same',[2] and by contrasting this external and tangible object with the visible object. The objects of sight are in some sense within the mind, and they act as signs or symbols of objects outside the mind, tangible objects.

This distinction between visible and tangible objects is not compatible with the view afterwards maintained in the *Principles*, that all sensible objects are 'ideas', existing in some sense within the mind. But this does not mean that Berkeley changed his view in the interval between writing the *Essay* and writing the *Principles*. It means rather that in the *Essay* he wishes to give only a partial version of his general theory. He speaks, therefore, as though visible objects were in the mind and tangible objects outside the mind. In the *Principles*, however, all sensible objects are brought within the mind, and it is no longer objects of sight alone which constitute a language determined by God. In other words, in the *Essay*, where he is primarily discussing a number of particular problems connected with perception, he introduces the reader to a part only of his general theory, and then only incidentally, whereas in the *Principles* he expounds the general theory. It should be added that even on Berkeley's general theory problems connected with our perception of distance, magnitude and situation can still be raised; but distance and situation can be, of course, only relative, and not absolute, if there are no mind-independent material things.

[1] *E.*, 147; II, p. 231.   [2] *E.*, 55; II. p. 191.

CHAPTER XII

BERKELEY (2)

Words and their meanings—Abstract general ideas—The esse
of sensible things is percipi—*Sensible things are ideas—
Material substance is a meaningless term—The reality of
sensible things—Berkeley and the representative theory of
perception.*

1. In the last chapter attention was drawn to Berkeley's concern
with language and with the meanings of words. In the *Philosophical Commentaries*, that is, in his notebooks, he remarks that
mathematics has this advantage over metaphysics and ethics, that
mathematical definitions are definitions of words not yet known
to the learner, so that their meaning is not disputed, whereas the
terms defined in metaphysics and ethics are for the most part
already known, with the result that any attempt to define them
may meet with preconceived ideas and prejudices about their
meanings.[1] Further, in many cases we may understand what is
meant by a term used in philosophy and yet be unable to give a
clear account of its meaning or define it. 'I may clearly and fully
understand my own soul, extension, etc., and not be able to define
them.'[2] And he attributes difficulty in defining and talking clearly
about things to 'the fault and scantiness of language' as much as
to confusion of thought.[3]

Linguistic analysis is, therefore, of importance in philosophy.
'We are frequently puzzled and at a loss in obtaining clear and
determined meanings of words commonly in use.'[4] It is not words
such as 'thing' or 'substance' which have caused mistakes so much
as 'the not reflecting on their meaning. I will be still for retaining
the words. I only desire that men would think before they speak
and settle the meaning of their words.'[5] 'The chief thing I do or
pretend to do is only to remove the mist or veil of words. This has
occasioned ignorance and confusion. This has ruined the Schoolmen and mathematicians, lawyers and divines.'[6] Some words do
not express any meaning, that is to say, their supposed meaning
vanishes under analysis; they are seen not to refer to anything.

[1] *P.C.*, 162; I, p. 22. [2] *P.C.*, 178; I, p. 24. [3] *Ibid.*
[4] *P.C.*, 591; I, p. 73. [5] *P.C.*, 553; I, p. 69. [6] *P.C.*, 642; I, p. 78.

'We have learned from Mr. Locke that there may be and that there are several glib, coherent, methodical discourses which nevertheless amount to just nothing.'[1] An example of Berkeley's meaning is given by a jotting expressing an idea which evidently occurred to him, though he did not develop it and indeed rejected the point of view to which he alludes. 'Say you the mind is not the perceptions but that thing which perceives. I answer you are abused by the words "that" and "thing"; these are vague, empty words without a meaning.'[2] We need analysis, therefore, to determine meanings when these are not clear and to reveal the meaninglessness of non-significant terms.

Berkeley applied this line of thought to Locke's doctrine of material substance. One can say that his attack on Locke's theory took the form of an analysis of material-object sentences. He argued that analysis of the meaning of sentences containing the names of sensible objects or bodies does not support the view that there is any material substance in Locke's sense, that is to say, a hidden and unknowable substrate. Things are simply what we perceive them to be, and we perceive no Lockean substance or substrate. Statements about sensible things can be analysed in terms of phenomena or translated into statements about phenomena. We can talk about substances if we simply mean things as we perceive them, but the term 'material substance' does not signify anything distinct from and underlying phenomena.

The whole matter is complicated, of course, by Berkeley's doctrine that sensible things are 'ideas'. But this doctrine can be left aside for the moment. And if we look at his procedure from one point of view only, we can say that for Berkeley those who believe in material substance have been misled by words. Because we predicate qualities of a rose, for example, philosophers such as Locke have been inclined to think that there must be some invisible substance which supports the perceived qualities. But Berkeley argues, as will be seen later, that no clear meaning can be attached to the word 'supports' in this context. He does not wish to deny that there are substances in any sense of the word, but only in the philosophical sense. 'I take not away substances. I ought not to be accused of discarding substance out of the reasonable world. I only reject the philosophic sense (which in effect is no sense) of the word "substance". . . .'[3]

Again, as we saw in the last chapter, Berkeley insisted on the

[1] *P.C.*, 492; I, p. 62.   [2] *P.C.*, 581; I, p. 72.   [3] *P.C.*, 517; I, p. 64.

need for a clear analysis of the word 'existence'. When he says of sensible things that their existence is to be perceived (*esse est percipi*), he does not intend to say that it is untrue that they exist; he is concerned to give the meaning of the statement that sensible things exist. 'Let it not be said that I take away Existence. I only declare the meaning of the word so far as I can comprehend it.'[1]

These remarks about language in the *Philosophical Commentaries* find their echo, of course, in the *Principles of Human Knowledge*; for the former contained preparatory material for the latter, as well as for the *Essay towards a New Theory of Vision*. In his introduction to the *Principles* Berkeley remarks that in order to prepare the mind of the reader for understanding his doctrine about the first principles of knowledge it is proper to say something first 'concerning the nature and abuse of language'.[2] And he has some interesting observations to make about the function of language. It is commonly supposed, he says, that the chief and indeed only function of language is the communication of ideas marked by words. But this is certainly not the case. 'There are other ends, as the raising of some passion, the exciting to, or deterring from an action, the putting the mind in some particular disposition; to which the former (that is, the communication of ideas) is in many cases barely subservient, and sometimes entirely omitted, when these can be obtained without it, as I think both not infrequently happen in the familiar use of language.'[3] Here Berkeley draws attention to the emotive use or uses of language. It is necessary, he thinks, to distinguish the various functions or purposes of language and of particular kinds of words and to discriminate between controversies which are purely verbal and those which are not, if one is to avoid 'being imposed on by words'.[4] This is obviously excellent advice.

2. It is in the setting of these general remarks about language that Berkeley discusses abstract general ideas. His contention is that there are no such things, though he is prepared to admit general ideas in some sense. 'It is to be noted that I do not deny absolutely there are general ideas, but only that there are any *abstract general ideas*.'[5] But this contention stands in need of some explanation.

In the first place there are no abstract general ideas, the

---

[1] *P.C.*, 593; I, p. 74.
[3] *Ibid.*, 20; II, p. 37.
[5] *Ibid.*, 12; II, p. 31.

[2] *P.*, Introduction, 6; II, p. 27.
[4] *Ibid.*, 24; II, p. 40.

emphasis being on the word 'abstract'. Berkeley is primarily concerned with refuting Locke's theory of abstract ideas. He mentions the Schoolmen too; but it is Locke whom he quotes. Further, he takes Locke to mean that we can form abstract general images, and he has, of course, no difficulty in refuting Locke's position when it is so understood. 'The idea of man that I frame to myself must be either of a white, or a black, or a tawny, a straight, or a crooked, a tall, or a low, or a middle-sized man. I cannot by any effort of thought conceive the abstract idea above described.'[1] I cannot, that is to say, frame an image of man which both omits and includes all the particular characteristics of real individual men. Similarly, 'what more easy than for anyone to look a little into his own thoughts, and there try whether he has, or can attain to have, an idea that shall correspond with the description that is here given of the general idea of a triangle, which is *neither oblique, nor rectangle, equilateral, equicrural, nor scalenon, but all and none of these at once?*'[2] I cannot have an idea (that is, an image) of a triangle which includes all the characteristics of different types of triangles and which at the same time is itself not classifiable as the image of a particular type of triangle.

This last illustration is taken directly from Locke, who speaks about forming the general idea of a triangle which 'must be neither oblique, nor rectangle, neither equilateral, equicrural, nor scalenon; but all and none of these at once'.[3] But Locke's accounts of abstraction and its products are not always consistent. Elsewhere he says that 'ideas become general by separating from them the circumstances of time, and place, and any other ideas, that may determine them to this or that particular existence. By this way of abstraction they are made capable of representing more individuals than one. . . .'[4] And he tells us that in the general idea of man the characteristics of individual men as individuals are omitted, only those characteristics being retained which all men have in common. Moreover, though Locke sometimes implies that abstract general ideas are images, he does not by any means always do so. Berkeley, however, who is himself speaking throughout of ideas of objects presented in sense-perception, persists in interpreting Locke as though the latter were speaking of abstract general images. And it is easy for him to show that there are no

---

[1] *P.*, Introduction, 10; II, p. 29.   [2] *Ibid.*, 13; II, p. 33.
[3] *Essay concerning Human Understanding*, 4, 7, 9.   [4] *Ibid.*, 3, 3, 6.

such things. True, he seems to suppose that composite images must be clearer than they are; but this does not alter the fact that there cannot be, for instance, an abstract general image of a triangle which fulfils all the conditions mentioned above. Nor, to take another example given by Berkeley, can we have an idea (image) of motion without a moving body and without any determinate direction or velocity.[1] But if we consider that part of Berkeley's theory which consists in an exegesis of Locke, we must say, I think, that he was definitely unfair to the latter, however much some admirers of the good bishop may have tried to dispose of this charge.

As we have seen, Berkeley appeals to introspection. And a natural comment to make is that on looking into his mind for abstract general ideas he sees only images and proceeds to identify the image with the idea. And as even the composite image is still a particular image, though it can be made to stand for a number of particular things, he denies the existence of abstract general ideas. This may, indeed, be true to a great extent; but Berkeley did not admit that we have universal ideas, if by this it is meant that we can have ideas, with a positive universal content, of sensory qualities which cannot be given alone in perception (such as motion without a moving body) or of purely general sensory qualities such as colour. If he had been accused of confusing images with ideas, he might have replied by challenging his critic to show that there are any abstract general ideas. It must be remembered that in Berkeley's philosophy 'essences' go by the board.

How, then, can Berkeley say that though he denies abstract general ideas he does not intend to deny general ideas absolutely? His view is that 'an idea, which considered in itself is particular, becomes general by being made to represent or stand for all other particular ideas of the same sort'.[2] Thus universality does not consist 'in the absolute, positive nature or conception of anything, but in the relation it bears to the particulars signified or represented by it'.[3] I can attend to this or that aspect of a thing; and if this is what is meant by abstraction, abstraction is obviously possible. 'It must be acknowledged that a man may consider a figure merely as triangular, without attending to the particular qualities of the angles, or relations of the sides. . . . In like manner

[1] *P.*, Introduction, 11; II, p. 31.   [2] *Ibid.*, 12; II, p. 32.
[3] *Ibid.*, 15; II, pp. 33-4.

we may consider Peter so far forth as man, or so far forth as animal. . . .'[1] If I consider Peter only in relation to the characteristics which he possesses in common with animals, abstracting or prescinding from the characteristics which he possesses in common with other men but not with animals, my idea of Peter can be made to represent or stand for all animals. In this sense it becomes a general idea; but universality belongs to it only in its function of representing or standing for. Considered in itself, with regard to its positive content, the idea is a particular idea.

If there are no abstract general ideas, it follows that reasoning must be about particulars. It obviously cannot be about abstract general ideas if there are none. The geometer makes a particular triangle stand for or represent all triangles, by attending to its triangularity rather than to its particular characteristics. And in this case properties demonstrated of this particular triangle are held to be demonstrated of all triangles. But the geometer is not demonstrating properties of the abstract general idea of triangularity; for there is no such thing. His reasoning is about particulars, and its universal scope is made possible by the power we have of rendering a particular idea universal, not by its positive content, but in virtue of a representative function.

Berkeley does not, of course, deny that there are general words. But he rejects Locke's theory that general words denote, as he says, general ideas, if we mean by this ideas which possess a positive universal content. A proper name, such as William, signifies a particular thing, while a general word signifies indifferently a plurality of things of a certain kind. Its universality is a matter of use or function. If we once understand this, we shall be saved from hunting for mysterious entities corresponding to general words. We can utter the term 'material substance', but it does not denote any abstract general idea; and if we suppose that because we can frame the term it must signify an entity apart from the objects of perception, we are misled by words. Berkeley's nominalism is thus of importance in his attack on Locke's theory of material substance. 'Matter' is not a name in the way in which William is a name, though some philosophers seem to have thought mistakenly that it is.

3. Already at the beginning of the *Principles* Berkeley speaks about sensory objects of knowledge as 'ideas'. But it will perhaps be better to leave aside this complicated subject for the moment

---

[1] *P.*, Introduction, 16; II, p. 35.

and to start with an approach to the theory that sensory objects have no absolute existence of their own apart from their being perceived, which does not necessarily involve talking about these objects as 'ideas'.

According to Berkeley, anyone can have knowledge of the fact that sensible things do not and cannot exist independently of being perceived if he attends to the meaning of the term 'exist' when applied to these things. 'The table I write on, I say, exists, that is, I see and feel it; and if I were out of my study I should say it existed, meaning thereby that if I was in my study I might perceive it, or that some other spirit actually does perceive it.'[1] Berkeley thus challenges the reader to find any other meaning for the proposition, 'the table exists', than 'the table is perceived or perceivable'. It is perfectly true to say, as any ordinary man would say, that the table exists when nobody is in the room. But what can this mean, asks Berkeley, save that if I were to enter the room I should perceive the table or that if another person were to enter the room he or she would, or could, perceive the table? Even if I try to imagine the table existing out of all relation to perception, I necessarily imagine myself or someone else perceiving it; that is to say, I covertly introduce a percipient subject, though I may not advert to the fact that I am doing so. Berkeley can say, therefore, that 'the absolute existence of unthinking things without any relation to their being perceived, that seems perfectly unintelligible. Their *esse* is *percipi*, nor is it possible they should have any existence out of the minds or thinking things which perceive them.'[2]

Berkeley's contention, therefore, is that to say of a sensible thing or body that it exists is to say that it is perceived or perceivable: in his opinion, there is nothing else that it can mean. This analysis, he maintains, does not affect the reality of things. 'Existence is *percipi* or *percipere*. The horse is in the stable, the books are in the study as before.'[3] In other words, he does not assert that it is untrue to say that the horse is in the stable when there is nobody about: he is concerned with the meaning of the statement. The following note has already been quoted, but it is worth re-quoting. 'Let it not be said that I take away Existence. I only declare the meaning of the word so far as I can comprehend it.'[4] Further, Berkeley considers that his analysis of existential statements about sensible things is in accordance with the outlook

[1] *P.*, I, 3; II, p. 42.   [2] *Ibid.*   [3] *P.C.*, 429; I, p. 53.   [4] *P.C.*, 593; I, p. 74.

of the plain man whose mind has not been misled by metaphysical abstractions.

It might well be objected, of course, that though the ordinary man would certainly agree that to say that the horse is in the stable when nobody is about means that if someone enters the stable he would or could have the experience which we call seeing a horse, he would boggle at the statement that the horse's existence is to be perceived. For when he admits that to say that the horse is in the stable 'means' that if someone entered the stable he would or could perceive a horse, he really only intends to say that the second statement is a consequence of the first. If the horse is in the stable, then anyone with normal eyesight who enters the stable can perceive the horse, given the other requisite conditions for perception. But it does not follow that the horse's existence consists in being perceived. Berkeley's position, however, seems to approach very closely to that of some of the modern neopositivists when they maintained that the meaning of an empirical statement is identical with the mode of its verification. To enter the stable and perceive the horse is a way of verifying the statement that there is a horse in the stable. And when Berkeley says that the latter statement can only mean that if a percipient subject enters the stable, he will have or could have certain sensory experiences, this seems to be another way of saying that the meaning of the statement that there is a horse in the stable is identical with the mode of its verification. This is not, of course, an adequate account of his view. For it omits all mention not only of his theory that sensible objects are ideas but also of his subsequent introduction of God as a universal and omnipresent perceiver. But as far as the linguistic analysis aspect of his doctrine goes, there does seem to be some similarity between his position and that of a number of modern neopositivists. And Berkeley's position is subject to the same sort of criticism which can be brought against the view of the neopositivists in question.[1]

Before we go any further it may be as well to draw attention to the two following points. First, when Berkeley says *esse est percipi*, he is talking only about sensible things or objects. Secondly, the full formula is, *esse est aut percipi aut percipere*, existence is either to be perceived or to perceive. Besides sensible 'unthinking' things, the existence of which consists in being perceived, there

---

[1] Cf., for example, Chapters III and IV of my *Contemporary Philosophy* (London, Burns and Oates, 1956).

are minds or percipient subjects, which are active and whose existence is to perceive rather than to be perceived.

4. Already in the *Philosophical Commentaries* we can find a statement of Berkeley's theory that sensible things are ideas or collections of ideas and of the conclusion which he draws, namely, that they cannot exist independently of minds. 'All significant words stand for ideas. All knowledge (is) about our ideas. All ideas come from without or from within.'[1] In the first case the ideas are called sensations, in the second, thoughts. To perceive is to have an idea. When, therefore, we perceive colours, for example, we are perceiving ideas. And as these ideas come from without, they are sensations. But 'no sensation can be in a senseless thing'.[2] Therefore ideas such as colours cannot inhere in material substance, an inert substrate. Hence it is quite unnecessary to postulate such a substance. 'Nothing like an idea can be in an unperceiving thing.'[3] To be perceived implies dependence on a perceiver. And to exist means either to perceive or to be perceived. 'Nothing properly but persons, i.e. conscious things, do exist; all other things are not so much existence as manners of the existence of persons.'[4] To show, therefore, that sensible objects are ideas is one of Berkeley's chief ways, if not the chief way, of showing the truth of the statement that the existence of these objects is to be perceived and of ruling out Locke's theory of material substance.

In the *Principles* Berkeley speaks of sensible things as collections or combinations of 'sensations or ideas' and draws the conclusion that they 'cannot exist otherwise than in a mind perceiving them'.[5] But though he asserts that it is evident that the objects of our knowledge are ideas,[6] he feels that this doctrine is not altogether in accordance with what most people believe. For he remarks that 'it is indeed an opinion strangely prevailing amongst men, that houses, mountains, rivers, and in a word all sensible objects have an existence natural or real, distinct from their being perceived by the understanding'.[7] But this strangely prevalent opinion is, none the less, a manifest contradiction. 'For what are the aforementioned objects but the things we perceive by sense, and what do we perceive besides our own ideas or sensations; and is it not plainly repugnant that any one of these or any combination of them should exist unperceived?'[8] The notion that these things can exist on their own, without relation to perception, 'will,

[1] *P.C.*, 378; I, p. 45.   [2] *Ibid.*   [3] *Ibid.*   [4] *P.C.*, 24; I, p. 10.
[5] *P.*, I, 3; II, p. 42.   [6] *P.*, I, I; II, p. 41.   [7] *P.*, I, 4; II, p. 42.   [8] *Ibid.*

perhaps, be found at bottom to depend on the doctrine of *abstrac. ideas*. For can there be a nicer strain of abstraction than to distinguish the existence of sensible objects from their being perceived, so as to conceive them existing unperceived?'[1]

Of course, if sensible things are ideas in the ordinary sense of the word, it is evident that they cannot exist apart from some mind. But what is the justification for calling them ideas? One line of argument pursued by Berkeley runs as follows. Some people make a distinction between secondary qualities, such as colour, sound and taste, and primary qualities, such as extension and figure. They admit that the former, as perceived, are not resemblances of anything existing outside the mind. They admit, in other words, their subjective character, that they are ideas. 'But they will have our ideas of the primary qualities to be patterns or images of things which exist without the mind, in an unthinking substance which they call *matter*. By matter therefore we are to understand an inert, senseless substance, in which extension, figure, and motion, do actually subsist.'[2] But this distinction will not do. It is impossible to conceive primary entirely apart from secondary qualities. 'Extension, figure, and motion, abstracted from all other qualities, are inconceivable.'[3] Further, if, as Locke thought, the relativity of secondary qualities provides a valid argument for their subjectivity, the same sort of argument can be employed with regard to the primary qualities. Figure or shape, for example, depends on the position of the perceiver, while motion is either swift or slow, and these are relative terms. Extension in general and motion in general are meaningless terms, depending 'on that strange doctrine of *abstract ideas*'.[4] In fine, primary qualities are no more independent of perception than are secondary qualities. The first no less than the second are ideas. And if they are ideas, they cannot exist or inhere in an unthinking substance or substrate. We can, therefore, get rid of Locke's material substance; and sensible things become clusters or collections of ideas.

Locke, as we saw earlier, did not actually say that secondary qualities are subjective. For in his technical terminology secondary qualities are the powers in things which produce in us certain ideas; and these powers are objective; that is, not dependent for their existence on our minds. However, if we mean by secondary qualities the qualities as perceived, colours, for example, we can

[1] *P.*, I, 5; II, p. 42.   [2] *P.*, I, 9; II, pp. 44–5.
[3] *P.*, I, 10; II, p. 45.   [4] *P.*, I, 11; II, p. 46.

say that for Locke they are subjective, being ideas in the mind. And it is from this point that Berkeley starts in the argument mentioned above. But the validity of the argument is certainly questionable. Berkeley seems to think that the 'relativity' of qualities shows that they are in the mind. There are no qualities in general, over and above the particular qualities perceived. And each particular quality perceived is perceived by and is relative to a particular subject. But it is not immediately evident that because the grass looks to me now green, now yellow or golden, the greenness and yellowness are ideas in the sense of being in my mind. Nor is it immediately evident that because a particular thing looks to me large in these circumstances and small in those circumstances or of one shape at one time and of another shape at another time, extension and figure are ideas. If, of course, we assume that, given the objectivity of qualities, things must necessarily appear the same to all people or to one person at all times and in all circumstances, it follows that if they do not so appear, they are not objective. But there does not seem to be any cogent reason for making this assumption.

5. However, if we assume that sensible things are ideas, it is evident that Locke's theory of a material substrate is an unnecessary hypothesis. But we can go further than this, according to Berkeley, and say that the hypothesis is not merely unnecessary but unintelligible. If we try to analyse the meaning of the term, we find that it consists of 'the idea of being in general, together with the relative notion of its supporting accidents. The general idea of being appeareth to me the most abstract and incomprehensible of all other; and as for its supporting accidents, this, as we have just now observed, cannot be understood in the common sense of those words; it must therefore be taken in some other sense, but what that is they do not explain.'[1] The phrase 'supporting accidents'[2] cannot be taken in its ordinary sense, 'as when we say that pillars support a building'. For material substance is supposed to be logically prior to extension, an accident, and to support it. 'In what sense therefore must it be taken?'[3] In Berkeley's opinion, no definite meaning can be given to the phrase.

The same line of thought is expressed more at length in the

[1] *P.*, I, 17; II, pp. 47-8.
[2] The word 'supporting' must be understood, of course, in an active sense. Material substance, that is to say, is said to support accidents.
[3] *P.*, I, 16; II, p. 47.

First Dialogue. Hylas is brought to acknowledge that the distinction between sensation and object, between an action of the mind and its object, is untenable when we are talking about perception. Sensible things are reducible to sensations; and it is inconceivable that sensations should exist in an unperceiving substance. 'But then on the other hand, when I look on sensible things in a different view, considering them as so many modes and qualities, I find it necessary to suppose a material *substratum*, without which they cannot be conceived to exist.'[1] Philonous then challenges Hylas to explain what he means by material substrate. If he means that it is spread under sensible qualities or accidents, it must be spread under extension. In this case it must itself be extended. And then we are involved in an infinite regress. Moreover, the same conclusion follows if we substitute the idea of standing under or supporting for the idea of being a substratum or of being spread under.

Hylas protests that he is being taken too literally. But Philonous retorts: 'I am not for imposing any sense on your words: you are at liberty to explain them as you please. Only I beseech you, make me understand something by them. . . . Pray let me know any sense, literal or not literal, that you understand in it.'[2] In the end Hylas finds himself compelled to admit that he cannot assign any definite meaning to phrases such as 'supporting accidents' and 'material substrate'.[3] The upshot of the discussion, therefore, is that the statement that material things exist absolutely, without dependence on the mind, is meaningless. 'The absolute existence of unthinking things are words without a meaning, or which include a contradiction. This is what I repeat and inculcate, and earnestly recommend to the attentive thought of the reader.'[4]

6. Berkeley is at pains to show that the statement that sensible things are ideas is not equivalent to the statement that sensible things possess no reality. 'Say you, at this rate all's nothing but idea, mere phantasm. I answer that every thing is as real as ever. I hope that to call a thing "idea" makes it not the less real. Truly I should perhaps have stuck to the word "thing", and not men-

---

[1] *D.*, 1; II, p. 197.   [2] *Ibid.*, p. 199.

[3] Hylas might perhaps have replied that the reason why he could not satisfy Philonous's request for a clear and definite meaning was that the latter was asking him to describe the relation between substance and accidents in terms of some relation other than itself. But Philonous (Berkeley) held, of course, that phenomena are ideas. And in this case they cannot inhere in unthinking, senseless substance.

[4] *P.*, 1, 24; II, p. 51.

ioned the word "idea", were it not for a reason, and I think a
good one too, which I shall give in the second Book.'[1] Again, 'On
my principles there is a reality, there are things, there is a *rerum
natura*'.[2] In the *Principles* Berkeley raises the objection that on
his theory 'all that is real and substantial in Nature is banished
out of the world: and instead thereof a chimerical scheme of ideas
takes place. . . . What therefore becomes of the sun, moon, and
stars? What must we think of houses, rivers, mountains, trees,
stones; nay, even of our own bodies? Are all these but so many
chimeras and illusions of the fancy?'[3] To this he answers that 'by
the principles premised, we are not deprived of any one thing in
Nature. Whatever we see, feel, hear, or any wise conceive or
understand, remains as secure as ever, and is as real as ever. There
is a *rerum natura*, and the distinction between realities and
chimeras retains its full force.'[4]

If, however, sensible things are ideas, it follows that we eat and
drink and are clothed with ideas. And this way of speaking sounds
'very harsh'. Of course it does, replies Berkeley; but the reason
why it sounds harsh and strange is simply that in ordinary discourse the word 'idea' is not normally used for the things which
we see and touch. The principal requirement is that we should
understand in what sense the word is being used in the present
context. 'I am not for disputing about the propriety, but the truth
of the expression. If therefore you agree with me that we eat and
drink and are clad with the immediate objects of sense which
cannot exist unperceived or without the mind: I shall readily
grant it more proper or conformable to custom, that they should
be called things rather than ideas.'[5]

What, then, is the justification for using the term 'idea' in a
sense which is admittedly not in accordance with common usage?
'I answer, I do it for two reasons: first, because the term *thing*, in
contradistinction to *idea*, is generally supposed to denote somewhat existing without the mind: secondly, because *thing* hath a
more comprehensive signification than *idea*, including spirits or
thinking things as well as ideas. Since therefore the objects of
sense exist only in the mind, and are withal thoughtless and
inactive, I chose to mark them by the word *idea*, which implies
those properties.'[6]

Because, therefore, Berkeley uses the word 'ideas' to refer to the

[1] *P.C.*, 807; I, p. 97.   [2] *P.C.*, 105; I, p. 38.   [3] *P.*, I, 34; II, p. 55.
[4] *Ibid.*   [5] *P.*, I, 38; II, p. 57.   [6] *P.*, I, 39; II, p. 57.

immediate objects of sense, and because he does not deny the
existence of the objects of sense-perception, he can maintain that
his theory of ideas makes no difference to the reality of the
sensible world. All that he gets rid of is Locke's material substance,
which is not an object of sense and which will therefore not be
missed by any ordinary man. 'I do not argue against the existence
of any one thing that we can apprehend, either by sense or
reflexion. That the things I see with mine eyes and touch with my
hands do exist, really exist, I make not the least question. The
only thing whose existence we deny, is that which philosophers call
matter or corporeal substance. And in doing of this, there is no
damage done to the rest of mankind, who, I dare say, will never
miss it. The atheist indeed will want the colour of an empty name
to support his impiety; and the philosophers may possibly find
they have lost a great handle for trifling and disputation.'[1]

It is arguable that there is some confusion or inconsistency in
Berkeley's use of the term 'idea'. In the first place he protests that
he simply uses the term to signify what we perceive, sensible
objects. And though this use of the term may be uncommon its
use does not affect the reality of the objects of sense-perception.
This suggests to the reader that the term is for Berkeley a purely
technical one. To call sensible things ideas in this purely technical
sense does not reduce them to ideas in the ordinary sense. At the
same time Berkeley speaks, as we have seen, of 'sensations or
ideas', as though the terms were synonymous. And, quite apart
from the general impropriety of equating ideas and sensations,
this inevitably suggests that sensible things are mere subjective
modifications of our minds. For the word 'sensation' refers to
something subjective and, indeed, to something private. It suggests that there is no real public sensible world, but rather as
many private sensible worlds as there are percipient subjects.
The sensible world then becomes something very like a dream
world.

At this point, however, it is relevant to introduce Berkeley's
distinction between ideas and images of things, even though it
means touching on aspects of his philosophy which will be considered in the next chapter. Ideas, that is, sensible things, are
said to be 'imprinted on the senses by the Author of Nature': they
are called 'real things'.[2] When, for example, I open my eyes and
see a piece of white paper, it does not depend on my choice that

[1] *P.*, 1, 35; 1, p. 55.   [2] *P.*, 1, 33; 11, p. 54.

I see a piece of white paper, except in the sense that I can choose to look in one direction rather than in another. I cannot look in the direction of the paper and see a piece of green cheese instead. In Berkeley's language the ideas or qualities which compose the piece of white paper are imprinted on my senses. I can, however, have images of things which I have seen, and I can combine images at will, to form, for example, the image of a unicorn. In ordinary language the piece of white paper which I see on my table is not called an idea, whereas we do talk about having the idea of a unicorn. But though in Berkeley's terminology the piece of white paper is spoken of as a collection or cluster of ideas, these ideas are not dependent on the finite mind in the same way that the image of a unicorn is dependent on it. And thus there is room in Berkeley's theory for a distinction between the sphere of sensible reality and the sphere of images. This distinction is of importance; for Berkeley insisted, as will be mentioned in the next chapter, that there is an 'order of Nature', a coherent pattern of ideas which does not depend on human choice. At the same time, though real things, sensible things that is to say, do not depend simply on the human perceiver, they are none the less ideas, and they cannot exist in absolute independence of a mind. For Berkeley, therefore, these two statements are both true and important, namely, that ideas (in his sense of the term) are not entirely dependent on the *human* mind and that they are none the less ideas and so dependent on some mind.

I do not suggest that this distinction clears up all difficulties and answers all possible objections. For one thing, it still seems to follow from Berkeley's theory that there are as many private worlds as there are percipient subjects, and that there is no public world. Berkeley was not, of course, a solipsist. But to say that he was not a solipsist is not the same thing as saying that solipsism cannot be derived from his premises. He believed, indeed, in a plurality of finite minds or spirits. But it is very difficult to see how on his premises he can assure himself of the validity of this belief. However, the distinction described in the last paragraph does at least help us to understand how Berkeley could feel justified in maintaining that on his theory there is still a *rerum natura* and that sensible things are not reduced to the level of chimeras, even if there is some discrepancy between the common-sense aspect of this theory (sensible things are simply what we perceive or can perceive them to be) and its idealist aspects (sensible things are ideas, equivalent to sensations). The discrepancy can be expressed in this way. Berkeley sets out to describe the world of the ordinary man, excluding the unnecessary and indeed meaningless additions of metaphysicians; but the result of his analysis is a proposition which, as Berkeley himself was aware, the ordinary man would not be disposed to accept.

7. As a conclusion to this chapter we can raise the question whether Berkeley's use of the term 'idea' implies the representative theory of perception. Locke frequently, though not always, speaks about perceiving ideas rather than things. And inasmuch as ideas for him often represent things, this way of speaking implies the representative theory of perception. This is one reason, of course, why Locke depreciates sensitive knowledge and physics in comparison with mathematics. The question is, therefore, whether Berkeley is involved in the same theory and in the same difficulties.

The proper answer to this question seems to be clear enough, provided that we attend to Berkeley's own philosophy rather than to the fact that Locke furnished him with a point of departure. If we consider merely the last-mentioned fact, we may easily be inclined to father on Berkeley the representative theory of perception. But if we attend carefully to his own philosophy, we shall recognize that he was not involved in this theory.

What Berkeley calls ideas are not ideas of things: they *are* things. They do not represent entities beyond themselves: they are themselves entities. In perceiving ideas we perceive, not images of sensible things, but sensible things themselves. In the *Philosophical Commentaries* Berkeley says explicitly: 'the supposition that things are distinct from ideas takes away all real truth and consequently brings in a universal scepticism, since all our knowledge and contemplation is confined barely to our own ideas'.[1] Again, 'the referring ideas to things which are not ideas, the using the term "idea of", is one great cause of mistake. . . .'[2] This is certainly not the representative theory of perception, which is indeed incompatible with Berkeley's philosophy. For on his premisses there is nothing for 'ideas' to represent. And, as can be seen from the first of the two quotations just given, he objects against the theory that it leads to scepticism. For if the immediate objects of sensible knowledge are ideas which are supposed to represent things other than themselves, we can never know that they do in fact represent things. Berkeley doubtless borrowed

[1] *P.C.*, 606; 1, p. 75.   [2] *P.C.*, 660; 1, p. 80.

from Locke the use of the term 'idea' for the immediate object of perception; but this does not mean that ideas fulfil the same function or have the same status in Berkeley's philosophy that they do in Locke's. With the latter, according at least to his prevalent way of speaking, ideas act as intermediaries between the mind and things, in the sense that though they are the immediate objects of knowledge, they represent external things which are not dependent on our minds. With the former ideas are not intermediaries; they are sensible things themselves.

CHAPTER XIII

BERKELEY (3)

*Finite spirits; their existence, nature and immortal character—
The order of Nature—Berkeley's empiricist interpretation of
physics, especially as seen in the* De motu*—The existence and
nature of God—The relation of sensible things to ourselves and
to God—Causality—Berkeley and other philosophers—Some
remarks on Berkeley's ethical ideas—A note on Berkeley's
influence.*

1. If sensible things are ideas, they can exist only in minds or
spirits. And spirits are thus the only substances. Ideas are passive
and inert: spirits, which perceive ideas, are active. '*Thing* or *being*
is the most general name of all, it comprehends under it two kinds
entirely distinct and heterogeneous, and which have nothing
common but the name, to wit, *spirits* and *ideas*. The former are
active, indivisible substances: the latter are *inert*, fleeting, dependent
beings, which subsist not by themselves, but are supported by[1]
or exist in minds or spiritual substances.'[2]

Spirits, therefore, cannot be ideas or like ideas. 'It is therefore
necessary, in order to prevent equivocation and confounding
natures perfectly disagreeing and unlike, that we distinguish
between *spirit* and *idea*.'[3] 'That this *substance* which supports or
perceives ideas should itself be an *idea* or like an *idea*, is evidently
absurd.'[4] Further, we cannot have, properly speaking, any idea
of spirit. Indeed, 'it is manifestly impossible there should be any
such *idea*'.[5] 'A spirit is one simple, undivided, active being: as it
perceives ideas, it is called the *understanding*; and as it produces
or operates about them, it is called the *will*. Hence there can be no
idea formed of a soul or spirit: for all ideas whatever, being passive
and inert, they cannot represent unto us, by way of image or
likeness, that which acts.'[6]

When he says that we can have no idea of spirit, Berkeley is
using the term 'idea' in his technical sense. He does not mean that

---

[1] It may seem that Berkeley is contradicting himself. But when he said, as
mentioned in the last chapter, that the term 'supporting accidents' is meaningless,
he was referring to the alleged relation between material substance and ideas.
Here he is speaking of the relation between spiritual substance or mind and ideas.

[2] *P.*, 1, 89; 11, pp. 79–80.   [3] *P.*, 1, 139; 11, p. 105.

[4] *P.*, 1, 135; 11, p. 103.   [5] *Ibid.*   [6] *P.*, 1, 27; 11, p. 52.

we have no knowledge of what is signified by the word 'spirit'. It must be admitted that 'we have some notion of soul, spirit, and the operations of the mind, such as willing, loving, hating, inasmuch as we know or understand the meaning of those words'.[1] A distinction is thus made by Berkeley between 'notion', namely, the mental or spiritual as object, and 'idea', namely, the sensible or corporeal as object. We can have a notion of spirit but not an idea in the technical sense. 'In a large sense indeed, we may be said to have an idea, or rather a notion of *spirit;* that is, we understand the meaning of the word; otherwise we could not affirm or deny anything of it.'[2] A spirit can be described as 'that which thinks, wills, and perceives; this, and this alone, constitutes the signification of that term'.[3] It will be remembered that an entry in Berkeley's notebooks[4] suggests that the possibility had occurred to him of applying to the mind the same sort of phenomenalistic analysis which he applied to bodies. But he rejected this idea. It seemed evident to him that if sensible things are reduced to ideas, there must be spirits or spiritual substances which have or perceive these ideas.

The question arises, how do we know of the existence of spirits, that is, of a plurality of finite spirits or selves? 'We comprehend our own existence by inward feeling or reflexion, and that of other spirits by reason.'[5] That I exist is, after all, evident; for I perceive ideas, and I am aware that I am distinct from the ideas which I perceive. But I know the existence of other finite spirits or selves only by reason, that is, by inference. 'It is plain that we cannot know the existence of other spirits, otherwise than by their operations, or the ideas excited by them in us. I perceive several motions, changes, and combinations of ideas, that inform me there are certain particular agents like myself, which accompany them, and concur in their production. Hence the knowledge I have of other spirits is not immediate, as is the knowledge of my ideas; but depending on the intervention of ideas, by me referred to agents or spirits distinct from myself, as effects or concomitant signs.'[6] Berkeley returns to this matter in *Alciphron.* 'In a strict sense I do not see Alciphron, i.e. that individual thinking thing, but only such visible signs and tokens as suggest and infer the being of that invisible thinking principle or soul.'[7] And he draws an analogy between our mediate knowledge of other finite spirits

---

[1] *P.*, I, 140; II, p. 105.   [2] *Ibid.*   [3] *P.*, I, 138; II, p. 104.
[4] *P.C.*, 581; I, p. 72.   [5] *P.*, I, 89; II, p. 80.   [6] *P.*, I, 145; II. p. 107.
[7] *A.*, 4, 5; III, p. 147.

and our mediate knowledge of God. In both cases it is through sensible signs that we come to know the existence of an active agent.

Apart from any other possible criticism, this account of our knowledge of the existence of other finite spirits or selves seems to labour under the following difficulty. According to Berkeley, 'when we see the colour, size, figure, and motions of a man, we perceive only certain sensations or ideas excited in our own minds: and these being exhibited to our view in sundry distinct collections serve to mark out unto us the existence of finite and created spirits like ourselves'.[1] 'We do not see a man, if by *man* is meant that which lives, moves, perceives, and thinks as we do: but only such a certain collection of ideas as directs us to think there is a distinct principle of thought and motion like to ourselves, accompanying and represented by it.'[2] But even if I do think in this way, can I be certain that the ideas produced in me which I attribute to other finite spirits are not really the effects of God? If God produces in me, without there being any material substance, the ideas which on the substance-accident theory would be regarded as accidents of material or corporeal substance, how can I be certain that he does not produce in me, without there being any other finite selves, the ideas which I take to be signs of the presence of such selves, that is, of spiritual substances other than myself?

At first sight Berkeley may appear to have felt this difficulty. For he asserts that the existence of God is more evident than the existence of human beings. But his reason for saying this is that the number of signs of God's existence is greater than the number of signs of any given man's existence. Thus Alciphron asks: 'What! Do you pretend you can have the same assurance of the being of a God that you can have of mine, whom you actually see stand before you and talk to you?'[3] And Euphranor answers: 'The very same, if not greater.' He goes on to state that whereas he is convinced of the existence of another finite self by only a few signs, 'I do at all times and in all places perceive sensible signs which evince the being of God.' Similarly, in the *Principles* Berkeley says that 'we may even assert, that the existence of God is far more evidently perceived than the existence of men; because the effects of Nature are infinitely more numerous and considerable than those ascribed to human agents'.[4] But he does not tell us how we can be certain that the ideas which we take to be signs of the presence

[1] *P.*, 1, 148; 11, p. 109.　[2] *Ibid.*　[3] *A.*, 4, 5; 111, p. 147.　[4] *P.*, 1, 147; 11, p. 108.

of finite spiritual substances really are what we think they are. Perhaps, however, he would reply that we do in point of fact discriminate between the particular effects which we ascribe to finite agents and the general order of Nature which is presupposed by these effects; and that his theory does not demand any further grounds for discrimination than those which we in fact possess and utilize. From ideas or observable effects which are analogous to those which we are conscious of producing, we infer the existence of other selves; and this is sufficient evidence. But if anyone is dissatisfied with such an answer and wishes to know what justification there is, on Berkeley's premises, for making this inference, he will not receive much help from Berkeley's writings.

Some of Berkeley's descriptions of the nature of a spirit have already been mentioned. But it can hardly be successfully claimed, I think, that his descriptions are always consistent. In the *Philosophical Commentaries* the suggestion is made that the mind is 'a congeries of perceptions. Take away perceptions and you take away the mind: put the perceptions and you put the mind.'[1] As has been noted, Berkeley did not pursue this phenomenalistic analysis of mind. But even later he says that the existence (*esse*) of spirits is to perceive (*percipere*), which implies that a spirit is essentially the act of perceiving. However, he also tells that the word 'spirit' means 'that which thinks, wills and perceives; this, and this alone, constitutes the signification of that term'.[2] Hence we can say in general that Berkeley rejected the idea of applying to mind the type of phenomenalistic analysis which he applied to bodies, and that he accepted Locke's theory of immaterial or spiritual substance.[3] And it is on this basis, of cause, that he maintains the immortality of the human soul or spirit.

If, as some held, the soul of man were a thin vital flame or a system of animal spirits, it would be corruptible like the body. It could not survive 'the ruin of the tabernacle, wherein it is enclosed'.[4] But 'we have shown that the soul is indivisible, incorporeal, unextended, and it is consequently incorruptible'.[5] This does not mean that the human soul is incapable of annihilation

---

[1] *P.C.*, 580; I, p. 72.   [2] *P.*, I, 138; II, p. 104.
[3] If the existence of bodies is defined as *percipi*, then it is natural to define the existence of spirits or minds as *percipere*. For the two are correlative. But inasmuch as bodies are said to be ideas which are imprinted on minds and perceived by them, it is natural to maintain that minds are substances which 'support' ideas and subjects which perceive ideas. Berkeley does not tidy up the confusion caused by his different ways of speaking.
[4] *P.*, I, 141; II, p. 105.   [5] *Ibid.*, p. 106.

even by the infinite power of God; 'but only that it is not liable to be broken or dissolved by the ordinary Laws of Nature or motion'.[1] This is what is meant by saying that the soul of man is naturally immortal; namely, that it cannot be affected by the motions, changes and decay 'which we hourly see befall natural bodies'.[2] The notion that the soul of man is corporeal and corruptible 'hath been greedily embraced and cherished by the worst part of mankind as the most effectual antidote against all impressions of virtue and religion'.[3] But the soul, as spiritual substance, is naturally immortal; and this truth is of great importance for religion and morality.

2. Returning from spirits to bodies, we have seen that according to Berkeley his analysis of the latter leaves intact the *rerum natura*. 'There is a *rerum natura*, and the distinction between realities and chimeras retains its full force.'[4] It is quite proper, therefore, to speak of laws of Nature. 'There are certain general laws that run through the whole chain of natural effects: these are learned by the observation and study of Nature. . . .'[5] Berkeley is thus quite ready to speak of 'the whole system, immense, beautiful, glorious beyond expression and beyond thought'.[6] We have to remember that for him sensible things or bodies are precisely what we perceive or can perceive them to be, and that he calls these phenomena 'ideas'. These ideas form a coherent pattern: we can discern more or less regular sequences. Regular sequences or series can be expressed in the form of 'laws', statements about the regular behaviour of sensible things. But connections in Nature are not necessary connections: they may be more or less regular, but they are always contingent. Ideas are imprinted on our minds in more or less regular series by the Author of Nature, God. And to say that Y regularly follows X is to say that that God imprints in us ideas in this order. And since all particular regular series, and the whole order of Nature in general, depend on the unceasing divine activity and will, what we call Nature is shot through and through, as it were, with contingency.

Physics, therefore, or natural philosophy is not denied by Berkeley. But physical laws which state, for example, that certain types of bodies attract one another state connections which are purely factual and not necessary. That certain bodies behave in a certain way depends on God; and though we may expect that God

---

[1] *P.*, I, 141; II, p. 105.   [2] *Ibid.*, p. 106.   [3] *Ibid.*, p. 105.
[4] *P.*, I, 34; II, p. 55.   [5] *P.*, I, 62; II, p. 67.   [6] *D.*, 2; II, p. 211.

will act uniformly for the most part we cannot know that He will always behave in the same way. If, generally speaking, *Y* always follows *X*, and if on a given occasion it does not do so, we may have to speak of a miracle. But if God acts miraculously, that is to say, in a manner quite different from the way in which He normally acts, He does not, so to speak, break a hard and fast law of Nature. For a law of Nature states the way in which things generally behave as a matter of fact, as far as our experience goes, not the way in which they must behave. 'By a diligent observation of the phenomena within our view, we may discover the general laws of Nature, and from them deduce the other phenomena. I do not say demonstrate; for all deductions of that kind depend on a supposition that the Author of Nature always operates uniformly, and in a constant observance of those rules we take for principles: which we cannot evidently know.'[1] In the language of ideas God is accustomed to imprint ideas on us in a certain order or in certain regular sequences. And this enables us to state 'laws of Nature'. But God is in no way bound to imprint ideas on us always in the same order. Miracles, therefore, are possible. They do not involve any interference with necessary connections between distinct ideas. For there are no such necessary connections. There is, indeed, a *rerum natura*, and there is an order of Nature, but it is not a necessary order.

3. In the foregoing section I assumed the existence of God and Berkeley's view of the way in which God acts. For I wished to bring out the fact that for him the order of Nature is not a necessary order. In the present section I wish to illustrate Berkeley's markedly empiricist, even positivistic, interpretation of physics, especially as seen in the *De motu*.

Berkeley's attack on abstract general ideas naturally has its repercussions in his interpretation of physics. He does not say that the use of abstract terms is illegitimate and serves no useful purpose; but he does suggest that the use of such terms may lead people to imagine that they possess more knowledge than they actually have, because they can employ a word to cover their ignorance. 'The great mechanical principle now in vogue is *attraction*. That a stone falls to the earth, or the sea swells towards the moon, may to some appear sufficiently explained thereby. But how are we enlightened by being told this is done by attraction?'[2] The physicist (Berkeley frequently speaks of 'mathematicians') or

---

[1] *P.*, I, 107; II, p. 88.   [2] *P.*, I, 103; II, p. 86.

natural philosopher may come to think that a term like 'attraction' signifies an essential quality inherent in bodies, which acts as a real cause. But it is no such thing. As a matter of pure empirical fact the observed relations between some bodies are of such a kind that we describe them as cases of mutual attraction; but the word 'attraction' does not signify an entity, and it is idle to suppose that the behaviour of bodies is explained by the use of such a term. The physicist is concerned with description and with the grouping of analogies under general 'laws' with a view to prediction and practical utility: but he is not concerned with causal explanation, if we mean by 'cause' an active efficient cause. And it is a great mistake to suppose that phenomena a, b and c are explained by saying that they are due to P, where P is an abstract term. For to suppose this is to misunderstand the use of the term. It does not signify any entity which could be an active efficient cause.

In the *De motu* Berkeley develops this point of view. He begins the treatise with the remark that 'in the pursuit of truth we must beware of being misled by terms which we do not rightly understand. Almost all philosophers utter the caution; few observe it.'[1] Take terms such as 'effort' and 'conation'. Such terms are properly applicable only to animate things: when applied to inanimate things they are used metaphorically and in a vague sense. Again, natural philosophers are accustomed to use abstract general terms, and there is a temptation to think they signify actual occult entities. Some writers speak, for example, of absolute space as though it were something, a distinct entity. But we shall find on analysis that 'nothing else is signified by these words than pure privation or negation, that is, mere nothing'.[2]

According to Berkeley, we ought to 'distinguish mathematical hypotheses from the natures of things'.[3] Terms such as 'force', 'gravity' and 'attraction' do not denote physical or metaphysical entities; they are 'mathematical hypotheses'. 'As for attraction, it is certainly employed by Newton, not as a true, physical quality, but only as a mathematical hypothesis. Indeed Leibniz, when distinguishing elementary effort or solicitation from impetus, admits that these entities are not really found in nature, but have to be formed by abstraction.'[4] Mechanics cannot progress without the use of mathematical abstractions and hypotheses, and their

---

[1] *D.M.*, 1; IV, p. 11.
[2] *D.M.*, 53; IV, p. 24.
[3] *D.M.*, 66; IV, p. 28.
[4] *D.M.*, 17; IV, p. 15.

use is justified by their success, that is, by their practical utility. But the practical usefulness of a mathematical abstraction does not prove that it denotes any physical or metaphysical entity. 'The mechanician employs certain abstract and general terms, imagining in bodies force, action, attraction . . . which are of great utility for theories and formulations, as also for computations about motion, even if in the truth of things, and in bodies actually existing, they would be sought in vain, just like the things which are fictions made by the geometers through mathematical abstraction.'[1]

One main reason why people are inclined to be misled by abstract terms as used in physics is that they think that the physicist is concerned with finding the true efficient causes of phenomena. They are inclined, therefore, to think that a word such as 'gravity' signifies an existent entity or quality which is the true efficient cause of certain motions and which explains the latter. But 'it does not belong to physics or mechanics to give efficient causes. . . .'[2] One reason why Berkeley says this is, of course, that in his view the only true causes are incorporeal agents. This is apparent in the following quotation. 'In physical philosophy we must seek the causes and solutions of phenomena from mechanical principles. Physically, therefore, a thing is explained not by assigning its truly active and incorporeal cause but by demonstrating its connection with mechanical principles, such as *action and reaction are always contrary and equal. . . .*'[3] What is meant by mechanical principles? The primary laws of motion, 'proved by experiments, developed by reasoning and rendered universal . . . are fittingly called principles, since from them are derived both general mechanical theorems and particular explanations of phenomena'.[4] To give a physical explanation of an event, therefore, is to show how it can be deduced from a high-level hypothesis. And explanations of this kind are concerned with behaviour rather than with existence. The existence of phenomena is explained in metaphysical philosophy by deriving it from its true efficient cause, which is incorporeal. The physicist is concerned to this extent with 'causes', that when he finds B constantly following A and never occurring when A has not preceded, where A and B are phenomena, he speaks of A as cause and B as effect. But phenomena are ideas, and ideas cannot be active efficient

---

[1] *D.M.*, 39; IV, p. 20.   [2] *D.M.*, 35; IV, p. 19.
[3] *D.M.*, 69; IV, p. 29.   [4] *D.M.*, 36; IV, p. 20.

causes; and if this is what is understood by causes, the physicist is not concerned with them.

Berkeley's contention, therefore, is that science is left unimpaired by his theory of ideas and by his metaphysics, provided that the nature of science is understood. Metaphysics must be eliminated from physics, and the two should not be confused. This elimination will purify physics of obscurities and vague verbiage and will save us from being misled by words which, however useful they may be, do not denote entities or actual qualities of entities. At the same time Berkeley did not eliminate metaphysics from physics in order to dissolve the former. His desire was rather to point the way to metaphysics. For if we once understand that physical science is not concerned with the truly active efficient causes of phenomena, we shall not only be saved from interpreting wrongly the function and meaning of words such as gravity and attraction but also be prompted to look elsewhere for the cause of the existence of phenomena. Berkeley spoke in a positivistic way about physics; but at the back of his mind was the desire to disabuse people of the notion that an adequate causal explanation of phenomena can be given in terms of gravity, attraction, and so on, which do not signify entities, or existent qualities, but are used for convenience in hypotheses which are validated by their success in grouping phenomena and deducing them from certain principles describing the behaviour of bodies. And he wished to disabuse people of a mistaken interpretation of the function of physical science because he wished to show them that the true causal explanations of phenomena can be found only in metaphysics, which establishes the relation of phenomena to God, the ultimate incorporeal and true efficient cause. 'Only by meditation and reasoning can truly active causes be brought out of the darkness with which they are surrounded and be so to some extent known. To deal with them pertains to first philosophy or metaphysics.'[1]

In this section reference has been made to physics or physical science, understood as including mechanics. But in the *De motu* Berkeley makes a curious distinction between physics and mechanics. 'In physics sense and experience, which reach only to apparent effects, hold sway; in mechanics the abstract notions of mathematicians are admitted.'[2] In other words, physics is concerned with the description of phenomena and their behaviour, while mechanics involves theorizing and explanatory hypotheses

---

[1] *D.M.*, 72; IV, p. 30.　　　　[2] *D.M.*, 71; IV, p. 30.

which employ mathematics. The reason why Berkeley makes this distinction is that he wishes to distinguish between the observed facts and the theories constructed to understand or explain these facts. For unless we make this last distinction, we shall be inclined to postulate occult entities corresponding to the abstract terms 'of the mathematicians'. Words such as 'gravity' or 'force' do not denote observable entities. Therefore, we may be inclined to think, there must be occult entities or qualities corresponding to these terms. 'But what an occult quality is, or how any quality can act or do anything, we can scarcely conceive—indeed we cannot conceive. . . . What is itself occult explains nothing.'[1] But if we distinguish carefully between observed effects and the hypotheses constructed to explain them, we shall be in a better position to understand the function of the abstract terms employed in these hypotheses. 'In part the terms have been invented by common habit to abbreviate speech, and in part they have been thought out for the purpose of teaching.'[2] In reasoning about sensible things we reason about particular bodies. But we require abstract terms for our universal propositions about particular bodies.

4. There is, therefore, for Berkeley an order of Nature, a system of phenomena or ideas which renders possible the construction of the natural sciences. But, as we have just seen, it is idle to look to the scientist for knowledge of the cause or causes of the existence of phenomena. And this suggests at once that Berkeley's proof of the existence of God will be an *a posteriori* proof, a variant of the causal argument. When he says in the *Philosophical Commentaries*, 'Absurd to argue the existence of God from his idea. We have no idea of God. 'Tis impossible,'[3] he is doubtless thinking primarily of his technical use of the word 'idea'. For it is obvious that there can be no idea of God, if 'God' means a spiritual being and 'idea' is used for the object of sense-perception. And when Alciphron is made to say that he is not to be persuaded by metaphysical arguments, 'such, for instance, as are drawn from the idea of an all-perfect being',[4] we have to remember that Alciphron is the 'minute philosopher' and the defender of atheism. Nevertheless, it is safe to say that Berkeley did not accept the so-called ontological argument, as used in different ways by St. Anselm and Descartes. His proof is a causal argument, based on the existence of sensible things. And the characteristic feature of Berkeley's argument for

[1] *D.M.*, 4 and 6; IV, p. 32.   [2] *D.M.*, 7; IV, p. 12.
[3] *P.C.*, 782; I, p. 94.   [4] *A.*, 4, 2; III, p. 142.

God's existence is the use which he makes of his theory of 'ideas'. If sensible things are ideas, and if these ideas are not dependent simply on our minds, they must be referred to a mind other than our own. 'It is evident to everyone, that those things which are called the works of Nature, that is, the far greater part of the ideas or sensations perceived by us, are not produced by, or dependent on the wills of men. There is, therefore, some other spirit that causes them, since it is repugnant that they should subsist by themselves.'[1]

In the *Dialogues* the proof of God's existence is put in this succinct form. '*Sensible things do really exist: and if they exist, they are necessarily perceived by an infinite mind: therefore there is an infinite mind, or God.* This furnishes you with a direct and immediate demonstration, from a most evident principle, of the *being of a God.*'[2] Berkeley does not enter at any length into the question of the unicity of God; he seems to proceed more or less straight from the statement that sensible things or ideas do not depend on our minds to the conclusion that they depend on one infinite mind. He practically takes it for granted that the system and harmony and beauty of Nature show that Nature is the product of one infinitely wise and perfect spirit, God, who upholds all things by His power. We do not, of course, see God. But we do not, for the matter of that, see finite spirits. We infer the existence of a finite spirit from 'some one finite and narrow assemblage of ideas', whereas 'we do at all times and in all places perceive manifest tokens of the divinity'.[3]

The blemishes and defects of Nature do not constitute any valid argument against this inference. The apparent waste of seeds and embryos, and the accidental destruction of immature plants and animals, may seem to point to faulty and careless management and organization, if we judge by human standards. But 'the splendid profusion of natural things should not be interpreted (as) weakness or prodigality in the agent who produces them, but rather be looked on as an argument of the riches of his power'.[4] And many things which appear to us to be evil, because they affect us painfully, can be seen to be good if they are regarded as part of the whole system of things. In *Alciphron* the speaker with this name is depicted as saying that while it may plausibly be alleged that a little evil in creation sets the good in a stronger light, this principle

---

[1] *P.*, I, 146; II, pp. 107-8.
[3] *P.*, I, 148; II, p. 109.
[2] *D.*, 2; II, p. 212.
[4] *P.*, I, 152; II, p. 111.

cannot account for 'blots so large and so black. . . . That there
should be so much vice and so little virtue upon earth, and that
the laws of God's kingdom should be so ill observed by His subjects, is what can never be reconciled with that surpassing wisdom
and goodness of the supreme Monarch.'[1] To this Berkeley answers
that moral faults are a result of human choice, and also that we
ought not to exaggerate the position of human beings in the
universe. 'It seems we are led not only by revelation, but by
common sense, observing and inferring from the analogy of
visible things, to conclude there are innumerable orders of intelligent beings more happy and more perfect than man.'[2]

It would be wrong to conclude from Berkeley's somewhat
summary exposition of the proof of God's existence that the
philosopher who was so ready to apply a critical analysis to terms
such as 'material substance' was blind to the difficulties which can
be encountered in analysing the meaning of the terms predicated
of God. Thus he makes Lysicles speak as follows: 'You must know
then that at bottom the being of God is a point in itself of small
consequence, and a man may make this concession without
yielding much. The great point is what sense the word God is to
be taken in.'[3] There have been people, says Lysicles, who have
maintained that terms such as wisdom and goodness, when
predicated of God, 'must be understood in a quite different sense
from what they signify in the vulgar acceptation, or from anything
that we can form a notion of or conceive'.[4] Thus they were able to
meet objections brought against the predication of such attributes
of God by denying that they were predicated in any known sense.
But this denial was equivalent to denying that the attributes
belonged to God at all. 'And thus denying the attributes of God,
they in effect denied His being, though perhaps they were not
aware of it.'[5] In other words, to assert that the terms predicated
of God are to be understood in a purely equivocal sense is to assert
agnosticism. Such people so whittled away the meaning of the
word 'God' by qualifications that 'nothing (was) left but the name
without any meaning annexed to it'.[6]

Lysicles takes it that this agnostic position was maintained by
a number of Fathers and Schoolmen. But Crito, with an apology
for introducing such unpolished and unfashionable writers as the
Schoolmen into good company, gives a summary historical account

[1] *A.*, 4, 23; III, p. 172.   [2] *Ibid.*   [3] *A.*, 4, 16; III, p. 163.
[4] *A.*, 4, 17; III, p. 164.   [5] *Ibid.*   [6] *Ibid.*

of the doctrine of analogical predication, in which he shows that the position of Schoolmen such as St. Thomas Aquinas and Suárez was not the same as that of the Pseudo-Dionysius. These School-men did not deny, for example, that knowledge can be attributed to God in a proper sense, but only that we can properly attribute to God the imperfections of knowledge as it is found in creatures. When, for instance, Suárez says that 'knowledge is said not to be properly in God it must be understood in a sense including im-perfection, such as discursive knowledge. . . . (But) of knowledge taken in general for the clear evident understanding of all truth, he expressly affirms that it is in God, and that this was never denied by any philosopher who believed a God.'[1] Similarly, when the Schoolmen said that God must not be supposed to exist in the same sense as created beings, they meant that He exists 'in a more eminent and perfect manner'.[2]

This represents Berkeley's own position. On the one hand, the terms which are first predicated of creatures and afterwards of God must be predicated of Him 'in the proper sense, . . . in the true and formal acceptation of the words. Otherwise, it is evident that every syllogism brought to prove those attributes or (which is the same thing) to prove the being of a God, will be found to consist of four terms, and consequently can conclude nothing.'[3] On the other hand, the terms predicated of God cannot be predi-cated in the same imperfect manner or degree in which they are predicated of creatures. My notion of God, Berkeley argues, is obtained by reflecting on my own soul, 'heightening its powers, and removing its imperfections'.[4] I conceive God according to the notion of spirit which I obtain by self-reflection. The notion remains essentially the same, though in conceiving God I remove the limitations and imperfections attaching to the notion of finite spirit as such.

It cannot be said that Berkeley carried the analysis of the meaning of the terms predicated of God any further than the Scholastics had done. Nor did he give much, if any, consideration to the possible objection that in the process of removing imper-fections we also remove the positive describable content of the term in question. He did, however, understand that there is a problem connected with the meaning of the terms predicated of God. And among the eminent modern philosophers who stood

---

[1] *A.*, 4, 20; III, pp. 168–9. [2] *Ibid.*
[3] *A.*, 4, 22; III, p. 171. [4] *D.*, 3; II, pp. 231–2.

outside the Scholastic tradition he was one of the very few who paid any serious attention to the problem. Analogy in this context was scarcely considered by the non-Scholastic philosophers. And this is one reason why discussion of the problem by analytic philosophers today not infrequently appears to believers as being purely destructive in character. On occasion, of course, it has been destructive. But one ought also to understand that this discussion represents the resuscitation of a problem with which the Schoolmen, and Berkeley, concerned themselves, but which was scarcely touched by the majority of the better-known modern philosophers.

5. Now, Berkeley frequently speaks of sensible things as though they existed in our minds. Thus we read that God 'excites those ideas in our minds',[1] and that ideas are 'imprinted on the senses'.[2] This suggests that the world is being constantly renewed or rather re-created. 'There is a mind which affects me every moment with all the sensible impressions I perceive.'[3] Again, though the metaphysical hypothesis of seeing all things in God is to be rejected, 'this optic language is equivalent to a constant creation, betokening an immediate act of power and providence'.[4] And Berkeley speaks of 'the instantaneous production and reproduction of so many signs, combined, dissolved, transposed, diversified, and adapted to such an endless variety of purposes. . . .'[5] It is also suggested, as has been already remarked, that there are as many private worlds as there are percipient subjects. And, indeed, Berkeley admits that while in the vulgar acceptation of the word 'same' we can be said to perceive the same objects, we do not do so, strictly speaking, any more than a given individual sees the same object which he touches or perceives the same object with the microscope that he perceives with the naked eye.[6]

But Berkeley also speaks of sensible things or ideas as existing in the mind of God. Natural things do not depend on me in the same way that the image of a unicorn depends on me. But, being ideas, they cannot subsist by themselves. Therefore 'there must be some other mind wherein they exist'.[7] Again, 'Men commonly believe that all things are known or perceived by God, because they believe the being of a God, whereas I on the other side, immediately and necessarily conclude the being of a God, because all sensible things must be perceived by Him'.[8] Berkeley was unwilling to deny all exteriority to sensible things; and he wished

[1] P., 1, 57; 11, p. 65.   [2] P., 1, 90; 11, p. 80: cf. P., 1, 1; 11, p. 41.
[3] D., 2; 11, p. 215.   [4] A., 4, 14; 111, p. 159.   [5] Ibid., pp. 159–60.
[6] D., 3; 11, pp. 245–7.   [7] D., 2; 11, p. 212.   [8] Ibid.

to give a meaning to the statement that things exist when no finite spirit is perceiving them. That is to say, he wished to give a further meaning to the statement that the horse is in the stable when nobody is perceiving it than the meaning which consists in saying that this statement is equivalent to the statement that anyone who entered the stable would or could have the experience which we call seeing a horse. And he can supply this further meaning only by saying that God is always perceiving the horse, even when no finite spirit is doing so. 'When I deny sensible things an existence out of the mind, I do not mean my mind in particular, but all minds. Now it is plain they have an existence exterior to my mind, since I find them by experience to be independent of it. There is therefore some other mind wherein they exist, during the intervals between the time of my perceiving them. . . . And as the same is true with regard to all other finite created spirits, it necessarily follows there is an *omnipresent eternal Mind*, which knows and comprehends all things, and exhibits them to our view in such a manner and according to such rules as he himself hath ordained, and are by us termed the *Laws of Nature*.'[1]

At first sight at least we are faced with two divergent views in which the statement that to exist is either to perceive or to be perceived assumes different meanings. On the first view to perceive refers to the finite subject, and to be perceived means to be perceived by this subject. On the second view to perceive refers to God and to be perceived means to be perceived by God. But Berkeley attempts to reconcile the two positions by means of a distinction between eternal and relative existence. 'All objects are eternally known by God, or which is the same thing, have an eternal existence in his mind: but when things before imperceptible to creatures are, by a decree of God, made perceptible to them; then they are said to begin a relative existence, with respect to created minds.'[2] Sensible things, therefore, have an 'archetypal and eternal' existence in the divine mind and an 'ectypal or natural' existence in created minds.[3] Creation takes place when the ideas receive 'ectypal' existence.

This distinction justifies Berkeley in saying that he does not share Malebranche's theory of the vision of ideas in God. For what we perceive are ideas as possessing relative or ectypal existence. These ideas come into being when they are imprinted on our minds by God. And they are thus distinct from the ideas as

---

[1] *D.*, 3; II, pp. 230–1.   [2] *Ibid.*, p. 252.   [3] *Ibid.*, p. 254.

eternally present in the divine mind. But it then appears to follow that we cannot speak of the ideas which we perceive as existing in the divine mind when we are not perceiving them. For they are not the same as the ideas which are present in the divine mind. If they were the same, it would be very difficult for Berkeley to escape embracing the theory of the vision of things in God, a theory which he emphatically rejects.

It may be said that this distinction should not be pressed to the extent of supposing that Berkeley postulated multitudinous sets of ideas; one set for each human percipient, all these sets possessing ectypal existence, and one set in the divine mind, possessing archetypal existence. What Berkeley means, it may be said, is simply that the same sensible things which, as perceived by a finite subject, possess ectypal or natural existence possess, as perceived by God, archetypal existence. After all, Berkeley speaks explicitly of objects eternally known by God and having an eternal existence in His mind as being made perceptible to creatures and thus beginning a relative existence.[1]

True, Berkeley does speak in this way, and I have no wish to question the fact. But it seems to me disputable whether it will fit in with his other ways of speaking. If we perceive objects existing in the mind of God, we have that vision of things in God which, according to Berkeley, we do not enjoy. If, however, sensible things are our sensations or if they are ideas imprinted on us by God, they must presumably be distinct from the ideas in God.

Berkeley's fundamental aim is, of course, to show that sensible things have no *absolute* existence independent of mind, and thus to cut the ground from under the feet of the materialists and atheists. And this involves for him getting rid of Locke's material substrate as a useless and indeed unintelligible hypothesis and by proving that sensible things are ideas. Then two points of view seem to manifest themselves. First, sensible things are ideas in finite minds, not in the sense that they are arbitrarily constructed by the latter, but in the sense that they are imprinted on or presented to finite minds by the unceasing divine activity. To say, therefore, that the horse is in the stable when nobody is there to perceive it is simply to say that if, given the requisite conditions, anyone were to enter the stable, God would imprint certain ideas on his mind. And this is a metaphysical way of saying that the

[1] *D.*, 3; II, p. 252.

statement that the horse is in the stable when nobody is there to perceive it means that if anyone were to enter the stable, then, given the requisite conditions, he would have the experience which we call seeing a horse. But this point of view seems to raise difficulties with regard to the existence of the sensible world before the advent of man. Hence Berkeley introduces a second point of view according to which ideas (sensible things) are always perceived by God. But this cannot mean that sensible things are perceived by God because they exist. For they would then be made independent of mind. They must exist because God perceives them. And this means that they must be ideas in the divine mind. But Berkeley does not wish to say that we enjoy the vision of things in God. Hence he introduces the distinction between ectypal or natural and archetypal existence, falling back on the old theory of 'divine ideas'. But in this case sensible things as our ideas are distinct from the ideas possessing archetypal existence in the divine mind. And it is not then proper to say that the horse is in the stable, when it is not perceived by a finite spirit, because God perceives it. For God does not have my ideas when I am not having them. I should not care to state dogmatically that these various ways of speaking cannot be reconciled. But it seems to me very difficult to reconcile them.

It is sometimes said that Berkeley's position is difficult to refute because of the difficulty in showing that God could not act in the way that he describes, namely, imprinting ideas on our minds or presenting them to us. But those who say this forget that they are presupposing God's existence, whereas Berkeley argues from *esse est percipi* to God's existence. He does not presuppose theism and use it to prove phenomenalism: he proceeds the other way round, maintaining that phenomenalism entails theism. This is a point of view which those philosophers who followed him in his empiricism and developed it can scarcely be said to have shared. But, quite apart from this question, his phenomenalism itself seems to contain two elements. First, there is the view that sensible things are simply what we perceive or can perceive them to be. This is what may be called the common-sense element inasmuch as the ordinary man never thinks of Locke's inert, unchanging and unknowable material substrate. (The exclusion of Locke's material substrate does not necessarily entail the exclusion of substance in any sense, of course.) Secondly, there is the view that sensible things are ideas. And in so far as this view cannot be reduced to a mere decision to use a word in an uncommon way, it can scarcely be said to represent the view of the ordinary man, whatever Berkeley may say. It is disputable whether these two elements are, as Berkeley thought they were, inseparable.

Finally, there is one topic which should be briefly mentioned in this section. It has sometimes been maintained that Berkeley came to substitute *esse est concipi* for *esse est percipi*, moving from empiricism to rationalism. And the main foundation of this contention is constituted by a number of remarks in *Siris* where he speaks in a deprecatory way of the senses in comparison with reason. Thus he says that 'we know a thing when we understand it; and we understand it when we can interpret or tell what it signifies. Strictly, the sense knows nothing. We perceive indeed sounds by hearing, and characters (letters) by sight; but we are not therefore said to understand them.'[1] And he blames 'the Cartesians and their followers, who consider sensation as a mode of thinking'.[2]

It seems, indeed, to be true that in *Siris* we can see a Platonic influence at work, leading to frequent disparaging remarks about the cognitive value of sensation by itself. And it also seems to be true that Berkeley felt that there was some difficulty in talking about God as 'perceiving' things. Alluding to Newton's idea of space as the divine *sensorium*, he remarks that 'there is no sense nor sensory, nor anything like a sense or sensory, in God. Sense implies an impression from some other being, and denotes a dependence in the soul which hath it. Sense is a passion; and passions imply imperfection. God knoweth all things as pure mind or intellect; but nothing by sense, nor in nor through a sensory. Therefore to suppose a sensory of any kind—whether space or any other—in God, would be very wrong, and lead us into false conceptions of His nature.'[3] But though the philosophical parts of *Siris* (most of this curious work is concerned with the virtues of tar-water) manifest a rather different atmosphere or mood from that of Berkeley's earlier writings, it is questionable if the book represents any such fundamental change of view as has been suggested. The distinction between sensation and thought may have been accentuated in *Siris*, but it was implicit in Berkeley's earlier writings. As we have seen, he insisted on the distinction between observation of phenomena and reasoning or theorizing about them. Again, Berkeley had already stated in express terms

[1] *Siris*, 253; v, p. 120. [2] *Siris*, 266; v, p. 125. [3] *Siris*, 289; v, pp. 134–5.

in the *Dialogues* that 'God, whom no external being can affect, who
perceives nothing by sense as we do . . . (cannot be affected by)
any sensation at all'.[1] God knows or understands all things, but
not by sense. Hence I do not think that it is correct to say that
Siris represents any fundamental change in Berkeley's philosophy.
The most we can say is that if certain lines of thought had been
followed out and developed, lines of thought which were already
implicit in earlier writings, a different version of his philosophy
might have been produced in which, for example, difficulties
arising from talk about God perceiving things and about 'ideas'
existing in the divine mind when we are not perceiving them would
have been cleared up.

6. We have already seen that Berkeley gives an empiricist or
phenomenalistic analysis of the causal relation as far as the
activity of sensible things is concerned. In fact, we cannot properly
speak of them as active causes at all. If *B* regularly follows *A* in
such a way that, given *A*, *B* follows and that, in the absence of
A, *B* does not occur, we speak of *A* as cause and of *B* as effect.
But this does not mean that *A* acts efficiently in the production
of *B*. The latter follows the former according to the disposition of
God. Ideas, being ideas, are passive and cannot, properly speaking, exercise efficient causality. The occurrence of *A* is the sign
of the coming occurrence of *B*. 'The connexion of ideas does not
imply the relation of *cause* and *effect*, but only of a mark or *sign*
with the thing *signified*. The fire which I see is not the cause of the
pain I suffer upon my approaching it, but the mark that forewarns
me of it.'[2]

There are, therefore, as one would expect, two elements in
Berkeley's analysis of the causal relation as far as sensible things
are concerned. There is first the empiricist element. All we observe
is regular sequence. There is secondly the metaphysical element.
A is a God-given prophetic sign of *B*; and the whole system of
Nature is a system of signs, a visual divine language, speaking to
our minds of God. Moreover, it is not that God established a system
in the beginning and then left it to operate 'as an artist leaves a
clock, to go thenceforward of itself for a certain period. But this
Visual Language proves, not a Creator merely, but a provident
Governor. . . .'[3] God produces each and every sign: He is con-
stantly active, constantly speaking to finite spirits through signs.
Perhaps it is not very easy to see why God should act in this way.

[1] *D.*, 3; II, p. 241.   [2] *P.*, I, 65; II, p. 69.   [3] *A.*, 4, 14; III, p. 160.

For visual signs can be of use only to spirits with bodies; and bodies, on Berkeley's principles, are themselves congeries of ideas, and so visual signs. But this difficulty is not cleared up.

In the *Third Dialogue* Hylas objects that if God is made the immediate author of all events in Nature, He is made the author of sin and crime. But to this Philonous answers, 'I have nowhere said that God is the only agent who produces motions in bodies'.[1] Human spirits are truly active efficient causes. Further, sin does not consist in the physical action 'but in the internal deviation of the will from the laws of reason and religion'.[2] The physical action of committing murder may be similar to the physical action of executing a criminal; but from the moral point of view the two actions are unlike one another. Where there is sin or moral turpitude there is a departure of the will from the moral law, and for this the human agent is responsible.

Thus Berkeley does not say that causality is nothing but regular sequence. What he says is that only spirits are truly active efficient causes. Nor does he say that God is the only true cause. What he says is that the only truly active causes are spirits. As so often with Berkeley, empiricism and metaphysics are combined.

7. Among the continental philosophers of the early modern period the one for whom one would naturally expect Berkeley to show most sympathy is Malebranche. But though he had studied Malebranche and, one must suppose, learned from him, Berkeley was at pains to draw a sharp distinction between his own philosophy and that of the French Oratorian. Several times in the notebooks he expresses disagreement with the latter. For example 'he (Malebranche) doubts of the existence of Bodies. I doubt not in the least of this.'[3] Again, apropos of Malebranche's occasionalism, he remarks: 'We move our legs ourselves. 'Tis we that will their movement. Herein I differ from Malebranche.'[4] And in the *Dialogues* he speaks at length about the remoteness of his philosophy from the 'enthusiasm' of the Frenchman. 'He builds on the most abstract general ideas, which I entirely disclaim. He asserts an absolute eternal world, which I deny. He maintains that we are deceived by our senses and know not the real natures or the true forms and figures of extended being; of all of which I hold the direct contrary. So that upon the whole there are no principles more fundamentally opposite than his and mine.'[5] Berkeley was,

---

[1] *D.* 3; II, p. 237.   [2] *Ibid.*   [3] *P.C.*, 800; I, p. 96.
[4] *P.C.*, 548; I, p. 69.   [5] *D.*, 2; II, p. 214.

of course, well aware of the comparisons which were sometimes drawn, and understandably drawn, between his writings and those of Malebranche, especially with regard to the latter's theory of the vision of all things in God. And these comparisons irritated him. At this distance of time it may, indeed, be a little difficult to understand this irritation, even if we allow for the fact that in his own mind Berkeley had dissociated himself from Malebranche from the start. But he evidently thought of Malebranche as an 'enthusiast' who paid little attention to strict philosophical argumentation. Thus he remarks, apropos of the existence of matter, that 'Scripture and possibility are the only proofs with Malebranche. Add to these what he calls a great propension to think so.'[1] Malebranche was not concerned, in Berkeley's opinion, to recall men from metaphysics to common sense; and he made great use of alleged general, abstract ideas. However, though Berkeley's critical attitude towards the Oratorian was doubtless sincere and an expression of his honest opinion, his concern to dissociate himself from Malebranche shows that he saw that grounds for making a comparison were not altogether wanting.

The philosophy of Descartes Berkeley found uncongenial, and he criticized it frequently. Referring to the former's view that we are not immediately certain of the existence of bodies, he exclaims: 'What a jest is it for a philosopher to question the existence of sensible things, till he hath it proved to him from the veracity of God. . . . I might as well doubt of my own being, as of the being of those things I actually see and feel.'[2] And for Spinoza and Hobbes he had little, if any, sympathy. In the *Dialogues* they are grouped with Vanini as atheists and 'abbettors of impiety',[3] while in the notebooks Berkeley declares that if his own doctrines are rightly understood 'all that philosophy of Epicurus, Hobbes, Spinoza, etc., which has been a declared enemy of religion, comes to the ground'.[4] 'Hobbes and Spinoza make God extended.'[5] And it was 'silly of Hobbes to speak of the will as if it were motion, with which it has no likeness'.[6] If Berkeley disapproved of Descartes, he disapproved much more strongly of Hobbes's materialism. Nor had he much use for the deists, as can be seen from the text of the *Theory of Vision Vindicated and Explained*.[7]

The chief influence on Berkeley as a philosopher was naturally the writings of Locke. For the latter he had a great respect. He

[1] *P.C.*, 686; I, p. 83. [2] *D.*, 3; II, p. 230. [3] *D.*, 2; II, p. 213. [4] *P.C.*, 824; I, p. 98.
[5] *P.C.*, 825; I, p. 98. [6] *P.C.*, 822; I, p. 98. [7] I, pp. 251f.

calls him 'as clear a writer as I have met with', and goes on to remark that 'such was the candour of this great man that I persuade myself, were he alive, he would not be offended that I differ from him, seeing that in so doing I follow his advice, viz. to use my own judgment, see with my own eyes and not with another's'.[1] Again, after referring to his reiterated and vain attempts to apprehend the general idea of a triangle he remarks that 'surely if anyone were able to introduce that idea into my mind, it must be the author of the *Essay concerning Human Understanding*; he who has so far distinguished himself from the generality of writers by the clearness and significancy of what he says'.[2] But though Berkeley felt a profound respect for Locke, and though the latter had furnished him to a great extent with his point of departure, his respect was, of course, accompanied by sustained criticism. In the notebooks he remarks that Locke would have done better to begin his *Essay* with the third book.[3] In other words, if the latter had begun with an examination and critique of language, he might not have fallen into his theory of abstract general ideas, which, according to Berkeley, was largely responsible for the doctrine of material substance. In general, we can say that Berkeley considered Locke to have been insufficiently empiricist and insufficiently observant of his own declared principles.

8. It is worth remarking that Berkeley was influenced by Locke's notion that ethics could be turned into a demonstrative science like mathematics. Thus he made a memorandum to consider well what Locke meant in saying of algebra 'that it supplies intermediate ideas. Also to think of a method affording the same use in Morals, etc., that this doth in mathematics'.[4] The notion that the mathematical method could be applied to ethics, rendering it a demonstrative science was, of course, common at the time, partly because of the prestige won by mathematics through its successful application in physical science and partly because it was widely thought that ethics had formerly depended on authority and needed a new rational basis. Berkeley saw, indeed, that ethics could not in any case be a branch of pure mathematics; but he shared, at one time at least, the hope of making it analogous to a branch of applied mathematics or, as he puts it, 'mixt Mathematics'.[5] This dream he never attempted to fulfil systematically;

---

[1] *P.C.*, 688; I, p. 84.   [2] *E.*, 125; I, p. 221.   [3] *P.C.*, 717; I, p. 87.
[4] *P.C.*, 697; I, p. 85.   [5] *P.C.*, 755; I, p. 92.

but he made some remarks which show that he differed from Locke in his view of what form ethical demonstration would take. For Locke mathematics studies the relations between abstract ideas and can pursue demonstration by means of 'intermediate ideas', but for Berkeley it considers the relations not between abstract ideas but between signs or symbols. Ethics, treated mathematically, would not demonstrate the relations between abstract ideas; it would concern words. It seems, he says, that all that is necessary to make ethics a demonstrative science is to make a dictionary of words and see which includes which.[1] The first important task, therefore, would be that of defining words.[2] It is clear, however, from some remarks in the notebooks that Berkeley realized even then that there is much more difficulty in attaining common agreement about the meaning of ethical terms than there is about the meaning of algebraic symbols. When one learns mathematics one learns the meaning of the symbols at the same time, without preconceptions about their meaning; but this is not the case with the terms used in ethics. This was possibly one of the reasons why Berkeley never wrote the part of the *Principles* which was to have dealt with ethics.

As it is, Berkeley's moral philosophy is fragmentary and un-developed. In his notebooks we find the surprising assertion that 'Sensual Pleasure is the Summum Bonum. This (is) the Great Principle of Morality'.[3] This seems at first sight to be the expression of a crass hedonism. But the words which follow immediately in the same entry show that this would be a rash conclusion to draw: 'This once rightly understood all the doctrines even the severest of the Gospels may clearly be demonstrated.' For if the statement that sensual pleasure is the *summum bonum* or supreme good is to be made consistent with the severest doctrines of the Gospels, it obviously cannot be taken in its prima facie sense. Moreover, in other entries Berkeley makes a distinction between different kinds of pleasure. 'Sensual pleasure qua pleasure is good and desirable by a wise man. But if it be contemptible, 'tis not qua pleasure but qua pain or cause of pain, or (which is the same thing) of loss of greater pleasure.'[4] Again, he states that 'he that acts not in order to the obtaining of eternal happiness must be an infidel; at least he is not certain of a future judgment'.[5] These entries may seem to be inconsistent; but by 'sensual pleasure' Berkeley apparently

---

[1] *P.C.*, 690; I, p. 84.　　[2] *P.C.*, 853; I, p. 101.　　[3] *P.C.*, 769; I, p. 93.
[4] *P.C.*, 773; I, p. 93.　　[5] *P.C.*, 776; I, p. 93.

means pleasure which is sensed or perceived (concrete pleasure) rather than the gratification of sensual appetite in an exclusive sense. If happiness is the end of human life, it must be something concrete, not a mere abstraction. 'What it is for a man to be happy, or an object good, every one may think he knows. But to frame an abstract idea of *happiness*, prescinded from all particular pleasure, or of *goodness*, from everything that is good, this is what few can pretend to. . . . And in effect, the doctrine of *abstraction* has not a little contributed towards spoiling the most useful parts of knowledge.'[1]

Berkeley came to make a distinction between 'natural' pleasures, suited to man as a rational as well as a sensitive being, and 'fantastical' pleasures, which feed desire without satisfying it. He supposed that self-love, as the desire for happiness, is the ruling motive in conduct; but he emphasized rational self-love and came to depreciate the pleasures of sense in comparison with the pleasures of reason, just as in his later writings, particularly in *Siris*, he depreciated sensation in comparison with rational knowledge.

Some of Berkeley's remarks appear to represent utilitarianism and the view that the common good, rather than private happiness, is the proper object of human endeavour. Thus he speaks of 'moral or practical truths being ever connected with universal benefit'.[2] And in the treatise on *Passive Obedience* we read that it is 'the general well-being of all men, of all nations, of all ages of the world, which God designs should be procured by the concurring actions of each individual'.[3] But insistence on the common good was not in Berkeley's opinion incompatible with insistence on the primacy of rational self-love. For the latter does not spell egoism; it includes what we call altruism. And God has so contrived things that the pursuit of happiness according to reason always contributes to the common good and welfare.

Further, being convinced that morality requires rational, moral laws, Berkeley maintained that reason can ascertain a natural moral law, implying human freedom and duty. But to assert the validity of universal standards and rules is not inconsistent with saying that everyone seeks his own interest. What the moral law commands is that we should seek our true interest according to reason, and it enables us to ascertain where our true

---

[1] *P.*, I, 100; II, pp. 84–5.   [2] *A.*, 5, 4; III, p. 178.
[3] *Passive Obedience*, 7; VI, p. 21.

interest lies. Thus, as Berkeley observes in *Alciphron*, 'everyone's true interest is combined with his duty' and 'wisdom and virtue are the same thing'.[1]

As Berkeley believed that rational self-love includes altruism, it is only to be expected that he would attack what he regarded as the narrow egoism of Hobbes. In *Alciphron* he also attacked Mandeville and Shaftesbury, the former in the second *Dialogue*, the latter in the third. Berkeley did not accept the theory of the moral sense, and in his view neither of these philosophers understood the function of reason in the moral life, nor did either of them provide an effective motive for altruistic conduct. The common defects of the two, and the special defects of each, illustrate the moral insufficiencies of the free-thinkers. To Shaftesbury at least Berkeley was definitely unfair, and he misrepresented his position. But his criticism of the free-thinkers is of interest because it shows his conviction that morality is not autonomous and that it must be linked with religion. 'Conscience always supposeth the being of a God.'[2] It may be that by the time he wrote *Alciphron* Berkeley had been influenced by the sermons of Bishop Butler; but it does not seem that this can be proved. However, he came to believe, as Butler believed, that rational and universal rules of morality have a real importance in the moral life and that ethics and religion are more closely connected than some writers supposed.

These remarks may suggest that Berkeley threw out a number of remarks about ethics and morality, and that he did not attempt to render them fully consistent, still less to develop them systematically. And it is indeed true that we cannot find in his writings anything which can properly be called a developed ethical system. At the same time we can find in the treatise on *Passive Obedience* what may be called perhaps prolegomena to Berkeley's ethical system. And it is perhaps worth while drawing attention, at the close of this section, to the relevant passages.

Self-love, as a principle of action, has the primacy. 'Self-love being a principle of all others the most universal, and the most deeply engraven in our hearts, it is natural for us to regard things as they are fitted to augment or impair our own happiness; and accordingly we denominate them *good* or *evil*.'[3] At first the human being is guided by the impressions of sense, and sensible pleasure

---

[1] *A.*, 3, 10; III, p. 129.   [2] *A.*, I, 12; III, p. 52.
[3] *Passive Obedience*, 5; VI, p. 19.

and pain are taken as the infallible characteristics of good and evil. But as the human being grows up, experience shows him that present pleasure is sometimes followed by a greater pain, and that present pain may be the occasion of procuring a greater future good. Further, when the nobler faculties of the soul display their activities, we discover goods which excel those of the senses. 'Hence an alteration is wrought in our judgments; we no longer comply with the first solicitations of sense, but stay to consider the remote consequences of an action, what good may be hoped, or what evil feared from it, according to the wonted course of things.'[1]

But this is but a first step. Consideration of eternity in comparison with time shows us that every reasonable man ought so to act as to contribute most effectively to his eternal interest. Further, reason shows that there is a God who can make man eternally happy or eternally miserable. And it follows from this that the reasonable man will conform his actions to God's expressed will. But Berkeley does not keep exclusively to this theological utilitarianism. If, he says, we consider the relation which God bears to creatures, we shall have to draw the same conclusion. For God, as maker and preserver of all things, is the supreme legislator. 'And mankind are, by all the ties of duty, no less than interest, bound to obey His laws.'[2] Duty and interest point in the same direction.

But how are we to know these laws, apart from revelation? 'Laws being rules directive of our actions to the end intended by the legislator, in order to attain the knowledge of God's laws we ought first to inquire what that end is which He designs should be carried on by human actions.'[3] The end must be good, for God is infinitely good. But it cannot be God's good; for God is already perfect. Hence the end must be the good of man. Now, it is moral goodness which makes this man rather than that man more acceptable to God. And moral goodness presupposes obedience to law. Hence the end envisaged by the legislator must logically precede all differentiations between individuals. And this means that the end must be the good, not of this or that particular man or nation, but of man in general; that is, of all men.

From this it follows that 'whatsoever practical proposition doth to right reason evidently appear to have a necessary connexion with the universal well-being included in it is to be looked upon

<hr>

[1] *Passive Obedience*, 5; VI, p. 19.   [2] *Ibid.*, 6; VI, p. 20.   [3] *Ibid.*, 7; VI, p. 20.

as enjoined by the will of God'.[1] These propositions are called 'laws of nature' because they are universal and derive their obligation from God, not from civil sanction. They are said to be stamped on the mind because they are well known by men and inculcated by conscience. They are termed 'eternal rules of reason' because 'they necessarily result from the nature of things, and may be demonstrated by the infallible deductions of reason'.[2]

This sketch of an ethical system is of some interest because it combines consideration of contemporary themes, such as the place of self-love in the moral life, the relation of duty to interest and the common good as the end of conduct, with traditional elements such as the idea of a natural moral law, determined not by the arbitrary will of God but by an objective end. It is also of interest as showing Berkeley's insistence on the function of reason in morality. On this matter it is possible that Berkeley was influenced, to some slight extent at least, by the Cambridge Platonists. As we have seen, he speaks of 'eternal rules of reason', and he asserts that 'in morality the eternal rules of action have the same immutable universal truth with propositions in geometry. Neither of them depend on circumstances or accidents, being at all times, and in all places, without limitations or exception, true.'[3] But though Berkeley's sketch is of some interest, he is not, as moral philosopher, of the same rank as Butler.

9. To understand Berkeley's own attitude towards his philosophy, we must bear in mind his concern to prove the existence and providential activity of God and the spirituality and immortality of the soul. He was convinced that through his criticism of the theory of material substance he had deprived materialism of its chief support. 'How great a friend material substance hath been to *atheists* in all ages, were needless to relate. All their monstrous systems have so visible and necessary a dependence on it, that when this corner-stone is once removed, the whole fabric cannot choose but fall to the ground.'[4] In order to see Berkeley's philosophy as he saw it, it is essential to remember his religious, apologetic and moral interests.

But it can scarcely be claimed that the metaphysical elements in Berkeley's philosophy have exercised much influence. It was the empiricist element which was most influential. Hume, as will be seen in the following chapters, developed his phenomenalistic

---

[1] *Passive Obedience*, 11; VI, p. 22.   [2] *Ibid.*, 12; VI, p. 23.
[3] *Ibid.*, 53; VI, p. 45.   [4] *P.*, 1, 92; II, p. 81.

analysis. And in the nineteenth century J. S. Mill praised his 'three first rate philosophical discoveries, each sufficient to have constituted a revolution in psychology, and which by their combination have determined the whole course of subsequent philosophical speculation'.[1] These three discoveries were, according to Mill, Berkeley's theory of visual perception (that is, the theory expounded in the *Essay towards a New Theory of Vision*), his doctrine that reasoning is always about particulars, and his view that reality consists of collections or groups of sensations. (Mill himself defined a corporeal thing as a permanent possibility of sensations.)

In speaking of Berkeley's importance Mill was quite justified. He remains as one of the three outstanding classical British empiricists, and his thought, in its empiricist aspect, has influenced, directly or indirectly, the subsequent development of English philosophy in this tradition. Today, when the movement of linguistic analysis is so strong in British thought, particular interest is taken in his anticipations of the theory and practice of this analysis. And it is important that this element in his thought should be brought out. But Berkeley himself would doubtless regret that the more metaphysical elements in his philosophy are generally considered unacceptable by those who esteem him on other grounds.

[1] *Dissertations and Discussions*, 4, 155.

CHAPTER XIV

HUME (1)

Life and writings—The science of human nature—Impressions and ideas—The association of ideas—Substance and relations—Abstract general ideas—Relations of ideas; mathematics—Matters of fact—The analysis of causality—The nature of belief.

1. LOCKE, as we have seen, combined an acceptance of the principle that all our ideas arise ultimately from experience with a modest metaphysics. Berkeley, though he carried empiricism further than Locke had done by rejecting the latter's conception of material substance, nevertheless utilized empiricism in the service of a spiritualist metaphysical philosophy. The task of completing the empiricist experiment and of presenting an uncompromising antithesis to continental rationalism was reserved for David Hume. It is to Hume, therefore, that modern empiricists look as the progenitor of the philosophy which they accept. I do not mean that the modern empiricist accepts all Hume's assertions or that he imitates all the latter's ways of expressing empiricist theories and analyses. But Hume remains for him the one outstanding philosopher up to the end of the eighteenth century who took empiricism seriously and who endeavoured to develop a consistent empiricist philosophy.

David Hume was born at Edinburgh in 1711. His family wished him to become a lawyer, but he tells that he was dominated by a passion for literature and felt 'an insurmountable aversion to everything but the pursuits of philosophy and general learning'. Hume's father was not, however, sufficiently wealthy to enable his son to follow his inclinations, and the latter went into business at Bristol. This was not a successful experiment, and after a few months of uncongenial work Hume went to France, resolved to devote himself to literary pursuits and to make a consistent frugality compensate for his lack of fortune. During the years which he spent in France, 1734-7, he composed his famous work, *A Treatise of Human Nature*. It was published in three volumes (1738-40) and according to its author's account it 'fell dead-born from the press', without even exciting 'a murmur among the zealots'.

After his return from France in 1737 Hume lived in Scotland with his mother and brother. In 1741-2 he published *Essays, Moral and Political*; and the success of this work stimulated him to set about re-writing the *Treatise* in the hope that in its new form it might prove more acceptable to the public. In 1745 Hume applied for the chair of ethics and pneumatic philosophy at the University of Edinburgh, but his reputation for scepticism and atheism helped to make his application unsuccessful. After a year as a private tutor he went abroad as secretary to General St. Clair, and he did not return home until 1749. In the meantime his revision of the first part of the *Treatise* had appeared in 1748 under the title of *Philosophical Essays concerning Human Understanding*. A second edition appeared in 1751, and Hume gave to the book the title which it now bears, *An Enquiry concerning Human Understanding*. In the same year he published *An Enquiry concerning the Principles of Morals*, which was more or less a recasting of the third part of the *Treatise* and which was regarded by its author as the best of his works. In 1752 he published his *Political Discourses*, which earned for him a considerable reputation.

In the same year, 1752, Hume became librarian to the Faculty of Advocates in Edinburgh and set up house with his sister in the city, his brother having married in the previous year. Helped by the use of his library, he now turned his attention to writing on the history of England. In 1756 he published a history of Great Britain from the accession of James I to the death of Charles I, and this was followed by the appearance in 1756 of a second volume which continued the history of Great Britain up to the revolution of 1688. His *History of England under the House of Tudor* was published in 1759, and in 1761 there appeared his *History of England from the Invasion of Julius Caesar to the Accession of Henry VII*. As far as philosophy is concerned, he did not publish much at this time, though his *Four Dissertations*, which included one on the natural history of religion, appeared in 1757.

In 1763 Hume went to Paris with the earl of Hertford, British Ambassador to France, and for some time he was secretary to the embassy. While in Paris he consorted with the group of French philosophers associated with the *Encyclopaedia*, and on returning to London in 1716 he brought back with him Rousseau, though the latter's suspicious character soon led to a break in their relations. For two years Hume was an Under-secretary of State, but in 1769 he returned to Edinburgh, where he died in 1776. His

Dialogues concerning Natural Religion, which had been written before 1752, were published posthumously in 1779. His essays on suicide and immortality appeared anonymously in 1777 and under Hume's name in 1783.

Hume's autobiography, edited by his friend Adam Smith, appeared in 1777. In it he describes himself in a frequently quoted passage as 'a man of mild disposition, of command of temper, of an open, social and cheerful humour, capable of attachment, but little susceptible of enmity, and of great moderation in all my passions. Even my love of literary fame, my ruling passion, never soured my temper, notwithstanding my frequent disappointments.' To judge by the memories of the earl of Charlemont, his appearance seems to have been remote from anything which the reader of his works would be likely to attribute to him spontaneously. For according to Charlemont, Hume looked much more like 'a turtle-eating Alderman than a refined philosopher'. We are also told that he spoke English with a very broad Scottish accent and that his French was far from exemplary. However, his personal appearance and his accent, though of interest to those who like to know such details about famous men, are clearly irrelevant to his importance and influence as a philosopher.[1]

2. In his Introduction to the *Treatise of Human Nature* Hume remarks that all the sciences have some relation to human nature. This is obvious, he says, in the case of logic, morals, criticism and politics. Logic is concerned with the principles and operations of man's faculty of reasoning and with the nature of our ideas; morals and criticism (aesthetic) treat of our tastes and sentiments; politics considers the union of men in society. Mathematics, natural philosophy and natural religion appear, indeed, to be concerned with subjects quite other than man. But they are known by man, and it is man who judges what is true and what is false in these branches of knowledge. Moreover, natural religion treats not only of the nature of the divine but also of God's disposition towards us and of our obligations towards Him. Human nature is thus the 'capital or centre' of the sciences, and it is of

---

[1] Page-references to Hume's *Treatise* and *Enquiries* will be given according to the editions by L. A. Selby-Bigge (Oxford, 1951 reprint of 1888 edition of the *Treatise* and 1951 impression of 1902 edition of the *Enquiries*). The *Treatise* will be referred to as *T.*; the *Enquiry concerning Human Understanding* as *E.*, and the *Enquiry concerning the Principles of Morals* as *E.M.* Page-references to the *Dialogues concerning Natural Religion* will be given according to the edition by Norman Kemp Smith (Edinburgh, second edition, 1947), and the work will be referred to as *D.*

paramount importance that we should develop a science of man. How is this to be done? By applying the experimental method. 'As the science of man is the only solid foundation for the other sciences, so the only solid foundation we can give to this science itself must be laid on experience and observation.'[1]

Hume's *Treatise* is thus inspired by no mean ambition. 'In pretending, therefore, to explain the principles of human nature, we in effect propose a complete system of the sciences, built on a foundation almost entirely new, and the only one upon which they can stand with any security.'[2] His point is that the experimental method which has been applied with such success in natural science should be applied also in the study of man. That is to say, we ought to start with a close observation of man's psychological processes and of his moral behaviour and endeavour to ascertain their principles and causes. We cannot, indeed, make experiments in this field in precisely the same way that we can in, for example, chemistry. We have to be content with the data as they are given to us in introspection and in observation of human life and conduct. But in any case we must start with the empirical data, and not with any pretended intuition of the essence of the human mind, which is something that eludes our grasp. Our method must be inductive rather than deductive. And 'where experiments of this kind are judiciously collected and compared, we may hope to establish on them a science which will not be inferior in certainty, and will be much superior in utility, to any other of human comprehension'.[3]

It is thus the intention of Hume to extend the methods of the Newtonian science, as far as this is possible, to human nature itself, and to carry further the work begun by Locke, Shaftesbury, Hutcheson and Butler. He sees, of course, that the science of human nature is in some sense different from physical science. He makes use, for instance, of the method of introspection, and he is obviously aware that this method is inapplicable outside the psychological sphere. At the same time he shares with the other philosophers of the pre-Kantian Enlightenment an insufficient understanding of the differences between the physical sciences and the sciences of the mind or 'spirit'. However, a better understanding was in part a result of the experiment of extending the general concepts of 'natural philosophy' to the science of man. And in view of the great advance in the natural sciences since the

[1] *T.*, Introduction, p. xx.   [2] *Ibid.*   [3] *Ibid.*, p. xxiii.

Renaissance it is no matter for surprise that the experiment was made.

In the *Enquiry concerning Human Understanding* Hume says that the science of human nature can be treated in two ways. A philosopher may consider man chiefly as born for action and concern himself with exhibiting the beauty of virtue with a view to stimulating men to virtuous conduct. Or he may consider man as a reasoning rather than as an active being and concern himself with enlightening man's understanding rather than with improving his conduct. Philosophers of this second type 'regard human nature as a subject of speculation, and with a narrow scrutiny examine it, in order to find those principles which regulate our understanding, excite our sentiments and make us approve or blame any particular object, action or behaviour'.[1] The first type of philosophy is 'easy and obvious', the second 'accurate and abstruse'. The generality of mankind naturally prefers the first type; but the second is requisite if the first is to possess any sure foundation. True, abstract and abstruse metaphysical speculation leads nowhere. 'But the only method of freeing learning at once from these abstruse questions is to inquire seriously into the nature of human understanding, and show, from an exact analysis of its powers and capacities, that it is by no means fitted for such remote and abstruse subjects. We must submit to this fatigue, in order to live at ease ever after; and (we) must cultivate true metaphysics with some care, in order to destroy the false and adulterate.'[2] Astronomers were once content with determining the motions and size of the heavenly bodies. But at last they succeeded in determining the laws and forces which govern the movements of the planets. 'The like has been performed with regard to other parts of nature. And there is no reason to despair of equal success in our inquiries concerning the mental powers and economy, if prosecuted with equal capacity and caution.'[3] 'True metaphysics' will drive out false metaphysics; but it will also establish the science of man on a sure basis. And to attain this end it is worth taking trouble and pursuing an accurate, even comparatively abstruse, analysis.

Hume is partly concerned in the first *Enquiry* with commending to his readers the lines of thought developed in the first part of the *Treatise*, which in his opinion failed to win due attention on its publication because of its abstract style. Hence his apologia

---

[1] *E.*, 1, 2, p. 6.   [2] *E.*, 1, 7, p. 12.   [3] *E.*, 1, 9, p. 14.

for a style of philosophizing which goes beyond moralistic edification. But he also makes it clear that he is taking up again the original project of Locke, to determine the extent of human knowledge. He shows, indeed, that he has in mind a purpose connected with morality, namely, to discover the principles and forces which govern our moral judgments. But he is also concerned with discovering the principles which 'regulate our understanding'. To emphasize Hume's role as moral philosopher is legitimate; but this aspect of his thought is over-emphasized if his role as epistemologist is pushed into the background.

3. Like Locke, Hume derives all the contents of the mind from experience. But his terminology is rather different from that employed by the former. He uses the word 'perceptions' to cover the mind's contents in general, and he divides perceptions into impressions and ideas. The former are the immediate data of experience, such as sensations. The latter are described by Hume as the copies or faint images of impressions in thinking and reasoning. If I look at my room, I receive an impression of it. 'When I shut my eyes and think of my chamber, the ideas I form are exact representations of the impressions I felt; nor is there any circumstance of the one, which is not to be found in the other. . . . Ideas and impressions appear always to correspond to each other.'[1] The word 'idea' is obviously used here to signify image. But, passing over this point, we can see immediately the general direction of Hume's thought. Just as Locke derived all our knowledge ultimately from 'simple ideas', so Hume wishes to derive our knowledge ultimately from impressions, from the immediate data of experience. But while these preliminary remarks illustrate the general direction of Hume's thought, they give a very insufficient account of it. And further explanation is required.

Hume describes the difference between impressions and ideas in terms of vividness. 'The difference betwixt these consists in the degrees of force and liveliness with which they strike upon the mind and make their way into our thoughts or consciousness. Those perceptions which enter with most force and violence we may name *impressions*; and, under this name, I comprehend all our sensations, passions and emotions, as they make their first appearance in the soul. By *ideas* I mean the faint images of these in thinking and reasoning; such as, for instance, are all the perceptions excited by the present discourse, excepting only those

[1] *T.*, I, I, I, p. 3.

which arise from the sight and touch, and excepting the immediate pleasure or uneasiness it may occasion.'[1] Hume proceeds to qualify this statement by adding that 'in sleep, in a fever, in madness, or in any very violent emotions of soul, our ideas may approach to our impressions: as, on the other hand, it sometimes happens that our impressions are so faint and low that we cannot distinguish them from our ideas'.[2] But he insists that in general the distinction holds good; and in the *Enquiry* he remarks that 'the most lively thought is still inferior to the dullest sensation'.[3] This distinction between impressions and ideas in terms of liveliness and force is, however, somewhat misleading. At least it can be misleading, if, that is to say, it diverts our attention from the fact that Hume is primarily concerned to distinguish between the immediate data of experience and our thoughts about these data. At the same time he regards ideas as copies of impressions or images of them, and it is perhaps natural that he stresses the difference in vividness between original and image.

As we have seen, Hume asserts that 'ideas and impressions appear always to correspond to each other'. But he goes on to qualify and correct this 'first impression'. He makes a distinction between simple and complex perceptions, a distinction which he applies to both kinds of perceptions, namely, both to impressions and to ideas. The perception of a red patch is a simple impression, and the thought (or image) of the red patch is a simple idea. But if I stand on the hill of Montmartre and survey the city of Paris, I receive a complex impression of the city, of roofs, chimneys, towers and streets. And when I afterwards think of Paris and recall this complex impression, I have a complex idea. In this case the complex idea corresponds in some degree to the complex impression; though it does not do so exactly and adequately. But let us take another case. 'I can imagine to myself a city as the New Jerusalem, whose pavement is gold, and walls are rubies, though I never saw any such.'[4] In this case my complex idea does not correspond to a complex impression.

We cannot say, therefore, with truth that to every idea there is an exactly corresponding impression. But it is to be noted that the complex idea of the New Jerusalem can be broken down into simple ideas. And we can ask whether every simple idea has a corresponding simple impression and every simple impression a corresponding simple idea. Hume answers, 'I venture to affirm

[1] *T.*, 1, 1, 1, p. 1. [2] *Ibid.*, p. 2. [3] *E.*, 2, 11, p. 17. [4] *T.*, 1, 1, 1, p. 3.

that the rule here holds without any exception, and that every simple idea has a simple impression which resembles it, and every simple impression a correspondent idea'.[1] This cannot be proved by examining all possible cases; but anyone who denies the statement can be challenged to mention an exception to it.

Are the impressions derived from ideas or ideas from impressions? To answer this question we need only examine the order of their appearance. It is clear that impressions precede ideas. 'To give a child an idea of scarlet or orange, of sweet or bitter, I present the objects, or, in other words, convey to him these impressions; but proceed not so absurdly as to endeavour to produce the impressions by exciting the ideas.'[2] However, Hume mentions an exception to the general rule that ideas are derived from corresponding impressions. Suppose a man who is familiar with all shades of blue except one. If he is presented with a graded series of blues, running from the deepest to the lightest, and if the particular shade of blue which he has never seen is absent, he will notice a blank in the continuous series. Is it possible for him to supply this deficiency by the use of his imagination and frame the 'idea' of this particular shade, though he has never had the corresponding impression? 'I believe there are few but will be of opinion that he can.'[3] Furthermore, it is obviously possible to form ideas of ideas. For we can reason and talk about ideas, which are themselves ideas of impressions. We then frame 'secondary ideas', which are derived from previous ideas rather than immediately from impressions. But this second qualification does not, strictly speaking, involve an exception to the general rule that impressions precede ideas. And if we make allowance for the exception mentioned in the first qualification, we can safely enunciate the general proposition that our simple impressions are prior to their corresponding ideas.

The following point, however, must be added. Impressions can be divided into impressions of sensation and impressions of reflection. 'The first kind arises in the soul originally from unknown causes.'[4] What, then, of impressions of reflection? These are derived, 'in great measure', from ideas. Suppose that I have an impression of cold, accompanied by pain. A 'copy' of this impression remains in the mind after the impression has ceased. This 'copy' is called an 'idea', and it can produce new impressions of aversion, for example, which are impressions of reflection. These

[1] T., I, I, I, p. 3.   [2] Ibid., p. 5.   [3] Ibid., p. 6.   [4] T., I, I, 2, p. 7.

again can be copied by the memory and imagination and become ideas; and so on. But even though in such a case impressions of reflection are posterior to ideas of sensation, they are prior to their corresponding ideas of reflection, and they are derived ultimately from impressions of sensation. In the long run, therefore, impressions are prior to ideas.

This analysis of the relation between impressions and ideas may appear to constitute a theory of purely academic interest and of little importance, except as a restatement of empiricism which excludes the hypothesis of innate ideas. But its importance becomes manifest if we bear in mind the way in which Hume applies it. For example, he asks, as will be seen later, from what impressions the idea of substance is derived. And he comes to the conclusion that we have no idea of substance apart from a collection of particular qualities. Again, his general theory about impressions and ideas is of great importance in his analysis of causality. Further, the theory can be used to get rid of what Hume calls 'all that jargon which has so long taken possession of metaphysical reasonings and drawn disgrace upon them'.[1] Philosophers may use terms which are vacuous, in the sense that they signify no determinate ideas and possess no definite meaning. 'When we entertain, therefore, any suspicion that a philosophical term is employed without any meaning or idea (as is but too frequent), we need but to inquire, *from what impression is that supposed idea derived?* And if it be impossible to assign any, this will serve to confirm our suspicion.'[2]

Hume's position can be expressed in a rather different way from that in which he actually expresses it. If a child comes across the word 'skyscraper', he may ask his father what it means. The latter can explain its meaning by definition or description. That is to say, he can explain to the child the meaning of the word 'skyscraper' by employing words such as 'house', 'tall', 'storey', and so on. But the child cannot understand the meaning of the description unless he understands the meanings of the terms employed in the description. Some of these terms can themselves be explained by definition or description. But ultimately we come down to words, the meaning of which must be learned ostensively. That is to say, the child must be shown examples of the way in which these words are used, instances of their application. In Hume's language, the child must be given 'impressions'. It is

---

[1] *E.*, 2, 17, p. 21.　　　　　　[2] *Ibid.*, p. 22.

possible, therefore, to explain Hume's point by the use of a distinction between terms, the meaning of which is learned ostensively, and terms, the meaning of which is learned by definition or by description. In other words, it is possible to substitute for Hume's psychological distinction between impressions and ideas a linguistic distinction between terms. But the main point, the priority of experience, of the immediately given, remains the same.

It is worth noting that Hume assumes that 'experience' can be broken into atomic constituents, namely, impressions or sense-data. But though this may be possible if considered as a purely abstract analysis, it is questionable whether 'experience' can profitably be described in terms of these atomic constituents. It is also worth noting that Hume uses the word 'idea' in an ambiguous way. Sometimes he is obviously referring to the image, and, given this sense of idea, it is not unreasonable to speak of ideas as copies of impressions. But at other times he is referring to the concept rather than to an image, and it is difficult to see how the relation of concept to that of which it is a concept can legitimately be described in the same terms as the relation of an image to that of which it is an image. In the first *Enquiry*[1] he uses the terms 'thoughts and ideas' as synonymous. And it is clear, I think, that his main distinction is between the immediately given, namely, impressions, and the derived, to which he gives the general name 'ideas'.

It has been said that Hume's theory of impressions and ideas excludes the hypothesis of innate ideas. But this statement needs some qualification in view of the way in which Hume employs the term 'innate idea'. If innate is taken as equivalent to natural, 'then all the perceptions and ideas of the mind must be allowed to be innate or natural'.[2] If by innate is meant contemporary with birth, the dispute whether there are innate ideas or not is frivolous; 'nor is it worth while to inquire at what time thinking begins, whether before, at or after our birth'.[3] But if by innate we mean copied from no precedent perception, 'then we may assert that all our impressions are innate, and our ideas not innate'.[4] Obviously, Hume did not assert that there are innate ideas in the sense in which Locke was concerned to deny that there are such things. To say that impressions are innate is merely to say that they are not themselves copies of impressions; that is, that they are not ideas in Hume's sense of the word.

[1] 2, 12, p. 18.   [2] *E.*, 2, 17, note, p. 22.   [3] *Ibid.*   [4] *Ibid.*

4. When the mind has received impressions, they can reappear, as Hume puts it, in two ways. First, they can reappear with a degree of vividness which is intermediate between the vividness of an impression and the faintness of an idea. And the faculty by which we repeat our impressions in this way is the memory. Secondly, they can reappear as mere ideas, as faint copies or images of impressions. And the faculty by which we repeat our impressions in this second way is the imagination.

Thus, just as Hume described the difference between impressions and ideas in terms of degrees of vividness, so now he describes the difference between ideas of the memory and ideas of the imagination in a similar manner. But he goes on to give another account of this difference, which is rather more satisfactory. Memory, he says, preserves not only simple ideas but also their order and position. In other words, when we say, for example, that a person has a good memory of a cricket-match, we mean that he recalls not only the various events taken singly but also the order in which they occurred. The imagination, however, is not tied down in this way. It can, for instance, combine simple ideas arbitrarily or break down complex ideas into simple ideas and then rearrange them. This is frequently done in poems and romances. 'Nature there is totally confounded, and nothing mentioned but winged horses, fiery dragons, and monstrous giants.'[1]

But though the imagination can freely combine ideas, it generally works according to some general principles of association. In memory there is an inseparable connection between ideas. In the case of the imagination this inseparable connection is wanting; but there is nevertheless a 'uniting principle' among ideas, 'some associating quality by which one idea naturally introduces another'.[2] Hume describes it as 'a gentle force, which commonly prevails'. Its causes are 'mostly unknown and must be resolved into *original* qualities of human nature, which I pretend not to explain'.[3] In other words, there is in man an innate force or impulse which moves him, though without necessity, to combine together certain types of ideas. What this 'gentle force' is in itself, Hume does not undertake to explain: he takes it as something given. At the same time we can ascertain the qualities which bring this gentle force into play. 'The qualities from which this association arises, and by which the mind is, after this manner, conveyed from one idea to another, are three, viz. *resemblance, contiguity* in

---

[1] *T.*, I, I, 3, p. 10.   [2] *T.*, I, I, 4, p. 10.   [3] *Ibid.*, p. 13.

time or place, and *cause* and *effect*.'¹ The imagination runs easily from one idea to another which resembles it. Similarly, by long custom the mind acquires the habit of associating ideas which are contiguous, immediately or mediately, in space and time. 'As to the connection that is made by the relation of *cause and effect*, we shall have occasion afterwards to examine it to the bottom, and therefore shall not at present insist upon it.'²

5. In the *Treatise* the section on the association of ideas is followed by sections on relations and on modes and substances. These are complex ideas which are asserted to be effects of the association mentioned above. In classifying complex ideas in this way Hume is adopting one of Locke's classifications. We can take the idea of substance first.

Hume asks, as we would expect, from what impression or impressions the idea of substance is derived, supposing that there is such an idea. It cannot be derived from impressions of sensation. If it is perceived by the eyes, it must be a colour; if by the ears, a sound; if by the palate, a taste. But nobody would say that substance is a colour, or a sound or a taste. If, therefore, there is an idea of substance, it must be derived from impressions of reflection. But these can be resolved into our passions and emotions. And those who speak of substances do not mean by the word passions or emotions. The idea of substance is derived, therefore, neither from impressions of sensation nor from impressions of reflection. It follows that there is, properly speaking, no idea of substance at all. The word 'substance' connotes a collection of 'simple ideas'. As Hume puts it, 'the idea of a substance . . . is nothing but a collection of simple ideas that are united by the imagination and have a particular name assigned them, by which we are able to recall, either to ourselves or others, that collection'.³ Sometimes the particular qualities which form a substance are referred to an unknown something in which they are thought to inhere; but even when this 'fiction' is avoided, the qualities are at least supposed to be closely related with one another by 'contiguity and causation'. Thus an association of ideas is set up in the mind, and when we perform the activity which we describe as discovering a new quality of a given substance, the new idea enters into the cluster of associated ideas.

Hume dismisses the subject of substance in a summary manner. It is clear that he accepts the general line of Berkeley's criticism

¹ *T.*, 1, 1, 4, p. 11.　　² *Ibid.*　　³ *T.*, 1, 1, 6, p. 16.

of Locke's notion of material substance, and that he does not consider that the theory of an unknown substratum needs further refutation. What is peculiar to him is that he also rejects Berkeley's theory of spiritual substance. That is to say, he extends the phenomenalistic interpretation of things from bodies to souls or minds. True, he evidently does not feel very happy about the resolution of minds into psychic events, united with the aid of the principle of association. But his general empiricist position obviously points to a consistent phenomenalism, to an analysis of all complex ideas into impressions, and he is involved in the attempt to treat spiritual substance in the same way as material substance. If he feels that his analysis leaves something out and suspects that his explanation of minds is an instance of explaining by explaining away, his doubts indicate either the insufficiency of phenomenalism in general or, at least, the inadequacy of his statement of phenomenalism. However, it is only in a later section of the *Treatise* that he deals with the mind or soul, under the heading of 'personal identity', and we may leave aside this problem for the moment, though it is useful to note at once that he does not confine himself, as Berkeley did, to a phenomenalistic analysis of the idea of material substance.

When discussing relations in the *Treatise* Hume distinguishes two senses of the word 'relation'. First, the word may be used to signify the quality or qualities 'by which two ideas are connected together in the imagination, and the one naturally introduces the other, after the manner above explained'.[1] These 'qualities' are resemblance, contiguity and the causal relation, and Hume calls them natural relations. In the case of natural relations, therefore, ideas are connected with one another by the natural force of association, so that the one tends naturally or by custom to recall the other. Secondly, there are what Hume calls philosophical relations. We can compare at will any objects, provided that there is at least some similarity of quality between them. In such comparison the mind is not impelled by a natural force of association to pass from one idea to another: it does so simply because it has chosen to institute a certain comparison.

Hume enumerates seven types of philosophical relation: resemblance, identity, relations of time and place, proportion in quantity or number, degrees in any quality, contrariety and causation.[2] It will be noted at once that there is a certain

---

[1] *T.*, 1, 1, 5, p. 13.   [2] *Ibid.*, pp. 14-15; cf. *T.*, 1, 3, 1, p. 69.

over-lapping between natural and philosophical relations. In fact, all three natural relations occur in the list of philosophical relations, though not, of course, as natural relations. But this over-lapping is not due to any oversight on Hume's part. He explains, for example, that no objects can be compared unless there is some resemblance between them. Resemblance is, therefore, a relation without which no philosophical relation can exist. But it does not follow that every resemblance produces an association of ideas. If a quality is very general and is found in a very great number of objects or in all objects, it does not lead the mind from one particular member of the class to any other particular member. For instance, all material things resemble one another in being material, and we can compare any material thing with any other material thing. But the idea of a material thing *as such* does not lead the mind by the force of association to any other particular material thing. Again, greenness is common to a great many things. And we can freely compare or group together two or more green things. But the imagination is not impelled, as it were, by natural force of association to move from the idea of green thing *X* to the idea of green thing *Y*. Again, we can compare any two things according to spatio-temporal relations, but it does not necessarily follow that the mind is impelled to do this by the force of association. In some cases it is (for example, when we have always experienced two things as spatially and immediately contiguous or as always succeeding one another immediately); but in very many cases there is no force of association at work. It may be that I am naturally, if not inevitably, impelled to think of St. Peter's when I think of the Vatican palace; but the idea of New York does not naturally recall the idea of Canton, though I can, of course, compare these two cities from a spatial point of view, asserting, for instance, that the one is so far distant from the other.

As for causation, Hume again postpones discussion of it. But it may be as well to remark here that in his view causation, considered as a philosophical relation, is reducible to such relations of space and time as contiguity, temporal succession and constant conjunction or togetherness. There is here no necessary connection between ideas; there are only factual spatio-temporal relations. Hence causation as a philosophical relation affords no ground for proceeding beyond experience by inferring transcendent causes from observed effects. In causation considered as a natural relation there is, indeed, an inseparable connection between ideas; but this element must be explained subjectively, with the aid of the principles of association.

6. Hume treats of general abstract ideas in the first part of the *Treatise*, in close connection, therefore, with his analysis of ideas and impressions. He begins by remarking that 'a great philosopher', namely, Berkeley, has asserted that all general ideas are 'nothing but particular ones annexed to a certain term, which gives them a more extensive signification, and makes them recall upon occasion other individuals, which are similar to them'.[1] This is not perhaps a very happy statement of Berkeley's position; but in any case Hume regards it as of one of the greatest and most valuable of recent discoveries and proposes to confirm it by some further arguments.

In the first place, abstract ideas are individual or particular in themselves. What Hume means can be illustrated by his arguments in favour of this proposition. First, 'the mind cannot form any notion of quantity or quality without forming a precise notion of degrees of each'.[2] For instance, the precise length of a line is not distinguishable from the line itself. We cannot form a general idea of a line without any length at all. Nor can we form the general idea of a line possessing all possible lengths. Secondly, every impression is determinate and definite. Since, therefore, an idea is an image or copy of an impression, it must itself be determinate and definite, even though it is fainter than the impression from which it is derived. Thirdly, everything which exists must be individual. No triangle, for instance, can exist, which is not a particular triangle with its particular characteristics. To postulate an existent triangle which is at the same time all and none of the possible kinds and sizes of triangle would be an absurdity. But what is absurd in fact and reality is absurd also in idea.

It is clear that Hume's view follows from his conception of ideas and of their relation to impressions. If the idea is an image or copy, it must be particular. He thus agrees with Berkeley that there are no *abstract* general ideas. At the same time he admits that what are called abstract ideas, though they are in themselves particular images, 'may become general in their representation'.[3] And what he tries to do is to define the way in which this extension of signification occurs.

When we have found a resemblance between things which we

---

[1] *T.*, I, I, 7, p. 17.   [2] *Ibid.*, p. 18.   [3] *Ibid.*, p. 20.

often observe, we are accustomed to apply the same name to them all, whatever the differences between them may be. For instance, having frequently observed what we call trees and having noticed resemblances between them, we apply the same word 'tree' to them all, in spite of the differences between oaks, elms, larches, tall trees, short trees, deciduous trees, evergreens, and so on. And after we have acquired the custom of applying the same word to these objects, the hearing of the word revives the idea of one of these objects, and makes the imagination conceive it. The hearing of the word or name cannot call up ideas of all the objects to which the name is applied: it calls up one of them. But at the same time it calls into play 'a certain custom', a readiness to produce any other individual resembling this idea, if occasion should demand it. For example, suppose that I hear the word 'triangle' and that this word calls up in my mind the idea of a particular equilateral triangle. If I then assert that the three angles of a triangle are equal to each other, 'custom' or 'association' calls up the idea of some other triangle which shows the falsity of this universal statement. To be sure, this custom is mysterious; and 'to explain the ultimate causes of our mental actions is impossible'.[1] But analogous cases can be cited to confirm the existence of such a custom. For example, if we have learned by heart a long poem, we do not recollect it all at once; but remembrance or hearing of the first line, possibly of the first word, puts the mind in readiness to recall all that follows as occasion demands; that is, in due order. We may not be able to explain how this association works, but there is no doubt about the empirical facts. Again, when we make use of terms such as *government* or *church*, we seldom conceive distinctly in our minds all the simple ideas of which these complex ideas are composed. But we can very well avoid talking nonsense about these complex ideas, and if someone makes a statement which is incompatible with some element of the full content of such an idea, we may recognize at once the absurdity of the statement. For 'custom' calls up the distinct component idea as occasion requires. Again, we may not be able to give any adequate causal explanation of the process; but none the less it occurs.

7. In the first *Enquiry* Hume asserts that 'all the objects of human reason or inquiry may naturally be divided into two kinds, to wit, *relations of ideas* and *matters of fact*. Of the first kind are the sciences of geometry, algebra and arithmetic, and, in short,

[1] *T.*, I, I, 7, p. 22.

every affirmation which is either intuitively or demonstratively certain. . . . Matters of fact, which are the second objects of human reason, are not ascertained in the same manner; nor is our evidence of their truth, however great, of a like nature with the foregoing.'[1] Hume means that all our reasoning concerns the relations between things. These relations are, as Locke stated, of two kinds, relations of ideas or matters of fact. An arithmetical proposition is an example of the former, while the statement that the sun will rise tomorrow is an example of the latter. In this section we are concerned with relations of ideas.

Of the seven philosophical relations only four, says Hume, depend solely on ideas; namely, resemblance, contrariety, degrees in quality and proportions in quantity or number. The first three of these are 'discoverable at first sight and fall more properly under the province of intuition than demonstration'.[2] As we are concerned with demonstrative reasoning, we are left, therefore, with proportions in quantity or number, namely, with mathematics. Mathematical propositions assert relations between ideas, and ideas only. In algebra, for example, it makes no difference to the certainty of the demonstrations and the truth of the propositions whether or not there are objects corresponding to the symbols employed. The truth of a mathematical proposition is independent of questions about existence.

Hume's account of mathematics is, therefore, rationalist and non-empiricist, in the sense that he maintains that the relations asserted are necessary. The truth of a mathematical proposition depends simply and solely on the relations between ideas, or, as we might say, on the meanings of certain symbols; and it requires no confirmation from experience. We should not, of course, understand Hume as meaning that mathematical ideas are innate in Locke's sense of the word. He was quite well aware of the ways in which we come to know the meanings of arithmetical and algebraic symbols. His point is that the truth of the propositions is quite independent of the ways in which we come to know the meanings of the symbols. Their truth cannot possibly be refuted by experience; for nothing is said about matters of fact. They are formal propositions, not empirical hypotheses. And though, of course, mathematics can be applied, the truth of the propositions is independent of this application. In this sense they can be called *a priori* propositions, though Hume does not use the term.

[1] *E.*, 4, 1, 20–1, p. 25.　　　[2] *T.*, 1, 3, 1, p. 70.

In the nineteenth century J. S. Mill tried to show that mathematical propositions are empirical hypotheses. But in the characteristic empiricism of the twentieth century it is the view of Hume rather than that of Mill which is accepted. The neo-positivists, for instance, interpret mathematical propositions as *a priori* and analytic propositions. At the same time, while not, of course, denying their applicability in science, they insist that in themselves they are void of factual, empirical content. To say that four plus three equals seven is not in itself to say anything about existent things: the truth of the proposition depends simply on the meanings of the terms. And this is the view maintained by Hume.

There is a further point to be noticed. In the *Treatise* Hume asserts that 'geometry falls short of that perfect precision and certainty which are peculiar to arithmetic and algebra, yet it excels the imperfect judgments of our senses and imagination'.[1] The reason he gives is that the first principles of geometry are drawn from the general appearances of things; and that appearances cannot give us certainty. 'Our ideas seem to give a perfect assurance that no two right lines can have a common segment; but if we consider these ideas, we shall find that they always suppose a sensible inclination of the two lines, and that where the angle they form is extremely small, we have no standard of a right line so precise as to assure us of the truth of this proposition.'[2] And the conclusion Hume draws is that 'there remain therefore algebra and arithmetic as the only sciences in which we can carry on a chain of reasoning to any degree of intricacy and yet preserve a perfect exactness and certainty'.[3] But there does not appear to be any adequate reason for treating geometry as an exception to a general interpretation of mathematics. If the truth of algebraic and arithmetical propositions depends solely on 'ideas' or on definitions, the same can be said of geometry, and sensible 'appearances' are irrelevant. Hume seems to have felt this himself; for in the first *Enquiry* geometry is placed on the same footing as algebra and arithmetic. And he remarks that 'though there never were a circle or triangle in nature, the truths demonstrated by Euclid would for ever retain their certainty and evidence'.[4]

8. Philosophical relations are divided by Hume into invariable and variable relations. Invariable relations cannot be changed without a change in the objects related or in the ideas of them.

[1] *T.*, 1, 3, 1, p. 71.   [2] *Ibid.*   [3] *Ibid.*   [4] *E.*, 4, 1, 20, p. 25.

Conversely, if the latter remain unchanged, the relation between them remains unchanged. Mathematical relations are of this type. Given certain ideas or meaningful symbols, the relations between them are invariable. In order to make an arithmetical or an algebraic proposition untrue, we should have to change the meanings of the symbols; if we do not do this, the propositions are necessarily true; that is, the relations between the ideas are invariable. Variable relations, however, can change without any change in the related objects or in their ideas being necessarily involved. For example, the spatial relation of distance between two bodies can vary, though the bodies and our ideas of them remain the same.

It follows that we cannot come to have certain knowledge of variable relations by pure reasoning; that is, simply by analysis of ideas and *a priori* demonstration: we become acquainted with them by experience and observation, or, rather, we depend upon experience and observation, even in those cases where inference is involved. We are here concerned with matters of fact, and not with purely ideal relations. And, as we have seen, we cannot attain the same degree of evidence about matters of fact which we attain about relations of ideas. A proposition which states a relation of ideas, in Hume's sense of the term, cannot be denied without contradiction. Given, for example, the meanings of the symbols 2 and 4, we cannot deny that $2+2=4$ without being involved in contradiction: the opposite is inconceivable. But 'the contrary of every matter of fact is still possible, because it can never imply a contradiction. . . . That the sun will not rise tomorrow is no less intelligible a proposition and implies no more contradiction than the affirmation that it will rise.'[1] Hume does not mean that it is untrue to say that the sun will rise tomorrow: he means that no logical contradiction is involved in saying that the sun will not rise tomorrow. Nor does he intend to deny that we may feel certain that the sun will rise tomorrow. He is maintaining, however, that we do not and cannot have the same grounds for assurance that the sun will rise tomorrow that we have for the truth of a proposition in pure mathematics. It may be highly probable that the sun will rise tomorrow, but it is not certain if we mean by a certain proposition one which is logically necessary and the opposite of which is contradictory and impossible.

Hume's position on this matter is of considerable importance.

---

[1] *E.*, 4, 1, 21, pp. 25–6.

Propositions asserting what he calls relations of ideas are now generally called analytic propositions. And propositions which assert matters of fact are called synthetic propositions. It is the contention of modern empiricists that all *a priori* propositions, the truth of which is known independently of experience and observation and the opposites of which are self-contradictory, are analytic propositions, their truth depending simply on the meanings of symbols. No synthetic proposition, therefore, is an *a priori* proposition; it is an empirical hypothesis, enjoying a greater or lesser degree of probability. The existence of synthetic *a priori* propositions, propositions, that is to say, which assert matters of fact but which at the same time are absolutely certain, is excluded. This general position represents a development of Hume's views.

A further point. We can make the following distinction between different kinds of variable or 'inconsistent' relations. According to Hume, 'we ought not to receive as reasoning any of the observations we may make concerning identity and relations of time and place; since in none of them the mind can go beyond what is immediately present to the senses, either to discover the real existence or the relations of objects'.[1] Thus I see immediately that this piece of paper is contiguous with the surface of the table. Here we have a case of perception rather than of reasoning. And I do not go beyond the actual perception by inferring the existence or activity of anything which transcends the actual perception. I can do so, of course; but in this case I introduce causal inference. In Hume's view, therefore, any 'conclusion (about matters of fact) beyond the impressions of our senses can be founded only on the connection of cause and effect'.[2] 'All reasonings concerning matter of fact seem to be founded on the relation of cause and effect. By means of that relation alone we can go beyond the evidence of our memory and senses.'[3] In other words, all reasoning in matters of fact, as contrasted with relations of ideas, is causal inference. Or, to put the matter more concretely, in mathematics we have demonstration, and in the empirical sciences we have causal inference. In view, therefore, of the important role played by causal inference in human knowledge we must inquire into the nature of the causal relation and the grounds which we have for proceeding by means of causal inference beyond the immediate testimony of the senses.

[1] *T*., I, 3, 2, p. 73.   [2] *Ibid*., p. 74.   [3] *E*., 4, I, 22, p. 26.

9. Hume approaches his examination of the causal relation by asking from what impression or impressions the idea of causation is derived. In the first place no quality of those things which we call 'causes' can be the origin of the idea of causation. For we cannot discover any quality which is common to them all. 'The idea then of causation must be derived from some *relation* among objects; and that relation we must now endeavour to discover.'[1]

The first relation which Hume mentions is contiguity. 'I find in the first place that whatever objects are considered as causes or effects are contiguous.'[2] He does not mean, of course, that the things which we consider to be causes and effects are always immediately contiguous; for there may be a chain or series of causes between thing A, which we call a cause, and thing Z, which we call an effect. But it will be found that A and B are contiguous, B and C, and so on, even though A and Z are not themselves immediately contiguous. What Hume rules out is action at a distance in the proper sense of the term. It must be added, however, that he is speaking of the popular idea of causation. It is popularly believed, he thinks, that cause and effect are always contiguous, either immediately or mediately. But he does not commit himself definitely in the third part of the *Treatise* to the statement that the relation of contiguity is essential to the causal relation. He says that we can take it that this is the case 'till we can find a more proper occasion to clear up this matter, by examining what objects are or are not susceptible of juxtaposition and conjunction'.[3] And later on he makes it clear that he does not regard spatial contiguity as essential to the idea of causation. For he maintains that an object can exist and yet be nowhere. 'A moral reflection cannot be placed on the right or on the left hand of a passion; nor can a smell or sound be either of a circular or a square figure. These objects and perceptions, so far from requiring any particular place, are absolutely incompatible with it, and even the imagination cannot attribute it to them.'[4] We certainly think of passions, for example, as entering into causal relations; but they cannot be said to be spatially contiguous with other things. Hume does not, therefore, regard spatial contiguity as an indispensable element in the causal relation.

The second relation which Hume discusses is that of temporal priority. He argues that the cause must be temporally prior to the effect. Experience confirms this. Further, if in any instance an

[1] *T.*, 1, 3, 2, p. 75.   [2] *Ibid.*   [3] *Ibid.*   [4] *T.*, 1, 4, 5, p. 236.

effect could be perfectly contemporary with its cause, this would be so in all instances of true causation. For in any instance in which it was not the case, the so-called cause would remain for some time in inactivity and would need some other factor to push it into activity. It would not then be a true or proper cause. But if all effects were perfectly contemporary with their causes, 'it is plain there would be no such thing as succession, and all objects must be coexistent'.[1] This is, however, patently absurd. We can take it, therefore, that an effect cannot be perfectly contemporary with its cause, and that a cause must be temporally prior to its effect.

But Hume is evidently not altogether sure of the cogency of this argument. For he goes on to say: 'If this argument appear satisfactory, it is well. If not, I beg the reader to allow me the same liberty which I have used in the preceding case, of supposing it such. For he shall find that the affair is of no great importance.'[2] It is thus untrue to say that Hume lays great emphasis on contiguity and on temporal succession as essential elements of the causal relation. He decided, indeed, to treat them as though they were essential elements, but there is another element of greater importance. 'Shall we then rest contented with these two relations of contiguity and succession, as affording a complete idea of causation? By no means. An object may be contiguous and prior to another, without being considered as its cause. There is a *necessary connection* to be taken into consideration; and that relation is of much greater importance than any of the other two above mentioned.'[3]

The question arises, therefore, from what impression or impressions is the idea of necessary connection derived. But in the *Treatise* Hume finds that he has to approach this question indirectly, by, as he says, beating about all the neighbouring fields in the hope that he may light on his quarry. This means that he finds it necessary to discuss first of all two important questions. 'First, for what reason (do) we pronounce it *necessary* that everything whose existence has a beginning, should also have a cause? Secondly, why (do) we conclude that such particular causes must *necessarily* have such particular effects; and what is the nature of that inference we draw from the one to the other, and of the belief we repose in it?'[4]

The maxim that whatever begins to exist must have a cause of

[1] *T.*, I, 3, 2, p. 76.   [2] *Ibid.*   [3] *Ibid.*, p. 77.   [4] *Ibid.*, p. 78.

its existence is, Hume maintains, neither intuitively certain nor demonstrable. He does not say much about the first point and to all intents and purposes contents himself with challenging anyone who thinks that it is intuitively certain to show that it is. As for the non-demonstrability of the maxim or principle, Hume argues first of all that we conceive an object as non-existent at one moment and as existent at the next moment without having any distinct idea of a cause or productive principle. And if we can conceive a beginning of existence in separation from the idea of a cause, 'the actual separation of these objects is so far possible, that it implies no contradiction nor absurdity; and is therefore incapable of being refuted by any reasoning from mere ideas, without which it is impossible to demonstrate the necessity of a cause'.[1] After this argument, which is connected with his theory of ideas as copies or images of impressions and with his nominalism, he proceeds to refute certain formulations of the pretended demonstration of the principle that everything which begins to be does so through the productive agency of a cause. For example, Clarke and others argued that if anything began to exist without a cause, it would cause itself; and this is obviously impossible, because to do so it would have to exist before itself. Again, Locke argued that a thing which came into being without a cause would be caused by nothing; and nothing cannot be the cause of anything. Hume's main criticism of arguments of this sort is that they all beg the question by presupposing the validity of the very principle which they are supposed to demonstrate, namely, that anything which begins to exist must have a cause.

If this principle is neither intuitively certain nor demonstrable, our belief in it must arise from experience and observation. But at this point Hume drops the subject, saying that he proposes to pass to his second question, why we believe that this particular cause must have this particular effect. Perhaps the answer to the second question will be found to answer the first as well.

In the first place, causal inference is not the fruit of intuitive knowledge of essences. 'There is no object which implies the existence of any other, if we consider these objects in themselves and never look beyond the ideas which we form of them. Such an inference would amount to knowledge, and would imply the absolute contradiction and impossibility of conceiving anything different. But as all distinct ideas are separable, it is evident there

[1] *T.*, I, 3, 3, p. 80.

can be no impossibility of that kind.'[1] For example, we do not, according to Hume, intuit the essence of flame and see its effect or effects as logically necessary consequences.

'It is therefore by *experience* only that we can infer the existence of one object from another.'[2] What does this mean in the concrete? It means that we frequently experience the conjunction of two objects, say, flame and the sensation which we call heat, and we remember that these objects have appeared in a regular recurrent order of contiguity and succession. Then, 'without any further ceremony we call the one *cause* and the other *effect* and infer the existence of the one from that of the other'.[3] The last remark shows that Hume is thinking of the ordinary man's idea of causality, and not simply of that of the philosopher. The ordinary man observes the 'constant conjunction' of A and B in repeated instances, where A is contiguous with B and is prior to B, and he calls A the cause and B the effect. 'When one particular species of events has always, in all instances, been conjoined with another, we make no longer any scruple of foretelling one upon the appearance of the other, and of employing that reasoning (causal inference) which can alone assure us of any matter of fact or existence. We then call the one object *cause*, the other *effect*.'[4] 'Suitably to this experience, therefore, we may define a cause to be *an object, followed by another, and where all the objects similar to the first are followed by objects similar to the second. Or, in other words, where, if the first object had not been, the second never had existed.'[5]

In saying that we 'remember' past instances Hume obviously goes beyond what common experience warrants him saying. For we may very well infer cause from effect or effect from cause without recalling any past instances. But Hume corrects this error presently, by means of the principle of association.

If our belief in regular particular causal connections rests on memory of past instances of constant conjunction, it appears that we are assuming the principle or at least acting as though we assumed the principle that 'instances of which we have had no experience must resemble those of which we have had experience, and that the course of nature continues always uniformly the same'.[6] But this principle is neither intuitively certain nor demonstrable. For the notion of a change in the course of nature

[1] *T.*, I, I, 3, 6, pp. 86–7. [2] *Ibid.*, p. 87. [3] *Ibid.*, p. 87.
[4] *E.*, 7, 2, 59, pp. 74–5. [5] *E.*, 7, 2, 60, p. 76. [6] *T.*, I, 3, 6, p. 89.

is not self-contradictory. Nor can the principle be established by probable reasoning from experience. For it lies at the basis of our probable reasoning. We always tacitly presuppose the uniformity. Hume does not mean that we ought not to assume the principle. To do this would be to adopt a scepticism which he considered incapable of being put into practice. He simply wishes to observe that we cannot prove the validity of our belief in causal inference by means of a principle which cannot itself be proved and which is not intuitively certain. At the same time we do in fact presuppose the principle, and we could neither act nor reason (outside pure mathematics) unless we tacitly presupposed it. This 'supposition that the future resembles the past is not founded on arguments of any kind, but is derived entirely from habit, by which we are determined to expect for the future the same train of objects to which we have been accustomed.'[1] Again, ''Tis not, therefore, reason which is the guide of life, but custom. That alone determines the mind, in all instances, to suppose the future conformable to the past. However easy this step may seem, reason would never, to all eternity, be able to make it.'[2] The idea of habit or custom plays a great part in Hume's final analysis of causality.

To return to the idea of constant conjunction. The statement that it is experience of constant conjunction which leads us to assert particular causal connections does not answer Hume's question, from what impression or impressions the idea of necessary connection is derived. For the idea of constant conjunction is the idea of the regular recurrence of two kinds of similar events according to a constant pattern of contiguity and succession, and this idea does not comprise that of necessary connection. 'From the mere repetition of any past impression, even to infinity, there never will arise any new original idea, such as that of a necessary connection; and the number of impressions has in this case no more effect than if we confined ourselves to one only.'[3] But we cannot, in Hume's opinion, derive the idea of necessary connection from observation of regular sequences or causal connections. We must say, therefore, either that there is no such idea or that it must be derived from some subjective source. Hume cannot adopt the first of these alternatives; for he has already laid stress on the importance of the idea of necessary connection. He must therefore adopt the second alternative; and this is in fact what he does.

To say that the idea of necessary connection is derived from a

[1] *T.*, 1, 3, 12, p. 134. [2] *Abstract*, 16. [3] *T.*, 1, 3, 6, p. 88.

subjective source is to say, within the framework of Hume's philosophy, that it is derived from some impression of reflection. But it does not follow that the idea is derived from the relation of the will to its effects, and that it is then extrapolated. 'The will, being here considered as a cause, has no more a discoverable connection with its effects than any material thing has with its proper effect. . . . In short, the actions of the mind are, in this respect, the same with those of matter. We perceive only their constant conjunction. . . .'[1] We must look, therefore, for another solution. Suppose that we observe several instances of constant conjunction. This repetition cannot, by itself alone, give rise to the idea of necessary connection. This point has been already admitted. To give rise to this idea, the repetition of similar instances of constant conjunction 'must either *discover* or *produce* something new, which is the source of that idea'.[2] But repetition does not make us discover anything new in the conjoined objects. Nor does it produce any new quality in the objects themselves. Observation of the repetition does, however, produce a new impression in the mind. 'For after we have observed the resemblance in a sufficient number of instances, we immediately feel a determination of the mind to pass from one object to its usual attendant. . . . Necessity, then, is the effect of this observation, and is nothing but an internal impression of the mind, or a determination to carry our thoughts from one object to another. . . . There is no internal impression which has any relation to the present business, but that propensity, which custom produces, to pass from an object to its usual attendant.'[3] The propensity, therefore, caused by custom or association, to pass from one of the things which have been observed to be constantly conjoined to the other is the impression from which the idea of necessary connection is derived. That is to say, the propensity, produced by custom, is something given, an impression, and the idea of necessary connection is its reflection or image in consciousness. This explanation of the idea of necessary connection is applicable both to external causal relations and to internal causal relations, such as the relation between the will and its effects.

We are now in a position to define the notion of cause more accurately. Causation, as was seen above, can be considered either as a philosophical or as a natural relation. Considered as a philosophical relation, it can be defined thus. A cause is 'an object

[1] *T.*, 1, 3, 14, pp. 632–3, Appendix.   [2] *Ibid.*, p. 163.   [3] *Ibid.*, p. 165.

precedent and contiguous to another, and where all the objects resembling the former are placed in like relations of precedency and contiguity to those objects that resemble the latter'.[1] Considered as a natural relation, 'a *cause* is an object precedent and contiguous to another, and so united with it that the idea of the one determines the mind to form the idea of the other, and the impression of the one to form a more lively idea of the other'.[2] It is to be noted that 'though causation be a *philosophical* relation, as implying contiguity, succession and constant conjunction, yet it is only so far as it is a *natural* relation and produces a union among our ideas, that we are able to reason upon it or draw any inference from it'.[3]

Hume has thus given an answer to his question 'why we conclude that such particular causes must necessarily have such particular effects, and why we form an inference from one to another'.[4] The answer is couched in psychological terms, referring to the psychological effect of observation of instances of constant conjunction. This observation produces a custom or propensity of the mind, an associative link, whereby the mind passes naturally from, say, the idea of flame to the idea of heat or from an impression of flame to the lively idea of heat. This enables us to pass beyond experience or observation. From the observation of smoke we naturally infer fire, even though the fire is not observed. If it is asked what guarantee we have of the objective validity of such an inference, the only ultimate answer which Hume can give is empirical verification. And in an empiricist philosophy this is the only answer which is really required.

Has Hume also answered the question, how experience gives rise to the principle that whatever begins to exist must have a cause of existence? His answer to the question why we conclude that this particular cause must have this particular effect suggests that it is custom which makes us expect every event to have some cause and which prevents us from maintaining that there can be absolutely uncaused events. And this is, I think, what he must say, given his premises. After giving his analysis of causality he remarks that in view of the resulting definitions of *cause* 'we may easily conceive that there is no absolute nor metaphysical necessity that every beginning of existence should be attended with such an object'.[5] We cannot demonstrate the truth of the principle in

---

[1] *T.*, I, 3, 14, p. 170.   [2] *Ibid.*, p. 170.   [3] *T.*, I, 3, 6, p. 94.
[4] *T.*, I, 3, 3, p. 82.   [5] *T.*, I, 3, 14, p. 172.

question. Yet he says in the first *Enquiry* that 'it is universally allowed that nothing exists without a cause of its existence'.[1] Our belief in this principle must, then, be due to custom. It is worth noting, however, that the sentence just quoted from the *Enquiry* goes on in this way: 'and that chance, when strictly examined, is a mere negative word, and means not any real power which has anywhere a being in nature'.[2] Now, 'chance' means for Hume a fortuitous or uncaused event. And not to believe in chance is to believe that every event has a cause. And to believe this is, for Hume, to believe that every cause is a necessary or determining cause. True, events may occur contrary to expectation. And this may lead the vulgar to believe in chance. But 'philosophers' (including, of course, scientists), finding on close examination in several instances that the unexpected event was due to the counteracting effect of a hitherto unknown cause, 'form a maxim that the connection betwixt all causes and effects is equally necessary, and that its seeming uncertainty in some instances proceeds from the secret opposition of contrary causes'.[3] Here the principle that every event has a cause is described as a maxim 'formed' by philosophers. But our belief in the maxim would seem to be the result of custom or habit.

Hume remarks that there can be only one kind of cause. 'For as our idea of efficiency is derived from the constant conjunction of two objects, wherever this is observed, the cause is efficient; and where it is not, there can never be a cause of any kind.'[4] The Scholastic distinction between formal, material, efficient and final causes is rejected. So is the distinction between cause and occasion, so far as these terms are used with different meanings. Further, just as there is only one kind of cause, so there is only one kind of necessity. The distinction between physical and moral necessity lacks any real foundation. 'It is the constant conjunction of objects, along with the determination of the mind, which constitutes a physical necessity: and the removal of these is the same thing with *chance*.'[5]

The foregoing sketch of Hume's analysis of causality indicates, I hope, the fact that he devoted considerable attention to the subject. It occupies a much more prominent position in the *Treatise* than is occupied by his treatment of substance. No doubt, he considered that the theory of material substance had already

---

[1] *E.*, 8, 1, 74, p. 95. [2] *Ibid.* [3] *T.*, 1, 3, 12, p. 132.
[4] *T.*, 1, 3, 14, p. 171. [5] *Ibid.*, p. 171.

been refuted by Berkeley. But the main reason why he devotes so much attention to causality is his understanding of the all-important role played by causal influence in the sciences and in human life in general. And the great merit of his analysis, which one can recognize whether one agrees with it or not, is his attempt to combine a consistent empiricism with a recognition of the meaning which we ordinarily attribute to causation. Thus he recognizes that when we say that X caused Y we mean something more than that X preceded Y temporally and was spatially contiguous with it. He faces up to the difficulty and tries to solve it on empiricist lines. This attempt to develop a consistent empiricist philosophy is his chief title to fame. What he said was by no means so novel as has been sometimes supposed. To take one example, Nicholas of Autrecourt[1] in the fourteenth century maintained that from the existence of one thing we cannot infer with certainty the existence of another thing, since, in the case of two distinct things, it is always possible without logical contradiction to affirm the existence of the one and deny the existence of the other. It is only analytic propositions, 'reducible' to the principle of non-contradiction, which are certain. Furthermore, Nicholas appears to have explained our belief in regular causal connections in terms of our experience of repeated sequences which gives rise to the expectation that if B has followed A in the past it will do so in the future. I am not suggesting, of course, that Hume knew anything at all about Nicholas of Autrecourt or similar thinkers of the fourteenth century. I am simply drawing attention to the historical fact that a number of Hume's positions had been anticipated in the fourteenth century, even though Hume was unaware of the fact. Nevertheless, it remains true that it is Hume, and not his early predecessors, who is the patron and father of modern empiricism. Terminology has changed since the eighteenth century, and the modern empiricist tries to avoid Hume's tendency to muddle up logic and psychology. But of the modern empiricist's direct or indirect debt to Hume there can be no doubt.

To emphasize Hume's historical importance is not necessarily to accept his analysis of causality. To take one example of a possible line of criticism, it seems to me that in spite of what Hume says on the matter we are conscious of interior causal production of a kind which cannot be explained simply in terms of his analysis. He seems to suppose that the notorious difficulty in

---

[1] For Nicholas of Autrecourt vol. III of this *History* may be consulted (pp. 135 f.).

explaining how our wills influence our bodily movements, or even how we perform at will certain interior operations, shows that even here causality, on the objective side, is simply constant conjunction, or at least that we perceive only constant conjunction. But this way of arguing appears to presuppose the validity of the position which had been maintained by the occasionalists that there is no productive causal efficacy or power unless we know not only that we act causally but also how we do so. And the validity of this contention is open to question. Again, it is important to distinguish between the question whether the scientist can get along with Hume's idea of causality and the question whether this idea represents an analysis that is adequate from the philosophical point of view. The physicist is not concerned, for instance, with the problem of the logical and ontological status of the principle that everything which begins to be does so through the agency of an extrinsic cause. It is not necessary for him to concern himself with such a problem. But the philosopher does ask this question. And Hume's treatment of it is open to criticism. For instance, even if one can imagine first a blank, as it were, and then X existing, it by no means follows necessarily that X can begin to exist without an extrinsic cause. Nor, from the fact that there is no verbal contradiction between the statements 'X began to exist' and 'X had no cause' does it necessarily follow that the statements are compatible when examined from the point of view of 'metaphysical analysis'. We have on the one hand analytic and 'formal' propositions and on the other empirical hypotheses: there is, in his scheme, no room for synthetic *a priori* propositions. And this is, indeed, the problem, whether or not there are propositions which are certain and yet informative about reality. But to discuss this matter adequately would mean discussing the nature and status of metaphysics. Once given Hume's premises and his conception of 'reason', something resembling his analysis of causality must follow. We cannot accept his premises and then add on a metaphysical doctrine of causality.

In criticizing Hume it is, however, important to remember that he does not deny that there are causal relations. That is to say, he does not deny the truth of the statement that flame causes heat. Nor does he deny even the truth of the statement that flame necessarily causes heat. What he does is to inquire into the meaning of these statements. And the question, in a discussion with Hume, is not whether there are causal relations, but what it means to say that there are causal relations. Again, the question is not whether there are any necessary connections, but what it means to say that there are necessary connections.

10. As we have seen, the uniformity of nature is not demonstrable by reason. It is the object of belief rather than of intuition or demonstration. We can say, indeed, as the ordinary man would say, that we know it, if the word *know* is used with the wide range of meaning that it has in common discourse. But if the word is used in a strict sense, to mean our apprehension of those propositions in the case of which all other alternatives are excluded, we cannot be said to have knowledge of the uniformity of nature. For Hume, we have analytic propositions on the one hand, which express relations between ideas, and synthetic propositions, which are based in some way on experience. But experience by itself gives us only factual data: it cannot tell us about the future. Nor can we prove by reason that our beliefs and expectations about the future are justified. Yet belief plays a very important part in human life. If we were confined to analytic propositions on the one hand and immediate empirical data, present or remembered, on the other, human life would be impossible. Every day we perform actions which are based on belief. It becomes necessary, therefore, to investigate the nature of belief.

Hume's account of belief illustrates his tendency to confuse logic and psychology. For he gives a psychological answer to the logical question about the grounds of that assurance which he calls belief. But he is perhaps bound to do this. For on his premisses there can be no logical grounds for our beliefs about the future course of events. He must, therefore, content himself with showing how we come to have these beliefs.

According to Hume, believing a proposition cannot be explained in terms of the operations of joining ideas. If, to take one of his examples, someone tells me that Julius Caesar died in his bed, I understand his statement and I join the same ideas as he does, but I do not assent to the proposition. We must look elsewhere for the difference between belief and incredulity. In Hume's view belief 'does nothing but vary the manner in which we conceive any object, it can only bestow on our ideas an additional force and vivacity. An opinion, therefore, or belief, may be most accurately defined, *a lively idea related to or associated with a present impression.*'[1] For example, when we infer the existence of one thing

_____
[1] *T.*, 1, 3, 7, p. 96.

from that of another (that is to say, when we believe as the result of inference that something exists), we pass from the impression of one object to the 'lively' idea of another; and it is this liveliness or vivacity of the idea which is characteristic of belief. In passing from the impression to the idea 'we are not determined by reason, but by custom, or a principle of association. But belief is something more than a simple idea. It is a particular manner of forming an idea; and as the same idea can only be varied by a variation of its degrees of force and vivacity, it follows upon the whole that belief is a lively idea produced by a relation to a present impression, according to the foregoing definition.'[1]

We can distinguish, therefore, between belief and fancies by referring to the manner in which we conceive the relevant ideas. 'An idea assented to *feels* different from a fictitious idea that the fancy alone presents to us: and this different feeling I endeavour to explain by calling it a superior *force*, or *vivacity*, or *solidity*, or *firmness*, or *steadiness*.'[2] Belief is 'a term that everyone sufficiently understands in common life';[3] but in philosophy we can describe it only in terms of feeling.

However, even if words like 'vivacity' and 'liveliness' suffice to distinguish propositions in which we believe from fancies which are known to be fancies, is it not true that we have many beliefs about which we have no strong feelings at all? We believe that the earth is not flat and that the moon is a satellite of the earth, but most of us have no strong *feelings* on these matters. It seems that in answer Hume must refer to the attributes of steadiness and firmness rather than to those of vivacity and liveliness. In Hume's view our assent to a proposition must be conditioned by the exclusion of alternatives. In the cases of an analytic proposition any contrary proposition is excluded because the denial of an analytic proposition is seen to be self-contradictory. In the case of a synthetic proposition the alternatives are excluded in proportion to the regularity with which the situation asserted in the proposition has occurred in the past, observation of this repetition having set up a custom and brought into play the principles of association. In the case of the statement that the moon is a satellite of the earth, we have always been told that it is true, nothing has occurred to make us doubt the truth of the statement, and any observations we may have made are compatible with its truth. We have, therefore, a firm and steady belief

---

[1] *T.*, I, 3, 7, p. 97.   [2] *Ibid.*, p. 629, Appendix.   [3] *Ibid.*

in the truth of the statement, even though we may not feel so strongly about it as we might feel, for example, about the honesty of an intimate friend when it has been maliciously impugned.

I have said that we have always been told that the moon is a satellite of the earth. This means that belief can be generated by education, and so by ideas. This Hume admits. 'All those opinions and notions of things, to which we have been accustomed from our infancy, take such deep root, that it is impossible for us, by all the powers of reason and experience, to eradicate them; and this habit not only approaches in its influence, but even on many occasions prevails over that which arises from the constant and inseparable union of causes and effects. Here we must not be contented with saying that the vividness of the idea produces the belief: we must maintain that they are individually the same. . . . I am persuaded that, upon examination, we shall find more than one half of those opinions which prevail among mankind to be owing to education, and that the principles which are thus implicitly embraced overbalance those which are owing either to abstract reasoning or experience. . . . Education is an artificial and not a natural cause.'[1]

According to Hume, therefore, 'when I am convinced of any principle, it is only an idea which strikes more strongly upon me. When I give the preference to one set of arguments above another, I do nothing but decide from my feeling concerning the superiority of their influence.'[2] Again, 'all our reasonings concerning causes and effects are derived from nothing but custom, and belief is more properly an act of the sensitive than of the cogitative part of our natures'.[3] How, then, can we decide between rational and irrational beliefs? Hume does not appear to give any very clear and explicit answer to this question; and when he is dealing with irrational beliefs, he tends to indicate how, in his opinion, the mind works rather than to make it clear how we are to distinguish between beliefs which are rational and those which are not. But his general answer to the problem seems to be more or less this. Many beliefs are the result of 'education', and some of them are irrational. The way to cure ourselves of them is to have recourse to experience or, rather, to test those beliefs by experience. Does the belief which is the result of our having been constantly told that it is true fit in with the beliefs which are founded on experience

[1] *T.*, 1, 3, 9, pp. 116–17.   [2] *T.*, 1, 3, 8, p. 103.   [3] *T.*, 1, 4, 1, p. 183.

of causal relations? If the former is incompatible or inconsistent with the latter, it should be discarded. Education is an 'artificial cause', and we should prefer the 'natural' cause of beliefs, causal relations in the philosophical sense, that is, constant or invariable conjunctions. Of course, we can form irrational beliefs, based on experience. Hume gives the example of generalizations about the members of some foreign nation which are the result of one or two encounters with foreigners. But the way to correct prejudices of this kind is obvious: it is the way by which such prejudices are in fact corrected, if they are corrected. Further, irrational beliefs can be generated by experience of uniformities or of constant conjunctions. But these can be corrected by reflection in the light of wider experience which reveals contrary instances or brings other factors to light. Tolstoy speaks somewhere of the belief of some peasants that the budding of the oak trees in the spring is due to a certain wind. And if the wind was contiguous with the trees and prior to their budding, the belief can be explained. But if experience reveals instances where the oaks bud even when this particular wind is not blowing, we do not entertain the peasants' belief. Again, even if in all instances oak trees budded only when the particular wind was blowing, the belief that the budding is caused by the wind might still be incompatible with our experience and observation of other cases of budding. The mind would not, then, form a habit or custom supplying, so to speak, the element of necessary connection; and we would not believe that the wind caused the budding of the oak trees.

If these remarks represent Hume's mind, a further difficulty arises. Hume often speaks as though custom not only does dominate but also ought to dominate in human life. At the same time he also speaks as though experience ought to be our guide. Thus he says that 'the experienced train of events is the great standard by which we all regulate our conduct. Nothing else can be appealed to in the field, or in the senate. Nothing else ought ever to be heard of in the school or in the closet.'[1] But perhaps the difficulty can be answered to some extent in this way. According to Hume, there are certain fundamental customary beliefs which are essential to human life; belief in the continuous and independent existence of bodies, and the belief that everything which begins to be has a cause. These fundamental customary beliefs dominate and ought to dominate, if, that is to say, human life is to be

[1] *E.*, 11, 110, p. 142.

possible. And they condition our more specific beliefs. But these latter are not inevitable and necessary: we are capable of testing and altering them. The test is the experienced course of events and consistency with beliefs which are themselves compatible with the experienced course of events.

CHAPTER XV

HUME (2)

Our belief in the existence of bodies—Minds and the problem of personal identity—The existence and nature of God—Scepticism.

1. AT the close of the last chapter we saw that belief in the continuing existence of bodies independently of the mind or of perception is for Hume a fundamental natural belief. But we must examine rather more closely what he has to say on this matter.

The main difficulty, Hume says, which arises in connection with our notion of a world of permanently existing objects independent of our perception, is that we are confined to the world of perceptions and enjoy no access to a world of objects existing independently of these perceptions. 'Now since nothing is ever present to the mind but perceptions, and since all ideas are derived from something antecedently present to the mind, it follows that it is impossible for us so much as to conceive or form an idea of anything specifically different from ideas and impressions. Let us fix our attention out of ourselves as much as possible; let us chase our imagination to the heavens, or to the utmost limits of the universe; we never really advance a step beyond ourselves, nor can conceive any kind of existence, but those perceptions which have appeared in that narrow compass. This is the universe of the imagination, nor have we any idea but what is there produced.'[1] Ideas are ultimately reducible to impressions, and impressions are subjective, pertaining to the percipient subject. We cannot, therefore, ever conceive what objects would be like, or are like, apart from our perceptions.

It is important to understand that Hume does not intend to deny the existence of body or bodies independently of our perceptions. He maintains, indeed, that we are unable to prove that body exists; but at the same time he insists that we cannot help assenting to the proposition. 'Nature has not left this to his (the sceptic's) choice, and has doubtless esteemed it an affair of too great importance to be trusted to our uncertain reasonings and speculations. We may well ask, *What causes induce us to believe in the existence of body?*, but it is in vain to ask *whether there be body or*

---

[1] *T.,* 1, 2, 6, pp. 67–8.

not. That is a point which we must take for granted in all our reasonings.'[1] The sceptic, as well as the non-sceptic, consistently acts as though body really exists; he cannot help believing in this, whatever academic doubts he may air in his study. We can only inquire, therefore, what is the cause or what are the causes which induce us to believe in the continued existence of bodies distinct from our minds and perceptions.

In the first place the senses cannot be the source of the notion that things continue to exist when they are unperceived. For in order for this to be the case, the senses would have to operate when they have ceased to operate. And this would involve a contradiction. Nor do the senses reveal to us bodies which are distinct from our perceptions; that is, from the sensible appearances of bodies. They do not reveal to us both a copy and the original. It may, indeed, seem that I perceive my own body. But 'properly speaking, it is not our body we perceive, when we regard our limbs and members, but certain impressions, which enter by the senses; so that the ascribing a real and corporeal existence to these impressions, or to their objects, is an act of the mind as difficult to explain as that which we examine at present'.[2] It is true that among the classes of impressions we ascribe a distinct and continuous existence to some and not to others. Nobody attributes distinct and continuous existence to pains and pleasures. The 'vulgar', though not 'philosophers', suppose that colours, tastes, sounds and, in general, the so-called secondary qualities possess such existence. Both philosophers and the vulgar alike suppose figure, bulk, motion and solidity to exist continuously and independently of perception. But it cannot be the senses themselves which lead us to make these distinctions; for, as far as the senses are concerned, all these impressions are on the same footing.

In the second place it is not reason which induces us to believe in the continuous and distinct existence of bodies. 'Whatever convincing arguments philosophers may fancy they can produce to establish the belief of objects independent of the mind, it is obvious these arguments are known but to very few; and that it is not by them that children, peasants, and the greatest part of mankind are induced to attribute objects to some impressions and deny them to others.'[3] Nor can we rationally justify our belief, once we have it. 'Philosophy informs us that everything which appears to the mind is nothing but a perception, and is interrupted and

---

[1] *T.*, 1, 4, 2, p. 187.   [2] *Ibid.*, p. 191.   [3] *Ibid.*, p. 193.

dependent on the mind.'[1] And we cannot infer the existence of objects from perceptions. Such an inference would be a causal inference. And for it to be valid we should have to be able to observe the constant conjunction of those objects with these perceptions. And this we cannot do. For we cannot get outside the series of our perceptions to compare them with anything apart from them.

Our belief in the continued and independent existence of bodies, and our habit of supposing that objective and independent counter-parts of certain impressions exist, must be due, therefore, neither to the senses nor to the reason or understanding but to the imagination. The question thus arises, which are the features of certain impressions that work on the imagination and produce our persuasion of the continued and distinct existence of bodies? It is useless to refer this belief or persuasion to the superior force or violence of certain impressions as compared with others. For it is obvious that the majority of people suppose that the heat of a fire, placed at a convenient distance, is in the fire itself, whereas they do not suppose that the intense pain caused by too great proximity to the fire is anywhere else but in the impressions of the percipient subject. Hence we have to look elsewhere for the peculiar features of certain impressions, which work upon the imagination.

Hume mentions two such peculiar features, namely, constancy and coherence. 'Those mountains and houses and trees which lie at present under my eye have always appeared to me in the same order; and when I lose sight of them by shutting my eyes or turn-ing my head, I soon after find them return upon me without the least alteration.'[2] Here we have constantly recurring similar impressions. But, obviously, bodies often change not only their positions but also their qualities. However, even in their changes there is a coherence. 'When I return to my chamber after an hour's absence, I find not my fire in the same situation in which I left it; but then I am accustomed, in other instances, to see a like alteration produced in a like time, whether I am present or absent, near or remote. This coherence, therefore, in their changes, is one of the characteristics of external objects, as well as their con-stancy.'[3] Hume's meaning is, I think, sufficiently clear. My impressions of the mountain which I can see through the window are constant, in the sense that, given the requisite conditions, they

[1] *T.*, 1, 4, 2, p. 193.   [2] *Ibid.*, p. 194.   [3] *Ibid.*, p. 195.

are similar. From the point of view of perception the mountain remains more or less the same. But the impression which I receive of the fire in my room at 9 p.m. is not the same as the impression which I receive when I return to the room at 10.30 p.m. The fire, as we say, has died down in the meantime. On the other hand, these two separate impressions agree with the two separate impressions which I receive at the same interval of time on another evening. And if I watch the fire for a stretch of time on two or more occasions, there is a regular pattern of coherence between the different series of impressions.

Hume is not, however, satisfied with an explanation of our belief in the continuous and independent existence of bodies, which rests simply and solely on the actual course of our impressions. On the one hand our impressions are in fact interrupted, while on the other hand we habitually believe in the continuous existence of bodies. And the mere repetition of interrupted, though similar, impressions cannot by itself produce this belief. We must look there for 'some other principles', and Hume, as we would expect, has recourse to psychological considerations. 'The imagination, when set into any train of thinking, is apt to continue even when its object fails it, and, like a galley put in motion by the oars, carries on its course without any new impulse.'[1] Once the mind begins to observe a uniformity or coherence among impressions, it tends to render this uniformity as complete as possible. The supposition of the continued existence of bodies suffices for this purpose and affords us a notion of greater regularity and coherence than is provided by the senses. But though coherence may give rise to the supposition of the continuous existence of objects, the idea of constancy is needed to explain our supposition of their distinct existence; that is, of their independence of our perceptions. When we have been accustomed to find, for example, that the perception of the sun recurs constantly in the same form as on its first appearance, we are inclined to regard these different and interrupted perceptions as being the same. Reflection, however, shows us that the perceptions are not the same. Therefore, to free ourselves from this contradiction, we disguise or remove the interruption 'by supposing that these interrupted perceptions are connected by a real existence, of which we are insensible'.[2]

These observations are not, it is true, very enlightening. And Hume endeavours to make his position more precise and clear.

[1] *T.*, 1, 4, 2, p. 198.　　　　[2] *Ibid.*, p. 199.

To do this, he distinguishes between the opinion of the vulgar and what he calls the 'philosophical system'. The vulgar are 'all the unthinking and unphilosophical part of mankind, that is, all of us at one time or other'.[1] These people suppose, says Hume, that their perceptions are the only objects. 'The very image which is present to the senses is with us the real body; and it is to these interrupted images we ascribe a perfect identity.'[2] In other words, the vulgar know nothing of Locke's material substance; material objects are for them simply what they perceive them to be. And to say this is, for Hume, to say that for the vulgar objects and perceptions are the same. This presupposed, we are then faced by a difficulty. On the one hand, 'The smooth passage of the imagination along the ideas of the resembling perceptions makes us ascribe to them a perfect identity'.[3] On the other hand, the interrupted manner of their occurrence or, as Hume says, appearance, leads us to consider them as distinct entities. But this contradiction gives rise to an uneasiness, and it must therefore be resolved. As we cannot bring ourselves to sacrifice the propensity produced by the smooth passage of the imagination, we sacrifice the second principle. It is true that the interruptions in the appearance of similar perceptions are often so long and frequent that we cannot overlook them; but at the same time 'an interrupted appearance to the senses implies not necessarily an interruption in the existence'.[4] Hence we can 'feign' a continued existence of objects. Yet we do not merely feign this; we *believe* it. And, according to Hume, this belief can be explained by reference to memory. Memory presents us with a great number of instances of similar perceptions which recur at different times after considerable interruptions. And this resemblance produces a propensity to look upon these interrupted perceptions as the same. At the same time it also produces a propensity to connect the perceptions by means of the hypothesis of a continued existence, in order to justify our ascription of identity to them and in order to avoid the contradiction in which the interrupted character of our perceptions seems to involve us. We have, therefore, a propensity to feign the continuous existence of bodies. Further, since this propensity arises from lively impressions of the memory, it bestows vivacity on this fiction, 'or, in other words, makes us believe the continued existence of body'.[5] For belief consists in the vivacity of an idea.

But though we are led in this way to believe in the continued

---

[1] *T.*, I, 4, I, p. 205. [2] *Ibid.* [3] *Ibid.* [4] *Ibid.*, pp. 207–8. [5] *Ibid.*, p. 209.

existence of 'sensible objects or perceptions', philosophy makes us
see the fallacy of the supposition. For reason shows us that our
perceptions do not exist independently of our perceiving. And
they have no more a continued than an independent existence.
Philosophers, therefore, have made a distinction between perceptions and objects. The former are interrupted and dependent on
the percipient subject: the latter exist continuously and independently. But this theory is arrived at by first embracing and then
discarding the vulgar opinion, and it contains not only all the
difficulties attaching to the latter but also some which are peculiar
to itself. For instance, the theory involves postulating a new set
of perceptions. We cannot, as has been seen earlier, conceive of
objects except in terms of perceptions. Hence, if we postulate
objects as well as perceptions, we merely reduplicate the latter
and at the same time ascribe to them attributes, namely, un-
interruptedness and independence, which do not belong to
perceptions.

The upshot of Hume's examination of our belief in the continued
and independent existence of bodies is, therefore, that there is no
rational justification for it. At the same time we cannot eradicate
the belief. We can take it for granted, 'whatever may be the
reader's opinion at this present moment, that an hour hence he
will be persuaded there is both an external and internal world'.[1]
It is only in the actual course of philosophical reflection that
scepticism on this point is possible, and even there it is only
theoretical. It is to be noted that Hume does not recommend the
theory that certain qualities (the so-called secondary qualities)
are subjective, while others (the primary qualities) are objective.
On the contrary, he maintains that 'if colours, sounds, tastes and
smells be merely perceptions, nothing we can conceive is possessed
of a real, continued and independent existence; not even motion,
extension and solidity, which are the primary qualities chiefly
insisted on'.[2] True, he agrees that 'when we reason from cause to
effect, we conclude that neither colour, sound, taste nor smell
have a continued and independent existence'.[3] But 'when we
exclude these sensible qualities, there remains nothing in the
universe which has such an existence'.[4] Hume certainly accepted
the main lines of Berkeley's criticism of Locke, but he did not
follow him further. For though Berkeley intended to refute the
sceptics, as well as the atheists and materialists, his arguments,

[1] *T.*, 1, 4, 1, p. 218.   [2] *T.*, 1, 4, 4, p. 228.   [3] *Ibid.*, p. 231.   [4] *Ibid.*

according to Hume, lead to scepticism in that 'they admit of no answer and produce no conviction. Their only effect is to cause that momentary amazement and irresolution and confusion, which is the result of scepticism.'[1] The retort can be made, of course, that Hume's position is more sceptical than Berkeley's, since he consciously underlines a fundamental and irreconcilable contradiction between the conclusions of philosophical reasoning and our natural belief. It is also arguable that he tends to misrepresent Berkeley to the extent that he depicts him as wishing to correct the opinions of 'the vulgar'. But, though all this may well be true, we must remember that Hume ultimately takes the side of the vulgar. His point is that we have an inevitable and ineradicable propensity to believe in the continuous and independent existence of bodies. This propensity produces belief, and this belief operates in the vulgar and the philosophical alike. All attempts to give a rational justification of this belief are failures. There may be something apart from our perceptions, but we cannot prove that this is the case. At the same time nobody does or can live his life on sceptical principles. Natural belief inevitably, and rightly, prevails.

It is clear, I think, that a good deal of the force of Hume's arguments depends on the premiss that it is our perceptions with which we are immediately acquainted. Moreover, he seems to use the word 'perception' in two senses, to signify, that is, the act of perceiving and the object perceived. It is obvious that our perceptions, in the first sense of the word 'perception', are interrupted and discrete. But the ordinary man is aware of this, and he does not identify, for example, two interrupted perceptions of the sun. If he can be said to identify his perceptions, he identifies them in the second sense of the word 'perception'. Hume might retort, of course, that to make this distinction is to beg the whole question; for it is the distinction itself which is the subject of dispute. At the same time the discussion cannot be profitably carried on unless linguistic distinctions are carefully sorted out. And Hume's discussion of the problem seems to me to suffer from the defect common to Locke's 'way of ideas' and its derivatives, namely, that a term such as 'idea' or 'perception' is used in an unusual sense without sufficient care being taken to discriminate between the unusual and the usual senses. And this point is of considerable importance. For momentous philosophical conclusions follow if

---

[1] *E.*, 12, I, 122, p. 155, note.

these words are taken in the unusual sense. It is, indeed, arguable that it is the empiricists who beg the whole question and that Hume's sceptical conclusions follow from his linguistic usage.

At the same time Hume's general position, that it is natural belief, analogous to animal 'belief', which does and should prevail in human life and that reason is powerless to justify these beliefs, if 'justify' is taken to mean something more than giving a psychological account of the genesis of the beliefs, is of great historical importance. It is probably this position which is characteristic of Hume and which sets him apart from both Locke and Berkeley. There are, indeed, some anticipations of the position in Locke; but Locke's philosophy had, as we have seen, a markedly rationalist element. It is Hume, above all other classical empiricists, who embodies the anti-rationalist current of thought. And it is a mistake to dwell so exclusively on his scepticism as to pass over or minimize the great emphasis which he places on the role of natural belief.

2. According to Hume, the problem of minds is not so complicated and difficult as the problem of bodies. 'The intellectual world, though involved in infinite obscurities, is not perplexed with any such contradictions as those we have discovered in the natural. What is known concerning it, agrees with itself; and what is unknown, we must be contented to leave so.'[1] Further reflection, as we shall see, led Hume to a less optimistic conclusion; but this is what he begins by saying.

Tackling first of all the subject of the immateriality of the soul, Hume suggests that the question whether perceptions inhere in a material or an immaterial substance is a meaningless question, in the sense that we can attach no clear meaning to it and cannot, therefore, answer it. In the first place, have we any idea of substance? If so, what is the impression which produces this idea? It may be said that we have an idea of substance because we can define it as 'something which may exist by itself'. But this definition will fit everything conceivable. For whatever is clearly and distinctly conceivable can exist by itself, as far as possibility is concerned. Hence the definition will not serve to distinguish substance from accident or soul from perceptions. In the second place, what is meant by 'inhesion'? 'Inhesion in something is supposed to be requisite to support the existence of our perceptions. Nothing appears requisite to support the existence of a perception. We have, therefore, no idea of inhesion.'[2] Perceptions cannot inhere

---

[1] *T.*, 1, 4, 5, p. 232.   [2] *Ibid.*, p. 234.

in a body. For in order to do so they would have to be present
locally. But it is absurd to speak of a passion, for example, being
situated locally in relation to a moral reflection, as being above or
below it, to the right or left of it. It does not follow, however, that
perceptions can inhere in an immaterial substance. 'That table,
which just now appears to me, is only a perception, and all its
qualities are qualities of a perception. Now the most obvious of
all its qualities is extension. The perception consists of parts.'[1]
But what does it mean to say that an extended perception inheres
in an immaterial substance? The supposed relation is inexplicable.
If it is said that perceptions must inhere in something, to say this
is to beg the question. In truth an object can exist and yet exist
nowhere. 'And I assert that this is not only possible but that the
greatest part of beings do and must exist after this manner.'[2]

. Hume's remarks about the table evidently presupposes that
what I know, when I know the table, is a perception. There may
be things other than perceptions; but, if so, we cannot know what
they are. We are confined to the world of perceptions. This presupposition is present also, I think, in his argument to show that
the theory of the soul as an immaterial substance is indistinguishable in the long run from what he calls, perhaps ironically, the
'hideous hypothesis' of Spinoza. There is, first, the universe of
objects or bodies. All these, according to Spinoza, are modifications of one substance or subject. There is, secondly, the universe
of thought, the universe of my impressions and ideas. These, we
are told by the 'theologians', are modifications of a simple, unextended substance, the soul. But we cannot distinguish between
perceptions and objects, and we can find no relation, whether of
connection or repugnance, which affects the one and does not
affect the other. If, therefore, we object against Spinoza that his
substance must be identical with its modifications and, further,
that it must be identical with incompatible modifications, exactly
the same line of objection can be urged against the hypothesis of
the theologians. The immaterial soul must be identical, for
instance, with tables and chairs. And if we have an idea of the soul,
this idea will itself be a perception and a modification. We shall
thus end up with Spinoza's theory of one substance. In fine, any
argument to show the absurdity of saying that all so-called
natural objects are modifications of one substance will also serve
to show the absurdity of saying that all impressions and ideas, that

[1] *T.*, I, 4, 5, p. 239.   [2] *Ibid.*, p. 235.

is, all perceptions, are modifications of an immaterial substance, the soul. And all arguments to establish that perceptions are modifications of the soul will also tend to establish the hypothesis of Spinoza. For we cannot distinguish between perceptions and objects and make statements about the one which will not apply to the other.

Of course, it is not Hume's intention to argue in favour of Spinoza's monism. He is engaged in an *argumentum ad hominem*, trying to show that the theological view of the soul is as open to criticism as is the theory of Spinoza. The conclusion which he draws is that 'the question concerning the substance of the soul is absolutely unintelligible. All our perceptions are not susceptible of a local union, either with what is extended or unextended; there being some of them of the one kind, and some of the other.'[1] The problem about the substance of the soul had, therefore, better be dismissed. For we can make no sense of it.

But if there is no substance, whether extended or unextended, which can be called the 'soul', what of personal identity? Hume is obviously compelled to deny that we have any idea of the self as distinct from our perceptions. Some philosophers, he tells us, imagine that we are always conscious of the self as something which remains in a permanent state of self-identity. But if we have any clear and intelligible idea of the self, it must be derived from an impression. Yet 'self or person is not any one impression, but that to which our several impressions and ideas are supposed to have a reference. If any impression gives rise to the idea of self, that impression must continue invariably the same, through the whole course of our lives; since self is supposed to exist after that manner. But there is no impression constant and invariable . . . and consequently there is no such idea.'[2] All our perceptions are distinguishable and separable, and we can discover no self apart from or underlying these perceptions. 'For my part, when I enter most intimately into what I call *myself*, I always stumble on some particular perception or other, of heat or cold, light or shade, love or hatred, pain or pleasure. I never catch *myself* at any time without a perception, and never can observe anything but the perception. . . . If anyone upon serious and unprejudiced reflection thinks he has a different notion of *himself*, I must confess I can reason no longer with him. All I can allow him is that he may be in the right as well as I, and that we are essentially different in this

[1] *T.*, I, 4, 5, p. 250. [2] *T.*, I, 4, 6, pp. 251–2.

particular. He may perhaps perceive something simple and continued, which he calls *himself*, though I am certain there is no such principle in me.'[1] Hume's conclusion is, therefore, that 'the mind is a kind of theatre where several perceptions successively make their appearance; pass, re-pass, glide away and mingle in an infinite variety of postures and situations. There is properly no *simplicity* in it at one time, nor *identity* in different; whatever natural propension we have to imagine that simplicity and identity. The comparison of the theatre must not mislead us. They are the successive perceptions only that constitute the mind; nor have we the most distant notion of the place where these scenes are represented or of the materials of which it is composed.'[2]

What, then, causes our propensity to attribute identity and simplicity to the mind? According to Hume, we tend to confuse the two ideas of identity and of a succession of related objects. For example, an animal body is an aggregate, and its component parts are constantly changing: in the strict sense it does not remain self-identical. But the changes are normally gradual and cannot be perceived from moment to moment. Further, the parts are related to one another, enjoying a mutual dependence on and connection with one another. The mind thus tends to neglect, as it were, the interruptions and to ascribe persistent self-identity to the aggregate. Now, in the case of the human mind there is a succession of related perceptions. Memory, by raising up images of past perceptions, produces a relation of resemblance among our perceptions: and the imagination is thus carried more easily along the chain, so that the chain appears to be a continued and persistent object. Further, our perceptions are mutually related by means of the causal relation. 'Our impressions give rise to their correspondent ideas: and these ideas in their turn produce other impressions. One thought chases another and draws after it a third, by which it is expelled in its turn.'[3] Here again memory is of primary importance. For it is only by memory that we are able to be aware of the causal relations between our perceptions. Hence memory is to be accounted the chief source of the idea of personal identity. Once given memory, our perceptions are linked by association in the imagination, and we attribute identity to what is in fact an interrupted succession of related perceptions. Indeed, unless corrected by philosophy, we may 'feign' a uniting principle,

[1] *T.*, 1, 4, 6, p. 252.   [2] *Ibid.*, p. 253.   [3] *Ibid.*, p. 261.

a permanent self distinct from our perceptions. If we rule out this 'fiction', all questions about personal identity 'are to be regarded rather as grammatical than as philosophical difficulties'.[1] That is to say, the question whether in any given instance it is proper to speak of a thing as identical or not, is a linguistic problem.

Given Hume's phenomenalistic analysis of the self, it is hardly worth discussing whether he believed in immortality. True he did not explicitly deny the possibility of survival. James Boswell records that in his last interview with Hume, on July 7th, 1776, he asked the philosopher whether he did not think it possible that there might be a future state. Hume replied that it was possible that a piece of coal put upon the fire would not burn. In other words, if Hume meant his remark to be taken seriously, survival is a logical possibility. He added, however, that it was a most unreasonable fancy that he should exist for ever. And it seems clear enough from what he has to say on the subject elsewhere not only that he did not think that immortality could be proved, either by metaphysical or moral arguments, but also that he himself did not believe in it. And this, it seems to me, is only what we would expect, if we bear in mind his account of the self.

It is important to add, however, that Hume realized that his account of the self presented difficulties. In his Appendix to the *Treatise* he admits that when it comes to explaining what binds together our distinct perceptions and makes us attribute to them a real simplicity and identity, 'I am sensible that my account is very defective, and that nothing but the seeming evidence of the precedent reasonings could have induced me to receive it. If perceptions are distinct existences, they form a whole only by being connected together. . . . But all my hopes vanish when I come to explain the principles that unite our successive perceptions in our thought or consciousness. I cannot discover any theory which gives me satisfaction on this head. In short, there are two principles which I cannot render consistent; nor is it in my power to renounce either of them, viz. *that all our distinct perceptions are distinct existences*, and *that the mind never perceives any real connection among distinct existences*. . . . For my part, I must plead the privilege of a sceptic and confess that this difficulty is too hard for my understanding.'[2] Hume might well feel some doubts about his account of the self and personal identity. Apart from objections which might be levelled against, for example, his ambiguous use

---

[1] *T.*, 1, 4, 6, p. 262.　　　　　　　[2] *T.*, pp. 635-6.

of the word 'identity',[1] he gives no real explanation of the function-ing of memory, though he emphasizes its importance. And some explanation is required. For it is not easy to see how memory is possible on his theory. Further, as he admits, if the mind can be said in some sense to collect the collection, how can it do this when it is identified with a collection, each member of which is a distinct thing? Does one perception enjoy awareness of others? If so, how? The difficulties do not seem to me to be in any way diminished if we adopt the modern empiricist device of talking about the mind as a 'logical construction' out of psychic events. In fact, precisely the same difficulties recur; and they must recur in any pheno-menalistic account of the self.

3. Before outlining Hume's views about the existence of God, it may be appropriate to say something about his general personal attitude towards religion. He was brought up as a Calvinist, but at a fairly early age he discarded the doctrines which he had been taught in boyhood. In spite, however, of his undoubted dislike for Calvinism, it would be a mistake to think of his attitude towards religion as being no more than the expression of a hostile reaction towards a theology and a religious discipline which had over-shadowed his early years. The truth seems to be that, once he had shed his initial Calvinism, religion was for him a purely external phenomenon which aroused little or no response within himself. In this sense he was an 'irreligious' man. Conscious of the part played by religion in the life of humanity, he was interested in its nature and power; but he was interested in it from the outside, as it were. Furthermore, he came to the conclusion that the influence of religion was far from beneficial. For instance, he thought that religion impairs morality by encouraging people to act for motives other than love of virtue for its own sake. In his essay on *The Natural History of Religion* he traces the development from poly-theism to monotheism. The multiple gods and goddesses of polytheism, who were simply magnified human beings, were progressively attributed with different perfections as by a species of flattery, until infinity was at length attributed to the divine, and this involved monotheism. But though in the course of religious development a lessening of superstition has been observable, the transition from polytheism to theism has also been accompanied by a growth of fanaticism, bigotry and intemperate zeal, as the

[1] He seems to imply, verbally at least, that we attribute identity to our per-ceptions. But we obviously do not do this, even if we regard them as acts of a persistent subject.

behaviour of Mohammedans and Christians shows. Again, the idea of the greatness and majesty of the infinite God has encouraged emphasis on attitudes of abasement and on practices of asceticism and mortification which were foreign to the pagan mentality. Further, whereas in ancient Greece, for example, there was no dogma, as Christians understand it, and philosophy was free and unencumbered by dogmatic theology, in the Christian world philosophy has been misused in the service of theological doctrines. Hume does not, indeed, reject all religion explicitly and in so many words: he distinguishes between true religion on the one hand and superstition and fanaticism on the other. But when we come to look in his writings for an account of what he understands by true religion we find that its content is tenuous in the extreme.

In the *Enquiry concerning Human Understanding* the eleventh section is devoted, according to its title, to the subject of a particular providence and of a future state. In order to give himself a free hand Hume puts what he has to say into the mouth of an Epicurean friend who, at Hume's request, delivers an imaginary speech to the Athenians. The speaker observes that the religious philosophers, instead of resting content with tradition, 'indulge a rash curiosity, in trying how far they can establish religion upon the principles of reason; and they thereby excite, instead of satisfying, the doubts which naturally arise from a diligent and scrutinous enquiry'.[1] He then remarks that 'the chief or sole argument for a divine existence is derived from the order of nature. . . . You allow that this is an argument drawn from effects to causes. From the order of the work you infer that there must have been project and forethought in the workman. If you cannot make out this point, you allow that your conclusion fails: and you pretend not to establish the conclusion in a greater latitude than the phenomena of nature will justify. These are your concessions. I desire to mark the consequences.'[2]

What are these 'consequences'? First, it is not permissible, when inferring a particular cause from an effect, to ascribe to the cause any qualities other than those which are required and which are sufficient to produce the effect. Secondly, it is not permissible to start with the inferred cause and infer other effects besides those already known. In the case of a human invention or work of art we can, indeed, argue that the author possesses certain attributes

---

[1] *E.*, 11, 104, p. 135.   [2] *E.*, 11, 105, pp. 135-6.

other than those immediately manifested in the effect. But we can do this only because we are already acquainted with human beings and with their attributes and capacities and ordinary ways of acting. In the case of God, however, this condition does not obtain. If I think that the world as I know it postulates an intelligent cause, I can infer the existence of such a cause. But I cannot legitimately infer that the cause possesses other attributes, moral qualities, for example, or that it can or will produce other effects than those already known to me. It may, of course, possess other attributes; but I do not know this. And even though conjecture may be permissible, it should be recognized as being mere conjecture, an assertion not of known fact but of mere possibility. Hume's 'friend' does not say that he regards the inference from the natural order to an intelligent designer and cause as valid and certain. On the contrary, 'it is uncertain; because the subject lies entirely beyond the reach of human experience'.[1] We can establish a causal relation only when we observe, and in so far as we observe, constant conjunction. But we cannot observe God at all, and natural phenomena remain what they are whatever explanatory hypothesis we adopt. 'I much doubt whether it be possible for a cause to be known only by its effect.'[2] The religious hypothesis is, indeed, one way of accounting for the visible phenomena of the universe; and it may be true, even though its truth is uncertain. At the same time it is not a hypothesis from which we can deduce any facts other than those which we already know. Nor can we derive from it principles and maxims of conduct. In this sense it is a 'useless' hypothesis. 'It is useless because our knowledge of this cause being derived from the course of nature, we can never, according to the rules of just reasoning, return back from the cause with any new inference, or, making additions to the common and experienced course of nature, establish any new principles of conduct and behaviour.'[3]

Substantially the same outlook is expressed at greater length in the *Dialogues concerning Natural Religion* which were published, according to Hume's wish, after his death. The participants in the *Dialogues* are named Cleanthes, Philo and Demea, and their conversation is reported by Pamphilus to Hermippus. Hume does not appear in his own person; nor does he state which of the particular views expressed is his own. Pamphilus alludes to 'the accurate philosophical turn of Cleanthes', the 'careless scepticism

---

[1] *E.*, 11, 110, p. 142.   [2] *E.*, 11, 114, p. 148.   [3] *E.*, 11, 110, p. 142.

of Philo' and 'the rigid inflexible orthodoxy of Demea'.[1] It has not infrequently been held, therefore, that Hume identifies himself with Cleanthes. Those who support this view can appeal to the concluding words of the *Dialogues* when Pamphilus remarks that 'upon a serious review of the whole I cannot but think that Philo's principles are more probable than Demea's, but that those of Cleanthes approach still nearer to the truth'.[2] Furthermore, writing to Sir Gilbert Elliot in 1751 Hume remarks that Cleanthes is 'the hero of the Dialogue' and that anything which Elliot can think of as strengthening Cleanthes' position will be 'most acceptable' to him. But if Hume is to be identified with Cleanthes, we must ascribe to him a firm belief in the argument from design. 'By this argument *a posteriori*, and by this argument alone, we do prove at once the existence of a Deity and his similarity to human mind and intelligence.'[3] But though Hume doubtless agreed with Cleanthes' rejection of what he calls *a priori* arguments and with the latter's contention that 'the words *necessary being* have no meaning, or, which is the same thing, none that is consistent',[4] it seems to me most improbable that he regarded the argument from design as conclusive. For this would hardly have been compatible with his general philosophical principles. Nor would it be consistent with the section of the first *Enquiry*, to which reference has been made above. For though in this section Hume produces an imaginary friend as speaker, it is in his own person that he remarks that 'I much doubt whether it be possible for a cause to be known only by its effect, as you have all along supposed'.[5] It seems to me that in the *Dialogues* it is Philo, not Cleanthes, who represents Hume, so far as any particular participant in the conversation can be said to represent him. Hume set out to develop a discussion of the problems of our knowledge of God's existence and nature, and it is unnecessary to suppose that he wished to identify himself exclusively either with Philo or with Cleanthes. But in so far as their views are opposed to one another, it seems to me only reasonable to associate Hume with the views of the former rather than with those of the latter. It would appear that Cleanthes is the hero of the *Dialogues* for Pamphilus rather than for Hume; and though when the latter showed Elliot an incomplete version of the work he could quite well invite Elliot to contribute ideas which would strengthen Cleanthes' position, in

---

[1] *D.*, Preface, p. 128. [2] *D.*, XII, p. 228. [3] *D.*, II, p. 143.
[4] *D.*, IX, p. 190. [5] *E.*, II, 115, p. 148.

order to maintain the dramatic interest of the dialogue, this does not alter the fact that the tendency of Part XII, the final section of the work, tends to strengthen Philo's position rather than that of Cleanthes, in spite of Pamphilus's concluding remarks.

If we assume, then, that where Philo and Cleanthes are really opposed to one another, it is the former who expresses Hume's mind more nearly than the latter, what conclusion do we arrive at concerning Hume's attitude towards our knowledge of God's existence and nature? The answer can be given in Philo's oft-quoted words. 'If the whole of natural theology, as some people seem to maintain, resolves itself into one simple, though somewhat ambiguous, at least undefined proposition, *that the cause or causes of order in the universe probably bear some remote analogy to human intelligence:* If this proposition be not capable of extension, variation or more particular explication: If it afford no inference that affects human life or can be the source of any action or for-bearance: And if the analogy, imperfect as it is, can be carried no farther than to the human intelligence, and cannot be transferred, with any appearance of probability, to the other qualities of the mind: If this really be the case, what can the most inquisitive, contemplative and religious man do more than give a plain, philosophical assent to the proposition as often as it occurs; and believe that the arguments on which it is established exceed the objections which lie against it?'[1] Here we are reduced to the simple proposition that the cause or causes of order in the world probably bear a remote analogy to human intelligence. No more can be said. No affirmation is made about the moral qualities of the 'cause or causes'. The proposition, moreover, is purely theoretical, in the sense that no conclusion can be legitimately drawn from it affecting human conduct, religious or moral. 'True religion' is reduced, therefore, to the recognition of a purely theoretical state-ment of probability. This is the position which fits the eleventh section of the first *Enquiry*, and it is as far as Hume is prepared to go.

Boswell records Hume's statement at the end of his life that he had never entertained any belief in religion since he began to read Locke and Clarke. Presumably he meant that when he began to study the rational defence of natural theology and of religion in the works of these philosophers he found their arguments so weak that he ceased to believe in the conclusions. It was Hume's view

---

[1] *D.*, XII, p. 227.

that religion originated in such passions as fear of disaster and hope of advantage or betterment when these passions are directed towards some invisible and intelligent power. In the course of time men attempted to rationalize religion and to find arguments in favour of belief; but most of these arguments will not stand up to critical analysis. This he thought to be true of the arguments adduced by Locke and Clarke and other metaphysicians. There is, however, a quasi-spontaneous tendency to regard the world as showing evidence of design; and, provided that we say no more, it is not unreasonable to say that it is probable that the cause or causes of phenomena, whatever these causes may be, bear some sort of an analogy with what we call intelligence. But in the long run, the world is an inscrutable mystery, and we cannot have any certain knowledge of ultimate causes.

The reader may expect a plain answer to the question whether Hume is to be regarded as an atheist, an agnostic or a theist. But it is not easy to give a 'plain answer' to this question. As already mentioned, he refused to recognize the validity of metaphysical arguments for God's existence; that is to say, he refused to allow that the existence of God is demonstrable. What he does is to examine the argument from design which he treats as leading to the 'religious hypothesis'. It is plain from the *Dialogues* that he disliked any form of the argument which is based principally on an analogy between human artificial constructions and the world. He admitted, however, that there are certain principles which operate in the world, namely, 'organization' or animal and vegetable life, instinct and intelligence. These principles are productive of order and pattern, and we know their effects by experience. But the principles themselves and their modes of operation are mysteries and inscrutable. However, there are points of analogy between them, to judge by their effects. And if by affirming God's existence we mean merely to affirm that the ultimate cause of order in the universe probably bears some remote analogy to intelligence, Hume is prepared to agree. This is not atheism in the sense of a categorical denial that there is anything besides phenomena; and Hume did not profess himself an atheist. Yet it is hardly to be called theism, not at least unless we read far more into Hume's admissions than he intended them to express. It might possibly be called agnosticism; but it must be remembered that Hume was not in a state of agnosticism about the existence of a personal God with moral attributes, as described by Christians in particular. The fact of the matter seems to be that Hume set out, as a detached observer, to examine the rational credentials of theism, maintaining in the meantime that religion rests on revelation, a revelation in which he personally certainly did not believe. The result of his investigation was, as we have seen, to reduce the 'religious hypothesis' to so meagre a content that it is difficult to know what to call it. It is a residuum which, as Hume was well aware, might be accepted by anyone who was not a dogmatic atheist. Its content is ambiguous, and Hume meant it to be ambiguous.

Emphasis is sometimes laid on the fact that Hume devoted his attention principally to theistic arguments as found in English writers such as Clarke and Butler. This is true enough; but if the implication is intended that Hume would have changed his mind, had he been acquainted with more satisfactory formulations of the arguments for the existence of God, it must be remembered that, given Hume's philosophical principles, especially his analysis of causality, he could not admit any cogent proofs of theism in a recognizable sense. In conclusion, it may be noted that Hume's analysis of the argument from design influenced Kant's final treatment of the matter, though the latter's attitude to theism was, of course, much more positive than that adopted by the former. Hume's thought was dissolvent of contemporary theological argument and apologetic, whereas Kant attempted to set belief in God on a new footing.

4. Some remarks on Hume's attitude towards scepticism may perhaps form a suitable conclusion to this chapter. And I shall begin by outlining the distinction which Hume draws in the *Enquiry concerning Human Understanding* between 'antecedent' and 'consequent' scepticism.

By antecedent scepticism Hume understands a scepticism which is 'antecedent to all study and philosophy'.[1] As an example he cites Cartesian doubt, taking this to involve doubt not only of all our particular previously held beliefs and opinions but also of the power of our faculties to attain truth. The definition of antecedent scepticism might suggest the sceptical attitude which may arise in the minds of non-philosophers rather than the Cartesian doubt which is part of a deliberately chosen philosophical method. However, it is, indeed, antecedent to the positive building-up of the Cartesian system; and in any case it is the example selected

[1] *E.*, 12, 1, 116, p. 149.

by Hume. According to Descartes, he says, we should entertain a universal doubt until we have reassured ourselves by means of a chain of reasoning deduced from some original principle which cannot itself be doubtful or fallacious. There is, however, no such original principle. And even if there were, we could not advance beyond it except by the use of the very faculties whose trustworthiness we have placed in doubt. Scepticism of this sort is not really possible; and, if it were, it would be incurable. But there is a more moderate and reasonable form of antecedent scepticism. That is to say, before pursuing philosophical inquiry we ought to free ourselves, so far as we can, from all prejudice and attain a state of impartiality. We ought to begin with clear and evident principles and advance carefully, examining all the steps of our reasoning. But this is a matter of common sense. Without such care and accuracy we cannot hope to make any sure progress in knowledge.

Consequent scepticism is scepticism which is 'consequent to science and enquiry'.[1] In other words, it is the result of the discovery, or supposed discovery, by philosophers either of the untrustworthy character of our mental faculties or, at least, of their unfitness for reaching any reliable conclusion 'in all those curious subjects of speculation about which they are commonly employed'.[2] And it may be divided into scepticism about the senses and scepticism about reason. In the *Treatise*[3] Hume discussed scepticism about the senses first, but in the first *Enquiry* the order of treatment is reversed.

What Hume calls the 'more trite topics' adduced by sceptics in all ages to show that the evidence of the senses is untrustworthy are dismissed in a rather summary manner. He refers to the familiar example of the oar which appears to be bent or crooked when partly immersed in water and to the double images which result from exerting pressure on one eye. All that such examples show, however, is that we may need to correct the immediate evidence of the senses by reason and by considerations based on the nature of the medium, the distance of the object, the disposition of the sense-organ, and so on. This is what we do in practice, and it is quite sufficient. 'There are other more profound arguments against the senses, which admit not of so easy a solution.'[4]

Men are led by a natural impulse to put faith in their senses,

---

[1] *E.*, 12, 1, 117, p. 150.   [2] *Ibid.*
[3] *T.*, 1, 4, 1–2, pp. 180–218.   [4] *E.*, 12, 1, 117, p. 151.

and from the start we suppose that there exists an external universe which is independent of the senses. Further, led by this 'blind and powerful instinct of nature',[1] men instinctively take the images presented by the senses to be the external objects themselves. 'But this universal and primary opinion of all men is soon destroyed by the slightest philosophy. And no man, who reflects, ever doubted that the existences which we consider when we say *this house* and *that tree* are nothing but perceptions in the mind and fleeting copies or representations of other existences which remain uniform and independent.'[2] To this extent, therefore, philosophy leads us to contradict or depart from our natural instincts. At the same time philosophy finds itself in an embarrassing situation when asked to give a rational defence of its position. For how can we prove that images or perceptions are representations of objects which are not themselves images or perceptions? 'The mind has never anything present to it but the perceptions and cannot possibly reach any experience of their connection with objects. The supposition of such a connection is, therefore, without any foundation in reasoning.'[3] To have recourse with Descartes to the divine veracity is useless. If the divine veracity were really involved, our senses would be always and entirely infallible. Moreover, if we once question the existence of an external world, how can we prove the existence of God or any of His attributes? We are faced, therefore, with a dilemma. If we follow the propensity of nature, we believe that perceptions or images are the external objects themselves; and this is a belief which reason refutes. If, however, we say that perceptions or images are caused by and represent objects, we cannot find any convincing argument, based on experience, to prove that the former are in fact connected with external objects. 'This is a topic, therefore, in which the profounder and more philosophical sceptics will always triumph, when they endeavour to introduce an universal doubt into all subjects of human knowledge and enquiry.'[4]

Scepticism about reason may concern either abstract reasoning or matters of fact. The chief sceptical objection to the validity of abstract reasoning is derived, according to Hume in the *Enquiry*, from examination of our ideas of space and time. Let us suppose that extension is infinitely divisible. A given quantity X contains within itself a quantity Y which is infinitely less than X. Similarly,

---

[1] *E.*, 12, 1, 118, p. 151.　　[2] *Ibid.*, p. 152.
[3] *E.*, 12, 1, 119, p. 153.　　[4] *E.*, 12, 1, 121, p. 153.

Y contains within itself a quantity *Z* which is infinitely less than *Y*. And so on indefinitely. A supposition of this kind 'shocks the clearest and most natural principles of human reason'.[1] Again, 'an infinite number of real parts of time, passing in succession and exhausted one after another, appears so evident a contradiction that no man, one should think, whose judgment is not corrupted, instead of being improved, by the sciences, would ever be able to admit it'.[2]

As for sceptical objections to 'moral evidence' or to reasonings concerning matters of fact, these may be either popular or philosophical. Under the former heading can be grouped objections derived from the variety of mutually incompatible opinions held by different men, the different opinions held by the same man at different times, the contradictory beliefs of different societies and nations, and so on. According to Hume, however, popular objections of this sort are ineffective. 'The great subverter of *Pyrrhonism* or the excessive principle of scepticism is action and employment and the occupations of common life.'[3] It may not be possible to refute these objections in the classroom, but in ordinary life they 'vanish like smoke and leave the most determined sceptic in the same condition as other mortals'.[4] More important are the philosophical objections. And chief among these is the objection deriving from Hume's own analysis of causality; for, given this analysis, we have no argument to prove that because *a* and *b* have always been conjoined in our past experience they will be similarly conjoined in the future.

Now, given Hume's view about mathematics and abstract reasoning, which concerns relations between ideas, he could not admit real grounds for scepticism in this field. Hence we find him saying 'how any clear, distinct idea can contain circumstances contradictory to itself or to any other clear, distinct idea is absolutely incomprehensible; and is, perhaps, as absurd as any proposition which can be formed. So that nothing can be more sceptical, or more full of doubt and hesitation, than this scepticism itself, which arises from some of the paradoxical conclusions of geometry or the science of quantity.'[5] He tried to avoid the antinomies which seemed to him to give rise to scepticism by denying that space and time are infinitely divisible in the sense alleged.[6] But whereas he felt bound to indicate a theoretical

---

[1] *E.*, 12, 2, 124, p. 156.   [2] *E.*, 12, 2, 125, p. 157.   [3] *E.*, 12, 2, 126, pp. 158–9.
[4] *Ibid.*, p. 159.   [5] *E.*, 12, 2, 125, pp. 157–8.
[6] Cf. *E.*, 12, 2, 125, note, p. 158, and *T.*, 1, 2, 1–2.

answer to scepticism about abstract reasoning, he pursued a different method with regard to thorough-going scepticism about the senses and about reasoning concerning matters of fact. As we have already seen when considering the problem of the existence of bodies, Hume remarked that scepticism on this point cannot be maintained in ordinary life. 'Carelessness and inattention alone can afford us any remedy. For this reason I rely entirely upon them.'[1] His remark that action and employment and the occupations of common life constitute the great subverter of Pyrrhonism has been quoted above in connection with popular objections to reasonings concerning matters of fact. Similarly, after speaking in the *Enquiry* about the principal philosophical objection against reasoning concerning matters of fact he observes that 'here is the chief and most confounding objection to *excessive* scepticism, that no durable good can ever result from it, while it remains in its full force and vigour. We need only ask such a sceptic, *What his meaning is? And what he proposes by all these curious researches?* He is immediately at a loss and knows not what to answer. A Copernican or Ptolemaic, who supports each his different system of astronomy, may hope to produce a conviction, which will remain constant and durable, with his audience. A Stoic or Epicurean displays principles which may not be durable but which have an effect on conduct and behaviour. But a Pyrrhonian cannot expect that his philosophy will have any constant influence on the mind; or if it had, that its influence would be beneficial to society. On the contrary, he must acknowledge, if he will acknowledge anything, that all human life must perish, were his principles universally and steadily to prevail. All discourse, all action would immediately cease; and men remain in a total lethargy, till the necessities of nature, unsatisfied, put an end to their miserable existence. It is true; so fatal an event is little to be dreaded. Nature is always too strong for principle.'[2] In the *Treatise*, after speaking of the intense realization of the manifold antinomies in which human reason is involved, he says: 'Most fortunately it happens that since reason is incapable of dispelling these clouds, nature herself suffices to that purpose. . . . I dine, I play a game of backgammon, I converse and am merry with my friends; and when after three or four hours' amusement, I would return to these speculations, they appear so cold and strained and ridiculous that I cannot find in my heart to enter into them any farther. Here then

---

[1] *T.*, 1, 4, 2, p. 218.   [2] *E.*, 12, 2, 128, pp. 159–60.

I find myself absolutely and necessarily determined to live and talk and act like other people in the common affairs of life.'[1]

Though Hume rejects, we may say, what he calls 'excessive' scepticism, he admits as 'both durable and useful' a 'mitigated' or 'academical' scepticism, which may be in part a result of Pyrrhonism (or excessive scepticism) when this has been 'corrected by common sense and reflection'.[2] This mitigated scepticism involves, for example, limiting our inquiries to those subjects for the consideration of which our mental capacities are adapted. 'It seems to me that the only objects of the abstract science or of demonstration are quantity and number, and that all attempts to extend this more perfect species of knowledge beyond these bounds are mere sophistry and illusion.'[3] As for inquiries about matters of fact and existence, we are here outside the sphere of demonstration. 'Whatever *is* may *not be*. No negation of a fact can involve a contradiction. . . . The existence, therefore, of any being can only be proved by arguments from its cause or its effect; and these arguments are founded entirely on experience. If we reason *a priori*, anything may appear able to produce anything.'[4]

Divinity or theology has a rational foundation in so far as it is supported by experience. 'But its best and most solid foundation is faith and divine revelation.'[5] What we are to think of this last proposition is made clear enough, I think, by the *Dialogues*. As for morals and aesthetics (which Hume calls 'criticism'), these are objects of taste and sentiment more than of the understanding. 'Beauty, whether moral or natural, is felt, more properly than perceived.'[6] We may, indeed, try to fix some standard, but then we have to consider some empirical fact, such as the general tastes of mankind.

Hume's famous conclusion deserves quotation here. 'When we run over libraries, persuaded of these principles, what havoc must we make? If we take in hand any volume; of divinity or school metaphysics, for instance; let us ask, *Does it contain any abstract reasoning concerning quantity or number?* No. *Does it contain any experimental reasoning concerning matter of fact and existence?* No. Commit it then to the flames: for it can contain nothing but sophistry and illusion.'[7]

Hume's remarks about scepticism, including 'Pyrrhonism', and about carelessness and inattention as the remedy for scepticism

[1] *T.*, 1 4, 7, p. 269.   [2] *E.*, 12, 3, 129, p. 161.   [3] *E.*, 12, 3, 131, p. 163.
[4] *E.*, 12, 3, 132, p. 164.   [5] *Ibid.*, p. 165.   [6] *Ibid.*   [7] *Ibid.*

should not be understood in a purely ironical sense or as indicating that the philosopher had his tongue in his cheek. Scepticism was a matter of importance in his eyes, partly because it was a living issue at the time, though more in France than in England, and partly because he was well aware of the sceptical conclusions which followed from the application of his own principles. For one thing, it was, he thought, a healthy antidote to dogmatism and fanaticism. Indeed, 'a true sceptic will be diffident of his philosophical doubts, as well as of his philosophical conviction'.[1] He will refrain from showing dogmatism and fanaticism in his scepticism. At the same time a thorough-going scepticism is untenable in practice. This fact does not prove its falsity; but it shows that in ordinary life we have inevitably to act according to natural belief or the propensities of our human nature. And this is how things should be. Reason is dissolvent; at least, there is very little that it leaves unshaken and unquestionable. And the philosophical spirit is the spirit of free inquiry. But human nature is very far from being governed and directed by reason alone. Morality, for example, is grounded on feeling rather than on the analytic understanding. And though the philosopher in his study may arrive at sceptical conclusions, in the sense that he sees how little reason can prove, he is at the same time a man; and in his ordinary life he is governed, and ought to allow himself to be governed if he wishes to live at all, by the natural beliefs which common human nature imposes on him as on others. In other words, Hume had little sympathy for any attempt to turn philosophy into a creed, a dogmatically propounded standard for belief and conduct. It is, if you like, a game; a game of which Hume was fond, and one which has its uses. But in the long run 'Nature is always too strong for principle'.[2] 'Be a philosopher; but, amidst all your philosophy, be still a man.'[3]

---

[1] *T.*, 1, 4, 7, p. 273.   [2] *E.*, 12, 2, 128, p. 160.   [3] *E.*, 1, 4, p. 9.

CHAPTER XVI

HUME (3)

Introductory—The passions, direct and indirect—Sympathy—The will and liberty—The passions and the reason—Moral distinctions and the moral sense—Benevolence and utility—Justice—General remarks.

1. HUME is chiefly famous for his epistemological analyses and for his examinations of causality and of the notions of the self and of personal identity; in other words, for the contents of the first book of the *Treatise*. But the *Treatise of Human Nature* was described by him as an attempt to introduce the experimental method of reasoning into moral subjects. In the Introduction he says that in the four sciences of logic, morals, criticism and politics 'is comprehended almost everything which it can any way import us to be acquainted with, or which can tend either to the improvement or ornament of the human mind'.[1] And he makes it clear that he hopes to lay the foundation of moral science. Towards the close of the first book he speaks of having been led into several topics which will 'prepare the way for our following opinions',[2] and he alludes to 'those immense depths of philosophy which lie before me'.[3] At the beginning of the third book he declares that 'morality is a subject that interests us above all others'.[4] It is true that he uses the term 'moral philosophy' to mean the science of human nature, and that he divides this into the study of man as 'a reasonable rather than as an active being' and the study of man 'chiefly as born for action'.[5] But there can be no doubt of the importance which Hume attached to moral philosophy in the ordinary sense. He thought of himself as carrying on the work of Shaftesbury, Hutcheson, Butler and so on, and as doing for morals and politics what others, such as Galileo and Newton, had accomplished for natural science. 'Moral philosophy is in the same condition as natural, with regard to astronomy before the time of Copernicus.'[6] The ancient astronomers invented intricate systems which were overloaded with unnecessary hypotheses. But these systems have at last given place to 'something more simple and

---

[1] p. xx.   [2] *T.*, 1, 4, 6, p. 263.   [3] *T.*, 1, 4, 7, p. 263.
[4] *T.*, 3, 1, 3, p. 455.   [5] *E.*, 1, 1–2, pp. 5–6.   [6] *T.*, 2, 1, 3, p. 282.

natural'.[1] So Hume wishes to discover the fundamental or elementary principles which operate in man's ethical life.

We have seen that according to Hume the basic assumptions on which we act, those fundamental beliefs, that is to say, which are necessary for practical life, are not conclusions drawn by the understanding from rational argument. This is not to say, of course, that people do not reason about their practical affairs: it is to say that the ordinary man's reflections and reasoning presuppose beliefs which are not themselves the fruit of reasoning. It is not surprising, therefore, that Hume should also minimize the part played by reason in morals. He is well aware, of course, that we do in fact reflect and reason and argue about moral problems and decisions; but he maintains that moral distinctions are derived ultimately, not from reasoning, but from feeling, from the moral sentiment. Reason alone is not capable of being the sole immediate cause of our actions. Indeed, Hume goes so far as to say that 'reason is, and ought to be the slave of the passions, and can never pretend to any other office than to serve and obey them'.[2]

I shall return later to the subject of the moral sentiment and to Hume's view of the part played by reason in morals. But if we bear in mind the general fact that he emphasizes the role of what we may call the emotional aspect of human nature in man's moral life, we can understand more easily why, before coming to ethics proper in the third book of the *Treatise*, he devotes the long second book to a discussion of the passions. I do not propose to enter in a detailed manner into his treatment of this subject; but something at least ought to be said about it. Before doing so, however, it may be as well to remark that the word 'passion' is not used by Hume to signify simply a burst of unregulated emotion, as when we speak of someone flying into a passion. The word is used by him, as by other philosophers of the period, to include emotions and affects in general. He is concerned with analysing the emotional aspect of human nature, considered as a source of action, not with moralizing about inordinate passions.

2. As we saw in Chapter XIV, Hume distinguished between impressions of sensation and impressions of reflection. This is the same as distinguishing between original and secondary impressions. 'Original impressions or impressions of sensation are such as without any antecedent perception arise in the soul, from the

---

[1] *T.*, 2, 1, 3, p. 282.   [2] *T.*, 2, 3, 3, p. 415.

constitution of the body, from the animal spirits, or from the application of objects to the external organs. Secondary, or reflective impressions are such as proceed from some of these original ones, either immediately or by the interposition of its idea. Of the first kind are all impressions of the senses, and all bodily pains and pleasure: of the second are the passions, and other emotions resembling them.'[1] Thus a bodily pain, such as the pain of gout, can produce passions like grief, hope and fear. Then we have passions, secondary impressions, derived from an original or primary impression, namely, a certain bodily pain.

I have said that Hume used the word 'passion' to cover all emotions and affects without confining it to unregulated bursts of emotion. But a qualification is needed. For he distinguishes between calm and violent reflective or secondary impressions. The sense of beauty and deformity in actions, in works of art and in natural objects belongs to the first class, while love and hatred, joy and grief, belong to the second. Hume admits, indeed, that 'this division is far from being exact,'[2] on the ground that the raptures of poetry and music may be very intense whereas 'those other impressions, properly called *passions*, may decay into so soft an emotion as to become, in a manner, imperceptible'.[3] But my point is that here he seems to restrict the word 'passion' to what he calls violent reflective impressions. And this is one reason why I said that my former statement stands in need of qualification. At the same time these 'violent' emotions, or passions in a restricted sense, are not necessarily disordered. Hume is thinking of intensity: he is not passing a moral judgment.

The passions are divided by Hume into direct and indirect passions. The former are those which arise immediately from the experience of pleasure or pain; and Hume mentions desire, aversion, grief, joy, hope, fear, despair and security. The pain of gout, for instance, produces direct passions. Hume also mentions direct passions which arise 'from a natural impulse or instinct, which is perfectly unaccountable. Of this kind is the desire of punishment to our enemies and of happiness to our friends; hunger, lust, and a few other bodily appetites.'[4] These passions are said to produce good and evil (that is, pleasure and pain) rather than to proceed from them as other direct passions do. Indirect passions do not arise simply from feelings of pleasure or pain; they arise from what

[1] *T.*, 2, 1, 1, p. 275.   [2] *Ibid.*, p. 276.
[3] *Ibid.*   [4] *T.*, 2, 3, 9, p. 439.

Hume calls 'a double relation of impressions and ideas'.[1] His meaning can best be explained by using examples, such as pride and humility, love and hatred.

In the first place we must distinguish between the object and the cause of a passion. The object of pride and humility is the self, 'that succession of related ideas and impressions, of which we have an intimate memory and consciousness'.[2] Whatever other objects we may have in mind when we feel pride or humility, they are always considered in relation to the self. And when self does not enter into consideration, there can be neither pride nor humility. But though the self is the object of these two passions, it cannot be their sufficient cause. If it were, a certain degree of pride would always be accompanied by a corresponding degree of humility, and conversely. Again, the object of love and hatred is some person other than the self. According to Hume, 'when we talk of *self-love*, it is not in a proper sense, nor has the sensation it produces anything in common with that tender emotion which is excited by a friend or mistress'.[3] But the other person is not the sole and sufficient cause of these passions. If it were, production of the one passion would involve production of the other.

In the second place we must distinguish, within the cause of a passion, between the quality which operates and the subject in which it is placed. To take an example given by Hume, when a man is vain of a beautiful house which belongs to him we can distinguish between the beauty and the house. Both are necessary component parts of the cause of the passion of vanity, but they are none the less distinguishable.

In the third place we must make the following distinction. The passions of pride and humility are 'determined to have self for their *object*, not only by a natural but also by an original property'.[4] The constancy and steadiness of the determination shows its 'natural' character. The self-regarding direction of pride and humility is 'original' in the sense that it is primary and cannot be further resolved into other elements. Similarly, the other-regarding determination of the passions of love and hatred is both natural and original. But when we turn from 'object' to 'cause', in the sense indicated above, we find a somewhat different situation. The causes of these passions are, according to Hume, natural, in the sense that the same sort of objects tend to give rise to the passions.

---

[1] *T.*, 2, 3, 9, p. 439. [2] *T.*, 2, 1, 2, p. 277.
[3] *T.*, 2, 2, 1, p. 329. [4] *T.*, 2, 1, 3, p. 280.

Material possessions and physical qualities tend to give rise, for example, to pride and vanity, in whatever epoch men may live. But the causes of pride and humility are not original in the sense of being 'adapted to these passions by a particular provision and primary constitution of nature'.[1] There is a vast number of causes, and many of them depend on human artifice and invention (houses, furniture and clothes, for instance); and it would be absurd to suppose that nature foresaw and provided for each possible cause of a passion. Hence, although it is from natural principles that a great variety of causes excites pride and humility, it is not true that each different cause is adapted to its passion by a different principle. The problem, therefore, is to discover among the various causes a common element on which their influence depends.

In his solution of this problem Hume invokes the principles of association of ideas and association of impressions. When one idea is present to the imagination, any other idea which is related to it by resemblance, contiguity or causality tends to follow. Again, 'all resembling impressions are connected together, and no sooner one arises than the rest immediately follow'.[2] (Impressions, unlike ideas, are associated only by resemblance.) Now, these two kinds of association assist one another and, 'both uniting in one action, bestow on the mind a double impulse'.[3] The cause of the passion produces in us a sensation. In the case of pride this is a sensation of pleasure, in the case of 'humility' or self-depreciation it is a sensation of pain. And this sensation or impression has a natural and original reference to the self as object or to the idea of the self. There is, therefore, a natural relation between impression and idea. And this permits a concurrent working of the two kinds of association—association of impressions and association of ideas. When a passion has been aroused it tends to call forth a succession of resembling passions by force of the principle of association of resembling impressions. Again, by force of the principle of association of ideas the mind passes easily from one idea (say, the idea of one aspect of the causes and object of pride) to another idea. And these two movements reinforce one another, the mind easily passing from one set to the other in virtue of the correlation between them. Suppose that a man has suffered an injury from another and that this has produced in him a passion. This passion (an impression) tends to call forth in him resembling passions. And

---

[1] *T.*, 2, 1, 3, p. 281.   [2] *T.*, 2, 1, 4, p. 283.   [3] *Ibid.*, p. 284.

this movement is facilitated by the fact that the man's idea of the causes and objects of the passion tend to call forth other ideas, which in turn are correlated with impressions. 'When an idea produces an impression, related to an impression, which is connected with an idea, related to the first idea, these two impressions must be in a manner inseparable, nor will the one in any case be unattended with the other.'[1]

Hume's intention is obviously that of explaining the complex emotional life of mankind with the aid of as few principles as possible. In treating of the indirect passions and of the transition from one passion to another he makes use of the principles of association. I say 'principles' rather than 'principle' because it is his view that the association of ideas by itself is not sufficient to give rise to a passion. He therefore speaks of indirect passions as arising from 'a double relation of impressions and ideas', and he explains the transition from one such passion to another as the effect of the concurrent operation of associated ideas and impressions. But he also emphasizes the influence of sympathy in our emotional life; and something must be said about this topic.

3. Our knowledge of the passions of others is gained by observation of the effects of these passions. 'When any affection is infused by sympathy, it is at first known only by its effects and by those external signs in the countenance and conversation which convey an idea of it.'[2] Now, the difference between ideas and impressions has been defined in terms of force and vivacity. A lively idea can, therefore, be converted into an impression. And this is what happens in the case of sympathy. The idea of a passion which is produced by observation of the latter's effects 'is presently converted into an impression and acquires such a degree of force and vivacity as to become the very passion itself'.[3] How does this conversion take place? Hume presupposes that 'nature has preserved a great resemblance among all human creatures, and that we never remark any passion or principle in others, of which, in some degree or other, we may not find a parallel in ourselves'.[4] Besides this general relation of resemblance there are other more specific relationships, such as blood-relationship, common membership of one nation, use of the same language, and so on. And 'all these relations, when united together, convey the impression or consciousness of our own person to the idea of the sentiments or passions of others and makes us conceive them in the strongest

[1] *T.*, 2, 1, 5, p. 289.   [2] *T.*, 2, 1, 11, p. 317.   [3] *Ibid.*   [4] *Ibid.*, p. 318.

and most lively manner'.[1] To each one of us his own self is, so to speak, intimately and always present. And when we observe the effects of the passions of others and so form ideas of these passions, these ideas tend to become converted into impressions; that is, into similar passions, to the degree that we associate ourselves with them in virtue of some relationship or relationships. 'In sympathy there is an evident conversion of an idea into an impression. This conversion arises from the relation of objects to oneself. Ourself is always intimately present to us.'[2]

Again, we may perceive the causes of a passion or emotion. Hume gives the example of seeing the preparations for a 'terrible' surgical operation (without anaesthetic, of course). These may excite in the beholder's mind, even though he is not the patient, a strong emotion of terror. 'No passion of another discovers itself immediately to the mind. We are only sensible of its causes or effects. From *these* we infer the passion: And consequently *these* give rise to our sympathy.'[3]

Whether all this fits in with Hume's phenomenalism is disputable. For he appears to postulate more than is warranted by his phenomenalistic analysis of mind. But it is clear at least that he was well aware of the intimate links between human beings. And he tries to explain the contagious character of the passions and emotions. In point of fact Hume's world is not a world of mutually sundered human atoms, but the world of ordinary experience in which human beings stand to one another in varying degrees of mutual relationships. This he takes for granted. It is the psychological mechanism of sympathy with which he is concerned. And he is sure that sympathetic communication is one important cause in the generation of passions.

4. Something having been said about the causes and mechanism of the passions, we can now turn to consider the relations between the will, the passions and the reason. And in the first place we can ask what Hume understands by will, and whether he recognizes free-will.

Hume speaks of the will as one of the immediate effects of pleasure and pain. It is not, however, properly speaking, a passion. He describes it as 'the internal impression we feel and are conscious of, when we knowingly give rise to any new motion of our body, or new perception of our mind'.[4] It cannot be defined, since it

---

[1] *T.*, 2, 1, 11, p. 318. [2] *Ibid.*, p. 320.
[3] *T.*, 3, 3, 1, p. 576. [4] *T.*, 2, 3, 1, p. 399.

cannot be further resolved, and it is needless to describe it any
further. We can, therefore, turn immediately to the problem of
freedom.

According to Hume, the union between motive and action
possesses the same constancy which we observe between cause and
effect in physical operations. Further, this constancy influences
the understanding in the same way that constant conjunction in
physical operations influences the understanding, namely, by
'determining us to infer the existence of one from that of another'.[1]
In fact, there is no known circumstance which enters into the
production of purely material operations which is not also found
in volition. Hence we have no good reason for attributing necessity
to the former and denying it of the latter. True, human action
often appears uncertain. Yet the more our knowledge is increased,
the clearer become the connections between character, motive and
choice. In any case we have no adequate reason for supposing that
there is a privileged sphere of freedom, where necessary connection
is wanting.

It is important to note that for Hume, as for some modern
empiricists, absence of necessity spells chance, so that to assert
liberty of indifference is to say that human choices are uncaused
and are due simply to chance. 'According to my definitions,
necessity makes an essential part of causation; and consequently
liberty, by removing necessity, removes also causes, and is the
very same thing with chance. As chance is commonly thought to
imply a contradiction, and is at least directly contrary to experience, there are always the same arguments against liberty or
free-will.'[2] It will be remembered that Hume recognized only one
type of causal relation, in which constant conjunction forms the
objective element and necessary connection the subjectively
contributed element. Once given this restricted view of causality,
it follows, of course, that free action would be uncaused action; if,
that is to say, assertion of freedom involves denial of necessity.
Hume admits, however, that the problem of freedom is to a certain
extent a linguistic problem, in the sense that though freedom must
be denied if it is defined in such a way as to exclude necessity, it
can be asserted if it is defined in another way. For instance, if
freedom is identified with spontaneity, there is freedom. For it is
clear that a great number of actions proceed from a man as a
rational agent without any external coercion. Indeed, spontaneity

is the only form of liberty which we should have any interest in asserting. For, Hume maintains, if so-called free actions are due to chance and are not caused by the agent, it would be unjust for God or man to hold human beings responsible for bad and vicious actions and to pass moral condemnation on the agents. For the agents would not in fact be agents at all in any proper sense. Obviously the validity of Hume's point of view on this matter depends on the validity of his notion of causality.

5. Having disposed of freedom, except when it is reduced to spontaneity, Hume attempts to prove the truth of two propositions. The first proposition is that 'reason alone can never be a motive to any action of the will', and the second is that reason 'can never oppose passion in the direction of the will'.[1] His defence of these two propositions arises out of the fact that 'nothing is more usual in philosophy, and even in common life, than to talk of the combat of passion and reason, to give the preference to reason and to assert that men are only so far virtuous as they conform themselves to its dictates'.[2]

In the first place, reason in the sense of the abstract understanding concerned with relations between ideas or with matters of demonstration is never the cause of any action. 'Mathematics, indeed, are useful in all mechanical operations, and arithmetic in almost every art and profession: but it is not of themselves they have any influence.'[3] They do not influence action unless we have a purpose or end which is not dictated or determined by mathematics.

The second operation of the understanding concerns probability, the sphere not of abstract ideas but of things related causally to one another, of matters of fact. Here it is obvious that when any object causes pleasure or pain we feel a consequent emotion of attraction or aversion and are impelled to embrace or avoid the object in question. But we are also impelled by the emotion or passion to reason concerning the objects which are or may be causally related with the original object. And 'according as our reasoning varies, our actions receive a subsequent variation'.[4] But the impulse which governs our actions is only directed by reason; it does not arise from it. 'It is from the prospect of pain or pleasure that the aversion or propensity arises towards any object.'[5]

Reason alone, therefore, can never produce any action. And

[1] T., 2, 3, 3. p. 413.   [2] Ibid.   [3] Ibid.
[4] Ibid., p. 414.   [5] Ibid.

Hume concludes from this to the truth of his second proposition. 'Since reason alone can never produce any action, or give rise to volition, I infer that the same faculty is as incapable of preventing volition, or of disputing the preference with any passion or emotion. This consequence is necessary.'[1] Reason could prevent volition only by giving an impulse in a contrary direction; but this is excluded by what has been already said. And if reason has no immediate influence of its own, it cannot withstand any principle, such as passion, which does possess efficacy. Hence 'we speak not strictly and philosophically when we talk of the combat of passion and of reason. Reason is, and ought only to be the slave of the passions, and can never pretend to any other office than to serve and obey them.'[2]

Now, this appears to be a paradoxical and strange position to adopt. For, as Hume admits, it is not only philosophers who speak of the combat between reason and passion. But the words quoted above, 'we speak not strictly and philosophically', ought to be noticed. Hume does not deny that there is something which is called the combat between reason and passion: what he maintains is that it is not accurately described when it is so called. And his analysis of the situation must be briefly explained.

Reason, Hume says, exerts itself without producing any sensible emotion. Now, there are also 'calm desires and tendencies which, though they be real passions, produce little emotion[3] in the mind and are more known by their effects than by the immediate feeling or sensation'.[4] These may be of two kinds. There are, according to Hume, certain instincts, such as benevolence and resentment, love of life and kindness to children, which are originally implanted in our nature. There are also the desire for good and aversion to evil, considered merely as such. When any of these passions are calm, they are easily taken as being operations of reason 'and are supposed to proceed from the same faculty, with that which judges of truth and falsehood'.[5] The calm passions do not prevail in everyone, it is true. And whether calm or violent passions prevail, depends on the general character and present disposition of a man. However, 'what we call strength of mind implies the prevalence of the calm passions above the violent'.[6]

In asserting this view of the subordination of the reason to the

---

[1] *T.*, 2, 3, 3, pp. 414–15.   [2] *Ibid.*, p. 415.
[3] Here Hume uses the word 'emotion' in a literal sense to mean a felt or apparent movement.
[4] *T.*, 2, 3, 3, p. 417.   [5] *Ibid.*   [6] *Ibid.*, p. 418.

passions Hume was obviously adopting an anti-rationalist position. Not reason but propensity and aversion, following experiences of pleasure and pain, are the fundamental springs of human action. Reason plays a part in man's active life, but as an instrument of passion, not as a sole sufficient cause. Of course, if we consider simply the theory that natural inclinations rather than the conclusions of the abstract reason are the influential factor in human conduct, we can scarcely call it a revolutionary or extravagant theory. It is opposed to Socratic intellectualism, but it is this intellectualism which is extravagant and which has always been attacked by its opponents as contrary to experience. Hume realized very clearly not only that man is not a kind of calculating machine but also that without the appetitive and emotional aspects of his nature he would not be man. At the same time it is arguable that his denial of liberty of indifference and his assertion of psychological determinism encouraged him to minimize in an exaggerated way the part played by the practical reason in human conduct.

6. That there are no moral distinctions whatsoever is not an opinion which is consonant with experience, common sense and reason. 'Let a man's insensibility be ever so great, he must often be touched with the images of Right and Wrong: and let his prejudices be ever so obstinate, he must observe that others are susceptible of like impressions.'[1] But though everyone makes some moral distinctions, the foundation of such distinctions is matter for dispute. Are they founded, as some claim, on reason, so that they are the same for every rational being? Or are they founded, as others claim, on a moral sense or sentiment, resting 'on the particular fabric and constitution of the human species'?[2] Arguments can be produced in favour of each theory. It may be said, on the one hand, that both in ordinary life and in philosophy disputes about good and evil, right and wrong, frequently occur. And the disputants produce reasons in favour of their several views. And how could such discussions take place and be accepted as a normal and sensible proceeding unless moral distinctions are derived from reason? On the other hand, it can be argued that the essence of virtue is to be amiable or lovable and of vice to be odious. And the attribution of such epithets must be the expression of affections or sentiments which are themselves grounded in the original constitution of man. Further, the end or purpose of moral

---

[1] *E.M.*, I, 133, p. 170.   [2] *E.M.*, I, 134, p. 170.

reasoning is action, the performance of duty. But reason alone cannot move to action. It is the passions or affections which constitute the springs of conduct.

We have already seen in the preceding section that according to Hume reason alone cannot affect conduct and that it is the passions or affections which are the fundamental springs of action. He is, therefore, committed, to this extent, to the second theory; that is, to the theory of a moral sense or sentiment. At the same time, however, he has no intention of denying that reason plays a part in morality. Hence he is willing to say that '*reason* and *sentiment* concur in almost all moral determinations and conclusions. The final sentence, it is probable, which pronounces characters and actions amiable or odious, praiseworthy or blameable; that which stamps on them the mark of honour or infamy, approbation or censure; that which renders morality an active principle and constitutes virtue our happiness and vice our misery: it is probable, I say, that this final sentence depends on some internal sense or feeling, which nature has made universal in the whole species. For what else can have an influence of this nature? But in order to pave the way for such a sentiment, and give a proper discernment of its object, it is often necessary, we find, that much reasoning should precede, that nice distinctions be made, just conclusions drawn, distant comparisons formed, complicated relations examined, and general facts fixed and ascertained.'[1] We examine, for instance, an action under its various aspects and in relation to various circumstances, and compare it with actions to which it bears a *prima facie* resemblance. But when we have, as it were, a clear view of the action, what ultimately influences our conduct is the feeling which we have towards the actions.

Examining the matter a little more closely, we find that Hume gives detailed arguments, both in the *Treatise* and in his first appendix to the *Enquiry concerning the Principles of Morals*, for saying that moral distinctions are not derived from reason. 'Reason judges either of *matter of fact* or of *relations*.'[2] 'As the operations of human understanding divide themselves into two kinds, the comparing of ideas, and the inferring of matter of fact, were virtue discovered by the understanding it must be an object of one of these operations, nor is there any third operation of the understanding which can discover it.'[3]

[1] *E.M.*, I, 137, pp. 172-3. [2] *E.M.*, Appendix I, 237, p. 287. [3] *T.*, 3, 1, 1, p. 463.

In the first place, moral distinctions are not derived from reason as concerned with matters of fact. 'Take an action allowed to be vicious: wilful murder, for instance. Examine it in all lights, and see if you can find that matter of fact, or real existence, which you call *vice*. In whichever way you take it, you find only certain passions, motives, volitions and thoughts. There is no other matter of fact in the case. . . . You can never find it, till you turn your reflection into your own breast and find a sentiment of disapprobation which arises in you towards this action. Here is a matter of fact; but it is the object of feeling, not of reason. It lies in yourself, not in the object.'[1] What Hume means is that the physical action of killing is or may be the same in a case of murder as it is in a case of justifiable homicide or of execution after judicial sentence.

In the second place, moral distinctions are not derived from reason as concerned with relations. 'There has been an opinion very industriously propagated by certain philosophers, that morality is susceptible of demonstration.'[2] In this case vice and virtue must consist in some relations. If it does, it must consist in resemblance, contrariety, degrees in quality or proportions in quantity and number. But these relations are found just as much in material things as in our actions, passions and volitions. Why is incest among human beings considered a criminal act, while we do not regard it as morally wrong when performed by animals? The relations, after all, are the same in both cases. The answer may be made that incest is not considered to be morally wrong if performed by animals because they lack the reason which is capable of discerning its wrongness, whereas man can do so. This answer, according to Hume, is patently useless. For before reason can perceive the wrongness, the wrongness must be there to perceive. Want of the reasoning faculty may prevent animals from perceiving duties and obligations, but it cannot hinder the duties and obligations from existing, 'since they must antecedently exist, in order to their being perceived. Reason must find them, and can never produce them. This argument deserves to be weighed, as being, in my opinion, entirely decisive.'[3] The same sort of argument appears in the second *Enquiry*. 'No, say you, the morality consists in the relation of actions to the rule of right, and they are denominated good or ill, according as they agree or disagree with it. What then is this rule of right? In what does it consist? How

---

[1] *T.*, 3, 1, 1, pp. 468–9.   [2] *Ibid.*, p. 463.   [3] *Ibid.*, p. 468.

is it determined? By reason, you say, which examines the moral relations of actions. So that moral relations are determined by the comparison of action to a rule. And that rule is determined by considering the moral relations of objects. Is not this fine reasoning?'[1]

If we make moral distinctions, and if they are not derived from reason, they must be derived from or founded on feeling. 'Morality, therefore, is more properly felt than judged of.'[2] Virtue arouses an 'agreeable' impression, vice an 'uneasy' impression. 'An action or sentiment or character is virtuous or vicious; why? because its view causes a pleasure or uneasiness of a particular kind.'[3] But, Hume insists, the pleasure caused by virtue and the pain caused by vice are pleasure and pain of a special kind. The term 'pleasure' covers many different types of sensation. 'A good composition of music and a bottle of good wine equally produce pleasure; and what is more, their goodness is determined merely by the pleasure. But shall we say upon that account that the wine is harmonious or the music of a good flavour? . . . Nor is every sentiment of pleasure or pain which arises from characters and actions of that *peculiar* kind which makes us praise or condemn.'[4] The moral sentiment is a feeling of approbation or disapprobation towards actions or qualities or characters. And it is disinterested. 'It is only when a character is considered in general, without reference to our particular interest, that it causes such a feeling or sentiment as denominates it morally good or evil.'[5] Aesthetic pleasure is, it is true, also disinterested. But though moral and natural beauty closely resemble one another, it is not precisely moral approbation which we feel, for example, for a beautiful building or a beautiful body.

Hume's 'hypothesis', therefore, 'defines virtue to be *whatever mental action or quality gives to a spectator the pleasing sentiment of approbation*; and vice the contrary'.[6] Does this view involve sheer relativism, on the principle that there is no dispute about tastes? It is evident that there are often differences between different people's moral judgments. But Hume seems to have thought that the general sentiments of morality are common to all men, not only in the sense that all normal human beings have moral feeling but also in the sense that there is a certain fundamental agreement in the operation of these feelings. When speaking of the legitimacy

[1] *E.M.*, Appendix 1, 239, pp. 288–9.   [2] *T.*, 3, 1, 2, p. 470.   [3] *Ibid.*, p. 471.
[4] *Ibid.*, p. 472.   [5] *Ibid.*   [6] *E.M.*, Appendix 1, 239, p. 289.

of rebelling against a tyrant, he remarks that only the most violent perversion of common sense can ever lead us to condemn resistance to oppression. He then adds: 'The general opinion of mankind has some authority in all cases; but in this of morals it is perfectly infallible. Nor is it less infallible because men cannot distinctly explain the principles on which it is founded.'[1] If the moral sentiments are due to the original constitution of men's minds, it is only natural that there should be some fundamental agreement. And if moral distinctions are founded on feelings rather than reason, we cannot go beyond an agreement in feeling and invoke a further criterion.

In the *Treatise* Hume raises the question 'why any action or sentiment upon the general view or survey gives a certain satisfaction or uneasiness'.[2] But the answer to this question is left for a discussion of the different virtues. For it may be that the reason why one type of action arouses the moral sentiment may not be precisely the same as the reason why another type of action does so. In any case, as Hume says in the second *Enquiry*, 'we can only expect success by following the experimental method and deducing general maxims from a comparison of particular instances'.[3] He holds, as we have seen, that what we call a moral judgment simply expresses the feeling of approval or disapproval which the man who makes the judgment has for the action or quality or character in question. And in this sense he maintains an emotive theory of ethics. But it still makes sense to ask what causes the feeling which is expressed in the judgment, even though the latter is not a statement that an action or quality or character causes the feeling. For though the judgment expresses feeling and does not make a statement about the cause of the feeling, we can very well make such statements, though they will be empirical rather than moral propositions.

It is not, however, possible to give a rational explanation of the ultimate ends of human action, if by rational explanation we mean an explanation in terms of higher or more remote principles. If we ask a man why he takes exercise, he may answer that he desires to preserve his health. And if he is asked why he desires this, he may answer that sickness is painful. But if we ask him why he dislikes pain, no answer can be given. 'This is an ultimate end, and is never referred to any other object.'[4] Similarly, if an answer

---

[1] *T.*, 3, 2, 9, p. 552.
[2] *T.*, 3, 1, 2, p. 475.
[3] *E.M.*, 1, 138, p. 174.
[4] *E.M.*, Appendix 1, 244, p. 293.

to a question is given in terms of pleasure, it is useless to ask why pleasure is desired. 'It is impossible there can be a progress *in infinitum*; and that one thing can always be a reason why another is desired. Something must be desirable on its own account, and because of its immediate accord or agreement with human sentiment and affection.'[1] This consideration can be applied to virtue. 'Now as virtue is an end and is desirable on its own account, without fee or reward, merely for the immediate satisfaction which it conveys, it is requisite that there should be some sentiment which it touches . . . which distinguishes moral good and evil. . . .'[2] But we can ask why this or that particular line of action causes moral satisfaction and is therefore esteemed virtuous. Hume stresses the importance of utility, and in this respect is a forerunner of the utilitarians. But he does not make utility the sole source of moral approbation. However, the meaning which he gives to utility and the degree of importance which he attributes to it are best illustrated by considering some particular virtues.

7. Let us take first the virtue of benevolence. Benevolence and generosity everywhere excite the approbation and goodwill of mankind. 'The epithets *sociable, good-natured, humane, merciful, grateful, friendly, generous, beneficent*, or their equivalents, are known in all languages and universally express the highest merit which *human nature* is capable of attaining.'[3] Further, when people praise the benevolent and humane man, 'there is one circumstance which never fails to be amply insisted on, namely, the happiness and satisfaction derived to society from his intercourse and good offices'.[4] This suggests that the utility of the social virtues 'forms at least a *part* of their merit, and is one source of that approbation and regard so universally paid to them. . . . In general, what praise is implied in the simple epithet *useful*! What reproach in the contrary!'[5]

It is to be noted that Hume does not say that benevolence is esteemed as a virtue simply because of its utility. Some qualities, such as courtesy, are immediately agreeable, without any reference to utility (which means with Hume a tendency to produce some further or ulterior good); and benevolence itself is immediately pleasing and agreeable. But the moral approbation which benevolence arouses is caused in part by its usefulness.

Before proceeding further with the subject of utility, we should

[1] *E.M.*, Appendix 1, 244, p. 293.   [2] *Ibid.*, 245, pp. 293-4.
[3] *E.M.*, 2, 1, 139, p. 176.   [4] *E.M.*, 2, 2, 141, p. 178.   [5] *Ibid.*, p 179.

note that Hume devotes an appendix to the second *Enquiry* to showing that there is such a thing as benevolence or, rather, that so-called benevolence is not merely a disguised form of self-love. The view that benevolence is really a form of self-love may range from cheap cynicism to a philosophical attempt to preserve the realities of the moral life while providing an analysis of the way in which self-love takes that particular form which we call benevolence. But Hume rejects this view in all its shapes. For one thing, 'the simplest and most obvious cause which can be assigned for any phenomenon is probably the true one'.[1] And there are certainly cases in which it is far simpler to believe that a man is animated by disinterested benevolence and humanity than that he is prompted to act in a benevolent way by some tortuous considerations of self-interest. For another thing, even animals sometimes show a kindness when there is no suspicion of disguise or artifice. And 'if we admit a disinterested benevolence in the inferior species, by what rule of analogy can we refuse it in the superior?'[2] Further, in gratitude and friendship and maternal tenderness we can often find marks of disinterested sentiments and actions. In general 'the hypothesis which allows of a disinterested benevolence, distinct from self-love, has really more *simplicity* in it, and is more conformable to the analogy of nature than that which pretends to resolve all friendship and humanity into this latter principle'.[3]

As there is such a thing as disinterested benevolence, it is obvious that when Hume finds in utility or usefulness a part-cause of the moral approbation accorded to benevolence, he is not thinking exclusively of usefulness to oneself. Perhaps we show more alacrity in praising benevolence when it benefits us personally; but we certainly praise it often enough when it does not do so. For instance, we feel moral approbation of benevolent actions performed by historic personages in other lands. And it is a 'weak subterfuge' to argue that when we do this we transport ourselves in imagination into that other land and period and imagine ourselves to be contemporaries benefiting from the actions in question. 'Usefulness is agreeable, and engages our approbation. This is a matter of fact, confirmed by daily observation. But, *useful*? For what? For somebody's interest, surely. Whose interest, then? Not our own only; for our approbation frequently extends farther. It must, therefore, be the interest of those who are served

---

[1] *E.M.*, Appendix 2, 251, p. 299.　　[2] *Ibid.*, 252, p. 300.　　[3] *Ibid.*, 253, p. 301.

by the character or action approved of; and these we may conclude, however remote, are not totally indifferent to us.'[1] Again, 'If usefulness, therefore, be a source of moral sentiment, and if this usefulness be not always considered with a reference to self, it follows that everything which contributes to the happiness of society recommends itself directly to our approbation and good-will. Here is a principle which accounts, in great part, for the origin of morality.'[2] It is unnecessary to ask why we have humanity or a fellow-feeling with others. 'It is sufficient that this is experienced to be a principle in human nature. We must stop somewhere in our examination of causes.'[3]

In maintaining that usefulness for others can be directly agree-able to us, indeed that 'everything which contributes to the happiness of society recommends itself directly to our approba-tion and goodwill', Hume seems to have modified, or rather changed, the view which he put forward in the *Treatise*. For there he said that 'there is no such passion in human minds as the love of mankind, merely as such, independent of personal qualities, of services, or of relation to oneself'.[4] The happiness or misery of another affects us, indeed, when it is not too far off and is repres-ented in lively colours; 'but this proceeds merely from sympathy'.[5] And sympathy is explained, as we saw in the last chapter, with the aid of the principles of association. But in the second *Enquiry* the idea of association of ideas drops into the background, and Hume maintains the view that the thought of the pleasures and pains of other people arouses directly in us the sentiments of humanity and benevolence. In other words, the pleasures of others and that which is 'useful' to them, producing pleasure in them, is or can be directly agreeable to us. And it is unnecessary to have recourse to an elaborate associative mechanism to explain altruistic senti-ments. In general, Hume tends, in the second *Enquiry*, to emphasize natural propensities, and the propensity to benevolence is one of them. It is probably not a derivative of self-love.

8. We have seen that according to Hume its utility is one of the reasons why benevolence wins our moral approbation. But it is not the only reason. He maintains, however, that 'public utility is the *sole* origin of justice, and that reflections on the beneficial con-sequences of this virtue are the *sole* foundation of its merit'.[6]

Society is naturally advantageous to man. Left to himself, the

[1] *E.M.*, 5, 1, 177, p. 218.   [2] *E.M.*, 5, 2, 178, p. 219.
[3] *E.M.*, 5, 2, 178 note, pp. 219-20.   [4] *T.*, 3, 2, 1, p. 481.
[5] *Ibid.*   [6] *E.M.*, 3, 1, 145, p. 183.

individual cannot provide adequately for his needs as a human being. Self-interest, therefore, drives men into society. But this alone is not sufficient. For disturbances inevitably arise in society if there are no conventions establishing and regulating the rights of property. There is need of 'a convention entered into by all the members of the society to bestow stability on the possession of those external goods, and leave everyone in the peaceable enjoyment of what he may acquire by his fortune and industry . . . it is by that means we maintain society, which is so necessary to their well-being and subsistence, as well as to our own'.[1] This convention should not be conceived as a promise. 'For even promises . . . arise from human conventions. It is only a general sense of common interest; which sense all the members of the society express to one another, and which induces them to regulate their conduct by certain rules.'[2] Once this convention about abstaining from the external goods of other people has been entered into, 'there immediately arise the ideas of justice and injustice'.[3] Hume does not mean, however, that there is a right of property which is antecedent to the idea of justice. He explicitly denies this. A 'general sense of common interest' expresses itself in the general principles of justice and equity, in fundamental laws of justice; and 'our property is nothing but those goods whose constant possession is established by the laws of society; that is, by the laws of justice. . . . The origin of justice explains that of property. The same artifice gives rise to both.'[4]

Justice, therefore, is founded on self-interest, on a sense of utility. And it is self-interest which gives rise to what Hume calls the 'natural obligation' of justice. But what gives rise to the '*moral* obligation, or the sentiment of right and wrong'?[5] Or why do we 'annex the idea of virtue to justice, and of vice to injustice'?[6] The explanation is to be found in sympathy. Even when injustice does not affect us personally as victims, it still displeases us, because we consider it as prejudicial to society. We share the 'uneasiness' of other people by sympathy. And since that which in human actions produces uneasiness arouses disapprobation and is called vice, while that which produces satisfaction is called virtue, we regard justice as a moral virtue and injustice as a moral vice. 'Thus self-interest is the original motive to the establishment of justice: but a sympathy with public interest is the source of the

---

[1] *T.*, 3, 2, 2, p. 489.   [2] *Ibid.*, p. 490.   [3] *Ibid.*
[4] *Ibid.*, p. 491.   [5] *Ibid.*, p. 498.   [6] *Ibid.*

moral approbation which attends that virtue.'[1] Education and the words of statesmen and politicians contribute to consolidate this moral approbation; but sympathy is the basis.

Hume does not give any clear definition of justice, nor even, as it seems to me, any really clear indication of what he understands by the term. In the second *Enquiry* he asserts that 'general peace and order are the attendants of justice or a general abstinence from the possessions of others';[2] and in the *Treatise*, under the general heading of justice and injustice, he considers first of all matters relating to property. He tells us that the three fundamental 'laws of nature' are those relating to stable possession of property, the transference of property by consent, and the performance of promises.[3] What is clear, however, is that in his opinion all the laws of justice, general and particular, are grounded on public utility.

We can now understand what Hume means by calling justice an 'artificial' virtue. It presupposes a human convention, based on self-interest. Justice produces pleasure and approbation 'by means of an artifice or contrivance which arises from the circumstances and necessity of mankind'.[4] The sense of justice arises from a convention which is a remedy for certain 'inconveniences' in human life. 'The remedy, then, is not derived from nature, but from *artifice*; or more properly speaking, nature provides a remedy in the judgment and understanding for what is irregular and incommodious in the affections.'[5] By using the word 'artifice' Hume does not mean that, given human beings as they are, it is a mere matter of taste or of arbitrary choice whether we regard justice as a virtue and institute laws of justice or not. 'The sense of justice and injustice is not derived from nature, but arises artificially, *though necessarily* (my italics), from education and human conventions.'[6] Justice is 'artificial' in the sense that it is an invention of man, invented as a remedy for human selfishness and rapacity combined with the scanty provision which nature has made for his wants. If these conditions did not obtain, there would be no virtue of justice. 'By rendering justice totally *useless*, you thereby totally destroy its essence and suspend its obligation upon mankind.'[7] But the conditions do obtain, and the 'invention' is required for man's benefit. 'And where an invention is obvious

---

[1] *T.*, 3, 2, 2, pp. 499–500.   [2] *E.M.*, Appendix 3, 256, p. 304.
[3] *T.*, 3, 2, 6, p. 526.   [4] *T.*, 3, 2, 1, p. 477.
[5] *T.*, 3, 2, 2, p. 489.   [6] *T.*, 3, 2, 1, p. 483.
[7] *E.M.*, 3, 1, 149, p. 188.

and absolutely necessary, it may as properly be said to be natural as anything that proceeds immediately from original principles, without the intervention of thought or reflexion. Though the rules of justice be *artificial*, they are not arbitrary. Nor is the expression improper to call them *Laws of Nature*; if by natural we understand what is common to any species, or even if we confine it to mean what is inseparable from the species.'[1]

The particular laws of justice and equity may, of course, operate in a manner prejudicial to the public benefit if we concentrate our attention on some one particular instance. For instance, an unworthy son may inherit a fortune from a wealthy father and use it for bad ends. But it is the general scheme or system of justice which is of public utility. And here we find a difference between a virtue such as benevolence and a virtue such as justice. 'The social virtues of humanity and benevolence exert their influence immediately by a direct tendency or instinct, which chiefly keeps in view the simple object, moving the affections, and comprehends not any scheme or system, nor the consequences resulting from the concurrence, imitation, or example of others. . . . The case is not the same with the social virtues of justice and fidelity. They are highly useful, or indeed absolutely necessary to the well-being of mankind: but the benefit resulting from them is not the consequence of every individual single act, but arises from the whole scheme or system concurred in by the whole, or the greater part of the society.'[2]

Hume, therefore, will not allow that there are eternal laws of justice, independent of man's conditions and of public utility. Justice is an artifice, an invention. At the same time it does not depend on a social contract, on a promise. For it is justice itself which gives rise to contracts and binding promises. It depends on felt utility, and this utility is real. Men establish the laws of justice out of a concern for their own and the public interest. But this concern is derived not from reasoning about the eternal and necessary relations of ideas but from our impressions and feelings. 'The sense of justice, therefore, is not founded on our ideas, but on our impressions.'[3] Men feel their interest in establishing a scheme of justice, and they feel approval for customary conventions which remedy the 'inconveniences' that accompany human life. But in elaborating particular rules reason is, of course,

[1] *T.*, 3, 2, 1, p. 484. [2] *E.M.*, Appendix 3, 255-6, pp. 303-4.
[3] *T.*, 3, 2, 2, p. 496.

employed. Hume thus brings the virtue of justice within the general pattern of his moral theory. Feeling is fundamental; but this does not mean that reason has no part to play in morality.

9. Hume set out to understand the moral life of mankind by studying the empirical data. That men make moral judgments is clear: it is an empirical fact which stands in need of no proof. But it is not immediately evident what men are doing when they make these judgments and what is the ultimate foundation of the judgments in question. Some philosophers have represented judgments of value as being the result of reasoning, as being conclusions of a logical process. They have tried to reconstruct the system of morals as a rational system akin to mathematics. But an interpretation of this sort bears little resemblance to the facts. Where there is a general agreement about values and moral principles, we can argue whether, for instance, a particular case falls under a given principle or not. And after we have made a moral judgment, we can look for reasons to support it. But the suggestion that moral judgments are in the first place a conclusion of reason, the conclusion of a deductive process akin to mathematics, does not fit the available data. In practice, of course, men's moral judgments are influenced by education and other external factors. But, if we leave aside the question what factors influence a man to make a particular moral judgment, it is clear, if we keep an eye on concrete moral experience, that when a man makes a moral judgment there is an element of immediacy which is not accounted for on the rationalist interpretation of ethics. Morality is more akin to aesthetics than to mathematics. It is truer to say that we 'feel' values than that we deduce values or arrive at our moral judgments by a process of logical reasoning from abstract principles.

In calling attention to the element of immediacy in the moral judgment Hume was emphasizing a valuable point. But in his further account of the matter he was hampered by his general psychology. Inasmuch as he refused to allow that moral distinctions are derived from either of the operations of reason which he recognized, he had to say that morality is more properly a matter of feeling than of judging and to reduce the judgment to an expression of feeling. But terms such as 'feeling' and 'moral sense', when used in this context, are analogical terms which may be useful for drawing attention to an aspect of man's moral life which was neglected by the rationalists but which need further examination than Hume accorded them. The elements of utilitarianism in his theory seem to me to suggest the desirability of revising Hume's conception of 'reason' rather than of resting content with terms such as 'feeling'. In other words, Hume's philosophy lacks a conception of the practical reason and of its mode of operation.

Hume was also hampered, I think, by his theory of relations. He refused to allow that reason can discern a relation between human acts and a rule of morality promulgated by reason. In fact, he thought that any such view of the matter involves one in circular reasoning. But his own insistence on the original constitution or fabric of human nature suggests that this nature is in some sense the foundation of morality or, in other words, that there is a natural law which is promulgated by reason apprehending human nature in its teleological and dynamic aspect. And an interpretation of morality on these lines can be developed without implying that men in general consciously 'reason' to general moral rules. Hume thought, of course, that if it is said that reason discerns relations which give rise to moral judgment, we shall also have to say that inanimate objects, for instance, are capable of morality. But it is difficult to see how this follows. For, after all, human acts are human acts; and it is these alone which are relevant. Hume, it is true, tended to say that acts are relevant to the moral judgment only as indicating motive and character. But this seems to be a way of saying that it is only human acts, acts which are deliberate, that are morally relevant. And the relation of such acts to a moral law are *sui generis*.

Perhaps it was only natural, given his interpretation of liberty, that Hume stressed above all character and qualities of character. For if liberty is reduced to spontaneity, an act has value either as a revelation of character or because of its 'utility'. Now, we are accustomed to regard characters and personal qualities as admirable or the reverse rather than as right or wrong, words which we reserve for acts. Hence, if we stress personal qualities rather than acts we shall probably be apt to assimilate the moral judgment or judgment of value to the aesthetic judgment. And in point of fact we find Hume slurring over the difference between moral qualities or virtues and natural gifts and talents. If, however, we look on acts as having value because of their utility, we shall tend to develop a utilitarian theory. And we find both lines of thought in Hume's analysis of morality.

It seems to me, therefore, that Hume's ethics is conditioned very largely by positions previously adopted, and that it contains different lines of thought. The utilitarian element was later developed by Bentham and the two Mills, while the insistence on feeling has found fresh life in modern empiricism in the emotive theories of ethics.

CHAPTER XVII

HUME (4)

Politics as a science—The origin of society—The origin of government—The nature and limits of allegiance—The laws of nations—General remarks.

I. HUME regarded politics as being in some sense of the word a science. As we have already seen, politics, which is described as considering men as united in society and dependent on each other, is classed with logic, morals and criticism as part of the science of man.[1] In an essay entitled *That Politics may be reduced to a Science* Hume remarks that 'so great is the force of laws and of particular forms of government, and so little dependence have they on the humours and tempers of men, that consequences almost as general and certain may sometimes be deduced from them as any which the mathematical sciences afford us'. At the end of the first *Enquiry* politics is separated from morals and criticism. 'Moral reasonings are either concerning particular or general facts'; and 'the sciences which treat of general facts are politics, natural philosophy, physic, chemistry, etc., where the qualities, causes and effects of a whole species of objects are enquired into.'[2] 'Morals and criticism,' however, 'are not so properly objects of the understanding as of taste and sentiment'.[3] Here, then, we have a different grouping from that in the introduction to the *Treatise*. Whatever Hume may have come to think about morals, he tries to conserve politics as a science, and he groups it with natural philosophy and chemistry. In the *Dialogues concerning Natural Religion*, however, politics is mentioned along with morals and criticism. 'So long as we confine our speculations to trade, or morals, or politics, or criticism, we make appeals, every moment, to common sense and experience, which strengthen our philosophical conclusions and remove (at least in part) the suspicion which we so justly entertain with regard to every reasoning that is very subtle and refined.'[4] Here economics, morals, politics and criticism or aesthetics are being contrasted with 'theological reasonings' in which we cannot, according to the

---

[1] *T.*, Introduction, pp. xix–xx. [2] *E.*, 12, 3, 132, pp. 164–5.
[3] *Ibid.*, p. 165. [4] *D.*, 1, p. 135.

speaker, the sceptically-minded Philo, confirm philosophical conclusions by appeals to common sense and experience.

Even if Hume's utterances about the relation of politics to
morals differ on different occasions, it is none the less clear that he
regards the former as a science or as capable of forming a science.
We can form general maxims and explanatory hypotheses, and it
is possible, within limits, to predict. But the unexpected may
happen, even though after the event we may be able to explain
it on the basis of already known principles. Thus in his essay *Of
some Remarkable Customs* Hume observes that 'all general maxims
in politics ought to be established with great caution', and that
'irregular and extraordinary appearances are frequently discovered in the moral as well as in the physical world. The former,
perhaps we can better account for after they happen, from springs
and principles of which everyone has, within himself or from
observation, the strongest assurance and conviction: but it is
often fully impossible for human prudence, beforehand, to foresee
and foretell them.' We cannot attain in politics the certainty
which is attainable in mathematics; for we are dealing mainly
with matters of fact. This is doubtless the reason why, when he
assimilates politics or mathematics in the passage quoted at the
beginning of this section, he inserts the saving word 'almost'.

2. As we have seen when considering the virtue of justice,
organized society came into existence because of its utility to man.
It is a remedy for the inconveniences of life without society.
'Society provides a remedy for these *three* inconveniences. By the
conjunction of forces, our power is augmented: By the partition
of employment, our ability increases: And by mutual succour we
are less exposed to fortune and accidents. It is by this additional
force, *ability* and *security* that society becomes advantageous.'[1]

It is important to understand, however, that Hume does not
imagine primitive human beings as thinking over the disadvantages of their lot without organized society, excogitating a remedy
and entering upon any explicit social contract or covenant. Apart
from the fact that he does not admit that promises and contracts
have binding force apart from society and the rules of justice, he
insists that the utility of society is originally felt rather than made
the subject of a reflective judgment. There can be a convention
or agreement between people although no explicit promises are
made. Speaking of the convention from which the ideas of justice,

[1] *T.*, 3, 2, 2, p. 485.

property and right arise, he uses a famous illustration which illustrates what he calls a 'common sense of interest', which is expressed in action rather than in word. 'Two men who pull the oars of a boat do it by an agreement or convention, though they have never given promises to each other. . . . In like manner are languages gradually established by human conventions without any promise.'[1]

In order that society should be formed, says Hume, it is necessary not only that it should be in fact advantageous to men but also that they should 'be sensible of these advantages'. And if we are not to picture primitive men arriving at this knowledge by reflection and study, how did they arrive at it? Hume's answer is that society arose through the family. Natural appetite draws members of the two sexes together and preserves their union until a new bond arises, their common concern for their offspring. 'In a little time, custom and habit operating on the tender minds of the children makes them sensible of the advantages which they may reap from society, as well as fashions them by degrees for it, by rubbing off those rough corners and untoward affections which prevent their coalition.'[2] The family, therefore (or, more accurately, the natural appetite between the sexes), is 'the first and original principle of human society'.[3] The transition to a wider society is effected principally by the felt need for stabilizing the possession of external goods.

As there is question of feeling a need rather than of consciously studying man's situation and arriving at a common and reflective judgment concerning the appropriate way of meeting it, and as this need is present practically from the beginning of human life on earth, it is understandable that Hume felt no more sympathy for the theory of a state of nature than for that of a social contract. He concludes that 'it is utterly impossible for men to remain any considerable time in that savage condition which precedes society, but that his very first state and situation may justly be esteemed social. This, however, hinders not but that philosophers may, if they please, extend their reasoning to the supposed *state of nature*; provided they allow it to be a mere philosophical fiction, which never had, and never could have any reality. . . . This *state of nature*, therefore, is to be regarded as a mere fiction.'[4] The same point is made in the second *Enquiry*. There, too, Hume speaks of

[1] *T.*, 3. 2. 2, p. 490.   [2] *Ibid.*, p. 486.
[3] *Ibid.*   [4] *Ibid.*, p. 493.

the state of nature as a philosophical fiction and remarks that 'whether such a condition of human nature could ever exist or, if it did, could continue so long as to merit the appellation of a *state*, may justly be doubted. Men are necessarily born in a family-society at least'.[1]

3. Similar statements may be made about the origin of government. If natural justice were sufficient to govern human conduct, if no disorder or wickedness ever arose, there would be no need for curtailing individual liberty by establishing governments to which we owe allegiance. 'It is evident that, if government were totally useless, it never could take place, and that the sole foundation of the duty of allegiance is the *advantage* which it procures to society by preserving peace and order among mankind.'[2] Its usefulness, therefore, is the foundation of the institution of government. And the principal advantage which it secures for mankind is the establishment and maintenance of justice. Thus in his essay *Of the Origin of Government* Hume begins by saying that 'Man, born in a family, is compelled to maintain society from necessity, from natural inclination and from habit. The same creature, in his further progress, is engaged to establish political society in order to administer justice, without which there can be no peace among them, nor safety, nor mutual intercourse. We are, therefore, to look upon all the vast apparatus of our government as having ultimately no other object or purpose but the distribution of justice.' In the *Treatise*, however, where Hume speaks more precisely, he observes that though the administration of justice and the settlement of controversies relating to matters of justice and equity are the principal advantages derived from government, they are not the only ones. Without government men would find it very difficult to agree about schemes and projects for the common good and to carry out such projects harmoniously. Organized society remedies such inconveniences. 'Thus bridges are built; harbours opened; ramparts raised; canals formed; fleets equipped; and armies disciplined; everywhere by the care of government.'[3]

Government, therefore, is an 'invention' of great advantage to men. But how does it arise? Is it so essential to society that there cannot be a society without government? In the *Treatise* Hume expressly says that he disagrees with those philosophers who

---

[1] *E.M.*, 3, 1, 151, p. 190.   [2] *E.M.*, 4, 164, p. 205.
[3] *T.*, 3, 2, 7, p. 539.

declare that men are incapable of social unity without government. 'The state of society without government is one of the most natural states of men, and must subsist with the conjunction of many families, and long after the first generation. Nothing but an increase of riches and possessions could oblige men to quit it.'[1] According to Hume, the existence of societies without regular government is empirically verified in the American tribes. And he seems, at first sight at least, to imply that primitive men, perceiving after a time the necessity of government, met together to choose magistrates, determine their power and promise them obedience. This would be because the 'laws of nature' (the fundamental principles of justice) and the binding character of promises are presupposed. They are antecedent to the establishment of government, though they are not antecedent to the establishment of the convention which lies at the root of society.

If it were really Hume's view that government owes its origin to an explicit compact or agreement, this would scarcely be consistent with his general outlook. For, as we have seen in connection with the origin of society, he lays stress on 'felt' utility and mistrusts the rationalistic theory of social contracts. But, however he may speak on occasion, I do not think that Hume intends to say that government originated through explicit agreements. In his view government probably originated, not through a simple development and enlargement of paternal authority or of patriarchal government, but through wars between different societies. Foreign war necessarily produces civil war in the case of societies without government. The first rudiments of government, then, as can be seen among the American tribes, is the authority enjoyed by the captain or tribal chieftain during a campaign. 'I assert the first rudiments of government to arise from quarrels, not among men of the same society, but among those of different societies.'[2] Thus in his essay *Of the Original Contract* Hume remarks that 'the chieftain, who had probably acquired his influence during the continuance of war, ruled more by persuasion than command; and till he could employ force to reduce the refractory and disobedient, the society could scarcely be said to have attained a state of civil government. No compact or agreement, it is evident, was expressly formed for general submission; an idea far beyond the comprehension of savages: each exertion of authority in the chieftain must have been particular, and called

[1] *T.*, 3, 2, 8, p. 541.   [2] *Ibid.*, pp. 539-40.

forth by the present exigencies of the case: the sensible utility resulting from his interposition made these exertions become daily more frequent; and their frequency gradually produced an habitual, and, if you please to call it so, a voluntary, and therefore precarious, acquiescence in the people.' Inasmuch, therefore, as government probably first arose through a gradual process, implying a progressive realization of its utility, it can be said to have been founded on a 'contract'. But if by 'contract' is meant an explicit agreement by which civil government was established all at once in a form which would be immediately recognized by us as civil government, there is no cogent evidence that any explicit agreement or contract of this kind was ever made. I think that this represents Hume's view of the matter, the hypothesis which he puts forward, though not dogmatically.

But though Hume seems to be willing to allow that in prehistoric times government probably originated in some sense through consent, and though he suggests that observation of the American tribes affords some empirical confirmation of this hypothesis, he has no use at all for the contract theory when its assertions go further than these modest admissions. In the essay *Of the Original Contract* he observes that some philosophers are not content with saying that government in its first beginnings 'arose from consent, or rather the voluntary acquiescence of the people'; they assert, too, that government always rests on consent, on promises, on a contract. 'But would these reasoners look abroad in the world, they would meet with nothing that in the least corresponds to their ideas or can warrant so refined and philosophical a system.' Indeed, 'almost all the governments which exist at present, or of which there remains any record in story, have been founded originally, either on usurpation or conquest or both, without any pretence of a fair consent or voluntary subjection of the people. . . . The face of the earth is continually changing, by the increase of small kingdoms into great empires, by the dissolution of great empires into smaller kingdoms, by the planting of colonies, by the migration of tribes. Is there anything discoverable in all these events but force and violence? Where is the mutual agreement or voluntary association so much talked of?' Even when elections take the place of force, what does it amount to? It may be election by a few powerful and influential men. Or it may take the form of popular sedition, the people following a ringleader who owes his advancement to his own impudence or to the momentary caprice of the crowd, most of whom have little or no knowledge of him and his capacities. In neither case is there a real rational agreement by the people.

Whatever, then, may be the case with regard to the authority in war of really primitive tribal chieftains and leaders, whom the people may be said to have followed voluntarily, the contract theory of the origin of government gains very little empirical support from the available data in historic times. The theory is a mere fiction, which is invalidated by the facts. This being the case, it is necessary to inquire into the foundations of the duty of political allegiance.

4. Granted that there is a duty of political allegiance, it is obviously idle to look for its foundation in popular consent and in promises if there is little or no evidence that popular consent was ever asked or given. As for Locke's idea of tacit consent, 'it may be answered that such an implied consent can only have place where a man imagines that the matter depends on his choice'.[1] But anyone who is born under an established government thinks that he owes allegiance to the sovereign by the very fact that he is by birth a citizen of the political society in question. And to suggest with Locke that every man is free to leave the society to which he belongs by birth is unreal. 'Can we seriously say that a poor peasant or artisan has a free choice to leave his country, when he knows no foreign language or manners and lives from day to day by the small wages which he acquires?'[2]

The obligation of allegiance to civil government, therefore, 'is not derived from any promise of the subjects'.[3] Even if promises were made at some time in the remote past, the present duty of allegiance cannot rest on them. 'It being certain that there is a moral obligation to submit to government, because everyone thinks so, it must be as certain that this obligation arises not from a promise, since no one whose judgment has not been led astray by too strict adherence to a system of philosophy has ever yet dreamt of ascribing it to that origin.'[4] The real foundation of the duty of allegiance is utility or interest. 'This interest I find to consist in the security and protection which we can enjoy in political society, and which we can never attain when perfectly free and independent.'[5] This holds good both of natural and of moral obligation. 'It is evident that, if government were totally

---

[1] *Of the Original Contract.*   [2] *Ibid.*   [3] *T.*, 3, 2, 8, p. 546.
[4] *Ibid.*, p. 547.   [5] *T.*, 3, 2, 9, pp. 550–1.

useless, it never could have place, and that the sole foundation of the duty of allegiance is the *advantage* which it procures to society by preserving peace and order among mankind.'[1] Similarly, in the essay *Of the Original Contract* Hume observes: 'If the reason be asked of that obedience which we are bound to pay to government, I readily answer, *Because society could not otherwise subsist*; and this answer is clear and intelligible to all mankind.'

The obvious conclusion to be drawn from this view is that when the advantage ceases, the obligation to allegiance ceases. 'As interest, therefore, is the immediate sanction of government, the one can have no longer being than the other; and whenever the civil magistrate carries his oppression so far as to render his authority perfectly intolerable, we are no longer bound to submit to it. The cause ceases; the effect must cease also.'[2] It is obvious, however, that the evils and dangers attending rebellion are such that it can be legitimately attempted only in cases of real tyranny and oppression and when the advantages of acting in this way are judged to outweigh the disadvantages.

But to whom is allegiance due? In other words, whom are we to regard as legitimate rulers? Originally, Hume thought or inclined to think, government was established by voluntary convention. 'The same promise, then, which binds them (the subjects) to obedience, ties them down to a particular person and makes him the object of their allegiance.'[3] But once government has been established and allegiance no longer rests upon a promise but upon advantage or utility, we cannot have recourse to the original promise to determine who is the legitimate ruler. The fact that some tribe in remote times voluntarily subjected itself to a leader is no guide to determining whether William of Orange or James II is the legitimate monarch.

One foundation of legitimate authority is long possession of the sovereign power: 'I mean, *long possession* in any one form of government, or succession of princes'.[4] Generally speaking, there are no governments or royal houses which do not owe the origin of their power to usurpation or rebellion and whose original title to authority was not 'worse than doubtful and uncertain'.[5] In this case 'time alone gives solidity to their right and, operating gradually on the minds of men, reconciles them to any authority and makes it seem just and reasonable'.[6] The second source of

[1] *E.M.*, 4, 164, p. 205.   [2] *T.*, 3, 2, 9, p. 551.   [3] *T.*, 3, 2, 10, p. 554.
[4] *Ibid.*, p. 556.   [5] *Ibid.*   [6] *Ibid.*

public authority is present possession, which can legitimize the possession of power even when there is no question of its having been acquired a long time ago. 'Right to authority is nothing but the constant possession of authority, maintained by the laws of society and the interests of mankind.'[1] A third source of legitimate political authority is the right of conquest. As fourth and fifth sources can be added the right of succession and positive laws, when the legislature establishes a certain form of government. When all these titles to authority are found together, we have the surest sign of legitimate sovereignty, unless the public good clearly demands a change. But if, says Hume, we consider the actual course of history, we shall soon learn to treat lightly all disputes about the rights of princes. We cannot decide all disputes in accordance with fixed, general rules. Speaking of this matter in the essay *Of the Original Contract*, Hume remarks that 'though an appeal to general opinion may justly, in the speculative sciences of metaphysics, natural philosophy or astronomy, be deemed unfair and inconclusive, yet in all questions with regard to morals, as well as criticism, there is really no other standard by which any controversy can ever be decided'. To say, for example, with Locke that absolute government is not really civil government at all is pointless if absolute government is in fact accepted as a recognized political institution. Again, it is useless to dispute whether the succession of the Prince of Orange to the throne was legitimate or not. It may not have been legitimate at the time. And Locke, who wished to justify the revolution of 1688, could not possibly do so on his theory of legitimate government being founded on the consent of the subjects. For the people of England were not asked for their opinion. But in point of fact William of Orange was accepted, and the doubts about the legitimacy of his accession are nullified by the fact that his successors have been accepted. It may perhaps seem to be an unreasonable way of thinking, but 'princes often *seem* to acquire a right from their successors as well as from their ancestors'.[2]

5. Inasmuch as it is to the interest of different political societies to carry on trade and commerce with one another and, in general, to enter into mutual relations, there arises a set of rules which Hume calls 'the laws of nations'. 'Under this head we may comprise the sacredness of the person of ambassadors, the declaration of war, the abstaining from poisoned arms, with other duties of

---

[1] *T.*, 3, 2, 10, p. 557.   [2] *Ibid.*, p. 566.

that kind, which are evidently calculated for the commerce that is peculiar to different societies.'[1]

These 'laws of nations' have the same foundation as the 'laws of nature', namely, utility or advantage, and they do not abolish the latter. Princes are, indeed, bound by moral rules. 'The same *natural* obligation of interest takes place among independent kingdoms, and gives rise to the same *morality*; so that no one of ever so corrupt morals will approve of a prince who voluntarily and of his own accord breaks his word or violates any treaty.'[2] At the same time, although the moral obligation of princes has the same extent as that of private persons, it does not possess the same *force*. For intercourse between different States is not so necessary or advantageous as that between individuals. Without society of some kind human life cannot subsist; but there is not the same degree of necessity for intercourse between States. Accordingly, the natural obligation to justice is not so strong with regard to the behaviour of one political society towards another as it is with regard to the mutual relations of two private members of the same society. And from this there follows a similar difference of strength in moral obligation. Hence, 'we must necessarily give a greater indulgence to a prince or minister who deceives another than to a private gentleman who breaks his word of honour'.[3] But if one is asked to state the exact proportion which obtains between the morality of princes and the morality of private persons, one can give no precise answer. 'One may safely affirm that this proportion finds itself, without any art or study of men; as we may observe on many other occasions.'[4] Hume is thus ready to find some truth in the principles of Machiavellian politics; but he is not prepared to state that there is one morality for princes and another for private persons.

6. One salient feature of Hume's political theory is his attention to empirical data and his refusal to accept philosophical hypotheses which are not confirmed by the known facts. This is particularly true of his attitude towards the contract theory or theories. He does, indeed, accept this theory to some extent as far as the first origins of government are concerned. But there he is thinking of a tribe voluntarily gathering round a leader in an inter-tribal war rather than of any formal contract or promise. And, apart from this concession, he has no use for contract theories. In place of such

[1] *T.*, 3, 2, 11, p. 567.   [2] *Ibid.*, pp. 568–9.
[3] *Ibid.*, p. 569.   [4] *Ibid.*

rationalistic theories he substitutes the idea of 'felt' interest or advantage.

There is a strong element of what we may call 'positivism' in Hume's political philosophy. He appeals to what actually happens or to what everyone thinks as a criterion rather than to any *a priori* reasonings. For example, political authority is frequently the result of usurpation, rebellion or conquest, and if the authority is stable and not obviously tyrannical and oppressive, it is in practice accepted as legitimate by the vast majority of the governed. This is sufficient for Hume. Subtle discussions about the legitimacy of such authority, and attempts to prove its legitimacy by means of 'philosophical fictions', are a waste of time. It is more profitable to inquire what are the titles to authority which are actually accepted as titles. Again, Hume is not disposed to spend time discussing ideal forms of commonwealth. In his essay on the *Idea of a Perfect Commonwealth* he does, indeed, remark that it is advantageous to know what is most perfect of its kind, that we may amend existing forms of constitution and government 'by such gentle alterations and innovations as may not give too great disturbance to society'. And he himself makes some suggestions under this heading. But he also observes that 'all plans of government which suppose great reformation in the manners of mankind are plainly imaginary. Of this nature are the *Republic* of Plato and the *Utopia* of Sir Thomas More.' But apart from the essay in question he shows himself more concerned with understanding what has been and is rather than with suggesting what ought to be And even when he does make suggestions towards improving the constitution, it is practical advantage and utility that he has in mind rather than conclusions deduced from eternal, abstract principles.

In his essay *Of the Original Contract* Hume mentions the position of those who maintain that since God is the origin of all authority the sovereign's authority is sacred and inviolable in all circumstances. He then comments as follows. 'That the Deity is the ultimate author of all government will never be denied by any who admit a general providence and allow that all events in the universe are conducted by an uniform plan and directed to wise purposes. . . . But since he (God) gave rise to it, not by any particular or miraculous interposition, but by his concealed and universal efficacy, a sovereign cannot, properly speaking, be called his vicegerent in any other sense than every power or force, being derived from him, may be said to act by his commission.' In other words, even if we grant the validity of the premiss, the conclusion drawn by those who maintain the divine right of kings does not follow. And, in general, it is clear that Hume did not think that there is much practical help to be gained by a process of deduction from metaphysical principles. God has made man so that government is highly advantageous, even necessary, to him; and in this sense God may be called the author of political authority. But in deciding what form of government to adopt or who possesses legitimate authority we must have recourse to other criteria than divine creation, preservation and providence.

But though Hume shows an admirable hard-headed common sense, his political theory seems to me to suffer from a weakness which is shared by his moral theory. It is all very well to appeal to utility and advantage and public benefit; but it is by no means self-evident what these terms mean in the concrete. And it is difficult to give them a meaning which will serve as a criterion without going further into a philosophical anthropology, and so into metaphysics, than Hume was prepared to go.

CHAPTER XVIII

FOR AND AGAINST HUME

Introductory remarks—Adam Smith—Price—Reid—Campbell
—Beattie—Stewart—Brown—Concluding remarks.

1. THE title of this chapter is perhaps rather misleading. For it suggests that at any rate immediately after Hume's death, if not during his lifetime, controversy raged about the validity of his philosophical theories. But this would scarcely be an accurate picture of the situation. In France he was acclaimed as the leading British man of letters and during his visits to that country he was lionized in the *salons* of Paris. But though his essays and historical writings were appreciated, his philosophy was not a success in his own country during his lifetime. And, apart from the scandal caused by his reputation for theological unorthodoxy, no very great interest was taken in it. If Hume is now generally regarded as the chief British philosopher, and certainly as the leading British thinker of his period, this is largely because his theories have come into their own, so to speak, in modern empiricism. He has undoubtedly exercised a profound influence on philosophical thought; but, if we except the influence which Hume's empiricism exercised on the mind of Kant, its more important manifestations were reserved for a later period.

In Hume's lifetime there were, however, a few thinkers in his own country who gave a more or less favourable reception to his philosophical ideas. And among these the most remarkable and the most appreciative was his personal friend, Adam Smith. Again, among Hume's critics some were, indeed, moderate and polite; and these included the moral philosopher, Richard Price. Further, a more extensive answer to Hume was proposed by Thomas Reid, the founder of the Scottish philosophy of common sense. It may be appropriate, therefore, to conclude the present part of the fourth volume of this *History* with a brief chapter on Smith, Price, Reid and Reid's followers.

2. Adam Smith (1723–90) went in 1737 to the University of Glasgow, where he attended Hutcheson's lectures. Three years later he went to Balliol College, Oxford. He seems to have become acquainted with Hume at Edinburgh about 1749, and in due course

he became the philosopher's close friend, the friendship lasting until Hume's death. In 1751 Smith was elected to the chair of logic at Glasgow, but in the following year he changed to the chair of moral philosophy, which had become vacant through the death of Hutcheson's successor. In 1759 he published his *Theory of Moral Sentiments*.

In 1764 Smith went to France as tutor-companion to the duke of Buccleuch, after having resigned from his university chair. While in Paris he consorted with Quesnay and other 'physiocrats' as well as with philosophers such as d'Alembert and Helvetius. The physiocrats were an eighteenth-century school of French economists who insisted that governmental interference with individual liberty should be reduced to the indispensable minimum. The reason for this insistence was that they believed in natural economic laws which produce prosperity and wealth if left to operate freely. Hence the word 'physiocracy' or rule of nature. Smith was influenced by them to some extent; but this influence should not be exaggerated. He did not borrow from them his leading ideas.

On returning to England in 1766 Smith retired to Scotland, and in 1776 there appeared his great work, *An Inquiry into the Nature and Causes of the Wealth of Nations*. He received a warm letter of congratulation from Hume. In this classic of economics Smith begins by insisting on the annual labour of a nation as the source of its supply of the necessities and conveniences of life. And he goes on to discuss the causes of improvement in the productiveness of labour and the distribution of its produce. The second book treats of the nature, accumulation and employment of stock; the third of the different progress of wealth in different nations; the fourth of systems of political economy; and the fifth of the revenue of the sovereign or commonwealth. And there are a large number of supplementary notes and dissertations.

In 1778 Smith was appointed one of the commissioners of customs in Scotland. In 1787 he was elected Lord Rector of Glasgow University. He died on July 17th, 1790.

We are not concerned here with Smith's economic theories, but with his moral philosophy. It is worth mentioning, however, that when he was lecturing at Glasgow his course was divided into four parts: natural theology, ethics, the part of morality relating to justice, and those political institutions, including those relating to finance and commerce, which are founded on 'expediency' rather than on the principle of justice and which tend to increase the riches and power of a State. For Smith, therefore, economics was a member of a total body of knowledge, of which ethics was another member.

One salient feature of Adam Smith's moral theory is the central place accorded to sympathy. To attribute ethical importance to sympathy was not, indeed, a novel position in British moral philosophy. Hutcheson had attributed importance to it, and Hume, as we have seen, made great use of the concept of sympathy. But Smith's use of it is more obvious in that he begins his *Theory of Moral Sentiments*[1] with this idea and thus gives his ethics from the very start a social character. 'That we often derive sorrow from the sorrow of others is a matter of fact too obvious to require any instances to prove it.'[2] The sentiment of sympathy is not confined to the virtuous and humane; it is found in all men to some degree.

Smith explains sympathy in terms of the imagination. 'As we have no immediate experience of what other men feel, we can form no idea of the manner in which they are affected, but by conceiving what we ourselves should feel in the like situation.'[3] When we sympathize with someone's great pain, 'by the imagination we place ourselves in his situation. . . .'[4] Thus sympathy, which means or can be used to mean 'our fellow-feeling with any passion whatever',[5] arises not so much from a view of the passion 'as from that of the situation which excites it'.[6] For example, when we feel sympathy with a madman, that is to say when we feel compassion and pity for his state, it is primarily his situation, that of being deprived of the normal use of reason, which excites our sympathy. For the madman himself may not feel any sorrow at all. He may even laugh and sing and appear quite oblivious of his pitiful condition. Again, 'we sympathize even with the dead'.[7]

However, if we assume the causes of sympathy, whatever they may be, we can say that it is an original sentiment of human nature. It is often excited so directly and immediately that it cannot reasonably be derived from self-interested affection, that is, from self-love. And there is no need to postulate a distinct 'moral sense' which expresses itself in moral approval or disapproval. For 'to approve of the passions of another, as suitable to their objects, is the same thing as to observe that we entirely

---

[1] This work will be referred to as *T.M.S.*

[2] *T.M.S.*, I, I, I, p. 2; 1812 edition.   [3] *Ibid.*   [4] *Ibid.*

[5] *Ibid.*, p. 5.   [6] *Ibid.*, p. 7.   [7] *Ibid.*, p. 8.

sympathize with them; and not to approve of them as such is the same thing as to observe that we do not entirely sympathize with them'.[1] Moral approbation and disapprobation, therefore, can ultimately be referred to the operation of sympathy. There are, indeed, cases in which we seem to approve without any sympathy or correspondence of sentiments. But even in these cases it will be found upon examination that our approbation is ultimately founded upon sympathy. Smith takes an example of what he calls a very frivolous nature. I may approve a jest and the consequent laughter, even though, for some reason or other, I do not myself laugh. But I have learned by experience what sort of pleasantry is most capable of amusing me and making me laugh, and I observe that the jest in question is one of this kind. And even though I am not now in the mood for laughing, I approve of the jest and of the company's merriment, this approval being the expression of 'conditional sympathy'. I know that, were it not for my present mood or perhaps illness, I should certainly join in the laughter. Again, if I see a passing stranger who shows signs of distress and sorrow and I am told that he has just lost his father or mother or wife, I approve of his sentiments, even though I may not actually share his distress. For I know by experience that a bereavement of this kind naturally excites such sentiments, and that if I were to take time to consider and enter into his situation, I should doubtless feel sincere sympathy.

Smith makes the sense of propriety the essential element in our moral judgments. And he speaks frequently of the suitableness or unsuitableness, propriety or impropriety of sentiments, passions and affections. Thus, he says that 'in the suitableness or un-suitableness, in the proportion or disproportion which the affection seems to bear to the cause or object which excites it, consists the propriety or impropriety, the decency or ungracefulness of the consequent action'.[2] Further, 'in the beneficial or hurtful nature of the effects which the affection aims at, or tends to produce, consists the merit or demerit of the action, the qualities by which it is entitled to reward, or is deserving of punishment'.[3] But when I disapprove of a man's resentment as being disproportionate to its exciting cause, I disapprove of his sentiments because they do not tally with my own or with what I think my own would be in a like situation. My sympathy does not reach to the man's degree of resentment, and I therefore disapprove of it as excessive. Again,

---

[1] *T.M.S.*, I, I, 3, p. 16.   [2] *Ibid.*, p. 20.   [3] *Ibid.*

when I approve of a man's act as meritorious, as entitled to reward, I sympathize with the gratitude which the action naturally tends to excite in the beneficiary of the action. Or, more accurately, my sense of the merit of the action is compounded of my sympathy with the agent's motive together with my sympathy with the gratitude of the beneficiary.

It may appear, says Smith, that it is the utility of qualities which first commends them to us. And consideration of utility, when we do come to consider it, doubtless enhances the value of qualities in our eyes. 'Originally, however, we approve of another man's judgment, not as something useful, but as right, as accurate, as agreeable to truth and reality, and it is evident we attribute those qualities to it for no other reason but because we find that it agrees with our own. Taste, in the same manner, is originally approved of, not as useful, but as just, as delicate, and as precisely suited to its object. The idea of the utility of all qualities of this kind is plainly an afterthought, and not what first recommends them to our approbation.'[1] If Smith rejected the idea of an original and distinct moral sense, so also did he reject utilitarianism. The concept of sympathy reigns supreme. Smith does, indeed, agree with an 'ingenious and agreeable author' (Hume) that 'no qualities of the mind are approved of as virtuous, but such as are useful or agreeable either to the person himself or to others; and no qualities are disapproved of as vicious but such as have a contrary tendency'.[2] Indeed, 'nature seems to have so happily adjusted our sentiments of approbation and disapprobation to the conveniency both of the individual and of the society that after the strictest examination it will be found, I believe, that this is universally the case'.[3] But it is not this utility which is the first or principal source of moral approbation or disapprobation. 'It seems impossible that the approbation of virtue should be a sentiment of the same kind with that by which we approve of a convenient and well-contrived building; or that we should have no other reason for praising a man than that for which we commend a chest of drawers.'[4] 'The sentiment of approbation always involves in it a sense of propriety quite distinct from the perception of utility.'[5]

To enter upon Smith's analyses of virtues and passions would be to devote to his ethics an excessive amount of space. But it is necessary to ask how he interprets the moral judgment which we

[1] *T.M.S.*, 1, 1, 4, p. 24.   [2] *T.M.S.*, 4, 2, p. 325.   [3] *Ibid.*
[4] *Ibid.*, p. 326.   [5] *Ibid.*

pass about ourselves if moral approbation is an expression of sympathy. And the answer is that in his opinion we cannot approve or disapprove of our own sentiments, motives or conduct except by placing ourselves in the position of another man and viewing our conduct from without, as it were. If a man were brought up on a desert island and had never at any time enjoyed human society, he could no more think 'of the propriety or demerit of his own sentiments and conduct than of the beauty or deformity of his own face'.[1] Our first moral judgments are made about the characters and conduct of other people. But we soon learn that they make judgments about us. Hence we become anxious to know how far we deserve their praise or blame; and we begin to examine our own conduct by imagining ourselves in the position of others, supposing ourselves to be the spectators of our own conduct. Hence, 'I divide myself, as it were, into two persons.... The first is the spectator.... The second is the agent, the person whom I properly call myself, and of whose conduct, under the character of a spectator, I was endeavouring to form some opinion.'[2] I can thus have sympathy with or antipathy towards my own qualities, motives, sentiments and actions.

One of the obvious objections against Smith's ethical theory of sympathy is that it seems to leave no room for any objective standard of right or wrong, good or evil. In answer to an objection of this kind Smith stresses the idea of the 'impartial spectator'. For example, he says that 'the natural misrepresentation of self-love can be corrected only by the eye of this impartial spectator'.[3] At the same time 'the violence and injustice of our own selfish passions are sometimes sufficient to induce the man within the breast to make a report very different from what the real circumstances of the case are capable of authorizing'.[4] Nature, however, has not left us to the delusions of self-love. We gradually and insensibly form for ourselves general rules concerning what is right and what is wrong, these rules being founded on experience of particular acts of moral approbation and disapprobation. And these general rules of conduct, 'when they have been fixed in our mind by habitual reflection, are of great use in correcting the misrepresentations of self-love concerning what is fit and proper to be done in our particular situation'.[5] Indeed, these rules are 'the only principle by which the bulk of mankind are capable of

[1] *T.M.S.*, 3, 1, p. 190. [2] *Ibid.*, p. 193. [3] *T.M.S.*, 3, 8, p. 231.
[4] *T.M.S.*, 3, 4, p. 266. [5] *Ibid.*, p. 273.

directing their actions'.[1] Further, nature impresses upon us an opinion, 'afterwards confirmed by reasoning and philosophy, that these important rules of morality are the commands and laws of the Deity, who will finally reward the obedient and punish the transgressors of their duty'.[2] And 'that our regard to the will of the Deity ought to be the supreme rule of our conduct can be doubted of by nobody who believes his existence'.[3] Conscience is thus the 'vicegerent' of God. Smith does not, however, claim infallibility for the moral judgment. He speaks at some length of the influence of custom on the moral sentiments.[4] Moreover, he tells us that the 'general rules of almost all the virtues . . . are in many respects loose and inaccurate, admit of many exceptions and require so many modifications, that it is scarce possible to regulate our conduct entirely by a regard to them'.[5] There is, indeed, one exception. 'The rules of justice are accurate in the highest degree.'[6]

As historians have pointed out, it is not always easy to reconcile Adam Smith's various statements. On the one hand, the impartial spectator, the man within the breast, will not deceive us if we listen to him attentively and respectfully. On the other hand, there are variations in moral approval from place to place and age to age, and bad customs can pervert or obscure the moral judgment. On the one hand, the majority of people are only capable of directing their conduct by general rules. On the other hand, as these rules, with the exception of the rules of justice, are loose and inaccurate and indeterminate, our conduct should be directed rather by a sense of propriety, by a certain taste for a particular way of acting, than by regard for a rule as such. It may, indeed, be possible to reconcile these diverse statements with one another. For example, it might be said that though the impartial spectator, if listened to attentively, never deceives, passion and bad custom (arising perhaps from external circumstances which seem to make the custom expedient) may very well prevent the requisite attention being given. In any case, however, it seems true to say with his critics that in his ethical treatise Smith displays his abilities to greater advantage as a psychological analyst than as a moral philosopher.

3. It has been already remarked that the philosophers of the moral sense theory tended to assimilate ethics to aesthetics, this

[1] *T.M.S.*, 3, 5, p. 276. [2] *Ibid.*, p. 279. [3] *Ibid.*, p. 291.
[4] *T.M.S.*, 5, 2. [5] *T.M.S.*, 3, 6, p. 299. [6] *Ibid.*, p. 301.

tendency being connected, I think, with their concentration on qualities of character rather than with acts. And to the extent that they assimilated ethics to aesthetics they tended to overlook the specifically ethical features of the moral judgment. I use the word 'tended' deliberately; for I do not intend to assert that they identified ethics and aesthetics or that they made no effort to distinguish them by isolating the specific feature or features of the moral judgment.

Adam Smith cannot, of course, be properly called a philosopher of the moral-sense theory. For despite his admiration for Hutcheson and his appreciation of the latter's achievements as a moralist he explicitly rejected 'every account of the principle of approbation, which makes it depend upon a peculiar sentiment, distinct from every other'.[1] At the same time Smith is akin to the philosophers of the moral sense theory in his tendency to dissolve ethics in psychology. (Again I use the word 'tendency' deliberately.) This tendency can be observed also in Hume, though in his moral philosophy, as we have seen, there was present a conspicuous element of utilitarianism.

The early utilitarians (and the same can be said of utilitarianism in general) tended to reduce the moral judgment to a statement about consequences. That is to say, they tended to interpret the specifically moral judgment as an empirical statement or hypothesis.

On the one hand, therefore, we have the moral sense school, with its psychologizing tendencies and its tendency to assimilate ethics to aesthetics, while on the other hand we have utilitarianism, which in its own way tended to strip the moral judgment of its specific character. It was only natural, then, that some thinkers at least should react to these tendencies by insisting on the part played by reason in morality and on the intrinsic nature of the rightness and wrongness of certain actions, quite apart from the thought of reward and punishment and other utilitarian considerations. Such a thinker was Richard Price, who in certain respects anticipated the position of Kant.

Richard Price (1723–91) was the son of a Nonconformist minister and himself entered the ministry. Besides publishing some sermons, he also wrote on financial and political matters. In addition, he carried on a controversy with Priestley, in which he upheld free-will and the immateriality of the soul. We are here

[1] *T.M.S.*, 7, 3, p. 579.

concerned, however, with his ethical ideas as expressed in his *Review of the Principal Questions in Morals* (1757). It shows clearly his debt to Cudworth and Clarke on the one hand and to Butler on the other, for whom he had a profound admiration.

Price disliked the moral sense theory, especially as developed by Hume. It favours subjectivism and abandons the direction of human conduct to instinct and feeling. Reason, not emotion, is authoritative in morals. And reason has every title to this position in that it discerns objective moral distinctions. There are actions which are intrinsically right and actions which are intrinsically wrong. Price does not mean that in ethics we should consider actions without any regard to the intention of the agent and the natural end of the action. But if we consider human acts in their totality, we can discern by reason their rightness or wrongness, which belong to the actions in question independently of consequences such as reward or punishment. There are at least some actions which are right in themselves and which need no further justification in terms of extraneous factors, just as there are some ultimate ends. 'There are, undoubtedly, some actions that are ultimately approved, and for justifying which no reason can be assigned; as there are some ends, which are ultimately desired, and for choosing which no reason can be given.'[1] If this were not the case, says Price, there would be an infinite regress.

In expounding the idea of an intellectual intuition of objective moral distinctions Price was reviving the views held by earlier writers such as Cudworth and Clarke. And the historical source of the neglect of this intellectual operation by the moral sense theorists and of the consequent subjectivism and empiricism of Hume was traced by Price to Locke's theory of ideas and to his concept of the understanding. Locke derived all simple ideas from sensation and reflection. But there are simple and self-evident ideas which are immediately perceived or intuited by the understanding. Among them are the ideas of right and wrong. If we confuse the understanding with the imagination, we shall necessarily tend to confine unduly the scope of the former. 'The powers of the imagination are very narrow; and were the understanding confined to the same limits, nothing could be known, and the very faculty itself would be annihilated. Nothing is plainer than that one of these often perceives where the other is blind . . . and in numberless instances knows things to exist of which the other can

[1] *Review,* 1, 3.

frame no idea.'[1] Reasoning, considered as a distinct intellectual operation, studies the relations between ideas which we already possess; but the understanding intuits self-evident ideas which cannot be resolved into elements derived from sense-experience.

In defence of the assertion that the understanding has original and self-evident ideas, Price appeals to 'common sense'. If a man denies that there are such ideas, 'he is not further to be argued with, for the subject will not admit of argument, there being nothing clearer than the point itself disputed to be brought to confirm it'.[2] In appealing to common sense and self-evident principles Price anticipates to some extent the position of the Scottish philosophy of common sense. But his insistence that the ideas of right and wrong are simple or 'single' ideas which are not further analysable recalls to mind later ethical intuitionism.

By rejecting the moral sense theory Price does not commit himself to rejecting the emotional element in morals. Right and wrong are objective attributes of human actions, and these attributes are perceived by the mind; but we certainly have feelings with regard to actions and human qualities, and these feelings find expression in the subjective ideas of moral beauty and deformity. What Price does, therefore, is to oust feeling from a central position and to keep it as an accompaniment of rational intuition. Another accompaniment of the intellectual perception of right and wrong in actions is the perception of merit and demerit in agents. To perceive merit in the agent is simply to perceive that his action is right and that he ought to be rewarded. On this matter Price follows Butler. He also insists that merit depends on the intention of the agent. Unless the action possesses 'formal rightness', unless, that is to say, it is performed with a good intention, it is not meritorious.

Right and obligatory seem to be synonymous for Price. The obligatory character of an intrinsically right action is founded simply on its rightness, without regard to reward or punishment. Benevolence is certainly a virtue, though not the only one; and there is such a thing as rational self-love. But a man, as a rational being, ought, in principle at least, to act simply out of respect for the dictates of reason, and not from instinct, passion or emotion. 'The intellectual nature is its own law. It has, within itself, a spring and guide of action which it cannot suppress or reject. Rectitude is itself an end, an ultimate end, an end superior to all other ends,

---

[1] *Review*, I, 2.   [2] *Ibid.*

governing, directing, and limiting them, and whose existence and influence depend on nothing arbitrary. . . . To act from affection to it, is to act with light, and conviction, and knowledge. But acting from instinct is so far acting in the dark, and following a blind guide. Instinct *drives* and *precipitates*; but reason *commands*.'[1] Hence an agent cannot properly be called virtuous 'except he acts from a consciousness of rectitude, and with a regard to it as his *rule* and *end*'.[2] In any case an agent's virtue is always less in proportion as he acts from natural propensity and inclination or from instinct instead of according to purely rational principles.[3] Price does, indeed, bring in consideration of reward and punishment to the extent that he expresses surprise that anyone should forget that by acting virtuously he may gain an infinite reward while by acting otherwise he may suffer infinite loss. And he insists that virtue itself is 'the object of the chief complacency of every virtuous man; the exercise of it is his chief delight; and the consciousness of it gives him his highest joy'.[4] But his insistence on acting in accordance with purely rational principles and out of consideration of the rightness of right acts, which oblige the agent, and his view that the virtue of a man is less in proportion to the degree in which he acts from instinct or natural inclination clearly approximate to a Kantian position. And Kant himself did not exclude all thought of reward from ethics. For though he considered that we should not do right and obligatory actions simply with a view to reward, he certainly thought that virtue should ultimately produce or be united with happiness. So for Price we must conceive happiness as the end envisaged by divine Providence. And virtue will produce happiness. But this happiness depends on 'rectitude', and we cannot be truly virtuous unless we do right actions because they are right.

4. Thomas Reid (1710–96), son of a Scottish minister, studied at Aberdeen. After some years as minister in the parish of New Machar he was elected to a post at King's College, Aberdeen, and in 1764 he published *An Inquiry into the Human Mind on the Principles of Common Sense*. Thus although Reid was a year older than Hume, his first work (apart from an essay on quantity) appeared much later than Hume's *Treatise* and *Enquiries*. Shortly after the publication of this work Reid was elected professor of moral philosophy at Glasgow in succession to Adam Smith. In 1785 he published a volume of *Essays on the Intellectual Powers of*

[1] *Review*, 8. [2] *Ibid*. [3] *Ibid*. [4] *Review*, 9.

Man, which was followed in 1788 by *Essays on the Active Powers of Man*. These two sets of essays have been reprinted together several times as *Essays on the Powers of the Human Mind*.

After reading part of the manuscript of Reid's *Inquiry*, transmitted to him by a Dr. Blair, Hume wrote a letter to the author which contained some innocuous comments. In the course of his reply Reid remarks: 'Your system appears to me not only coherent in all its parts, but likewise justly deduced from principles commonly received among philosophers: principles which I never thought of calling in question, until the conclusions you draw from them in the *Treatise of Human Nature* made me suspect them.' It was Reid's contention that Hume's philosophy was 'a system of scepticism, which leaves no ground to believe any one thing rather than its contrary'.[1] In fact, it constituted, in Reid's opinion, the *reductio ad absurdum* of scepticism. At the same time it was the result of a consistent development of the implications of certain principles, or of a certain principle, which had been shared by writers such as Locke and Berkeley, and even by Descartes, who were not so consistent or rigorous as Hume in drawing the appropriate conclusions from their premises. Hence it was necessary to examine the starting-point of the process of reasoning which had led in the end to a contradiction of the beliefs upon which all men of common sense must act in common life.

The root of the whole trouble Reid finds in what he calls 'the theory of ideas'. In his first essay,[2] as indeed elsewhere, Reid distinguishes several senses of the word 'idea'. In popular language the word signifies conception or apprehension. Reid means the act of conceiving or apprehending. 'To have an idea of anything is to conceive it. To have a distinct idea is to conceive it distinctly. To have no idea of it is not to conceive it at all. . . . When the word idea is taken in this popular sense, no man can possibly doubt whether he has ideas.'[3] But the word is also given a 'philosophical' meaning; and then 'it does not signify that act of the mind which we call thought or conception, but some object of thought'.[4] Thus according to Locke ideas are nothing but the immediate objects of the mind in thinking. Now, 'Bishop Berkeley, proceeding upon this foundation, demonstrated very easily that there is no material

---

[1] Dedication to the *Inquiry*.
[2] References to the *Essays on the Powers of the Human Mind* are given according to the three-volume edition of 1819, while references to the *Inquiry* are also given according to 1819 edition.
[3] *Essays*, I, I, 10; I, p. 38.   [4] *Ibid.*, p. 39.

world. . . . But the Bishop, as became his order, was unwilling to give up the world of spirits. . . . Mr. Hume shows no partiality in favour of the world of spirits. He adopts the theory of ideas in its full extent; and, in consequence, shows that there is neither matter nor mind in the universe; nothing but impressions and ideas.'[1] In fact, 'Mr. Hume's system does not even leave him a *self* to claim the property of his impressions and ideas'.[2] Ideas, therefore, which 'were first introduced into philosophy in the humble character of images or representatives of things' have by degrees 'supplanted their constituents and undermined the existence of everything but themselves', the 'triumph of ideas' being completed by Hume's *Treatise*, which 'leaves ideas and impressions as the sole existence in the universe'.[3]

In attacking the theory of ideas Reid characteristically employs two ways of approaching the matter. One way is to appeal to common sense, to the universal belief or persuasion of ordinary people. Thus the ordinary man is convinced that what he perceives is the sun itself, and not ideas or impressions. But Reid does not content himself with an appeal to the beliefs of 'the vulgar'. He also argues, for example, that there are no such things as ideas in the 'philosophical' sense of the word; they are fictions of the philosophers, or of some philosophers, and it is in no way necessary to postulate them. Why, then, did philosophers invent this fiction? In Reid's opinion one fundamental error was Locke's assumption that 'simple ideas' are the elementary data of knowledge. The 'ideal system' 'teaches us that the first operation of the mind about its ideas is simple apprehension; that is, the bare conception of a thing without any belief about it; and that after we have got simple apprehensions, by comparing them together, we perceive agreements or disagreements between them; and that this perception of the agreement or disagreement of ideas is all that we call belief, judgment or knowledge. Now this appears to me to be all fiction, without any foundation in nature. . . . Instead of saying that the belief or knowledge is got by putting together and comparing the simple apprehensions, we ought rather to say that the simple apprehension is performed by resolving and analysing a natural and original judgment.'[4] Locke and Hume started with the supposed elements of knowledge, simple ideas in the case of the former and impressions in the case of the latter, and then

---

[1] *Essays*, 2, 12; 1, pp. 266–7.   [2] *Ibid.*, p. 267.
[3] *Inquiry*, 2, 6, pp. 60–1.   [4] *Inquiry*, 2, 4, pp. 52–3.

depicted knowledge as being essentially the result of combining
these elementary data and perceiving their agreement or disagreement. But the so-called elementary data are the result of analysis:
we first have original, fundamental judgments. 'Every operation
of the senses, in its very nature, implies judgment or belief, as well
as simple apprehension. . . . When I perceive a tree before me, my
faculty of seeing gives me not only a notion or simple apprehension
of the tree, but a belief of its existence, and of its figure, distance,
and magnitude; and this judgment or belief is not got by comparing ideas, it is included in the very nature of the perception.'[1]

These 'original and natural judgments are therefore a part of
that furniture which nature hath given to the human understanding. They are the inspiration of the Almighty, no less than
our notions or simple apprehensions. . . . They are a part of our
constitution, and all the discoveries of our reason are grounded
upon them. They make up what is called *the common sense of mankind*; and what is manifestly contrary to any of those first principles is what we call *absurd*.'[2] If philosophers maintain that ideas
are the immediate objects of thought, they will be forced to conclude in the end that ideas are the only objects of our minds.
Locke did not draw this conclusion. He used the word 'idea' in
several senses, and there are different, and indeed incompatible,
elements in his writings. But Hume eventually drew the logical
conclusions from Locke's premises (which can be referred back
to Descartes). And in so doing he has to deny the principles of
common sense, the original and natural judgments of mankind.
His conclusions, therefore, were absurd. The remedy is to recognize the principles of common sense, the original judgments of
mankind, and to acknowledge that the 'theory of ideas' is a useless
and harmful fiction.

By judgments of nature and principles of common sense Reid
means self-evident principles. 'We ascribe to reason two offices,
or two degrees. The first is to judge of things self-evident; the
second to draw conclusions that are not self-evident from those
that are. The first of these is the province, and the sole province of
common sense.'[3] The name 'common sense' is appropriate because
'in the greatest part of mankind no other degree of reason is to be
found'.[4] The power to deduce conclusions from self-evident principles in an orderly and systematic way is not found in everyone,

[1] *Inquiry*, 7, 4, p. 394.   [2] *Ibid.*, pp. 394-5.
[3] *Essays*, 6, 2; ii, pp. 233-4.   [4] *Ibid.*, p. 234.

though many people can learn to do so. But the power to see self-evident truths is found in all beings who qualify for being called rational. And it is 'purely the gift of Heaven':[1] it cannot be acquired if one does not possess it.

What relation does common sense in this special meaning of the term bear to common sense in the 'popular' meaning of the term? Reid's answer is that 'the same degree of understanding which makes a man capable of acting with common prudence in the conduct of life makes him capable of discovering what is true and what is false in matters that are self-evident and that he distinctly apprehends'.[2]

According to Reid, therefore, there are 'common principles which are the foundation of all reasoning and of all science. Such common principles seldom admit of direct proof, nor do they need it. Men need not to be taught them; for they are such as all men of common understanding know; or such, at least, as they give a ready assent to, as soon as they are proposed and understood.'[3] But what are these principles? Reid distinguishes between necessary truths, the opposite of which is impossible, and contingent truths, the opposite of which is possible. Each class includes 'first principles'. Among first principles belonging to the first class there are logical axioms (for example, every proposition is either true or false), mathematical axioms, and the first principles of morals and metaphysics. One of the examples of moral first principles given by Reid is that 'no man ought to be blamed for what it was not in his power to hinder'.[4] These moral axioms 'appear to me to have no less evidence than those of mathematics'.[5] Under the heading of metaphysical first principles Reid considers three, 'because they have been called in question by Mr. Hume'.[6] The first is that 'the qualities which we perceive by our senses must have a subject, which we call body, and that the thoughts we are conscious of must have a subject, which we call mind'.[7] This principle is recognized as true by all ordinary men, and this recognition is expressed in ordinary language. The second metaphysical principle is that 'whatever begins to exist must have a cause which produced it'.[8] And the third is that 'design and intelligence in the cause may be inferred from marks or signs of it in the effect'.[9]

Among the first principles of contingent truths we find 'that

[1] *Essays*, 6, 2; 11, p. 234.   [2] *Ibid.*, p. 223.   [3] *Essays*, 1, 2; 1, p. 57.
[4] *Essays*, 8, 3, 5; 11, p. 338.   [5] *Ibid.*   [6] *Essays*, 8, 3, 6; 11, p. 339.
[7] *Ibid.*   [8] *Ibid.*, p. 342.   [9] *Ibid.*, p. 352.

those things did really happen which I distinctly remember';[1] 'that those things do really exist which we distinctly perceive by our senses, and are what we perceive them to be';[2] 'that the natural faculties by which we distinguish truth from error are not fallacious';[3] and 'that in the phenomena of nature what is to be will probably be like to what has been in similar circumstances'.[4] That we have some degree of power over our actions and over the determinations of our will, and that there is life and intelligence in our fellow-men with whom we converse, are also among the first principles mentioned by Reid.

Now, it is evident, I think, that these first principles are of different types. Among logical axioms Reid mentions the proposition that whatever can be truly affirmed of a genus can be truly affirmed of the species. Here we have an analytic proposition. We have only to learn the meanings of the terms 'genus' and 'species' in order to see that the proposition is true. But can the same be said of the validity of memory or of the existence of the external world? Reid can hardly have thought that it could; for he classifies the relevant propositions as first principles of contingent truths. In what sense, then, are they self-evident? Reid obviously means at the very least that there is a natural propensity to believe them. Speaking of the statement that the things really exist which we perceive by the senses and that they are what we perceive them to be, he remarks: 'It is too evident to need proof, that all men are by nature led to give implicit faith to the distinct testimony of their senses, long before they are capable of any bias from prejudices of education or of philosophy.'[5] Again, when speaking of the principle relating to the uniformity, or probable uniformity, of nature, he observes that it cannot be simply the result of experience, though it is confirmed by experience. For 'the principle is necessary for us before we are able to discover it by reasoning, and therefore is made a part of our constitution, and produces its effects before the use of reason'.[6] In other words, we have a natural propensity to expect that the course of nature will probably prove to be uniform.

Propositions which are obviously tautological cause no difficulty. Given the meanings of the terms, they cannot be denied without absurdity. And though the existence of informative necessary propositions is a matter of controversy, Reid is perfectly entitled

[1] *Essays*, 6, 5, 3; II, p. 304.   [2] *Essays*, 6, 5, 5; II, p. 308.
[3] *Essays*, 6, 5, 7; II, p. 314.   [4] *Essays*, 6, 5, 12; II, p. 328.
[5] *Essays*, 6, 5, 5; II, p. 308.   [6] *Essays*, 6, 5, 12; II, p. 329.

to his opinion that there are such propositions. I mean, the issue between Reid and Hume on this matter can be clearly expressed. But the issue is not at all so clear when it comes to natural belief in what Reid calls the first principles of contingent truths; nor has Reid made it clear. Hume never denied that there are natural beliefs; and he was perfectly well aware that these natural beliefs form a basis or framework for practical life. He does, indeed, sometimes make ontological assertions, as when he says that people are nothing but bundles or collections of different perceptions; but, generally speaking, he is concerned, not with denying a given proposition, but with examining our grounds for asserting the proposition. For instance, Hume does not say that there is no external world or that the course of nature will be so entirely unexpected that we can rely on no uniformity at all: he is concerned with examining the rationally assignable grounds for beliefs which he shares in common with other people. Hence in so far as Reid appeals to natural belief, to natural propensities and to the common consent of mankind, his observations have not much relevance as against Hume. Reid does, indeed, recognize that Hume speaks of natural beliefs; but he tends to represent the latter as denying what he does not in fact deny. If Reid had maintained that what he calls first principles were susceptible of proof, the issue with Hume would be sufficiently clear-cut. For example, can the validity of memory be proved or can it not? But Reid did not think that his first principles were susceptible of proof. Speaking of the validity (in principle) of memory, he says that the principle possesses one of the surest marks of a first principle, namely, that no one has pretended to prove it, though no sensible man questions it. But Hume was well aware that people are naturally prone to believe that memory is in principle reliable. Reid refers to the acceptance of testimony in the courts of law and remarks that 'what is absurd at the bar (that no heed at all should be paid to testimony) is so in the philosopher's chair'.[1] But Hume never dreamed, of course, of suggesting that testimony about remembered facts should never be accepted, and that no one should ever trust his or her memory. Reid does, indeed, proceed to admit that 'Mr. Hume has not, as far as I remember, directly called in question the testimony of memory',[2] though he adds immediately that Hume has laid down the premises by which the authority of memory is overthrown, leaving it to his reader to

---

[1] *Essays*, 6, 5, 3, p. 305.   [2] *Ibid*.

draw the logical conclusion. But it is a mistake to assume that Hume intended, even by implication, to destroy that degree of reliance on memory which is given it by prudent common sense. He no more intended this than he intended to deny that there are any causal relations and to suggest that no reliance should in practice be put on causal laws. In general, then, we can say that Reid's criticism of Hume is sometimes deprived of force by his misunderstanding of what Hume was about.

It is not, of course, a fair presentation of Reid's position if he is depicted as appealing simply to the persuasion or opinion of non-philosophers as a proof of the truth of his first principles. What he does is to regard universal consent, when coupled with an inability to doubt, save perhaps in the sceptical philosopher's chair, as an indication that a given proposition is a first principle. First principles cannot be proved; otherwise they would not be first principles. They are known intuitively. But Reid does not give, as it seems to me, any very clear and consistent account of the way or ways in which we come to know the different types of first principles. In some cases he does, indeed, explain his view. For example, 'the evidence of mathematical axioms is not discerned till men come to a certain degree of maturity of understanding. A boy must have formed the general conception of *quantity*, and of *more* and *less* and *equal*, of *sum* and *difference*; and he must have been accustomed to judge of these relations in matters of common life, before he can perceive the evidence of the mathematical axiom, that equal quantities, added to equal quantities, make equal sums. In like manner our moral judgment, or conscience, grows to maturity from an imperceptible seed, planted by our Creator.'[1] Here we have a reasonably straightforward account. In the course of experience a man obtains certain notions or learns the meaning of certain terms, and he can then see the self-evident truth of certain propositions containing or presupposing those terms. If the principles are said to belong to the constitution of human nature, this means that we have a natural power of discerning the evident truth of these principles, but not that the latter are known antecedently to experience. But when talking about the proposition that perceived sensible qualities and thoughts of which we are conscious must have subjects, namely, body and mind, Reid speaks of 'principles of belief in human nature, of which we can give no other account but that they necessarily

---

[1] *Essays*, 5, 1; III, p. 451.

result from the constitution of our faculties'.[1] And this principle, like mathematical axioms, is classed as a first principle of necessary truths. And when we turn to first principles of contingent truths we find him saying with regard to the principle of the uniformity of nature, that it is 'a part of our constitution and produces its effects before the use of reason'.[2] The principle is antecedent to experience, 'for all experience is grounded upon a belief that the future will be like the past'.[3] We are determined by our nature to expect that the future will be like the past. There is a kind of irresistible natural expectation.

Perhaps these ways of speaking can be made consistent. Speaking of the principle that the natural faculties by which we distinguish truth from error are not fallacious, Reid remarks that 'we are under a necessity of trusting to our reasoning and judging powers', and that doubt on this point cannot be maintained 'because it is doing violence to our constitution'.[4] He also asserts that 'no man ever thinks of this principle, unless when he considers the grounds of scepticism; yet it invariably governs his opinions'.[5] He seems to be saying, therefore, first that there is a natural and irresistible propensity to trust our rational powers, and secondly that this proposition is not explicitly recognized as true from the beginning. And he might make analogous statements, not only about the principle of the uniformity of nature, but also about the principle of causality, which he regards as a metaphysical and necessary principle. But he tends, I think, to leave his readers with the impression that principles such as the validity of memory and the existence of the external world are self-evident in the sense that we have a natural and irresistible impulse to believe them, whereas mathematical axioms, for instance, are self-evident in the sense that once we have the meanings of certain terms we see necessary relations between them. What I suggest, therefore, is that Reid asserts the existence of a considerable number of first principles of different types without providing an unambiguous explanation of the precise sense or senses in which they are said to be self-evident, first principles, and a part of the constitution of our nature. It may be possible to reconcile his various ways of speaking and provide an account which will cover all his first principles; but I do not think that Reid provided it. And if he wished to give different accounts of the different sets of

---

[1] *Essays*, 6, 6, 6; ii, p. 341.   [2] *Essays*, 6, 5, 12; ii, p. 329.   [3] *Ibid.*
[4] *Essays*, 6, 5, 7; ii, p. 316.   [5] *Ibid.*, p. 317.

first principles, he might have made the point clearer than he in fact did.

Reid sometimes tends to play to the gallery by practically making fun of certain philosophers (Berkeley, for example) and by announcing that he takes his stand with 'the vulgar'. But his philosophy of common sense is by no means a mere acceptance of the opinions of the multitude and a rejection of academic philosophy. It was his view that philosophy must be grounded in common experience and that if it reaches paradoxical conclusions which contradict common experience and conflict with the beliefs on which everyone, even sceptical philosophers, necessarily base their lives in practice, there must be something wrong with it. And this is a perfectly reputable view of philosophy. It is not invalidated by Reid's historical inaccuracies and misrepresentations of other points of view.

It must be added that Reid did not adhere invariably to common sense, if by common sense we mean the spontaneous belief of the man in the street. For example, when speaking of colour he first says that 'by colour all men, who have not been tutored by modern philosophy, understand, not a sensation of the mind, which can have no existence when it is not perceived, but a quality or modification of bodies, which continues to be the same, whether it is seen or not'.[1] He then goes on to distinguish between 'the appearance of colour' and colour itself, as a quality of a body. The latter is cause of the former, and it is unknown in itself. But the appearance of scarlet, for example, is so closely united in imagination with its cause that 'they are apt to be mistaken for one and the same thing, although they are in reality so different and unlike that one is an idea in the mind, the other is a quality of body. I conclude, then, that colour . . . is a certain power or virtue in bodies that in fair daylight exhibits to the eye an appearance. . . .'[2] Indeed, Reid does not hesitate to say that 'none of our sensations are resemblances of any of the qualities of bodies'.[3] It is perhaps rather surprising to hear such utterances from the lips of a champion of 'the vulgar'. But the truth is, of course, that though Reid maintained that in the 'unequal contest betwixt common sense and philosophy the latter will always come off both with dishonour and loss',[4] he by no means confined himself to repeating the views of people innocent of all philosophy and science.

[1] Inquiry, 6, 4, p. 153. [2] Ibid., pp. 156-7.
[3] Inquiry, 6, 6, p. 163. [4] Inquiry, 1, 4, p. 32.

5. Among Reid's friends was George Campbell (1719–96), who became Principal of Marischal College, Aberdeen, in 1759 and professor of divinity at that college in 1771. In his *Philosophy of Rhetoric* he includes under the general heading of propositions the truth of which is known intuitively mathematical axioms, truths of consciousness and first principles of common sense. Some mathematical axioms, he points out, merely exhibit the meanings of terms, though this is not true, in his opinion, of all mathematical principles. Truths of consciousness include, for instance, assurance of one's existence. As for principles of common sense, these include the principle of causality, the principle of the uniformity of nature, the existence of body, and the validity of memory when it is 'clear'. He thus gave to common sense a more restricted meaning than that given it by Reid.

6. Better known than Campbell are James Oswald (d. 1793), author of *An Appeal to Common Sense in behalf of Religion*, and James Beattie (1735–1803). In 1760 the latter was elected professor of moral philosophy and logic at Marischal College, Aberdeen; and in 1770 he published his *Essay on Truth*. In it he not only criticized Hume's opinions but also indulged in declamation and diatribe in passages which were doubtless the expression of sincere indignation but which seem rather out of place in a philosophical work. Hume was angry; and some of his comments have been reported. Of the *Essay on Truth* he remarked: 'Truth! there is no truth in it; it is a horrible large lie in octavo.' And of its author he spoke as 'that silly bigoted fellow, Beattie'. But the work enjoyed a great success. King George III was pleased, and he rewarded the author with an annual pension. Oxford University conferred on Beattie the doctorate of civil law.

In the first part of the *Essay on Truth* Beattie considers the standard of truth. He distinguishes between common sense, which perceives self-evident truth, and reason (reasoning). The first principles of truth, of which there are a considerable number, 'rest upon their own evidence, perceived intuitively by the understanding'.[1] But how are we to distinguish between first principles of common sense and mere prejudices? This question is treated in the second part. Reflection on mathematics shows us that the criterion of truth is that principle which forces our belief by its own intrinsic evidence.[2] In natural philosophy this principle is 'well-informed sense'. When is sense well-informed? First, I must be

---

[1] *Essay*, 1, 2, 9, p. 93; 1820 edition.   [2] *Essay*, 2, 1, 1; p. 117.

disposed, of my own accord, to confide in it without hesitation. Secondly, the sensations received must be 'uniformly similar in similar circumstances'.[1] Thirdly, I must ask myself 'whether, in acting upon the supposition that the faculty in question is well-informed, I have ever been misled to my hurt or inconvenience'.[2] Fourthly, the sensations communicated must be compatible with one another and with the perceptions of my other faculties. Fifthly, my sensations must be compatible with those of other men. The third part of the *Essay* is professedly devoted to answering objections against Beattie's theories. But the latter takes the opportunity of giving us his opinions about a large number of philosophers, and in most cases this opinion is very low. For Aristotle he shows an obvious respect; and Reid is naturally immune from attack. But the Schoolmen are depicted as mere verbal wranglers, and the greater number of modern philosophical systems are represented as contributing to or as examples of sceptical systems, 'those unnatural productions, the vile effusions of a hard heart'.[3] Beattie tends to give the impression that he has very little use for philosophy except as a means of attacking philosophies and philosophers.

7. Of more account than Beattie was Dugald Stewart (1753–1828). After studying at Edinburgh University he taught mathematics there, and in 1778 he took the class in moral philosophy during the absence of the professor, Adam Ferguson.[4] When the latter resigned his chair in 1785, Stewart was appointed to succeed him. In 1792 he published the first volume of *Elements of the Philosophy of the Human Mind*, of which the second and third volumes did not appear until 1814 and 1827 respectively. *Outlines of Moral Philosophy* was published in 1793, and *Philosophical Essays* in 1810. In 1815 and 1821 appeared the two parts of his *Dissertation exhibiting the Progress of Metaphysical, Ethical and Political Philosophy since the Revival of Letters in Europe* which was written for the supplement of the *Encyclopaedia Britannica*. Finally, his *Philosophy of the Active and Moral Powers* was published in 1828, a few weeks before his death. Stewart was an eloquent and influential lecturer, attracting students even from abroad. And after his death a monument to his memory was

---

[1] *Essay*, 2, 1, 2, p. 140.   [2] *Ibid.*, p. 141.   [3] *Essay*, 3, 3, p. 385.
[4] Adam Ferguson (1723–1816) published an *Essay on the History of Civil Society* (1767), *Institutes of Moral Philosophy* (1769), a *History of the Progress and Termination of the Roman Republic* (1783) and *Principles of Moral and Political Science* (1792). Hume had a high opinion of him and left him a legacy in his will.

erected in Edinburgh. He was not a particularly original thinker; but he was a man of wide culture, and he was gifted with a power of exposition.

In the introduction to his *Outlines of Moral Philosophy* Stewart remarks that 'our knowledge of the laws of nature is entirely the result of observation and experiment; for there is no instance in which we perceive such a necessary connection between two successive events, as might enable us to infer the one from the other by reasoning *a priori*. We find, from experience, that certain events are invariably conjoined, so that when we see the one, we expect the other, but our knowledge in such cases extends no farther than the fact.'[1] We have to use observation and controlled experiment to arrive inductively at general laws, from which we can reason deductively ('synthetically') to effects.

This point of view may seem to be very out of keeping with the outlook of Reid. But though Reid maintained that the truth of the proposition that everything which begins to be has a cause is known intuitively, he did not maintain that experience can inform us about particular necessary connections in Nature. 'General maxims, grounded on experience, have only a degree of probability proportioned to the extent of our experience, and ought always to be understood so as to leave room for exceptions if future, experience shall discover any such.'[2] According to Reid, we can infer the existence of God, as cause of contingent and mutable things, with absolute certainty. But apart from this truth, from self-evident first principles and from what can be strictly deduced from them, we are left to experience and probability. He instances the law of gravitation as a probable law, in the sense that exceptions are in principle possible. Hence Stewart's view of natural philosophy is not so alien to Reid's outlook as might appear at first sight.

Stewart notes that the 'reformation' in physics which has taken place during the last two centuries has not been extended in the same degree to other branches of knowledge, in particular to the knowledge of the mind. 'As all our knowledge of the material world rests ultimately on facts ascertained by observation, so all our knowledge of the human mind rests ultimately on facts for which we have the evidence of our own consciousness. An attentive examination of such facts will lead in time to the general principles

---

[1] *Outlines*, Introduction, 1. 3; 11, p. 6. All page references are to the edition of Stewart's *Collected Works* by Sir William Hamilton, 1854–8.

[2] *Essays*, 6, 6, 6; 11, p. 345.

of the human constitution, and will gradually form a science of mind not inferior in certainty to the science of body. Of this species of investigation, the works of Dr. Reid furnish many valuable examples.'[1]

The general aim proposed by Stewart for inquiries into psychology is, therefore, that of giving to this branch of study the character of a science. And this involves applying to psychology the methods which have proved so successful in physics. The data studied are, of course, different from the data studied by physicists. But an analogous scientific method should be used. And if psychology is to acquire the character of a science, it is most important that it should not be confused with metaphysics. Natural philosophers or physicists 'have, in modern times, wisely abandoned to metaphysicians all speculations concerning the nature of that substance of which it (the material world) is composed; concerning the possibility or impossibility of its being created; . . . and even concerning the reality of its existence, independent of that of percipient beings: and have confined themselves to the humbler province of observing the phenomena it exhibits, and of ascertaining their general laws. . . . This experimental philosophy no one now is in danger of confounding with the metaphysical speculations already mentioned. . . . A similar distinction takes place among the questions which may be stated relative to the human mind. . . . When we have once ascertained a general fact, such as the various laws which regulate the association of ideas, or the dependence of memory on that effort of the mind which we call Attention; it is all we ought to aim at in this branch of science. If we proceed no farther than facts for which we have the evidence of our own consciousness, our conclusions will be no less certain than those in physics. . . .'[2]

Stewart restricts unduly the scope of psychology and regards as 'metaphysical' some inquiries which would not ordinarily be classified in this way.[3] But the interesting point about his discussion of the science of mind is his inductive approach and his insistence on not confounding science with speculation. And even though he tends sometimes to restrict unduly the scope and range of psychological inquiry, this does not mean that he is blind to the need for constructive hypotheses. On the contrary, he reproves those Baconians who reject hypotheses and appeal to Newton's

[1] *Outlines*, Introduction, 2, 11; 11, p. 8.
[2] *Elements*, Introduction, 1; 11, pp. 48–52.
[3] In another sense psychology has a very broad range for Stewart.

famous *Hypotheses non fingo*, understood in a literal sense. We must distinguish between 'gratuitous' hypotheses and those which are supported by presumptions suggested by analogy. The utility of an hypothesis is shown when conclusions derived from it are verified or confirmed. But even an hypothesis which is subsequently shown to be false may prove to have been of great use. Stewart quotes[1] Hartley's remark in his *Observations on Man*[2] that 'any hypothesis which possesses a sufficient degree of plausibility to account for a number of facts, helps us to digest these facts in proper order, to bring new ones to light, and to make *experimenta crucis* for the sake of future inquirers'.

In his approach to psychology, therefore, Stewart adopted what we may call a frankly empiricist approach. But this does not mean that he rejects Reid's theories of first principles or principles of common sense. True, he regards the term 'common sense' as too vague and as calculated to give rise to misunderstanding and misrepresentation. But he accepts the idea of principles, the truth of which is perceived intuitively. These he classifies under three headings. First, there are axioms of mathematics and physics. Secondly, there are first principles relating to consciousness, perception and memory. Thirdly, there are 'those fundamental laws of human belief, which form an essential part of our constitution; and of which our entire conviction is implied, not only in all speculation, but in all our conduct as acting beings'.[3] Among 'laws' of this first class are the truths of the existence of the material world and of the uniformity of nature. 'Such truths no man ever thinks of stating to himself in the form of propositions; but all our conduct and all our reasonings proceed on the supposition that they are admitted. The belief of them is necessary for the preservation of our animal existence; and it is accordingly coeval with the first operations of the intellect.'[4] Stewart distinguishes, therefore, between judgments which 'are formed as soon as the terms of the proposition are understood' and judgments which 'result so necessarily from the earliest constitution of the mind, that we act upon them from our earliest infancy, without ever making them an object of reflection'.[5] In addition, there are judgments which are arrived at by reasoning.

The judgments which result from the earliest constitution of the mind are called by Stewart 'fundamental laws of human

---

[1] *Elements*, 2, 1, 4, p. 301.　　　[2] 1, 5.　　　[3] *Outlines*, 1, 9, 71; 11, p. 28.
[4] *Ibid*.　　　[5] *Outlines*, 1, 9, 70; p. 27.

belief'. The word 'principle' is, in his opinion, misleading. For we cannot draw any inferences from them for the enlargement of human knowledge. 'Abstracted from other data, they are perfectly barren in themselves.'[1] They should not be confused with 'principles of reasoning'. They are involved in the exercise of our rational powers; but it is with the rise of philosophical reflection that they are thought about, becoming objects of the mind's attention. As for the criterion by which we can distinguish fundamental laws of belief, universality of belief is not the only one. Stewart mentions with approval two criteria proposed by Buffier.[2] First, the truths in question should be such that it is impossible either to attack or to defend them except by means of propositions which are neither more evident nor more certain than they are. Secondly, the practical influence of the truths must extend even to those who theoretically dispute their authority.

It is clear that Stewart is more careful than Reid in trying to state his position exactly. And this care can be frequently seen in his treatment of particular points. For example, he explains with care that though the immediate evidence of consciousness assures us of the present existence of sensations or of affections, desires, and so on, we are not immediately conscious of the mind itself in the sense of enjoying a direct intuition of the mind. True, 'the very first exercise of consciousness necessarily implies a belief, not only of the present existence of what is felt, but of the present existence of *that* which feels and thinks. . . . Of these facts, however, it is the former alone of which we can properly be said to be conscious, agreeably to the rigorous interpretation of the expression.'[3] Consciousness of the self as subject of sensation or feeling is posterior in the order of nature, if not in the order of time, to consciousness of the sensation or feeling. In other words, awareness of our existence is 'a concomitant or accessory of the exercise of consciousness'.[4] Again, when writing about our belief in the uniformity of nature, Stewart is careful to discuss the meaning of the word 'law' when we talk about laws of nature. When used in experimental philosophy, 'it is more correctly logical to consider it as merely a statement of some general fact with respect to the order of nature—a fact which has been found to hold uniformly in

---

[1] *Elements*, 2, I, I, 2, 4; III, p. 45.
[2] Claude Buffier (1661–1737), a French Jesuit, published a *Traité des vérités premières* (1717) in which he treated of the maxims of common sense.
[3] *Elements*, 2, I, I, 2, I; III, p. 41.
[4] *Ibid.*

our past experience, and on the continuance of which, in future, the constitution of our mind determines us confidently to rely'.[1] We should beware of conceiving so-called laws of nature as acting in the capacity of efficient causes.

The moral faculty is 'an original principle of our constitution which is not resolvable into any other principle or principles more general than itself; in particular, it is not resolvable into self-love or a prudential regard to our own interest'.[2] 'There are, in all languages, words equivalent to *duty* and to *interest*, which men have constantly distinguished in their signification.'[3] By this faculty we perceive the rightness or wrongness of actions. And we must distinguish between this perception and the accompanying emotion of pleasure or pain which varies according to the degree of a person's moral sensibility. We must also distinguish the perception of the merit or demerit of the agent. Hutcheson went wrong by making no distinction between the rightness of an action as approved by our reason and its aptitude to excite a man's moral emotions. Again, Shaftesbury and Hutcheson tended to neglect the fact that the objects of moral approbation are actions, not affections. In other words, Stewart disliked the tendency of the moral sense theorists to turn ethics into aesthetics, though he also thought that some writers, such as Clarke, had paid too little attention to our moral feelings. As for the term 'moral sense', considered in itself, Stewart has no objection to its retention. As he remarks, we habitually speak of a 'sense of duty' and it would be pedantic to object to 'moral sense'. At the same time he insists that when a man asserts that an act is right he intends to say something which is true. Moral discrimination is a rational operation, just as much as is perception of the fact that the three angles of a triangle together equal one right angle. 'The exercise of our reason in the two cases is very different; but in both cases we have a perception of *truth*, and are impressed with an irresistible conviction that the truth is immutable and independent of the will of any being whatever.'[4]

Stewart considers the obvious objection to the theory that rightness and wrongness are qualities of actions, which are perceived by the mind; namely, the objection that people's ideas of what is right and wrong have varied from country to country and

---

[1] *Elements*, 2, 1, 2, 4, 2; III, pp. 159–60.
[2] *Active and Moral Powers*, 2, 3; VI, p. 233.
[3] *Ibid.*, 2, 2; VI, p. 220.
[4] *Ibid.*, 2, 5, 1; VI, p. 299

from age to age. And he thinks that this variety can be explained in a manner which leaves his theory of objective moral qualities intact. Physical conditions, for instance, may influence the moral judgment. Where nature produces in abundance the necessities of life, it is only to be expected that men should have looser ideas about the rights of property than those which prevail elsewhere. Again, different speculative opinions or convictions can influence people's perceptions of right and wrong.

On the subject of moral obligation Stewart expresses his agreement with Butler's insistence on the supreme authority of conscience. And he commends the statement of a Dr. Adams that '*right* implies duty in its ideas'. Stewart's point is that 'it is absurd to ask *why* we are bound to practise virtue. The very notion of virtue implies the notion of obligation.'[1] Obligation cannot be interpreted simply in terms of the notions of reward and punishment. For these presuppose the existence of obligation. And if we interpret obligation in terms of the divine will and command, we shall find ourselves involved, in Stewart's opinion, in a vicious circle.

In conclusion, we can consider very briefly Stewart's line of argument for the existence of God. The process of reasoning, he tells us, 'consists only of a single step, and the premises belong to that class of first principles which form an essential part of the human constitution. These premises are *two* in number. The one is, that everything which begins to exist must have a cause. The other, that a combination of means conspiring to a particular end implies intelligence.'[2]

Stewart accepts Hume's contention that every attempt to demonstrate the truth of the first premiss involves assuming what has to be proved. He also accepts Hume's analysis of causality, so far as natural philosophy is concerned. 'In natural philosophy, when we speak of one thing being the cause of another, all that we mean is, that the two things are *constantly conjoined*, so that when we see the one we may expect the other. These conjunctions we learn from experience alone. . . .'[3] Causes in this sense can be called 'physical causes'. But there is also a metaphysical sense of causality, in which the word implies necessary connection. And causes in this sense can be called 'metaphysical or efficient causes'. As for the question how this idea of causation, power or efficacy

[1] *Active and Moral Powers*, 2, 6; VI, p. 319.
[2] *Ibid.*, 3, 1; VII, p. 11.
[3] *Ibid.*, 3, 2, 1; VII, p. 24.

is acquired, Stewart says that 'the most probable account of the matter seems to be that the idea of Causation or Power necessarily accompanies the perception of change in a way somewhat analogous to that in which sensation implies a being who feels, and thought a being who thinks'.[1] In any case the truth of the proposition that everything which begins to exist must have a cause is intuitively perceived. And in applying this principle Stewart is prepared to admit that all the events which constantly take place in the material universe are the immediate effects of divine causation and power, God being the constantly operative efficient cause in the material world. Stewart is thus in agreement with Clarke's view that the course of nature is, strictly speaking, nothing but the will of God producing certain effects in a continuous, regular and uniform manner. In other words, we can consider nature from the point of view either of the physicist or of the metaphysician. In the first case the empiricist analysis of causality is all that is required. In the second case (that is to say, if we grant the reality of active power in the material world), we must see natural events as effects of a divine agency. But for this argument to have any cogency, it is obviously necessary to suppose that we cannot discern active power and efficient causes (in Stewart's sense of the term) in nature. Further, as Stewart notes, this line of reasoning does not of itself show the unicity of God.

Stewart then turns to consider our apprehension of intelligence or design as manifested in the 'conspiration' of different means to a particular end. He argues first that we have intuitive knowledge of the connection between observed evidence of design and a designer or designers. That the combination of a variety of means to produce a particular effect implies design is not a generalization from experience; nor can it be demonstrated. We perceive its truth intuitively. Secondly, Stewart argues that there are evidences of design in the universe. He cites, for example, the way in which Nature repairs, in many cases, injuries to the human body. Thirdly, he argues that there is one uniform plan, which proves the unicity of God. He subsequently goes on to consider the moral attributes of the Deity.

In his writings Stewart manifests his wide reading and his power of using material taken from a great variety of philosophers in developing his system. But the essential features of his system are

---

[1] *Active and Moral Powers*, 3, 2, 1; VII, p. 18.

evidently derived mainly from Reid. What he does is to systema-
tize and develop Reid's ideas, even though he criticizes him from
time to time. Of Kant, Stewart knew comparatively little, as he
himself observes. He shows, indeed, some appreciation of the
German philosopher, and he concedes that Kant had a glimpse of
the truth. But he was evidently both revolted and mystified by
Kant's style, and in his *Philosophical Essays*[1] he speaks of Kant's
'scholastic barbarism' and of the 'scholastic fog through which he
delights to view every object to which he turns his attention'.
Reid, if he had been able to, might have learned something from
Kant; but it is obvious that the former was, in Stewart's opinion, a
superior philosophical thinker.

8. We have seen that Stewart, and indeed Reid before him,
accepted Hume's analysis of causality as far as natural philosophy
is concerned. Thomas Brown (1778–1820), a pupil of Stewart and
his successor in the chair of moral philosophy at Edinburgh,
proceeded further in the empiricist direction. Indeed, he may be
regarded as a link between the Scottish philosophy of common
sense and the nineteenth-century empiricism of J. S. Mill and
Alexander Bain.

In his *Inquiry into the Relation of Cause and Effect* (1804, later
revised and enlarged), Brown defines a cause as 'that which immediately precedes any change, and which, existing at any time
in similar circumstances, has been always, and will be always,
immediately followed by a similar change'.[2] The elements, and the
only elements combined in the idea of cause are priority in the
observed sequence and invariable antecedence. Power is only
another word for expressing 'the antecedent itself, and the invari-
ableness of the relation'.[3] When, therefore, we say 'that A is the
cause of B, it may be allowed that we mean only that A is followed
by B, has always been followed by B, and, we believe, will be
always followed by B'.[4] Similarly, 'when I say that I have mentally
the power of moving my hand, I mean nothing more than that,
when my body is in a sound state, and no foreign force is imposed
on me, the motion of my hand will always follow my desire to
move it'.[5] Thus in mental phenomena, as in physical phenomena,
causality is to be analysed in the same way.

Brown rejects Stewart's distinction between physical and
efficient causality. 'The *physical* cause which has been, is, and

---

[1] Cf., *Works*, v, pp. 117–18, note, and p. 422.　　[2] i, 1; 1835 edition, p. 13.
[3] *Ibid.*, p. 14.　　[4] *Ibid.*, i, 3, p. 32.　　[5] *Ibid.*, p. 38.

always will be, followed by a certain change is the *efficient* cause of that change; or if it be not the efficient cause of it, it is necessary that a definition of efficiency should be given us, which involves more than the certainty of a particular change, as consequent in instant sequence. Causation is efficiency; and a cause which is not efficient, is truly no cause whatever.'[1] The defenders of the distinction between efficient and physical causes have merely asserted that there is a distinction without explaining its nature. It is true that God is the ultimate cause of all things; but this is no reason for saying that there are no other efficient causes.

Given this analysis of causality, it may well be asked with what justification Brown is classified with the philosophers of 'common sense' rather than as a follower of Hume. The answer is that though Brown accepts Hume's analysis of causal relation in terms of invariable or uniform sequence, he rejects the latter's account of the origin of our belief in necessary connection and in causation in general. According to Brown, there is an original belief in causation, which is antecedent to any effects of custom and association. 'The belief of regularity of sequence is so much the result of an original principle of the mind, that it arises constantly, on the observation of change, whatever the observed antecedents and consequents may have been, and requires the whole counter-acting influence of our past knowledge to save us from the mistakes into which we should thus, at every moment, be in danger of falling.'[2] Further, 'the uniformity of the course of Nature, in the similar returns of future events, is not a conclusion of reason . . . but is a single intuitive judgment that, in certain circumstances, rises in the mind inevitably and with irresistible conviction. Whether true or false, the belief is in these cases felt, and it is felt without even the possibility of a perceived customary conjunction of the particular antecedent and the particular consequent.'[3] Belief in the uniformity of nature is not the result of custom and association; it is antecedent to observed sequences. What experience of customary succession does is to enable us to determine particular antecedents and their particular consequents. The trouble with Hume is his determination to derive all ideas from impressions, which forces him to explain belief in necessary connection and in the uniformity of nature in terms of observation of single sequences. But this belief is prior to such observation, and

---

[1] *Inquiry into the Relation of Cause and Effect*, 1, 5; 1835 edition, p. 89.
[2] *Ibid.*, 4, 2, pp. 286–7.   [3] *Ibid.*, p. 290.

it is intuitive in character. 'In ascribing the belief of efficiency to such a principle, we place it, then, on a foundation as strong as that on which we suppose our belief of an external world, and even of our own identity, to rest.'[1] Brown goes further than Reid or Stewart in accepting Hume's analysis of causality, which he is prepared to extend to the mental sphere, and even to divine power. But he endeavours to combine this acceptance with an acceptance of the doctrine of intuitive beliefs, which was characteristic of the Scottish philosophy of common sense. In so doing he gives a new colouring to Reid's first principles. He tells us, for instance, that 'the proposition, *Everything which begins to exist must have had a cause of its existence,* is not itself an independent axiom, but is reducible to this more general law of thought, *Every change has had a cause of its existence in some circumstance, or combination of circumstances, immediately prior*'.[2]

In his *Lectures on the Philosophy of the Human Mind*, which were published after his death, Brown assimilates the study of mental phenomena to that of physical phenomena. 'The same great objects are to be had in view, and no other—the analysis of what is complex, and the observation and arrangement of the sequences of phenomena, as respectively antecedent and consequent.'[3] In both cases our knowledge is confined to phenomena. 'The philosophy of mind and the philosophy of matter agree in this respect, that our knowledge is, in both, confined to the mere phenomena.'[4] Brown does not question the existence of matter or the existence of mind; but we use these words, he insists, to connote the unknown causes of the respective sets of phenomena. Our knowledge of mind and matter is relative. We know matter as it affects us and mind in the varying mental phenomena of which we are conscious. A science of mind, therefore, so far as it is open to us, will consist in the analysis of mental phenomena and in the observation and systematic arrangement of causal sequences, that is, of regular sequences, in these phenomena.

The announcement of this programme does not mean, however, that Brown has abandoned belief in primary truths or intuited principles. He does, indeed, remark that the assertion of such principles can be carried to 'an extravagant and ridiculous length —as, indeed, seems to me to have been the case in the works of Dr. Reid and some other Scotch philosophers, his contemporaries

[1] *Inquiry into the Relation of Cause and Effect*, 4, 7, pp. 377–8.
[2] *Ibid.*, Note H, p. 435.   [3] *Ibid.*, Lecture 9; vol. 1, p. 178, 1824 edition.
[4] *Ibid.*, Lecture 10; 1, p. 194.

and friends'.[1] If this habit is indulged, it only encourages mental laziness. At the same time 'it is not less certain that of our mental nature such principles are truly a part'.[2] Brown does not attempt to give a list of those principles, but among first principles of belief he mentions 'that on which I conceive the conviction of our identity to be founded'.[3] Our belief in our identities as permanent beings is universal, irresistible and immediate; and it is prior to, or presupposed by, reasoning. It is, therefore, an intuitive belief. Brown finds that it is 'another form of the faith which we put in memory':[4] it is 'founded on an essential principle of our constitution, in consequence of which it is impossible for us to consider our successive feelings[5] without regarding them as truly our successive feelings, states, or affections of our thinking substance'.[6]

In the same *Lectures* Brown vigorously criticizes Reid's refutation of the 'theory of ideas'. In his opinion Reid attributed to the majority of philosophers a view which they did not in fact maintain, namely, that ideas are entities which occupy a position intermediate between perceptions and the things perceived. In reality, Brown maintains, these philosophers understood by ideas the perceptions themselves. Further, he finds himself in agreement with the view of these philosophers that it is sensations and perceptions of which we are immediately aware, and not of an independent material world. Sensations, when referred to an external cause, are called perceptions. The question arises, therefore, what is this reference, in consequence of which a new name is given to sensations? For Brown, 'it is the suggestion of some extended resisting object, the presence of which had before been found to be attended with that particular sensation, which is now again referred to it'.[7] In other words, our primary knowledge of the material is due to touch. More accurately, it is due to muscular sensations. The child encounters resistance and, guided by the principle of causation, it finds the cause of this resistance in something other than itself. Brown distinguished between muscular sensations and other feelings commonly ascribed to the sense of touch. 'The feeling of resistance is, I conceive, to be ascribed, not to our organ of touch, but to our muscular frame, to which I have already more than once directed your attention as forming a distinct organ of sense.'[8] Our notion of extension is originally due

---

[1] *Lectures on the Philosophy of the Human Mind*, Lecture 13; 1, p. 265.
[2] *Ibid.*, p. 268. [3] *Ibid.* [4] *Ibid.*, p. 273.
[5] Brown gives to the word 'feeling' a very wide range of meaning.
[6] *Ibid.*, p. 275. [7] *Ibid.*, Lecture 25; 1, p. 546. [8] *Ibid.*, Lecture 22; 1, p. 460.

to muscular sensations as known in time. If a child gradually stretches its arm or closes its hand, it has a succession of feelings, and this gives it the notion of length. The notions of breadth and depth can be analogously explained. But in order to arrive at belief in an independent material reality the muscular feeling of resistance must be added to the notion of extension. 'Extension, resistance—to combine these simple notions into something which is not ourselves, and to have the notion of matter, are precisely the same thing.'[1] The feelings of extension and resistance are referred to an external, material world; but this independent world, considered in itself, is unknown to us.

From what has been said hitherto it is clear that Brown was very far from simply carrying on the positions adopted by Reid and Stewart. Indeed, he frequently adopted a critical attitude towards their opinions. We would expect him, then, to show a similar vigorous independence in his ethical reflections. In Brown's opinion moral philosophy has suffered from the making of distinctions which seemed to those who made them to be the result of accurate analysis, but which were only verbal. For example, some have thought that questions such as, what makes an action virtuous, what constitutes the moral obligation to perform certain actions, and what constitutes the merit of the agent of such actions, are distinct questions. But 'to say that any action which we are considering is right or wrong, and to say that the person who performed it has moral merit or demerit, are to say precisely the same thing'.[2] 'To have merit, to be virtuous, to have done our duty, to have acted in conformity with obligation—all have reference to one feeling of the mind, that feeling of approbation which attends the consideration of virtuous actions. They are merely, as I have said, different modes of stating one simple truth; that the contemplation of anyone, acting as we have done in a particular case, excites a feeling of moral approval.'[3] We can ask, of course, why it seems to us virtuous to act in this or that way. Why do we have a feeling of obligation? And so on. But 'the only answer which we can give to these questions is the same to all, that it is impossible for us to consider the action without feeling that, by acting in this way, we should look upon ourselves, and others would look on us, with approving regard; and that if we were to act in a different way we should look upon ourselves, and

---

[1] *Lectures on the Philosophy of the Human Mind,* Lecture 24; I, p. 508.
[2] *Ibid.,* Lecture 73; III, p. 529.   [3] *Ibid.,* p. 532.

others would look upon us, with abhorrence, or at least with disapprobation'.[1] If we say that we regard an action as virtuous because it tends to the public good or because it represents the divine will, similar questions will recur, and a like answer will have to be given. Certainly, we can and do consider actions in themselves, apart from any particular agent, and we can and do consider virtuous qualities or dispositions in themselves; but here we have abstractions, useful abstractions no doubt, but still abstractions.

Brown insists, however, that when he says that it is vain to ask why we feel the obligation to perform certain actions, he is speaking of inquiry into the nature of the mind. If we look beyond the mind itself, we can find the answer. The case of our belief in the uniformity of nature presents us with an analogous situation. If we consider the mind alone, we cannot say why we expect future events to resemble past events: we can only say that the mind is so constituted. But there are obvious reasons why the mind has been so constituted. For example, if we had been constituted with the opposite expectation, we could not live; we could not provide for the future, nor could we take steps to avoid dangers by learning from past experience. Similarly, if we had no feelings of moral approbation and disapprobation, if there were no virtue or vice, no love of God or man, human life would be wretched in the extreme. 'We know, then, in this sense, why our mind has been so constituted as to have these emotions; and our inquiry leads us, as all other inquiries ultimately lead us, to the provident goodness of him by whom we were made.'[2]

Given this view of moral approbation, Hume's utilitarian interpretation of morality is naturally rejected by Brown. 'That virtuous actions do all tend in some greater or less degree to the advantage of the world, is indeed a fact, with respect to which there can be no doubt.'[3] But 'the approbation which we give to actions as virtuous, whether we be ourselves the agents, or merely consider the actions of others, is not given to them simply as useful. Utility, in either case, is not the measure of moral approbation. . . .'[4] For the matter of that, conduciveness to the public good is itself an object of moral approbation. The reason why thinkers such as Hume find it easy to slip into a utilitarian interpretation of morality is that there is an 'independent pre-

[1] Lectures on the Philosophy of the Human Mind, Lecture 73; III, p. 533.
[2] Ibid., p. 543.   [3] Ibid., Lecture 77; IV, p. 29.   [4] Ibid., p. 51.

established relation of virtue and utility',[1] established, that is to say, by God.

Does this mean that Brown accepts the theory of a moral sense? If by the word 'sense' were meant merely susceptibility, then, inasmuch as we undoubtedly possess a susceptibility for moral feelings, we could speak of a moral sense. In this case, however, we should have to speak of as many 'senses' as there are distinguishable kinds of feeling. But the moral sense theorists understood something more by 'sense' than mere susceptibility. They were thinking of a peculiar moral sense analogous to the various senses such as sight and touch. And Brown can 'discover no peculiar analogy to perceptions or sensations, in the philosophical meaning of those terms, and the phrase "moral sense", therefore, I consider as having had a very unfortunate influence on the controversy as to the original moral differences of actions, from the false analogies which it cannot fail to suggest'.[2] Hutcheson's great mistake was to believe that there are certain moral qualities in actions, which excite in us ideas of those qualities in the same way that external things give us ideas of colour, form and hardness. But right and wrong are not qualities of things. 'They are words expressive only of relation, and relations are not existing parts of objects or things. . . . There is no right nor wrong, virtue nor vice, merit or demerit, existing independently of the agents who are virtuous or vicious; and, in like manner, if there had been no moral emotions to arise on the contemplation of certain actions, there would have been no virtue, vice, merit or demerit, which express only relations to these emotions.'[3]

There is another error to which some philosophers have been prone. In considering the aesthetic emotions they suppose that there is a universal beauty which is diffused, as it were, in all beautiful things. Similarly, they have imagined that there must be one universal virtue, diffused in all virtuous actions. Hence some have made of benevolence a universal virtue. 'There is no virtue, however, as I have already repeatedly said; there are only virtuous actions; or, to speak still more correctly, only virtuous agents: and it is not one virtuous agent only, or any number of virtuous agents, acting in one uniform manner, that excite our moral emotion of regard; but agents acting in many different ways —in ways that are not less different in themselves, on account of

---

[1] *Lectures on the Philosophy of the Human Mind*, Lecture 77; IV, p. 54.
[2] *Ibid.*, Lecture 82; IV, pp. 149–50.
[3] *Ibid.*, pp. 161–2.

the real or supposed simplicity of the generalizations and classifications which we may have made.'[1] Brown does not deny, of
course, that we can generalize and classify. But he rejects any
attempt to reduce all virtuous actions to one class.

Brown's 'empiricist' tendency shows itself in what he has to say
on evidence for God's existence. He remarks several times that he
rejects all *a priori* reasonings on this matter, and, indeed, all
metaphysical arguments except in so far as they can be reduced
to what he calls the physical argument. 'The arguments commonly
termed metaphysical I have always regarded as absolutely void of
force, unless in as far as they proceed on a tacit assumption of the
physical argument.'[2] By the physical argument Brown means the
argument from design. 'The universe exhibits indisputable marks
of design, and is, therefore, not self-existing, but the work of a
designing mind. There exists, then, a great designing mind.'[3]
Brown argues that the universe exhibits a harmony of relations,
and that to perceive this harmony is to perceive design. 'That is
to say, it is impossible for us to perceive them without feeling
immediately, that the harmony of parts with parts, and of their
results with each other, must have had its origin in some designing
mind.'[4] But Brown seems to take it for granted that this argument
also shows the existence of God as maker or author of the universe.
He does not appear to realize that the argument from design,
considered by itself, shows only that there is a designer, not that
there is, in the strict sense, a creator.

When speaking of the divine unity, Brown again rejects all
metaphysical arguments as, at best, 'a laborious trifling with
words, which either signify nothing or prove nothing'.[5] Hence the
only divine unity which we can prove is 'wholly relative to that
one design which we are capable of tracing in the frame of the
universe'.[6] And this anti-metaphysical attitude comes out again
in his treatment of the divine goodness. That God is not malevo-
lent 'the far greater proportion of the marks of benevolent intention sufficiently indicates'.[7] In other words, Brown argues that if
we weigh the proportion of good to evil in the universe, we shall
find that the former exceeds the latter. As for the moral goodness
of God, His character is manifested in His gift to man of moral
feelings. And we on our part are led by our very nature to regard

[1] *Lectures on the Philosophy of the Human Mind*, Lecture 82; IV, p. 169.
[2] *Ibid.*, Lecture 93; IV, p. 387.   [3] *Ibid.*, Lecture 92; IV, p. 369.
[4] *Ibid.*, Lecture 93; IV, pp. 387–8.   [5] *Ibid.*, p. 391.
[6] *Ibid.*   [7] *Ibid.*, p. 407.

what we look on with moral approbation or disapprobation as 'objects of approbation or disapprobation, not to all mankind only, but to every being whom we imagine to contemplate the actions, and especially to him who, as quickest to perceive and to know, must, as we think, by this very superiority of discernment, be quickest also to approve and condemn'.[1]

Obviously, if anyone accepts the kind of metaphysical arguments which Brown rejects, he will look on the latter's natural theology as constituting one of the weakest, or more probably the weakest, parts of his philosophy. If, however, he thinks that propositions about God are at best empirical hypotheses, he will presumably sympathize with Brown's general attitude, even if he does not regard the latter's arguments as cogent.

9. Kant's opinion of the Scottish philosophers of common sense was not a high one. His remarks about them in the introduction to the *Prolegomena to any Future Metaphysic* have been often quoted. Hume's opponents, says Kant, such as Reid, Oswald and Beattie, missed the point altogether. For they assumed what he doubted and undertook to prove what he never thought of disputing. Further, they appealed to common sense as to an oracle, using it as a criterion of truth when they had no rational justification to offer for their opinions. In any case 'I should think Hume might fairly have laid as much claim to sound sense as Beattie, and besides to a critical understanding such as the latter did not possess. . . .'

This judgment was doubtless prompted primarily by Beattie's performance; and he was far from being the best representative of the Scottish School. However, there is obviously some justification for Kant's remarks. After all, Brown, himself a Scottish philosopher, drew attention to the undesirability of laying down a multitude of inviolable first principles of common sense. We cannot set bounds in this dogmatic way to critical analysis. Further, both Stewart and Brown noted that Hume had often been misunderstood by the earlier philosophers of the common-sense tradition. And they were justified in doing so.

Further, it may appear that the development of the Scottish common-sense philosophy provides empirical evidence for the soundness of Kant's criticism. For, as we have seen, this movement which began, in large part at least, as a vigorous reaction against Hume's theories, gradually came nearer, on several important

[1] *Lectures on the Philosophy of the Human Mind*, Lecture 95; IV, p. 444.

points, to the latter's philosophy. Moreover, from some of Brown's positions to the position of J. S. Mill there was no great step to be taken. For example, though Brown affirmed the existence of an independent material world, matter in itself was, in his opinion, unknown by us. We know sensations, and belief in the independent material world arises through a combination of the acquired notion of extension and the notion of external reference acquired by muscular experience of resistance. The distance does not seem to be so very great from this position to Mill's view of the world as a permanent possibility of sensations. It is thus arguable that in proportion as the employment of critical analysis advanced within the common-sense School, this philosophy approximated more and more to empiricism, and that this is an indication of its untenable character in the earlier forms which were attacked by Kant.

Yet the common-sense philosophy obviously had something to say for itself. Reid's attack on the 'theory of ideas' was not entirely without point. It is true, as Brown remarks, that Reid inclined to treat the philosophers who spoke of perceiving ideas as though they all held pretty much the same theory, namely, that the ideas which we perceive are intermediate entities between minds and things. And this interpretation does not fit Berkeley, for instance, who called sensible things 'ideas'. But it is applicable to Locke, if we concentrate on one of his ways of speaking. In any case it is arguable that the language of ideas was unfortunate, that the philosophers who used this language became victims of their own way of speaking and that what Reid was doing was to recall philosophers to the position of common sense and to underline the need for delimiting carefully the meanings of terms such as 'idea' and 'perception'. Again, when Reid objected to the epistemological atomism of Locke and Hume and drew attention to the fundamental role of judgment, maintaining that the supposed elements of cognition were obtained by analytic abstraction from a larger whole, he was putting forward a point of view which certainly merited attention.

As for the general recall to common sense, some distinctions must, I think, be made. In so far as the Scottish philosophers were suggesting that we should regard with some suspicion those theories which are incompatible with common experience or which are plainly at variance with the beliefs and presuppositions which are necessary for life, their point of view was sound. At the same time people like Beattie do not seem to have understood that David Hume was not concerned to reject natural beliefs or to deny the standpoint of common sense. He was concerned to examine the theoretical reasons which can be adduced to support these beliefs. And even when he thought that no valid theoretical reasons or proofs could be adduced, he did not suggest that we should abandon these beliefs. Indeed, his point of view was that in practice belief must prevail over the dissolvent effects of the critical reason. Hence the Scottish philosophers' criticism of Hume frequently missed the mark altogether. It was not sufficient to offer a large number of principles of common sense, especially when the tendency was to depict these principles as representing inevitable propensities of the human mind. What they should have done, if they wished to refute Hume, was to show either that the validity of Hume's natural beliefs, which he accounted for with the aid of association, could be theoretically proved or that the so-called principles of common sense really were intuitively perceived self-evident rational principles. Or, more accurately, they should have concentrated on the second alternative, since in their view the first principles of common sense could not be demonstrated. It was not enough merely to assert the principles. For it would have been open to Hume to retort that in some cases at least what were called principles of common sense simply expressed natural beliefs which could be accounted for psychologically but which could not be philosophically proved, however necessary they might be for practical life. It is really no great matter for surprise that the Scottish philosophy of common sense was overshadowed in the nineteenth century by empiricism on the one hand and idealism on the other. And when something resembling a philosophy of common sense came again to the fore in contemporary British thought it took a new form, namely, the form of linguistic analysis.

On the continent of Europe the Scottish movement was not without success. Through Victor Cousin (1792–1867) in particular it exercised a very considerable influence on what was for a time the official philosophy of France. The French philosophers who were influenced by the Scottish movement saw further than the features which excited Kant's critical comments. They saw, for example, and approved the direction of the mind towards ethical and practical questions, the use of the experimental method, and the tendency to concentrate on available factual data rather than on abstract speculations. And it is true in a sense that for the

Scottish thinkers philosophy was less of a game than it was for their great compatriot, Hume. It would, indeed, be misleading to suggest that for Hume philosophy was no more than a game. He thought, for example, that an analytic and critical philosophy can be a powerful instrument for diminishing fanaticism and intolerance. And, on the positive side, he envisaged the rise of a science of man which might be analogous to the physical science of Galileo and Newton. At the same time he did sometimes speak of his philosophy, especially in what appeared to Reid as its more destructive aspects, as a matter for the study, as having little connection with practical life. Reid and Stewart, however, evidently regarded philosophy as of importance for man's ethical and political life; and they were concerned not merely to investigate why people think and speak as they do, but to reinforce the convictions which they regarded as valuable. And their French admirers, accustomed to see in philosophy a guide to life, found this element in their thought congenial.

Reid's great thesis, so far as his attack on Hume was concerned, was that the latter simply drew in a clear and consistent manner the conclusions which followed from the premises laid down by his predecessors. And he was thus partly responsible for a common and influential interpretation of the development of classical British empiricism. To a certain extent this thesis was shared by Kant, to the extent at least of considering that a fresh hypothesis should be prepared and that a fresh explanation was needed of man's cognitive life and of his moral and aesthetic judgments. But though Hume provided, in part, a point of departure not only for Reid but also for Kant, the latter is of vastly more importance in the history of philosophy than the philosopher of common sense. And his system will be considered at some length in the next volume.

APPENDIX

A SHORT BIBLIOGRAPHY

For general remarks and for General Works see the Bibliography at the end of Volume IV, *Descartes to Leibniz*.

Chapters I–II: Hobbes

Texts

Hobbes: *Opera philosophica quae latine scripsit*. Edited by W. Molesworth. 5 vols. London, 1839–45.

The English Works of Thomas Hobbes. Edited by W. Molesworth. 11 vols. London, 1839–45.

The Metaphysical System of Hobbes. Selections edited by M. W. Calkins. Chicago, 1905.

Hobbes: Selections. Edited by F. J. E. Woodbridge. New York, 1930.

The Elements of Law, Natural and Politic (together with *A Short Treatise on First Principles* and parts of the *Tractatus opticus*), edited by F. Tönnies. Cambridge, 1928 (2nd edition).

De Cive or the The Citizen. Edited by S. P. Lamprecht. New York, 1949.

Leviathan. Edited with an introduction by M. Oakeshott. Oxford, 1946.

Leviathan. With an introduction by A. D. Lindsay. London (*E.L.*).

Of Liberty and Necessity, edited with an introduction and notes by Cay von Brockdorff. Kiel, 1938.

Studies

Battelli, G. *Le dottrine politiche dell' Hobbes e dello Spinoza*. Florence, 1904.

Bowle, J. *Hobbes and His Critics: A Study of Seventeenth-Century Constitutionalism*. London, 1951.

Brandt, F. *Thomas Hobbes' Mechanical Conception of Nature*. London, 1928.

Brockdorff, Cay von. *Hobbes als Philosoph, Pädagoge und Soziologe*. Kiel, 1929.
     Die Urform der Computatio sive Logica des Hobbes. Kiel, 1934.

Gooch, G. P. *Hobbes*. London, 1940.

Gough, J. W. *The Social Contract: A Critical Study of Its Development*. Oxford, 1936 (revised edition, 1956).

Hönigswald, R. *Hobbes und die Staatsphilosophie*. Munich, 1924.

Laird, J. *Hobbes*. London, 1934.

Landry, B. *Hobbes*. Paris, 1930.

Levi, A. *La filosofia di Tommaso Hobbes*. Milan, 1929.

Lyon, G. *La philosophie de Hobbes*. Paris, 1893.

Polin, R. *Politique et philosophie chez Thomas Hobbes*. Paris, 1953.

Robertson, G. C. *Hobbes*. Edinburgh and London, 1886.

Rossi, M. M. *Alle fonti del deismo e del materialismo moderno*. 1, *Le origini del deismo*. 2, *L'evoluzione del pensiero di Hobbes*. Florence, 1942.

Stephen, L. *Hobbes*. London, 1904.

Strauss, L. *The Political Philosophy of Hobbes*. Translated by E. M. Sinclair. Oxford, 1936.

Taylor, A. E. *Thomas Hobbes*. London, 1908.

Tönnies, F. *Thomas Hobbes: Leben und Lehre*. Stuttgart, 1925 (3rd edition).

Vialatoux, J. *La cité de Hobbes. Théorie de l'État totalitaire. Essai sur la conception naturaliste de la civilisation*. Paris, 1935.

Chapter III: Herbert of Cherbury and the Cambridge Platonists

1. Lord Herbert of Cherbury

Texts

The Autobiography of Edward, Lord Herbert of Cherbury, with introduction and notes by S. L. Lee. London, 1886.

Tractatus de veritate. London, 1633.

De veritate. Translated with an introduction by M. H. Carré. Bristol, 1937.

De causis errorum. London, 1645.

De religione gentilium. Amsterdam, 1663 and 1670; London, 1705.

De religione laici. Translated with a critical discussion of Lord Herbert's life and philosophy and a comprehensive bibliography of his works by H. R. Hutcheson. New Haven (U.S.A.) and London, 1944.

A Dialogue between a Tutor and His Pupil. London, 1768.

Studies

De Rémusat, C. *Lord Herbert of Cherbúry, sa vie et ses œuvres*. Paris, 1853.

Güttler, C. *Edward, Lord Herbert of Cherbury*. Munich, 1897.

Köttich, R. G. *Die Lehre von den angeborenen Ideen seit Herbert von Cherbury*. Berlin, 1917.

2. Cudworth

Texts

The True Intellectual System of the Universe. London, 1743 (2 vols.),
    1846 (3 vols). There is an edition (London, 1845) by J. Harrison
    with a translation from the Latin of Mosheim's notes.
Treatise concerning Eternal and Immutable Morality. London, 1731.
A Treatise of Free Will. Edited by J. Allen. London, 1838.

Studies

Aspelin, G. Cudworth's Interpretation of Greek Philosophy. Bonn,
    1935.
Beyer, J. Cudworth. Bonn, 1935.
Lowrey, C. E. The Philosophy of Ralph Cudworth. New York, 1884.
Passmore, J. A. Cudworth, an Interpretation. Cambridge, 1950.
Scott, W. R. An Introduction to Cudworth's Treatise. London, 1891.

3. Henry More

Texts

Opera omnia. 3 vols. London, 1679.
Enchiridion metaphysicum. London, 1671.
Enchiridion ethicum. London, 1667.
The Philosophical Writings of Henry More. Selected by F. I.
    Mackinnon. New York, 1925.

Studies

Reimann, H. Henry Mores Bedeutung für die Gegenwart. Sein Kampf
    für Wirken und Freiheit des Geistes. Basel, 1941.

4. Cumberland

Text

De legibus naturae disquisitio philosophica. London, 1672. English
    translation by J. Maxwell. London, 1727.

Studies

Payne, S. Account of the Life and Writings of Richard Cumberland.
    London, 1720.
Spaulding, F. E. Richard Cumberland als Begründer der englischen
    Ethik. Leipzig, 1894.

5. Other Works

Texts

The Cambridge Platonists. Selections from Whichcote, Smith and
    Culverwel, edited by E. T. Campagnac. London, 1901.

Studies

Cassirer, E. *The Platonic Renaissance in England*. Translated by J. P. Pettegrove. Edinburgh and London, 1953.

De Pauley, W. C. *The Candle of the Lord: Studies in the Cambridge Platonists*. New York, 1937.

De Sola Pinto, V. *Peter Sterry; Platonist and Puritan, 1613–1672. A Biographical and Critical Study with Passages selected from His Writings*. Cambridge, 1934.

Mackinnon, F. I. *The Philosophy of John Norris*. New York, 1910.

Muirhead, J. H. *The Platonic Tradition in Anglo-Saxon Philosophy*. London, 1920.

Powicke, F. J. *The Cambridge Platonists: A Study*. London, 1926.

Tulloch, J. *Rational Theology and Christian Philosophy in England in the Seventeenth Century: II, The Cambridge Platonists*. Edinburgh and London, 1872.

Chapters IV–VII: Locke

Texts

The Works of John Locke. 9 vols. London, 1853.

The Philosophical Works of John Locke (*On the Conduct of the Understanding, An Essay concerning Human Understanding, the controversy with Stillingfleet, An Examination of Malebranche's Opinion, Elements of Natural Philosophy* and *Some Thoughts concerning Reading*). Edited by J. A. St. John. 2 vols. London, 1854, 1908.

Locke: Selections. Edited by S. P. Lamprecht. New York, 1928.

An Essay concerning Human Understanding. Edited with introduction and notes by A. C. Fraser. 2 vols. Oxford, 1894.

An Essay concerning Human Understanding. Abridged and edited by A. S. Pringle-Pattison. Oxford, 1924.

An Essay concerning Human Understanding. Abridged and edited by R. Wilburn. London (*E.L.*).

An Early Draft of Locke's Essay, together with Excerpts from His Journal. Edited by R. L. Aaron and J. Gibb. Oxford, 1936.

An Essay concerning the Understanding, Knowledge, Opinion and Assent. Edited by B. Rand. Cambridge (U.S.A.), 1931. (These two last-mentioned works are early drafts of Locke's *Essay*. According to Professor von Leyden, 'the text of the draft edited by Rand can only be considered authentic in a small degree. . . .' See *Notes concerning Papers of John Locke in the Lovelace Collection* by W. von Leyden in *The Philosophical Quarterly*, January 1952, pp. 63–9. The Lovelace Collection is now housed in the Bodleian Library.)

Two Treatises of Government (containing also Filmer's *Patriarcha*, edited by T. I. Cook). New York, 1947.

Two Treatises of Civil Government. With an introduction by W. S. Carpenter. London (*E.L.*).

Second Treatise of Civil Government and Letter on Toleration. Edited by J. W. Gough. Oxford, 1948.

John Locke: Essays on the Law of Nature. Latin text with translation, introduction and notes by W. von Leyden. Oxford, 1954.

Original Letters of Locke, Sidney and Shaftesbury. Edited by T. Forster. London, 1847 (2nd edition).

The Correspondence of John Locke and Edward Clarke. Edited by B. Rand. Cambridge (U.S.A.), 1927. (See the remarks of Professor von Leyden in the article referred to above in the passage in brackets.)

Lettres inédites de John Locke à ses amis N. Thoynard, Ph. van Limborch et E. Clarke. Edited by H. Ollion. The Hague, 1912.

(R. Filmer's *Patriarcha and other Political Works*, edited by P. Laslett, were published at Oxford in 1949.)

Studies

Aaron, R. I. *John Locke*. Oxford, 1955 (2nd edition). (This study can be highly recommended.)
> *Great Thinkers: X, Locke* (in *Philosophy* for 1937).

Alexander, S. *Locke*. London, 1908.

Aspelin, G. *John Locke*. Lund, 1950.

Bastide, C. *John Locke*. Paris, 1907.

Bianchi, G. F. *Locke*. Brescia, 1943.

Carlini, A. *La filosofia di G. Locke*. 2 vols. Florence, 1920.
> *Locke*. Milan, 1949.

Christophersen, H. O. *A Bibliographical Introduction to the Study of John Locke*. Oslo, 1930.

Cousin, V. *La philosophie de Locke*. Paris, 1873 (6th edition).

Fowler, T. *Locke*. London, 1892 (2nd edition).

Fox Bourne, H. R. *The Life of John Locke*. 2 vols. London, 1876.

Fraser, A. C. *Locke*. London, 1890.

Gibson, J. *Locke's Theory of Knowledge and Its Historical Relations*. Cambridge, 1917.

Gough, J. W. *John Locke's Political Philosophy*. Oxford, 1950.
> *The Social Contract* (see *Hobbes*).

Hefelbower, S. G. *The Relation of John Locke to English Deism*. Chicago, 1918.

Hertling, G. V. *Locke und die Schule von Cambridge*. Freiburg i. B., 1892.

Hofstadter, A. *Locke and Scepticism*. New York, 1936.

Kendall, W. *John Locke and the Doctrine of Majority-Rule.* Illinois, 1941.

King, Lord. *The Life and Letters of John Locke.* 2 vols. London, 1858 (3rd edition).
(This work includes some extracts from Locke's journals and an abstract of the *Essay*.)

Klemmt, A. *John Locke: Theoretische Philosophie.* Meisenheim, 1952.

Krakowski, E. *Les sources médiévales de la philosophie de Locke.* Paris, 1915.

Lamprecht, S. P. *The Moral and Political Philosophy of John Locke.* New York, 1918.

MacLean, K. *John Locke and English Literature of the Eighteenth Century.* New Haven (U.S.A.), 1936.

Marion, H. *John Locke, sa vie et son œuvre.* Paris, 1893 (2nd edition).

O'Connor, D. J. *John Locke.* Penguin Books, 1952.

Ollion, H. *La philosophie générale de Locke.* Paris, 1909.

Petzäll, A. *Ethics and Epistemology in John Locke's Essay concerning Human Understanding.* Göteborg, 1937.

Tellkamp, A. *Das Verhältnis John Lockes zur Scholastik.* Münster, 1927.

Thompson, S. M. *A Study of Locke's Theory of Ideas.* Monmouth (U.S.A.), 1934.

Tinivella, G. *Giovanni Locke e i pensieri sull'educazione.* Milan, 1938.

Yolton, J. W. *John Locke and the Way of Ideas.* Oxford, 1956.

Chapter VIII: Boyle and Newton

1. Boyle

Texts

The Works of the Honourable Robert Boyle. Edited by T. Birch. 6 vols. London, 1772 (2nd edition).

Studies

Farrington, F. *A Life of the Honourable Robert Boyle.* Cork, 1917.

Fisher, M. S. *Robert Boyle, Devout Naturalist: A Study in Science and Religion in the Seventeenth Century.* Philadelphia, 1945.

Masson, F. *Robert Boyle.* Edinburgh, 1914.

Meier, J. *Robert Boyles Naturphilosophie.* Munich, 1907.

Mendelssohn, S. *Robert Boyle als Philosoph.* Würzburg, 1902.

More, L. T. *The Life and Works of the Hon. Robert Boyle.* Oxford, 1945.

2. *Newton*

Texts

Opera quae existunt omnia. Edited by S. Horsley. 5 vols. London, 1779–85.

Philosophiae naturalis principia mathematica. Edited by R. Cotes. London, 1713, and reprints.

Mathematical Principles of Natural Philosophy and System of the World. Translated by A. Motte, revised and annotated by F. Cajori. Cambridge, 1934.

Opticks. London, 1730 (4th edition); reprint New York, 1952.

Sir Isaac Newton: Theological Manuscripts. Selected and edited by H. McLachlan. Boston, 1950.

Newton's Philosophy of Nature. Selections from his writings edited by H. S. Thayer. New York, 1953.

Studies

Andrade, E. N. da C. *Sir Isaac Newton.* London, 1954.

Bloch, L. *La Philosophie de Newton.* Paris, 1908.

Clarke, G. N. *Science and Social Welfare in the Age of Newton.* Oxford, 1949 (2nd edition).

De Morgan, A. *Essays on the Life and Work of Newton.* Edited by F. E. B. Jourdain. London, 1914.

Dessauer, F. *Weltfahrt der Erkenntnis. Leben und Werk Isaak Newtons.* Zürich, 1945.

McLachlan, H. *The Religious Opinions of Milton, Locke and Newton.* Manchester, 1941.

More, L. T. *Isaac Newton, A Biography.* New York, 1934.

Randall, J. H., Jr. *Newton's Natural Philosophy: Its Problems and Consequences* (in *Philosophical Essays in Honor of Edgar Arthur Singer, Jr.* Edited by F. P. Clark and M. C. Nahm. Philadelphia, 1942, pp. 335–57).

Rosenberger, I. *Newton und seine physikalischen Prinzipien.* Leipzig, 1893.

Steinmann, H. G. *Ueber den Einfluss Newtons auf die Erkenntnistheorie seiner Zeit.* Bonn, 1913.

Sullivan, J. W. N. *Isaac Newton, 1642–1727.* London, 1938.

Volkmann, P. *Ueber Newtons Philosophia Naturalis.* Königsberg, 1898.

Whittaker, E. T. *Aristotle, Newton, Einstein.* London, 1942.

3. *General Works*

Burtt, E. A. *The Metaphysical Foundations of Modern Physical Science. A Historical and Critical Essay.* London, 1925; revised edition, 1932.

Cassirer, E. *Das Erkenntnisproblem in der Philosophie und Wissenschaft der neueren Zeit.* 3 vols. Berlin, 1906–20; later edition, 1922–3.

Dampier, W. C. *A History of Science and its Relations with Philosophy and Religion.* Cambridge, 1949 (4th edition).

Mach, E. *The Science of Mechanics.* Translated by T. J. MacCormack. La Salle (Illinois), 1942 (5th edition).

Strong, E. W. *Procedures and Metaphysics: A Study in the Philosophy of Mathematical Physical Science in the Sixteenth and Seventeenth Centuries.* Berkeley, U.S.A., 1936.

Chapter IX: Religious Problems

1. *Clarke*

Texts

Works. With a preface by B. Hoadley. 4 vols. London, 1738–42.

Œuvres philosophiques. Translated by C. Jourdain. Paris, 1843.

A Demonstration of the Being and Attributes of God. London, 1705.

A Discourse concerning the Unchangeable Obligations of Natural Religion. London, 1706.

One hundred and Twenty Three Sermons. Edited by J. Clarke. 2 vols. Dublin, 1734.

A Collection of Papers which passed between the late learned Mr. Leibniz and Dr. Clarke. London, 1717.

Studies

Le Rossignol, J. E. *The Ethical Philosophy of Samuel Clarke.* Leipzig, 1892.

Zimmermann, R. *Clarkes Leben und Lehre.* Vienna, 1870.

2. *Toland*

Texts

Christianity not Mysterious. London, 1696.

Pantheisticon. London, 1720.

3. *Tindal*

Text

Christianity as Old as the Creation. London, 1730.

4. Collins

Texts

A Discourse of Free-thinking. London, 1713.

Philosophical Enquiry concerning Human Liberty and Necessity. London, 1715.

A Discourse of the Grounds and Reasons of the Christian Religion. London, 1724.

A Dissertation on Liberty and Necessity. London, 1729.

5. Dodwell

Text

An Epistolary Discourse, proving from the Scriptures and the First Fathers that the Soul is a Principle naturally Mortal. London, 1706.

6. Bolingbroke

Texts

The Philosophical Works of the Right Hon. Henry St. John, Lord Viscount Bolingbroke. Edited by D. Mallet. London, 1754 (5 vols.), 1778, 1809; Philadelphia (4 vols.), 1849.

Letters on the Study and Use of History. London, 1738 and 1752.

Studies

Brosch, M. Lord Bolingbroke. Frankfurt a M., 1883.

Hassall, A. Life of Viscount Bolingbroke. London, 1915 (2nd edition).

James, D. G. The English Augustans: I, The Life of Reason: Hobbes, Locke, Bolingbroke. London, 1949.

Merrill, W. McIntosh. From Statesman to Philosopher. A Study of Bolingbroke's Deism. New York, 1949.

Sichel, W. Bolingbroke and His Times. London, 1902.

7. Deism in General

Carrau, L. La philosophie religieuse en Angleterre depuis Locke jusqu'à nos jours. Paris, 1888.

Farrar, A. S. A Critical History of Free Thought. London, 1862.

Lechler, G. V. Geschichte des englischen Deismus. 2 vols. Stuttgart, 1841.

Leland, J. A View of the Principal Deistical Writers. 2 vols. London, 1837.

Noack, L. *Die englischen, französischen und deutschen Freidenker.* Berne, 1853–5.

Sayous, A. *Les déistes anglais et le christianisme rationaliste.* Paris, 1882.

Stephen, L. *History of English Thought in the Eighteenth Century.* 2 vols. London, 1876.

8. *Butler*

Texts

Works. Edited by J. H. Bernard. 2 vols. London, 1900.

Works. Edited by W. E. Gladstone. 2 vols. London, 1910 (2nd edition).

The analogy of Religion, natural and revealed, to the Constitution and Cause of Nature, with an introduction by R. Bayne. London (*E.L.*).

Fifteen Sermons upon Human Nature, or Man considered as a Moral Agent. London, 1726, 1841, etc.

Fifteen Sermons (and *Dissertation on Virtue*). Edited by W. R. Matthews. London, 1949.

Studies

Broad, C. D. *Five Types of Ethical Theory.* (Chapter III, 'Butler', pp. 53–83.) London, 1930.

Collins, W. L. *Butler.* Edinburgh and London, 1889.

Duncan-Jones, A. *Butler's Moral Philosophy.* Penguin Books, 1952.

Mossner, E. C. *Bishop Butler and the Age of Reason.* New York, 1936.

Norton, W. J. *Bishop Butler, Moralist and Divine.* New Brunswick and London, 1940.

Chapter X: Problems of Ethics

1. *Shaftesbury*

Texts

Characteristics. Edited by J. M. Robertson. 2 vols. London, 1900.

Studies

Brett, R. L. *The third Earl of Shaftesbury: A Study in Eighteenth-Century Literary Theory.* London, 1951.

Elson, C. *Wieland and Shaftesbury.* New York, 1913.

Fowler, T. *Shaftesbury and Hutcheson.* London, 1882.

Kern, J. *Shaftesburys Bild vom Menschen.* Frankfurt a M., 1943.

Lyons, A. *Shaftesbury's Principle of Adaptation to Universal Harmony*. New York, 1909.
Meinecke, F. *Shaftesbury und die Wurzeln des Historismus*. Berlin, 1934.
Osske, I. *Ganzheit, Unendlichkeit und Form. Studien zu Shaftesburys Naturbegriff*. Berlin, 1939.
Rand, B. *Life, Unpublished Letters and Philosophical Regimen of Anthony, Earl of Shaftesbury*. London, 1900.
Spicker, G. *Die Philosophie des Grafen von Shaftesbury*. Freiburg i. B., 1871.
Zani, L. *L'etica di Lord Shaftesbury*. Milan, 1954.

2. *Mandeville*

Texts

The Grumbling Hive or Knaves turned Honest. London, 1705.
The Fable of the Bees or Private Vices Public Benefits. London, 1714, and subsequent editions.
The Fable of the Bees. Edited by F. B. Kaye. Oxford, 1924.

Studies

Hübner, W. *Mandevilles Bienenfabel und die Begründung der praktischen Zweckethik der englischen Aufklärung* (in *Grundformen der englischen Geistesgeschichte*. Edited by P. Meissner. Stuttgart, 1941, pp. 275–331).
Stammler, R. *Mandevilles Bienenfabel*. Berlin, 1918.

3. *Hutcheson*

Texts

Works. 5 vols. Glasgow, 1772.

Studies

Fowler, T. *Shaftesbury and Hutcheson*. London, 1882.
Rampendal, R. *Eine Würdigung der Ethik Hutchesons*. Leipzig, 1892.
Scott, W. R. *Francis Hutcheson, His Life, Teaching and Position in the History of Philosophy*. London, 1900.
Vignone, L. *L'etica del senso morale in Francis Hutcheson*. Milan, 1954.

4. *Butler*

For *Texts* and *Studies* see Bibliography under Chapter IX.

5. *Hartley*

Texts

Observations on Man, His Frame, His Duty and His Expectations.
Edited by J. B. Priestley. 3 vols. London, 1934 (3rd edition).

Studies

Bower, G. S. *Hartley and James Mill*. London, 1881.
Heider, M. *Studien über David Hartley*. Bonn, 1913.
Ribot, T. *Quid David Hartley de consociatione idearum senserit*.
Paris, 1872.
Schoenlank, B. *Hartley und Priestley, die Begründer des Assozia-
tionismus in England*. Halle, 1882.

6. *Tucker*

Text

The Light of Nature Pursued. Edited, with a Life, by H. P. St. John
Mildmay. 7 vols. London, 1805 and reprints.

Study

Harris, W. G. *Teleology in the Philosophy of Joseph Butler and
Abraham Tucker*. Philadelphia, 1942.

7. *Paley*

Texts

Paley's *Works*, first published in 8 vols., 1805–8, have been repub-
lished several times, the number of volumes varying from eight
to one (1851).
The Principles of Moral and Political Philosophy. London, 1785, and
subsequent editions.
*Natural Theology, or Evidences of the Existence and Attributes of the
Deity collected from the Appearances of Nature*. London, 1802,
and subsequent editions.

Study

Stephen, L. *History of English Thought in the Eighteenth Century*.
2 vols. London, 1876. (For Paley see I, pp. 405f., and II, pp.
121f.)

8. *General Works*

Texts (Selections)

Rand, B. *The Classical Moralists*. *Selections*. London, 1910.
Selby-Bigge, L. A. *British Moralists*. 2 vols. Oxford, 1897.

Studies

Bonar, J. *Moral Sense*. London, 1930.
Mackintosh, J. *On the Progress of Ethical Philosophy, chiefly during the XVIIth and XVIIIth Centuries*. Edited by W. Whewell. Edinburgh, 1872 (4th edition).
Martineau, J. *Types of Ethical Theory*. 2 vols. Oxford, 1901 (3rd edition, revised).
Moskowitz, H. *Das moralische Beurteilungsvermögen in der Ethik von Hobbes bis J. S. Mill*. Erlangen, 1906.
Raphael, D. Daiches. *The Moral Sense*. Oxford, 1947.
(This work deals with Hutcheson, Hume, Price and Reid.)
Sidgwick, H. *Outlines of the History of Ethics for English Readers*. London, 1931 (6th edition).

Chapters XI–XIII: Berkeley

Texts

The Works of George Berkeley, Bishop of Cloyne. Edited by A. A. Luce and T. E. Jessop. 9 vols. London, 1948 (critical edition).
The Works of George Berkeley. Edited by A. C. Fraser. 4 vols. Oxford. 1901 (2nd edition).
Philosophical Commentaries, generally called the Commonplace Book. An *editio diplomatica* edited with introduction and notes by A. A. Luce. London, 1944.
(The *Philosophical Commentaries* are also contained in the critical edition of the *Works*, vol. i.)
A New Theory of Vision and other Select Philosophical Writings (*Principles of Human Knowledge* and *Three Dialogues*), with an introduction by A. D. Lindsay. London (*E.L.*).
Berkeley: Selections. Edited by M. W. Calkins. New York, 1929.
Berkeley: Philosophical Writings. Selected and edited by T. E. Jessop. London, 1952.
Berkeley: Alciphron ou le Pense-menu. Translated with introduction and notes by J. Pucelle. Paris, 1952.

Studies

Baladi, N. *La pensée religieuse de Berkeley et l'unité de sa philosophie*. Cairo, 1945.
Bender, F. *George Berkeley's Philosophy re-examined*. Amsterdam, 1946.
Broad, C. D. *Berkeley's Argument about Material Substance*. London, 1942.

Cassirer, E. *Berkeley's System.* Giessen, 1914.

Del Bocca, S. *L'unità del pensiero di Giorgio Berkeley.* Florence, 1937.

Fraser, A. C. *Berkeley.* Edinburgh and London, 1881.

Hedenius, I. *Sensationalism and Theology in Berkeley's Philosophy.* Oxford, 1936.

Hicks, G. Dawes. *Berkeley.* London, 1932.

Jessop, T. E. *Great Thinkers: XI, Berkeley* (in *Philosophy* for 1937).

Johnston, G. A. *The Development of Berkeley's Philosophy.* London, 1923.

Joussain, A. *Exposé critique de la philosophie de Berkeley.* Paris, 1920.

Laky, J. J. *A Study of George Berkeley's Philosophy in the Light of the Philosophy of St. Thomas Aquinas.* Washington, 1950.

Luce, A. A. *Berkeley and Malebranche: A Study in the Origins of Berkeley's Thought.* New York, 1934.
  Berkeley's Immaterialism: A Commentary on His Treatise concerning the Principles of Human Knowledge. London, 1945.
  The Life of George Berkeley, Bishop of Cloyne. London, 1949.

Metz, R. *G. Berkeleys Leben und Lehre.* Stuttgart, 1925.

Oertel, H. J. *Berkeley und die englische Literatur.* Halle, 1934.

Olgiati, F. *L'idealismo di Giorgio Berkeley ed il suo significato storico.* Milan, 1926.

Penjon, A. *Étude sur la vie et sur les œuvres philosophiques de George Berkeley, évêque de Cloyne.* Paris, 1878.

Ritchie, A. D. *George Berkeley's 'Siris'* (British Academy Lecture). London, 1955.

Sillem, E. A. *George Berkeley and the Proofs for the Existence of God.* London, 1957.

Stäbler, E. *George Berkeleys Auffassung und Wirkung in der deutschen Philosophie bis Hegel.* Dresden, 1935.

Stammler, G. *Berkeleys Philosophie der Mathematik.* Berlin, 1922.

Testa, A. *La filosofia di Giorgio Berkeley.* Urbino, 1943.

Warnock, G. J. *Berkeley.* Penguin Books, 1953.

Wild, J. *George Berkeley: A Study of His Life and Philosophy.* London, 1936.

Wisdom, J. O. *The Unconscious Origins of Berkeley's Philosophy.* London, 1953.
  See also *Hommage to George Berkeley.* A commemorative issue of *Hermathena.* Dublin, 1953. And the commemorative issue of the *British Journal for the Philosophy of Science.* Edinburgh, 1953.

Chapters XIV–XVII: Hume

Texts

The Philosophical Works of David Hume. Edited by T. H. Green and
T. H. Grose. 4 vols. London, 1874–5.

A Treatise of Human Nature. Edited by L. A. Selby-Bigge. Oxford,
1951 (reprint of 1888 edition).

A Treatise of Human Nature. With an introduction by A. D. Lindsay.
2 vols. London (*E.L.*).

An Abstract of a Treatise of Human Nature, 1740. Edited by J. M.
Keynes and P. Sraffa. Cambridge, 1938.

*Enquiries concerning the Human Understanding and concerning the
Principles of Morals.* Edited by L. A. Selby-Bigge. Oxford,
1951 (reprint of second edition, 1902).

Dialogues concerning Natural Religion. Edited with an introduction
by N. K. Smith. London, 1947 (2nd edition).

The Natural History of Religion. Edited by H. Chadwick and with
an introduction by H. E. Root. London, 1956.

Political Essays. Edited by C. W. Hendel. New York, 1953.

Hume: Theory of Knowledge. (Selections.) Edited by D. C. Yalden-
Thomson. Edinburgh and London, 1951.

Hume: Theory of Politics. (Selections.) Edited by E. Watkins.
Edinburgh and London, 1951.

Hume: Selections. Edited by C. W. Hendel. New York, 1927.

The Letters of David Hume. Edited by J. V. T. Grieg. 2 vols. Oxford,
1932.

New Letters of David Hume. Edited by R. Klibansky and E. C.
Mossner. Oxford, 1954.

Studies

Bagolini, L. *Esperienza giuridica e politica nel pensiero di David
Hume.* Siena, 1947.

Brunius, T. *David Hume on Criticism.* Stockholm, 1952.

Church, R. W. *Hume's Theory of the Understanding.* London, 1935.

Corsi, M. *Natura e società in David Hume.* Florence, 1954.

Dal Pra, M. *Hume.* Milan, 1949.

Della Volpe, G. *La filosofia dell' esperienza di David Hume.* Florence,
1939.

Didier, J. *Hume.* Paris, 1912.

Elkin, W. B. *Hume, the Relation of the Treatise Book I to the Inquiry.*
New York, 1904.

Glatke, A. B. *Hume's Theory of the Passions and of Morals.* Berkeley,
U.S.A., 1950.

Greig, J. V. T. *David Hume.* (Biography.) Oxford, 1931.

Hedenius, L. *Studies in Hume's Aesthetics.* Uppsala, 1937.

Hendel, C. W. *Studies in the Philosophy of David Hume*. Princeton, U.S.A., 1925.

Huxley, T. *David Hume*. London, 1879.

Jessop, T. E. *A Bibliography of David Hume and of Scottish Philosophy from Francis Hutcheson to Lord Balfour*. London, 1938.

Kruse, V. *Hume's Philosophy in His Principal Work, A Treatise of Human Nature*. Translated by P. E. Federspiel. London, 1939.

Kuypers, M. S. *Studies in the Eighteenth-Century Background of Hume's Empiricism*. Minneapolis, U.S.A., 1930.

Kydd, R. M. *Reason and Conduct in Hume's Treatise*. Oxford, 1946.

Laing, B. M. *David Hume*. London, 1932.
 Great Thinkers: XII, Hume (in *Philosophy* for 1937).

Laird, J. *Hume's Philosophy of Human Nature*. London, 1932.

Leroy, A-L. *La critique et la religion chez David Hume*. Paris, 1930.

MacNabb, D. G. *David Hume: His Theory of Knowledge and Morality*. London, 1951.

Magnino, B. *Il pensiero filosofico di David Hume*. Naples, 1935.

Maund, C. *Hume's Theory of Knowledge: A Critical Examination*. London, 1937.

Metz, R. *David Hume, Leben und Philosophie*. Stuttgart, 1929.

Mossner, E. C. *The Forgotten Hume: Le bon David*. New York, 1943.
 The Life of David Hume. London, 1954. (The fullest biography to date.)

Passmore, J. A. *Hume's Intentions*. Cambridge, 1952.

Price, H. H. *Hume's Theory of the External World*. Oxford, 1940.

Smith, N. K. *The Philosophy of David Hume*. London, 1941.

Chapter XVIII: For and Against Hume

1. *Adam Smith*

Texts

Collected Works. 5 vols. Edinburgh, 1811–12.

The Theory of Moral Sentiments. London, 1759, and subsequent editions.

The Wealth of Nations. 2 vols. London, 1776, and subsequent editions.

The Wealth of Nations. With an introduction by E. R. A. Seligman. 2 vols. London (*E.L.*).

Studies

Bagolini, L. *La simpatia nella morale e nel diritto: Aspetti del pensiero di Adam Smith*. Bologna, 1952.

Chevalier, M. *Étude sur Adam Smith et sur la fondation de la science économique.* Paris, 1874.
Hasbach, W. *Untersuchungen über Adam Smith.* Leipzig, 1891.
Leiserson, A. *Adam Smith y su teoría sobre il salario.* Buenos Aires, 1939.
Limentani, L. *La morale della simpatia di Adam Smith nella storia del pensiero inglese.* Genoa, 1914.
Paszhowsky, W. *Adam Smith als Moralphilosoph.* Halle, 1890.
Rae, J. *Life of Adam Smith.* London, 1895.
Schubert, J. *Adam Smiths Moralphilosophie.* Leipzig, 1890.
Scott, W. R. *Adam Smith as Student and Professor.* Glasgow, 1937.
Small, A. W. *Adam Smith and Modern Sociology.* London, 1909.

2. Price

Text

A Review of the Principal Questions in Morals. Edited by D. Daiches Raphael. Oxford, 1948.

Study

Raphael, D. Daiches. *The Moral Sense.* Oxford, 1947. (This work deals with Hutcheson, Hume, Price and Reid.)

3. Reid

Texts

Works. Edited by D. Stewart. Edinburgh, 1804.
Works. Edited by W. Hamilton. 2 vols. Edinburgh, 1846. (6th edition, with additions by H. L. Mansel, 1863.)
Œuvres complètes de Thomas Reid. Translated by T. S. Jouffroy. 6 vols. Paris, 1828–36.
Essays on the Intellectual Powers of Man. (Abridged.) Edited by A. D. Woozley. London, 1941.
Philosophical Orations of Thomas Reid. (Delivered at Graduation Ceremonies.) Edited by W. R. Humphries. Aberdeen, 1937.

Studies

Bahne-Jensen, A. *Gestaltanalytische Untersuchung zur Erkenntnislehre Reids.* Glückstadt, 1941.
Dauriac, L. *Le réalisme de Reid.* Paris, 1889.
Fraser, A. C. *Thomas Reid.* Edinburgh and London, 1898.
Latimer, J. F. *Immediate Perception as held by Reid and Hamilton considered as a Refutation of the Scepticism of Hume.* Leipzig, 1880.

Peters, R. *Reid als Kritiker von Hume.* Leipzig, 1909.
Sciacca, M. F. *La filosofia di Tommaso Reid con un'appendice sui rapporti con Gallupi e Rosmini.* Naples, 1936.

4. Beattie

Texts

Essay on the Nature and Immutability of Truth. Edinburgh, 1770, and subsequent editions.
Dissertations Moral and Critical. London, 1783.
Elements of Moral Science. 2 vols. Edinburgh, 1790–3.

Study

Forbes, W. *An Account of the Life and Writings of James Beattie.* 2 vols. Edinburgh, 1806 (2nd edition, 3 vols., 1807).

5. Stewart

Texts

Collected Works. Edited by W. Hamilton. 11 vols. Edinburgh, 1854–8.
Elements of the Philosophy of the Human Mind. 3 vols. Edinburgh, 1792–1827, and subsequent editions.
Outlines of Moral Philosophy. Edinburgh, 1793 (with notes by J. McCosh, London, 1863).
Philosophical Essays. Edinburgh, 1810.
Philosophy of the Active and Moral Powers of Man. Edinburgh, 1828.

Study

A Memoir by J. Veitch is included in the 1858 edition of Stewart's *Works.* The latter's eldest son, M. Stewart, published a Memoir in *Annual Biography and Obituary*, 1829.

6. Brown

Texts

An Inquiry into the Relation of Cause and Effect. London, 1818.
Lectures on the Philosophy of the Human Mind. Edited by D. Welsh. 4 vols. Edinburgh, 1820, and subsequent editions.
Lectures on Ethics. London, 1856.

Study

Welsh, D. *Account of the Life and Writings of Thomas Brown.* Edinburgh, 1825.

7. General Works

Text

Selections from the Scottish Philosophy of Common Sense. Chicago, 1915.

Studies

Jessop, T. E. *A Bibliography of David Hume and of Scottish Philosophy from Francis Hutcheson to Lord Balfour.* London, 1938.

Laurie, H. *Scottish Philosophy in its National Development.* Glasgow, 1902.

McCosh, J. *Scottish Philosophy from Hutcheson to Hamilton.* London, 1875.

Pringle-Pattison, A. S. *Scottish Philosophy: A Comparison of the Scottish and German Answers to Hume.* Edinburgh and London, 1885 and subsequent editions.

INDEX

(The principal references are in heavy type. Asterisked numbers refer to bibliographical information. References in ordinary type to a continuous series of pages, e.g. 33–43, do not necessarily indicate continuous treatment. References to two persons together are usually under the person criticized or influenced. Footnote abbreviations given in italics, e.g. *A.*, are referred to the pages explaining them fully.)

[1] At the time dealt with in this book philosophy and science were not so clearly distinguished as they are today. Hence identical matters may be mentioned and indexed under different names. This should be borne in mind when looking up any of the following subjects: natural philosophy; philosophy, experimental; philosophy of Nature; physics; science, experimental.

---

[1] See footnote on page 429.

[1] See footnote on page 429.

[1] See footnote on page 429.